**Soviet Cinema in the
Silent Era, 1918–1935**

Texas Film Studies Series
Thomas Schatz, Editor

Soviet Cinema in the Silent Era, 1918–1935

by
Denise J. Youngblood

University of Texas Press
Austin

For Ethan

Contents

Preface

Silent cinema is one of the most interesting—yet most poorly understood—aspects of Soviet society in the twenties. Although the prerevolutionary Russian film industry had been virtually destroyed by the depredations of the World War, Revolution, and Civil War, by the end of the first decade of Soviet power, Soviet cinema was renowned the world over. Film historians in fact consider this period the Golden Age of Soviet cinema, pointing to the achievements of such geniuses as Sergei Eisenstein, Vsevolod Pudovkin, Lev Kuleshov, Dziga Vertov, and Aleksandr Dovzhenko.

Yet how much is known about this Golden Age? The traditional historiographical view of the twenties is as a period of relative political and economic freedom that the ascendancy of Stalin and the initiation of the First Five Year Plan abruptly ended. According to this interpretation, in the chaotic years following the Revolution, the avant-garde dominated until the arts were forced under state control. Cinema has also been interpreted this way, in part because directors like Pudovkin, Vertov, and Eisenstein, who were indeed innovators, are the only directors with whom even Russian and Soviet specialists are familiar.

This idealized picture of Soviet society during the twenties is only partially correct and has been the subject of fairly extensive historiographic revision in recent years—a reevaluation which has not, however, included cinema.[1] Can the encroaching authoritarianism on the "cinema front"—as it was called in the battle jargon of the time—be explained away as yet another manifestation of Stalin's will to totally dominate every aspect of Soviet life? Although it would be naive to undervalue the role of the Party in this or any other period of Soviet history, the "Stalin Revolution" was responding to a malaise in Soviet society and enjoyed "grass-roots" support, as true in the cinema world as in other spheres.

Soviet cinema presents a unique opportunity for studying the dynamics of change in Soviet society in this pivotal period. Cinema is more than a cultural phenomenon—it is also an industry requiring a fiscal base, sophisticated equipment, and technical expertise. A writer can create his world on a scrap of paper; indeed, the chronic paper shortages of the twenties have been advanced—not entirely lightheartedly—as the basis for the popularity of poetry over the novel in this period. A filmmaker, on the other hand, cannot realize *his* artistic vision without film stock, cameras, lights (and large quantities of electricity), and a horde of trained technical personnel, not to speak of the projectors, screens, electrical generators, and projectionists needed for the finished film to reach its audience. Therefore, to a much greater degree than any other art, cinema had to engage in a struggle for money and material in order to survive.

Structure

This work is conceived as a history of Soviet cinema from its inception in 1918 through the end of the silent period, concentrating on the critical years 1924-30. In order to bring the complex, often subtle (and essential) interconnections in developments into the sharpest possible relief, institutional changes, theoretical and polemical issues, and the films themselves are discussed in more or less chronological order. While the topics under consideration would have lent themselves to compartmentalized discussion, *ocherki* style, the inherent drama of the story—and its historical significance—would have been lost.

Sources

Choice of sources is critical in determining the character of any study. Because this is a look at the film industry "from below," I eschewed reviews and articles in the general press, although cultural publications like *New Spectator, The Life of Art, On Literary Guard, Revolution and Culture, Lef,* and *New Lef* were reviewed. In my year of research in Moscow, I read nearly every cinema book and film journal from the twenties from cover to cover. I was privileged to work in the Central State Archive of Literature and Art (TsGALI), and to be the first Westerner granted access to film archives from the period, primarily those *fondy* dealing with Sovkino and the Association of Revolutionary Cinematography (ARK). I also viewed about one hundred rare silent films at the All-Union State Institute of Cinematography in Moscow and the Pacific Film Archive in Berkeley. The omission of current Soviet monographs and articles from the notes and bibliography comes not from lack of familiarity but because their usefulness is limited due to the still considerable politicization of cinema scholarship.

Most students of the Soviet Union run into roadblocks and blind alleys in the quest for sources. A limitation *not* imposed by the vagaries of archival access politics is the concentration herein on full-length feature films (primarily fiction) from the Russian Republic. Although the more widely distributed nonfiction feature films and films from the non-Russian republics are discussed, mainstream cinema culture, the subject of this work, was fictional and centered in the RSFSR, so the impact of these omissions is slight.

Other omissions are not deliberate and carry potentially serious implications; it can only be hoped that major errors of interpretation have been avoided. Leningrad filmmakers pursued a consistently independent course, and although I had no special trouble obtaining films made in the Leningrad studios, I was consistently denied access to periodicals and archival materials pertaining to them. I was also forbidden the archive of the Society of Friends of Soviet Cinema (ODSK), an organization which I had considered the least important of the period, but about which judgment must now be reserved. All films which were denied me are indicated in the text. Illustrations are from *Cinema Week* (1924) and *Soviet Screen* (1928), the majority from the latter.

Translation and Transliteration

In the hope of making an admittedly specialized work more accessible to the non-Russian speaker, references in the text are in English (followed by the Russian in the first citation only). Titles in the notes and bibliography, however, are exclusively in Russian.

Transliteration is the bane of all scholars using Russian language sources. I have followed the Library of Congress system, with two exceptions—in the text, the soft sign (') in personal names has been omitted, and "Eizenshtein" has been rendered the usual "Eisenstein."

Acknowledgments

Thanks are due to Terence Emmons, for believing that a "real" historian could study film; to Edward J. Brown, for forcing me to prove my thesis to his satisfaction; to Sofia Donskaya, for providing answers to arcane questions about Soviet culture; to Stanley B. Youngblood, for being as critical a lay reviewer as one could hope to find; and to Steven Kovacs, for introducing me to the possibilities of the subject.

The bulk of the research upon which this work is based was made possible by a grant from the International Research and Exchanges Board (IREX) and the USSR Ministry of Higher Education. I am especially grateful for the assistance I received in Moscow from the All-Union State Institute of Cinematography, the Central State Archive of Literature and Art, and the Lenin Library.

Finally, I am indebted to the Pacific Film Archive of the Art Museum of the University of California, Berkeley—and especially to Linda Artel—for so generously sharing its collection of silent films; and to Wojciech Zalewski and the Stanford University Libraries, for obtaining rare materials for me.

Preface to the Paperback Edition

The preceding words were written in Palo Alto, California in December 1984, literally on the eve of the great turning point in the Soviet Union—and in Soviet cinema studies. My hopes for the recognition of this field as a significant area of scholarly endeavor have been realized to a greater extent than I dared believe possible. While this is not the place for an encyclopedic accounting of recent work on the first fifty years of Russian and Soviet cinema, it does seem appropriate to draw attention to a few of my colleagues' more outstanding accomplishments.

The indefatigable Richard Taylor, who may truly be said to have inaugurated the reevaluation of early Soviet cinema in 1979 with his book *The Politics of the Soviet Cinema, 1917–1929*, has earned the debt of cinema scholars in many ways. His magisterial document collection *The Film Factory: Russian and Soviet Cinema in Documents, 1896–1939* (1988, in collaboration with Ian Christie) is arguably the most important of these. If that achievement were not more than enough, Taylor has also translated a volume of Eisenstein and written several insightful articles on the cinema of the early '30s, all of which have contributed to our understanding of a period even less investigated than the '20s.

Vance Kepley, Jr., who has written prolifically on the early avant-garde (and indeed, still professes partiality to the pantheon), has expanded the boundaries of the conventional through his superb biography of Oleksandr Dovzhenko, *In the Service of the State* (1986) as well as through his studies of early Soviet film education and cinema in workers' clubs. Other recent books of note include François Albera and Roland Cosandey, *Boris Barnet* (1985); Vlada Petric, *Constructivism in Film* (1987); Judith Mayne, *Kino and the Woman Question* (1989); François Albera, Ekaterina Khokhlova, and Valerie Posner, *Koulechov et les siens* (1990); and Nicholas Galichenko, *Glasnost—Soviet Cinema Responds*, edited by Robert Allington (1991).

Works in press which will contain important new material on this period include Taylor and Christie's *Inside the Film Factory* and Anna Lawton's *The Red Screen*, based on the conference she organized at the Kennan Institute in 1986, the first in this country devoted to the subject of Soviet cinema. Books on the way include Peter Kenez's study of cinema in the Stalin era, Richard Taylor's history of the '30s, and my own work on the popular cinema of the New Economic Policy period.

This selective overview includes only works by "Western" scholars. Perhaps the most gratifying change over the past few years has been the opportunity to work closely with Soviet cinema scholars, who are now engaged in a number of exciting projects, particularly at VNIIK, the All-Union Institute for Cinema Research in Moscow. Expanded opportunities for conference participation have been invaluable, and the 1990 British Inter-University History Film Consortium Conference "Soviet Cinema: Continuity and Change" (organized by Richard Taylor and Derek Spring) is a case in point. Having the opportunity to draw upon the collective knowledge of Maya Turovskaya, Ekaterina Khokhlova, Yuri Tsivian, Viktor Listov, Leonid Kozlov, Mikhail Yampolsky, and Rashid Yangirov adds immeasurably to the ongoing processes of investigation and discovery.

If I were writing this book today, there are a few places in which I would be more judicious in my conclusions or more charitable in my acknowledgments, and there are more places in which I would strive for more graceful prose. Yet there is a story here which has not been told elsewhere in all its gritty and impassioned detail. It still needs to be heard, because despite the efflorescence of Soviet studies in the '80s, we have few studies of reasonably ordinary people struggling as best they could to deal with extraordinary times.

Soviet society is once again a society in transition, and the cultural and economic politics of the '20s (in large part the subject of this book) have never been quite as relevant as they are at present. The resemblance between the tensions of freedom and poverty then and now are uncanny, and the "lessons" that may be derived from this story of institutional and ideological conflict are certainly not restricted to the cultural arena, let alone the purely cinematic.

It gives me great pleasure to acknowledge the assistance I have received in bringing *Soviet Cinema in the Silent Era* back into print. Peter Kenez has been the book's most fervent champion, but I would also like to thank Anna Lawton, Richard Stites, and Richard Taylor for their support. Thanks are due my editor at UMI Research Press, Bradley Taylor, for his help in the process of transferring the rights. It was Vladimir Padunov who first proposed the idea of a reprint to me, and so this edition is dedicated to him.

Burlington, Vermont
January 1991

Introduction

The history of the Soviet film industry in the twenties may be described as the inexorable move from organizational chaos to total centralization and from aesthetic radicalism to Socialist Realism. How these twin objectives were achieved in little more than a decade, and why these ends seemed desirable, is the subject of this study. It is a convoluted tale of warring interest groups set against a backdrop of political, social, and economic upheaval. The film industry may be viewed as a microcosm of Soviet society, but its unique configurations should also be recognized.

The first confused years after the Revolution, roughly the period between 1917 and 1921, saw the end of World War I, a great Civil War, and a terrible famine. Misery was widespread, but so was revolutionary enthusiasm. It was at this time that cinema was first seized upon as the art of the Soviet future.

Political radicals, who supported the aims of the Revolution whether or not they were Bolsheviks, were drawn to cinema because they considered it, unlike theater, an art of the *people*, a mass medium. They embraced it with special fervor because unlike printed mass media, cinema required minimal literacy, a critical factor in a country where the illiteracy rate was extremely high (75-80 percent). Cinema was rarely considered a vehicle for propaganda even by the most political of its supporters except in the broadest sense, as a cultural tool for the enlightenment of the masses.

Artistic radicals were also drawn to cinema but considered it revolutionary for fundamentally different reasons. Cinema for them was a *new* art, an art with few ties to the corrupted culture of the tsarist past, a technological art, an abstract art. Yet from the beginning, the artistic left in cinema was more diverse than it has been portrayed. It was divided into those who supported fiction films with weakly developed narratives and those—the most radical—who rejected the fiction film altogether, advocating the nonfiction film in its place. While the importance of the former faction would persist, the influence of the latter had all but ended by 1924 as revolutionary romanticism was eschewed by young film activists more intent on rebuilding a shattered industry than indulging in sloganeering and the writing of aesthetic platforms.

Nonetheless, the artistic debates of this first phase of Soviet cinema lay the groundwork for developments in the future. Throughout the decade, critics and directors struggled to formulate aesthetic principles for a fiction film which would both appeal to the mass audience while exhibiting distinctly Soviet characteristics. What "Soviet" meant was a divisive issue in the polemics of the silent film era, whether the subject was the role of the professional movie actor, the shortage of suitable scripts, or the importance of narrative realism in cinema.

With the end of the Civil War, Lenin decided that the draconian state control of the economy known as War Communism should be abandoned in favor of what came to be known as the New Economic Policy (NEP). Inaugurated in 1921, NEP meant a return to a limited free market and a toleration of bourgeois specialists and fellow travellers. Although cinema had been nationalized in 1919 and remained under state control during NEP, NEP in cinema led to the reopening of private theaters and more importantly, to the return of the old specialists to filmmaking. As the economy slowly improved as a result of NEP, the state cinema enterprise Goskino was able to import foreign films in greater quantities, thereby satisfying the demands of the commercial theaters, even though domestic film production still was virtually nonexistent.

In 1924, with the economy stabilized, Goskino became the object of intensive critical scrutiny. As a result, Goskino was replaced by Sovkino, a joint stock company with a considerably broader mandate and a sounder financial base (although it was undercapitalized by Western standards). Sovkino, which was run by Party members of long standing, quickly established itself as the enemy of enthusiastic—but inexperienced—young filmmakers, whether they supported the fiction or nonfiction film, whether they looked upon cinema as an intellectual art, a cultural-educational tool for the rural masses, or something in between.

The enforced inactivity on the cinema front had created a pent-up demand for filmmaking, a demand that Sovkino consistently thwarted by backing the massive importation of foreign films and the limitation of Soviet films to a few large budget extravaganzas, made by established "bourgeois" directors. The rationale behind Sovkino's policy was a purely economic one. Since the Party had made it abundantly clear that little fiscal (or even moral) support for the film industry would be forthcoming, Sovkino had to look out for its own interests. Its administrators argued that foreign films were what the public wanted to see—thus guaranteeing good returns at the box office—and that Russian costume dramas appealed not only to the home audience, but also to that in the West, thus maximizing the marketability of Soviet-produced films. Sovkino justified its favoritism to the "old specialists" by arguing that without them the infant Soviet film industry did not have enough experienced personnel to sustain its development—though it could not deny that there was an abundance of talent among the young.

So while novice directors of various political and artistic persuasions *did* make movies under Sovkino's aegis, the constant struggle for the means to do so turned aesthetic positions into weapons in a power struggle. Canonizing the fiction or nonfiction film, acted or nonacted, realistic or avant-garde, seemed to be a way of ensuring access to funding for future projects. Because of this, aesthetic debates became connected to institutional developments to a quite remarkable degree.

While Sovkino's justification for its "line" was a reasonable one—the films of "revolutionary" young Soviet directors were proven time and again to be unprofitable, if justly admired by the critics—it is easy to imagine the resentment that this policy caused. A filmworker did not have to be politically active or particularly radical to wonder what had happened to the aims of the Revolution during the "Thermidor" of NEP, and Sovkino became the central antagonist in many group conflicts. In fact, the history of the film industry in this period is one of conflict—between insiders and outsiders, the young and the established, the educated and the half-educated. Yet another important aspect of the conflict was the bureaucratic struggle between Sovkino and the Commissariat of Enlightenment, the department of the government under whose nominal control cinema affairs fell. Furthermore, the relationship among the studios, the cinema press, and the Association of Revolutionary Cinematography (ARK, the chief professional organization) was complex and interconnected.

What was the role of the Party in these internecine struggles? Certainly, no one position can be attributed to the Party in the twenties, for Party members among filmworkers ran the gamut from aesthetic rightists, like Sovkino's I. P. Trainin, to political leftists, like Nikolai Lebedev, the founder of ARK. The truth of this may best be indicated by the fact that although the Association of Revolutionary Cinematography was often described as being iconoclastic and apolitical, its membership in this period included a significant number of Party members (40 percent).[1]

While the Party did use cinema as propaganda during the Civil War, with the advent of NEP, its attention was turned to rebuilding the economy, and even before the death of Lenin in 1924, to the power struggle for control of the Party. By 1927, the right wing of the Party (supporters of NEP and the reconciliation with old specialists) seemed to emerge victorious, since the Left Opposition had been decisively defeated and its leader Trotskii ousted from the Party. Yet almost immediately following his victory over the Left, Stalin announced his plans to abandon NEP (and the coexistence with bourgeois specialists) and to forge ahead with rapid industrialization and full-scale collectivization. Just as cinema had been seen as a useful tool during the Civil War, so now it was seen as a useful tool in the class war known as the "cultural revolution" which accompanied the First Five Year Plan.

This renewed attention to cinema, which began in late 1927 as the Party was laying its plans for the industrialization campaign, occurred at a time when the malaise in the film industry was all but overwhelming. From the point of view of the industry rank-and-file, NEP had not worked. They were not willing to proceed toward socialism "at a snail's pace" (in the words of the Rightist leader Bukharin); they wanted to seize control of the studios. Yet the crisis in cinematography was more than just a crisis of means. It was also a crisis of revolutionary faith, which helps explain the fervor with which many filmworkers embraced the tenets of the cultural revolution. While it cannot be denied that Stalin's decision to co-opt the policies of the Left had, of course, complicated political motivations, conditions and attitudes in Soviet society that had been developing throughout the twenties came to their grimly logical conclusion with the changes instituted by the Party.

The film industry is an ideal context in which to examine the development of Soviet society in this decade. It was a cultural phenomenon, which allows us the opportunity to compare the aesthetic debates in cinema with those in the other arts. It was an industry, which made it subject to the ebbs and flows of the national economy. It was an institution, the personnel of which—both leaders and cadres—were profoundly affected by political and social currents. But perhaps most importantly, the film industry provides us with the rare opportunity to see Soviet citizens *who were not political figures* as participants in the turbulent events of the twenties.

1

Beginnings (1918-23)

The first film organization of the new Soviet government was the Cinema Subsection of the Extracurricular Section of the Commissariat of Enlightenment, formed in 1918 and headed by Lenin's wife, N. K. Krupskaia. In March 1918 cinema committees were created by both the Moscow and Petrograd Soviets to deal not only with ideological problems, but also with the more pressing practical ones, like halting the flow of equipment and personnel from Moscow or trying to obtain enough electricity to keep the theaters running.[1] The attitude of the government toward nationalization of the industry was as yet confused, but in any case, it was powerless to halt the dismantling of the studios. Electricity was in even shorter supply than films, and under these circumstances, it is easily imagined that viewing conditions were very difficult.[2]

Amazingly, by mid-1918 enough film stock had been scraped together, from the blackmarket or through a process of re-using positive stock by re-emulsification, to begin the first Soviet productions—short propaganda films called *agitki* which were shown around the country on agit-trains.[3] The film industry, such as it was, was nationalized on August 27, 1919, and placed under the control of Narkompros, the Commissariat of Enlightenment,[4] but the Commissariat lacked the power to enforce the government's order. The ramifications of nationalization would not be felt for some years.

The Civil War and After

The year 1919 was one of bitter hardship, yet there was still film work done in Moscow despite extreme cold and hunger. An example of this inexplicable urge to make movies regardless of conditions was a film by the Rus studio, *Polikushka*, to be discussed below.[5] But *Polikushka*, based on Lev Tolstoi's story, was a rare fiction film, for until the end of the Civil War and the establishment of a mixed economy with the New Economic Policy (NEP), almost all films made were short agit-films for use at the front. Few of these are extant, but they provided good technical training for a number of cameramen, and important directors like Lev Kuleshov and Dziga Vertov got their start in movies making Civil War agit-films and newsreels. (Sergei Eisenstein was also on the agit-trains, but as a poster artist, not filmmaker.)

The end of the Civil War and the beginnings of the limited private enterprise of the New Economic Policy did not, of course, lead to the immediate flourishing of cinema. Most experts had fled, taking their equipment with them; every scrap of raw film stock had been used and reused; theaters and studios had decayed.[6] With famine (especially bad in 1921), the rebellion at Kronstadt, and economic collapse, film production could hardly seem to anyone to be of special importance, least of all to the harassed Party. Huge sums of foreign currency or gold would be required to import the necessary materials. Moreover, the making and showing of movies required electricity, in woefully short supply in the cities and nonexistent in most of the country.

Halfhearted attempts in 1921-22 to ensure cinema's self-sufficiency failed, and at the end of 1922 the Council of People's Commissars authorized the creation of Goskino, the Central State Photo-Cinema Enterprise, which was based on the former VFKO, the Photo-Cinema Section of the Commissariat of Enlightenment. On paper, Goskino had a distribution monopoly in order to earn money for production,[7] but the organization's uncertain situation was not helped by its competition for films and materials with other Soviet organizations, particularly Sevzapkino, Rus, and Proletkino in the Russian Republic, and VUFKU and Goskinprom Gruzii in the Ukraine and Georgia, respectively. In 1918, the government had been bilked out of one million gold rubles in an attempt to get film equipment, an experience which made Goskino administrators wary of further foreign dealings.[8] Reinforcing this reluctance, the foreign films Goskino imported were ridiculed not only for faulty ideology but also for being a bad bargain. These twin concerns of sound ideology and fiscal shrewdness would prove troublesome to Goskino and its successors.

Bourgeois Remnants *(Cinema Life)*

By 1922, with the establishment of Goskino, there were signs of revival in the film world. A few journals had appeared. Yet one would never imagine from looking at the first issue of *Cinema Life* (*Kino-zhizn'*), published in May 1922, that there had ever been a revolution. *Cinema Life* featured photo layouts of prerevolutionary stars and had advertisements for lipstick, face powder, and medical remedies. It was a pulp movie magazine, designed for the audience of "Hottentots" who wanted to see *The Human Beast* (*Chelovek-zver'*) and *The Woman Who Invented Love* (*Zhenshchina kotoraia izobrela liubov'*), both starring the glamorous prerevolutionary film star Vera Kholodnaia.

Although *Cinema Life* was supposed to be a "weekly," its second issue did not appear until September 1922, four months later. The cover still featured the late, lamented Vera Kholodnaia, and the content was basically the same, but the editorial, amusingly enough, claimed that Russian cinema should fill a propaganda function. It also deplored the conversions of movie theaters to "legitimate" theaters, since theaters served the NEP bourgeoisie and could not be as forceful a propaganda vehicle as cinema.[9] Yet later in this same issue we read that the public only wanted to see Vera Kholodnaia.[10]

Indeed, who else was there to see? Soviet productions were few and not very interesting, but by October 1922, thanks to the New Economic Policy and despite inflation, a few foreign movies began appearing on the commercial screen in Moscow.[11] The big hit of the year was a picture that the Russian star Ivan Mozhukhin made abroad, *Child of the Carnival* (*Dit'ia karnavala*).[12]

The situation in Petrograd was bleaker; *Cinema Life*'s correspondent noted that the same movies were running over and over, since there were as yet no private theaters in the city. The best movies went to the privately owned city theaters, such as those in Moscow, so viewers in the provinces clamored for the new pictures, the "hits" (*boeviki*) to no avail.[13] This was the first hint of the chronic distribution problem which would plague the industry throughout the twenties.

Cinema Life was obviously not a socially responsible publication born of the Revolution. It was a survival from the previous era, and it terminated in March 1923, after less than a year of sporadic output. While the exact circumstances of its demise are unclear, it seems unlikely that it was shut down by the authorities—rampant inflation would have been enough to force its closure. Moreover, in these early years of genuine revolutionary enthusiasm, *Cinema Life* was more than a bit out of touch with the times. One of its last issues featured advertisements for movies with "colossal mass scenes" and "shooting among wild beasts," as well as the promise of a questionnaire for readers on the burning topic of the day: "Romanticism or the Detective Story?"[14] While this undoubtedly interested some viewers, hopeful young filmmakers entertained loftier notions of the place of cinema in a socialist society. There had indeed been a revolution, though its implications for cinema were not always clear.

The Leftists

The Cinema Constructivists

When one thinks of Soviet culture in the early twenties, one does not think of a magazine like *Cinema Life*, but of mass street theater, futurist poets, and constructivist art and architecture. This tendency was expressed in cinema through the constructivist journal *Cinema-photo (Kino-fot)*, which first appeared in August 1922. Aleksei Gan, the constructivist critic, was the journal's editor and the acknowledged leader of a loose group known as the cinema-constructivists, which seemed to consist of anyone who at one time or another wrote for *Cinema-photo*. In any case, Gan alone could make noise enough for many, and he immediately established his journal at the forefront of the artistic avant-garde with his first editorial, "Cinema and Cinematography" ("Kinematograf i kinematografiia"). In Gan's view, cinematography under Soviet power must be entirely new. "*Kinematograf*" (an obsolete word for cinema—replaced by *kino*) was, on the other hand, the art of the past, living photography, filmed theater, a tool of capitalism. The cinema of the future was inseparable from technology, both to be at the service of the first proletarian government.[15]

Gan saw cinema as anti-art, part of the veritable abolition of art in the machine age, and trumpeted this notion throughout the brief and boisterous life of *Cinema-photo*. For the constructivists, cinema was the quintessentially modern art: "Between cinema and the twentieth century there is an equal sign," cinema having the "power of the machine." (Such rhetoric was typical of the enthusiasms of the movement.)[16]

If cinema were the art of the future, then what was the art of the past, and what should its fate be? This too concerned the *Cinema-photo* "group." Bourgeois art was a passive appreciation of beauty, a product of individualism and an addiction to cottage industry (*kustarnichestvo*, in this case alluding to private studios). Although the Revolution would eventually revolutionize all art, according to these cinema avant-gardists, cinema was in particular danger from the depredations of the bourgeoisie. Since theater was dying, the bourgeoisie, still a powerful force, wanted to co-opt cinema as its own.

To these radical leftists on the cinema front, Soviet cinema would be agit-cinema, but this did not mean propagandistic cinema in any but the loosest sense. It would stand in bold contrast to bourgeois cinema, free of static theatrics, symbolism, or fantasy. It would be dynamic treatment of "only the most real, the most contemporary material." Thanks to the Revolution, cinema had reached, like all the arts, the stage where it was either "revolutionary" or "reactionary." The terms "high" and "low" art no longer had any meaning.[17]

Because of their antagonism to anything "bourgeois," the Cinema-photoists were extremely concerned about the effect of NEP on the nascent film industry. A mixed economy in their opinion could only be bad. New cinema must be constructed on socialist principles, and the fate of art (since cinema was its vanguard) hinged on the success of cinema activists in battling the dark forces of private enterprise.[18]

Aleksei Gan and his followers believed that "private enterprise" had infiltrated the Commissariat of Enlightenment and was already adversely affecting cinema.[19] Believing these "moles" more dangerous than the obvious threat NEPmen posed, the Cinema-photoists adopted a militaristic jargon appropriate to the battle they saw raging:

> Be firm and courageous, believe, for not all have enough courage, not all have enough faith, *under the temptations* of NEP, many leave. But of those who remain, from those who enter, *comes* a real *cinema-army*, an army of iron will and great knowledge. Let the army forge ahead, let the army believe in itself, in its work, in the idea of precise cinematography and victory. The army will conquer.[20]

The "army" had to fight against the old "specialists" who supported the old ways, as well as for material needs.[21] This resentment against specialists and "fellow travellers" surfaced in the other arts, and indeed, in all aspects of Soviet society during NEP, but the question of poverty assumed an importance for the cinema that cannot be overstressed. Writers can still write in times of need. Filmmakers *cannot* make movies. The competition for raw materials became a struggle for artistic survival during the twenties. With this in mind, the fanaticism of the Cinema-photoists and those to follow becomes easier to comprehend.

In October 1922, a manifesto appeared in *Cinema-photo* that is worth reproducing in full since it vividly illustrates the estrangement of this avant-garde group not only from NEP society, but also from the cinema community.

> We know that our comrades do not hear us.
> We know that the citizenry in whose midst we live do not love us.
> But we directly and steadfastly go about our business.
> Tomorrow 1,000 Russian and foreign fiction films could appear.
> The day after tomorrow, dozens of film journals.
> It is not terrible for us, for our business is the business of a culture being born in which cinema does not occupy last place.
> What will the new art-cinema pictures do?
> They will poison with putrid breath the broad masses and enrich the cinema businessmen.
> What will the film journals do in the hands of cinema junk dealers, cinema gout-sufferers, and cinema speculators?
> They will muddy the already dirty waters of senile cinematography and trample the fresh shoots on the young plants of our cinematography.
> Comrades, build.
> The hour of new battle advances.
> We need a blow.
> With the first number of *Cinema-photo*, we struck at the moldy comforts of cinema-art-speculation. With the fifth, we strike at the skulls of gout-sufferers and paralytics, *who are trying* with all their strength to protect the ulcer of old cinematography.
> Comrades, build.
> We will fight![22]

The Cinema-photoists became the champions of the director who most closely typified their ideals, Dziga Vertov. Just as *Cinema-photo* was the most belligerently "leftist" of all cinema journals, so Vertov was the most vociferous and dogmatic of all Soviet silent film directors. He fought against the fiction film throughout his career and he represented the radical fringe group of modern art. To most, he was undeniably an artist, yet he himself abjured the very idea of art. Vertov had shot newsreels during the Civil War and was now engaged in producing his *Cinema Truth* (*Kino-pravda*) newsreel series. Vertov's well-known philosophy being that the mechanical eye of the camera was truer than the human eye, he called his production collective the Cinema-eyes (*Kinoki*).

Cinema-photo editor Aleksei Gan was a particular admirer of Vertov's work, for in it he recognized the director's devotion to the contemporary, to fixing the details of the new way of life,[23] an intrinsic part of Gan's own notion of modern "art." Vertov contributed a characteristic article to *Cinema-photo*: a denunciation of those sybarites who called themselves "documentarists" but nonetheless received commissions from the Photo-Cinema Section of the Commissariat of Enlightenment (VFKO) and expected such luxuries as a car, a regular cameraman, a laboratory, and even *film*.[24]

It is indicative of the relative tolerance of the times that a radical journal like *Cinema-photo* also offered a forum for Lev Kuleshov, the "father" of the Soviet fiction film. Kuleshov shared the revolutionary enthusiasm and some of the ideas of Gan's group, but not their machine-age jargon and their rejection of art. Kuleshov agreed with the Cinema-photoists that cinema was the art of the future. He found the other contemporary arts foundering, dilettantish, and hopelessly divorced from contemporary life; cinema on the other hand was absolutely *specific*—in time, space, organization, and material.[25] Thus far, there is not much to distinguish him from the "leftists."

But Kuleshov had distinctly original traits. He was a great admirer of the American movie—particularly the detective film—as maligned then as now among "serious" film lovers. "High brows" explained the success of these pictures with the mass viewer as evidence of the public's poor taste, but Kuleshov, with his remarkable instinct for what is cinematographic, realized that the key to the perennial success of these films was their *dynamism*. As he wrote in "Amerikanshchina" (which Ronald Levaco has aptly translated as "Americanitis")[26]: "*For cinematography, there is no more harmful appearance of literariness than psychologism, that is, the external inactivity of the plot* [*siuzhet*, sometimes translated as plot-theme]." Did American cinema achieve dynamism simply through choice of "active" subject matter? Kuleshov's answer (which he had articulated somewhat earlier but which achieved fame through this essay) had enormous impact on the history of cinema. It marked the beginning of Russian "montage" theory, which Kuleshov, ironically enough, called "American montage."

Montage means editing or cutting. All films are edited; that is, made of shots and scenes spliced together. Kuleshov did not, of course, invent editing, nor was he the first to practice it for artistic effect. He was, rather, the articulator and elaborator of the idea, being, like Vertov, a director-theorist, a peculiarly Soviet phenomenon. The essence of his theory is this:

> One must search for the organizing basis of cinematography, not within the limits of the shot, but in the changing of these shots...the essence of cinema, its means of achieving the maximum impression, is *montage*.[27]

Kuleshov was cautious about what NEP would mean for cinema. He was not as negative as others who wrote for *Cinema-photo*, because he believed that the cinema situation would improve with or without NEP, since it could not have gotten much worse. Yet he feared the renewed development of large commercial firms which would attract speculators and restrict experimentation because of the need to make a profit. Even in these days of cruelly limited resources, Kuleshov spoke out strongly in favor of experimentation. He felt that it could be accomplished economically and was vital for the development of a Soviet film art:

> Experiments are now extremely necessary for cinematography. This is most essential and valuable....The experiment for an honorable cinematographer is more important than bread.[28]

Coming from Kuleshov, this was not hyperbole, for no one could deny that his collective was totally devoted to filmmaking, no matter the hardship. He himself had begun cinema work in 1916 as a set designer for Evgenii Bauer, a director with the Khanzhankov studio. In 1919-20 Kuleshov shot agit-films, helped organize GTK, the state film school, and founded his own collective, which included his wife, the actress Aleksandra Khokhlova, the future directors Vsevolod Pudovkin and Boris Barnet, and actors Sergei Podobed, Sergei Komarov, and Vladimir Fogel.[29]

Kuleshov's most famous montage experiment was the one known as the "Mozhukhin effect." He took a single shot of the prerevolutionary star Mozhukhin and cut it with shots of different objects, which caused viewers to believe that the actor's expression was changing.[30] To offer training in his theory of the actor-model (*akter-naturshchik*), which required rigorous physical discipline, Kuleshov had the collective stage "films without film," sketches done in the cinematographic style since there was no film stock for shooting. Kuleshov and Khokhlova remembered that these presentations were well attended despite ticket prices of 10-30,000 rubles.[31]

As such prices indicate, inflation was ravaging Soviet society. The last issue of *Cinema-photo*, which appeared in early 1923, cost 350 rubles. Gan understandably enough viewed the New Year gloomily. There was still a dearth of trained personnel, little equipment, and no relief in sight because of the economic crisis. While "films without film" might have proved the devotion of the Kuleshov collective, they also vividly illustrated the seeming hopelessness of their predicament.

Yet even in time of material want, Gan characteristically worried about ideological leadership. He did not feel that there was any government support for the development of a truly revolutionary cinema art, and he believed that a choice had to be made immediately. For him, Soviet culture was at the crossroads: along one path "slowly moves the aesthetic gravedigger smelling like Dostoevskii or Tolstoi"; along the other strode the healthy young constructivists, who "see the real world," human society, and technology.[32] Gan continued to defend the utility of proclamation writing, but as early as 1923 support had evaporated for such utopianism.

A persistent stereotype of Soviet cinema in the twenties is that it consisted of propaganda, anti-art slogans, and unrealistic projects. This was only true of *Cinema-photo* during its short life. Its impact was negligible—its most important contribution lay in providing Lev Kuleshov a forum, ironic considering that Kuleshov was not a radical. Its support of Dziga Vertov was also noteworthy and undoubtedly aided in the publicizing of his career, but Vertov was in the end his own most effective spokesman.

Cinema-photo was not only estranged from the moderate "mainstream" of Soviet cinema, it purposefully disengaged itself from the "Left Front" of the arts as well. Gan was sharply critical of the "Left Front," which included all the artistic "-ists"—Stankists, suprematists, non-objectivists, futurists, immanentists, and expressionists—*except* the constructivists. He charged that the "left" artistic groups, although condemning the old art, posited nothing new in its place: "On the 'Left Front' there is no reflection of *new* life. In all this time, we have seen only an endless row of formal experiments." (Gan chose not to explain how the constructivists had achieved "new life.")

Cinema constructivists, wrote Gan, were interested neither in experimentation nor in finding new forms. Cinema must be wrested from the clutches of both capitalism (into which its "industrial connections" had led it) and the corrupted arts. He said:

> The sooner we accept that cinema is not art [then] the closer we will come to the battle, the truer we will begin to accomplish the necessary work on the path of our young, revolutionary cinematography.[33]

The *Cinema-photo* group represented an interesting but essentially isolated phenomenon in Soviet cinema, as we shall see. Their revolutionary enthusiasm, disdain for old art, and admiration for technology did not address the concrete problems of building a film industry and articulating a new aesthetic. Their fractionalism in fact discredited their position with other cinema workers.

The Futurists

Despite Gan's avowals to the contrary, one familiar with the futurists will recognize certain common attitudes. Poet Vladimir Maiakovskii's journal *Lef* (for "Left Front") was not a film journal, but three of the seven signers of the first *Lef* manifesto—Maiakovskii, Osip Brik, and Sergei Tretiakov—had a more than passing interest in cinema,[34] and another, B. Arvatov, had contributed to *Cinema-photo*.[35] Brik, Maiakovskii, and Tretiakov all wrote scripts; Brik and Tretiakov were able film critics; and Maiakovskii acted.

The militant views of the Lefists and the Cinema-photoists on the sorry state of the old culture were similar, as was their certainty that a new art must come from the new society.[36] It was hardly fair of Gan to charge that the futurists had no concrete answers, for who had? In the cinema world, where the economic situation was especially precarious, there was still no opportunity for hopefuls to put their ideas into practice.

Since ideas were all anyone could offer in 1923, it is worth examining two essays published that year in *Lef*. The articles appeared in the same issue, one following the other; while this juxtaposition must have enraged Dziga Vertov, it was most appropriate, for the problems posed in these two pieces formed the central theoretical conflict of cinema in the decade: should fact or fiction be the basis of the film art of the future? The question had been skirted in the first Soviet film tract *Cinema* (*Kinematograf*)[37] and summarily dismissed in *Cinema-photo*.

Boris Kushner, one of the original Lefists, addressed the question in "Izopovest'." The title is a neologism meaning "pictorial story," which was how he attempted to define the domain of cinema (as opposed to that of theater). Kushner came out squarely in favor of narrative cinema as an "amazing, witty, and entertaining storyteller." According to Kushner, cinema was so far from being a step-cousin of the arts that even literature should emulate the way cinema combined pictorial concreteness with its story-telling techniques.[38]

Vertov's *Lef* article, "Cinema-eyes: Coup" ("Kinoki: Perevorot") expressed a completely different point of view and is one of the most famous expositions of his theory. It is also an excellent example of the difficult, innovative, and quarrelsome style which was his trademark. He began by declaring that everything in cinema needed to become exactly the opposite of what it had been. He therefore absolutely condemned fiction cinema, whether psychological, detective, or satirical, as being a "literary skeleton plus cinema illustrations."[39] Vertov decried the tenacity of the old forms of the cinema drama, pointing out that the new productions with their NEPmen heroes were no more than remakes of old pictures with bourgeois heroes.[40]

Thus far, the essay could have been written by Gan; Vertov was, however, a thoroughgoing revolutionary. He made it very clear that the machine was not equal but *superior* to man, writing:

> The end point is: *the use of the movie camera as a cinema-eye, more perfect than the human eye, for the investigation of the chaos of visual phenomena which resemble space.*
> The cinema-eye lives and moves in time and space, perceives and fixes impressions in a new way completely unlike the human eye.... We cannot make our eyes better than they are, but we can endlessly perfect the movie camera.[41]

This is an astonishing statement, the ultimate extension of the constructivist ideal of art as the embodiment of the machine age. Vertov's modernism definitely diminishes man; the machine—in this case the movie camera—is better because it is more "truthful."

Did this mean that the role of man in the movie-making process was simply to hold the camera? Here Vertov provided his own version of Kuleshov's montage theory, boldly recognizing that montage was more than just the organizational and aesthetic basis of cinema. Montage, according to Vertov, is the manipulation of the viewer. He boasted that he could take a shot of a person in Chicago in 1923 and "place" him in Petrograd in 1918 and even went so far as to point out examples from his own *Cinema Truth* "newsreels":

> They lower the coffins of people's heroes to the grave (shot in Astrakhan in 1918), fill up the grave (Kronstadt, 1921), cannon gun salute (Petrograd, 1920), eternal memory, they take off their caps (Moscow, 1922)—such things go together even with "ungrateful," not specially shot material (see *Cinema Truth*, No. 13). Here it is proper to cut from montage of a welcoming crowd and a welcoming car to Comrade Lenin (*Cinema Truth*, No. 14), shot in different places, at different times.

Vertov apparently saw nothing ironical about the title of his films and his cinematic practices.

Such was his confidence in the power montage gave the filmmaker that he could write:

> I am the cinema-eye. I am the builder. I placed you, today created by me, in a room which did not exist until this moment, also created by me.... I am the cinema-eye; I create a person more perfect than Adam.... I am the cinema-eye. I am the mechanical eye. I am the machine which shows you the world as only I can see it.[42]

The basic problem with Vertov is that he could make such statements while at the same time staking an apparently sincere claim for his own objectivity, for example:

> From today, in cinema we need neither psychological nor detective dramas; from today, we do not need theatrical productions shot on film; from today, we do not adapt Dostoevskii or Nat Pinkerton [for the screen]. Everything enters into a new understanding of the newsreel.[43]

But what was this "new understanding?" The Vertov controversy, one of the key aesthetic debates of the coming years, centered on how well he lived up to his own declared standards of objectivity. The fate of the Soviet nonfiction feature film was intimately connected with the fate of Dziga Vertov.

FEKS

Although they were interested in cinema, the Lefists did not form a cinema group. At the time of the publication of their manifesto, *Eccentrism* (*Ekstsentrizm*) in 1922, FEKS, the Workshop of the Eccentric Actor, was neither a cinema group nor were its members particularly interested in cinema. Even so, FEKS must be considered at the end of a discussion of "left" trends in cinema, because its leaders, Grigorii Kozintsev and Leonid Trauberg, were shortly to become important film directors, and they transformed FEKS from a theater to a cinema collective.

Extreme youth characterized the "left wing" of cinema, and FEKS leaders Kozintsev and Trauberg and their colleague Sergei Iutkevich (later a film director in his own right), were the youngest of all. When the group was organized in 1921, Kozintsev was sixteen years old; Trauberg, nineteen; Iutkevich, seventeen. Due to their long collaboration, Kozintsev and Trauberg are generally remembered as the sole leaders of the group but Iutkevich was also an important contributor to the manifesto.

FEKS, unlike the cinema constructivists, was not anti-art. They simply wanted to deflate art; as Kozintsev put it, they wanted "art without capital letters."[44] They therefore sought inspiration in the most "popular"—in the sense of most "accessible"—forms of acted art: the circus, the street player, the music hall. In the pictorial arts, they admired the poster and the advertisement.

They also regarded the author irreverently, as merely an "inventor-builder." The traditional actor likewise was a target for diminution, as "mechanized action." Emphasizing their break from tradition, Kozintsev declared that "Charlo [Chaplin]'s back is dearer to us than the hand of Eleonora Duse."[45] FEKS admired the dynamism and unpretentiousness of American popular culture even more than did Kuleshov; the art of the future, they declared, would be a Russian version of American "vulgarity."[46]

FEKS bluntly refused to ally itself with the other left groups, and properly so, since FEKS did not worship technology and altogether presented a disarmingly human face of avant-garde art. Like Gan, Iutkevich in fact poked fun at all the "isms" of modern art, saying that these were a "complete break from life, through their concentration on form rather than plotted action [*siuzhet*]."[47] Art, according to FEKS, should be contemporary and "boulevardized," that is, it should cater to the tastes of the people. (Despite this credo, FEKS' films were not to prove easily accessible to the masses.)

Although FEKS did not offer much by way of theory, it did express the irrepressible youth and energy and good spirits found in cinema and the other arts in the first years of the revolution. The FEKS collection crackles with the audacity of extreme youth; Iutkevich declared that their motto was that of the Italian futurist Marinetti: "The old are always wrong, even when right, but the young are always right, even when wrong."[48] Cinema was attractive to bright young people with artistic interests precisely because it had so poor a past. In Soviet Russia, due to the traumas of the past years, cinema was very nearly a *new* art; and film lovers could make of it whatever they wanted. The world, so they thought, was theirs.

The Centrists *(Cinema Gazette)*

To this point, we have considered the first hesitant steps toward the re-establishment of a film industry and the formulation of a film aesthetic. The position of the government and Party was not clearly defined, although the blatantly "bourgeois" style of *Cinema Life* was permanently eclipsed. There were some amorphous left-wing groupings in cinema; chief among these were Aleksei Gan and *Cinema-photo* and Dziga Vertov's Cinema-eye collective. A number of Lefists were interested in cinema, and in Petrograd FEKS formed the basis for an important avant-garde film collective of the future. This, the most avant-garde period of Soviet cinema, was characterized by wishful thinking, due to the lack of raw materials needed to make films, but even among stridently left-wing publications, there was room for diversity of opinion.

Although these avant-garde "groups" were less alike than they appeared on the surface, it would be a mistake to assume that they represented mainstream opinion. By 1923, the center consisted of moderates concerned with the rebuilding of Russian cinema and reviving public interest in it. Their forum was the Moscow newspaper *Cinema Gazette* (*Kino-gazeta*). The following anecdote about a lively discussion in Moscow's most lavish movie palace, the Malaia Dmitrovka theater, illustrates the jaundiced view of many film activists toward extreme leftists like Gan and Vertov: "D. Vertov, as usual, began and ended addressing all workers in cinematography abusively," after which A. Anoshchenko "pinned them [the Cinema-eyes] to the wall" with his witty sallies, and Lev Kuleshov proved, to the joy of most present, that there was nothing new about the montage in Vertov's *Cinema Truth* series. When Gan tried to speak, he was whistled down. And in the end, the "Cinema-eyes and their friends, the constructivists, were finally unmasked."[49] To the moderates, Soviet cinema had problems more serious than those posited by Vertov.

The first concern addressed was that of economics, and the picture was a gloomy one. Before there could be any discussion of the kinds of movies to make, practical problems had to be faced. Vertov may have thought the question of film stock and laboratories philistine, but Kuleshov believed that it was financially and technically impossible to make a good modern film in Soviet Russia. He also supported the production of films that would be marketable abroad, because although he personally favored "revolutionary" movies as the mainstay of Soviet production, historical movies were more likely to find foreign purchasers.[50]

The state film enterprise Goskino, as mentioned earlier, was in a precarious position due to lack of founding capital. As early as 1923 (less than a year after its founding) it was perceived as being incapable of solving the problems of Soviet cinema. *Cinema Gazette*'s "line" in these days was that Goskino must be replaced by a film syndicate,[51] but unfortunately there was very little concrete information offered about the economic situation and Goskino's role in the crisis.

Another specific concern was foreign movies. Although they were potentially harmful ideologically, this was not viewed as a problem since they could be re-edited and the titles rewritten to be "critically" illuminating.[52] More worrisome from the economic and organizational point of view was that "a significant percentage" of foreign films (for which much precious hard currency had been paid) had been banned by the censors, indicating a costly lack of communication between the censorship and Goskino.[53]

The third major issue that surfaced in 1923 was one of the enduring problems of the decade, the "scenario crisis"—the shortage of suitable scripts. This was first articulated not in *Cinema Gazette*, but in *Prolet-cinema* (*Proletkino*), a short-lived journal connected with the slightly less short-lived production company of the same name, which was dedicated to the furthering of proletarian cinema. According to *Prolet-cinema* there was still no "Soviet" cinema, only recycled ideas and "pseudo-revolutionary" films, made by people connected with the prerevolutionary movie industry.[54]

Prolet-cinema therefore issued a call to "new authors" for "healthy" stories, especially about the revolutionary epoch.[55] Goskino, too, was quite concerned about getting enough scripts, having budgeted 3,000 *gold* rubles for this purpose through July 1, 1924. To stir public interest, it planned to hold a contest with fifty *chervonets* (500 rubles) as first prize.[56] The Leningrad production company Sevzapkino also announced that they were accepting scripts, though without mention of remuneration.[57]

At the end of 1923 an important article appeared in *Cinema Gazette* calling for the establishment of a "new cinema front" to end the general malaise:

> We need a group of active people: first, those who are committed to the affairs of the revolution, and second, those who love cinematography, know it, and work in it. Only such an avant-garde might lead cinematography along the path of modernity in the service of the Revolution.

The proposed organization was to be called the Association of Revolutionary Cinematography (ARK);[58] within a year these plans would come to fruition through the efforts of *Cinema Gazette*'s editor Nikolai Lebedev.

Films

Agit-films

Film production was limited during this period and almost none have survived due to the fragility of nitrate stock and the very poor quality of what the Soviets had at their disposal.[59] That any were made at all in these early years was something of a miracle. It was inevitable that the Revolution would offer new topics, and it is interesting to see how "revolutionary ideas" were perceived and popularized by film directors, a group not known for political perspicacity. The most important genre for this period, as indicated earlier, was the agit-film needed for propaganda on the front. One of the very first Soviet-made films was a film of this type, *Overcrowding (Uplotnenie,* 1918), produced by the Petrograd Cinema Committee, directed by Aleksandr Panteleev, and based on Commissar of Enlightenment A. V. Lunacharskii's first cinema script. (In fact, the movie begins with a shot of Lunacharskii boyishly grinning at the camera.) It is the story of a pampered professor (played by D. I. Leshchenko, the head of the Commissariat's Cinema Section [VFKO] in 1919) who has to give up some rooms in his large house to workers; after a rough start, all turns out well. The professor begins teaching science to a workers' club, and his son falls in love with a proletarian girl who has moved in with them. *Overcrowding* is a perfect example of an agit-film, for it has a rudimentary plot, a simple message supporting the regime, and limited character development. Even with such restricted aims, the action and relationship of the characters are confusing; for example, people are constantly seen reading letters, but the viewer is never apprised of the content.[60] Soviet cinema had humble beginnings indeed.

Vladimir Gardin's 1921 *Sickle and Hammer* (*Serp i molot*) is a better example of the agit-film, except that at six reels it is considerably longer than the norm (which was about two reels, or twenty minutes). It is primitive and easily understandable with clichéd characters in a stock plot. A priest is shown cleaning pictures of the tsar, unsubtly making the connection between religion and autocracy. Rich peasants (*kulaks*) hoard bread, as children die of hunger; they buy forged "invalid" documents to keep from serving in the Red Army; and they seduce women and wring their hands villainously. The purpose of this picture (featuring the future director Vsevolod Pudovkin as a worker whose baby dies) was to effect a reconciliation between town and country, although this idea was executed most banally. Nonetheless, the use of hackneyed cinematic conventions was not naive. If the masses had ever before seen a movie, this was the style to which they were accustomed, and, as cinema activists were already aware, making movies comprehensible to the peasants was no easy task. As we shall see again and again, peasants had great difficulty understanding any but the most simple films.

Literary Adaptations

A more noteworthy example of the "miracle" of early Soviet filmmaking is *Polikushka* (1919, directed by Aleksandr Sanin), an adaptation of Lev Tolstoi's story starring the famous theater actor Ivan Moskvin in his first screen role. Screen adaptations of Russian classics had been a popular prerevolutionary genre, and the trend would continue. In this case, the adaptation could actually be said to be Soviet in character: not only is there a socially uplifting theme —on the depredations of drink—but the picture of rural poverty is a grim one.

This is perhaps Moskvin's best screen performance; he managed to overcome his intrinsic theatricality to create a memorable Polikushka. His death scene—suicide by hanging—is shot in slow motion, thus revealing some of the artistic possibilities of the medium. *Polikushka* was one of the first Soviet films to become popular abroad, and it is important for the politics of later film production that Hungarian film critic Bela Balasz pinned the film's success to its theatricality and its Moscow Art Theater star.[61]

Revolutionary Films

There were two kinds of films in the "revolutionary" genre that aimed higher than the "vulgar" propaganda of the agit-films. These were the "historical-revolutionary" films and the "international revolutionary" films. *Arsen Dzhordzhiashveli* (1921; Ivan Perestiani, director) has the distinction of being the first attempt at the former type, a romantic film of the revolutionary past. It was also the first film on a Georgian theme with Georgian actors.[62] Just as Vsevolod Pudovkin was getting his start in the movies as an actor, so the future Georgian director Mikhail Chiaureli played Arsen, the film's protagonist, a member of the underground during the 1905 Revolution. In many ways the plot is indistinguishable from that of an agit-film: the workers plan a strike; there is a traitor in the group, and as a result the committee is arrested. Arsen and two of his friends escape, the two cohorts deciding that someone should kill the governor-general.

Arsen—quite properly from a Bolshevik point of view—has mixed feelings about an act of individual terror, but he loses the straw vote and must kill the general. At this point the movie becomes interesting, due to a large extent to Chiaureli's attempts to define his character as a real person. Arsen is tormented by his fate, *not* because such acts of terror are politically wrong, but because he is passionately in love. He overcomes his personal feelings, kills the general, and dies heroically (an officer executes him after the firing squad refuses to shoot).

Arsen Dzhordzhiashveli was the first movie to try to develop a revolutionary theme in a narrative form more complex than that of the agit-film. The tendentiousness of the theme is enlivened by the love interest, played with breast-heaving passion and fluttering eyelids; and by a good dose of brutality, as when Arsen is caught or when the stool pigeon is thrown from a bridge into the path of a train. There is also a well-cut chase scene with the dramatic touch of a bloody hand streaking a wall. But most importantly, *Arsen Dzhordzhiashveli* attempted to depict a realistic hero, a man beset by doubts and reluctant to die. In fact, this film represents an ideal rarely achieved in Soviet silent cinema—it was both entertaining and economically made.

Perestiani was not an inspired filmmaker, but he had at least a rudimentary knowledge of cinematographic principles. Another example of the revolutionary film, *Locksmith and Chancellor* (*Slesar' i kantsler*, 1923) directed by Vladimir Gardin, is a puzzlingly bad picture, puzzling because the personnel involved were experienced; not only the director, Gardin, but his assistant, Olga Preobrazhenskaia, had had considerable careers in prerevolutionary cinema (Preobrazhenskaia was an actress of some repute and had directed on her own).

Locksmith and Chancellor is nonetheless a truly terrible picture, a revolutionary fable based on the play by the Commissar of Enlightenment, A.V. Lunacharskii. The setting is a foreign country populated by decadent women and homosexual soldiers. There is a badly shot strike scene which merely shows a lot of people milling around, and even the moving camerawork is boring, lacking dynamism and focus. The self-conscious revolutionary cliches and nonexistent plot make it an example of the worst of the decade. The critical opinion of the time concurred. Valentin Turkin, a prerevolutionary scenarist who continued to be important in the early Soviet period as writer, critic, and teacher, wrote:

> ... the picture represents unbroken directorial confusion with regard to the methods of work in cinematography.... All the principles of constructing screen action have fallen before absolutely total absurdity.[63]

Comedies

Comedies were also considered a desirable genre, especially to express anti-religious ideas. According to his sister, Lenin's favorite movie was Aleksandr Panteleev's 1922 anti-religious comedy *Miracle Worker* (*Chudotvorets*). It is clear from memoirs that Lenin did not see many movies, which makes his famous saying "Cinema is for us the most important of all arts" undoubtedly apocryphal. Nonetheless, if *Miracle Worker* were indeed his favorite film, it may tell us something about his character, for it is a vulgar comedy of a phony miracle. The peasants play jokes on their cruel mistress, such as throwing horse manure through a window or putting a pig with her nightcap on its head in her bed. The film is "correct" in that it sets the peasants against both landlords and the Church, the peasants coming off as cunning but extremely uncouth. The making of anti-religious movies would continue to pose stylistic problems; long after the worst clichés had disappeared from other genres, anti-religious films were consistently crude.

The second comedy to be considered here, the 1922 film *Commander Ivanov* (*Kombrig Ivanov*) directed by Aleksandr Razumnyi, also has strong anti-religious overtones. It was one of the few films the financially strapped Proletkino studio managed to complete and is a curious effort from an organization dedicated to making "proletarian" films: the tale of how a Bolshevik commissar manages to overcome the petty-bourgeois resistance of a priest's daughter (played by Olga Tretiakova, a vocal spokeswoman for actors' rights) to "living in sin." One could of course argue that it represents the "new morality" which had not yet fallen into disgrace and was therefore consonant with proletarian aims, but its lascivious slyness makes its American title *The Beauty and the Bolshevik* fitting (it was later criticized for being shown abroad under such a title). *Commander Ivanov* is good-natured, even in its attack against religion, but shallow, and not particularly compelling. A major flaw which must have hampered its reception with the semi-literate mass audience were the titles; very long and literary, they disturbed the continuity of the action.

In fact, the popular reception of *Commander Ivanov* is open to some dispute. One report was that peasants rejected the picture for its lack of realism, the argument being that a few flaws could seriously damage the credibility of cinema with the literal-minded peasant audience.[64] Another report was that workers, while rejecting the primitive moralizing of agit-films, liked *Commander Ivanov* very much.[65] Although concrete reports of audience response were rare, it is clear that the pessimism of critics about the quality of Soviet cinema was justified.

First Successes

By 1922, however, two productions gave cause for hope. One was the first number of Dziga Vertov's *Cinema Truth* series of newsreels.[66] The other could not have been more different, a lively adventure story of children in the Civil War, directed by the Georgian Ivan Perestiani (who made the revolutionary adventure discussed above, *Arsen Dzhordzhiashveli*). This historic film, *Little Red Devils* (*Krasnye d'iavoliata*), was a truly delightful movie which was enormously popular with the viewers (named their favorite film as late as 1925).

Little Red Devils begins with the ironic touch of the boy-hero reading James Fenimore Cooper's *The Pathfinder* and imagining himself chased by Indians while his sister is reading Romain Rolland and envisioning herself as a bombthrower. Of course, they do not need to rely on imagination since they are in the midst of a real-life adventure. Makhno's anarchist "Greens" are attacking their Ukrainian town; the gang members look like comic-strip villains. The tone of the movie in fact constantly fluctuates between the humorous and the serious, for the bandits, despite their satirically depraved appearance, are truly violent killers.

One of the early victims is the children's father, who exhorts them with his dying words to remember their brother who was a mutineer on the *Aurora*. In the course of various comic adventures (like the slapstick robbery of a peasant couple), the children join forces with a Negro boy, Tom Jackson (whose appearance in the Ukraine is bizarre, to say the least). The girl, Dunia, is tortured on hot coals before justice triumphs, but at last the villain (who sports sunglasses throughout) dies.

Cinema Gazette extolled this droll adventure as the "first film of the revolution," pointedly noting that it was a production of the Georgian production company Goskinprom Gruzii, thus by implication chastising the Russian studios. The newspaper advised that in order for everybody to see the picture, one hundred copies should be made, an extraordinary demand considering the severe stock shortage (ordinarily ten copies of a film were made). *Cinema Gazette*'s view of the virtues of the movie was most revealing: *Little Red Devils* could

> ... cure film workers of the sick pessimism caused by the lack of success of the past years; it will serve as a strong and hopeful weapon in the hands of the supporters of the revolutionary

art film, will attract to cinema the still greater attention of Soviet public opinion, and will deprive the cinema producers of the right to make potboilers, alluding to our technical poverty as an excuse.[67]

This statement made an important point about the status of cinema in Soviet society. The time for self-flagellation was passing; the inferiority complex must be overcome to spur the sluggish development of cinema. Some had claimed that Soviet cinema technology was only advanced enough for the nonfiction film; *Little Red Devils* showed that this was not true, and *Cinema Gazette*, as a supporter of the fiction film, found cause at last to rejoice.

Despite the dreams, promises, and slow beginnings, very little had happened in Soviet cinema from 1919 to 1923 in terms of establishing a film industry. A diverse and lively discussion was taking place concerning the *possibilities* of cinema, and gifted young people were attracted by the notion of making a revolutionary art from a lowly entertainment medium. More important, some were even rejecting philosophizing to take stock of an extremely unpleasant reality: the poor physical condition of a practically nonexistent "industry." Literally everything was in the future.

The Turning Point (1924)

Despite the surprising success of *Little Red Devils*, cinema activists were far from optimistic at the outset of the year 1924. In the cities, where most theaters were, theaters suffered from chaotic finances, high taxes, and a shortage of movies. From all indications, conditions were primitive. Showings were never on time,[1] and some German visitors considered even Moscow's theaters (the country's finest) shockingly old-fashioned, most of them lacking orchestras.[2] Provincial theaters suffered from a glut of petty-bourgeois films (according to a *Cinema Week* [*Kino-nedelia*] critic), and Grigorii Boltianskii noted that theaters were either closed or extremely decrepit.[3] Nikolai Lebedev wrote that there was as yet no revolutionary cinematography, only "brisk trade of foreign trash" and "nasty domestic hack-work."[4] Doubtless most would have agreed with him, whether examining the scene from an artistic or ideological point of view (and the movies just discussed would corroborate this).

Concerns up to this point had been mainly theoretical, but in 1924 there was a shift away from the exuberant revolutionary manifestoes of previous years toward a more realistic appraisal of the vast problems facing Soviet cinema. Pessimism was still rampant:

> Up to now we have had no organization. Up to now we have not known how to cope with the bureaucratism, chancellory-itis [*kantseliarshchina*], slovenliness, and superficiality which reign in part of our cinema organization. Up to now we have not freed ourselves from speculators and pseudo-specialists who consciously or unconsciously hamper our cinema work....
> Up to now we have had neither cinema politics nor normal economics.
> We have still *not created the preconditions for production.*
> ... That is why our cinema spring is so sad.[5]

The formalist critic and writer Viktor Shklovskii, recently returned from exile abroad for his socialist revolutionary connections, declared that the time for watching poor pictures merely because they were Russian was past, caustically noting that "only Finland and Poland will watch 'their' films from patriotism."[6] This new spirit was articulated by many others.[7] The time had come to make movies.

Goskino and the Economy

In the spring of 1924, the All-Union Conference of Cinema Organizations was convened to review the findings of the Mantsev Commission (which had been appointed in September 1923 to study the organizational problems of the industry). While the conference resolutions dealt mainly with the "monopoly question," they also revealed some general directives for future action. Although the government monopoly on distribution would be retained and extended to encompass all Soviet republics the better to exploit the internal market, it was suggested that film organizations should unify through a joint-stock company. The conference accepted the Mantsev Commission's recommendations on the necessity of reorganizing the industry, except that the Commissariat of Enlightenment was to remain in charge of cinema.[8]

The basic form the new "practicality" on the cinema front took was a critical examination of Goskino. Could Goskino pull itself out of its difficulties? The Conference of Cinema Organizations believed not, the question being what should replace it. At the end of 1923 *Cinema Gazette* had favored a union of existing organizations; now it began to re-evaluate this. Goskino's capital, it charged, was capital on paper only, the "real" money backing the organization estimated at 27,000 rubles. Should the "dead" capital of Goskino be joined with the "living," that is, should Goskino receive more money?

According to *Cinema Gazette*, providing Goskino with more funds would be tantamount to jumping on a sinking ship. There should be no union of studios with Goskino, but instead the "creation of an authoritative regulatory organ and the transfer to it of the right of monopoly" to aid the development of Soviet cinema.[9] *Cinema Gazette* therefore campaigned for the fall of Goskino, attributing the crisis in cinema and the inactivity of production and distribution to Goskino's "monopoly." (A better argument could be made that these problems stemmed from Goskino's fiscal weakness.)

Goskino's alleged monopoly illustrated the dangers of "*glavkism*," central bureaucratic control. Where central bureaucratic control was weakest, claimed *Cinema Gazette*, cinema was doing best, both in production and distribution: "The free initiative of separate *Soviet* enterprises will defeat the remains of '*glavkism.*'"[10] Calls like this, for decentralization, were rarely seen in the pages of the cinema press except in the Leningrad newspaper *Cinema Week* where they would continue until 1925.

Cinema Week, the organ of the Leningrad studio Sevzapkino, was, if anything, more strongly opposed to Goskino than was its Moscow counterpart

Cinema Gazette, labelling Goskino the "evil genius" of Soviet cinema in one editorial. Goskino, it agreed with *Cinema Gazette*, had not put the industry on firm footing; worse yet, Goskino was flooding Soviet screens with terrible foreign pictures: "petty-bourgeois [*meshchanskie*], stupid, dull, marshy films." According to *Cinema Week*, the crisis exemplified the evils of monopoly; it could only be remedied by involving more people in the decision-making process, specifically OSPK (Society of Builders of Proletarian Cinema, see below), the Artistic Council on Cinema Affairs in the Commissariat of Enlightenment, Soviet public opinion, and collective labor in cinema production.[11]

Cinema Week was also quite interested in the specifics of the economic situation (and with workers in general, as one might expect in Leningrad, where the Russian labor movement had started). In an attempt to approach problems more rationally, it tried to quantify production costs.[12] Economic questions concerned everyone in the film community, and an important, long-hoped-for change occurred in May 1924 when the Council of People's Commissars (Sovnarkom) lowered the tax on movie tickets from 30 percent to 10 percent. That was the only concrete step taken to solve the industry's financial problems, although Sovnarkom empowered the Supreme Council of the National Economy (Vesenkha) to "take measures" to solve the chronic shortage of raw materials for cinema production.[13]

Any discussion of which organization should control distribution was rather academic. Due to the shortage of raw materials, there was little production and therefore little to distribute. "Film hunger" (even "starvation") was a chronic problem, and because demand exceeded supply, film rental was expensive. In prerevolutionary times theaters had paid for films by the meter; now they had to turn over a percentage of their proceeds as well, ranging from 30 to 50 percent. In the opinion of many, rental prices had to be lowered to prevent the failure and closure of theaters. Furthermore, especially in provincial theaters, there was no choice of films. Provincial theaters were forced to accept what was sent, and, adding to their woes, the films arrived late (allowing no opportunity for advertising), or not at all.[14]

With little domestic production, it is easy to imagine that the dilemma facing the industry regarding foreign films was as much economic as ideological. Of course it was recognized that foreign (and prerevolutionary) films were not made to satisfy communist ideology, but it must be emphasized that what caused greater concern at this point was that the latest American hits still had not been seen (because they were too expensive to purchase).[15]

Good or bad, more than 95 percent of the films in distribution in 1924 were foreign films. Worry over the possible political ramifications of this "infiltration" of foreign ideology increased, and as mentioned earlier, the aesthetically dubious solution was to re-edit foreign films for the Soviet audience. This practice proved good training for a generation of Soviet film editors, including the distinguished compilation-documentarist Esfir Shub, although there were complaints that the re-editing was done hastily by "accidental people [who] not only [are] politically illiterate, neither can they write Russian correctly [for the titles]." In addition, the newly written titles were ridiculously long and boring in an effort to inject revolutionary ideology in the movies. To overcome these shortcomings, it was recognized that the ranks of film editors had to be strengthened with people who were politically and grammatically literate. This could be achieved in two ways: by increasing wages and by putting the name of the editor in the credits.[16] (The Revolution notwithstanding, people apparently still hungered for money and fame.)

The Labor Force

The difficulty of attracting competent film editors was a single facet of a larger problem. Just as there was a shortage of money and raw materials for the cinema, so was there a shortage of trained personnel on all levels. The nascent Soviet cinema had become a director's cinema, in the sense that there was a tacit recognition that the director was the central figure in the movie-making process. But many believed the prerevolutionary directors who had remained were not working out entirely satisfactorily,[17] while the young were unskilled technically. So few new directors had technical mastery, in fact, that one writer charged many cameramen were actually making the films[18] (presumably benefitting from their Civil War experience). This notwithstanding, the general opinion was that the "salvation of Soviet cinematography" lay not with "old specialists" but with youth. The young simply needed to learn.[19]

Discontent with "specialists" was a characteristic of Soviet society not unique to cinema. One school of thought maintained, however, that working without directors was actually a *strong* point of Soviet cinema, since in a socialist society the collective should be the "ideal of cinema production."[20] This was hardly a workable solution. Collectives like Kuleshov's, Vertov's, or Kozintsev's and Trauberg's were very much directed and led. Leo Mur, one of the more colorful characters in Soviet cinema, a former revolutionary whose years in exile had led him to filmwork in New York and Hollywood, answered the question this way: there should be collectives (a collective "machine," as he phrased it), but standing "over the collective must be a single thought and will. . . . " In view of Soviet conditions, the director should be a "team leader," but the idea of working without a director was as dangerous as working without rules.[21] The question of the director's role in filmmaking persisted as an important problem. The form the issue was taking—the charges of a "dictatorship" of the director—could lead to some glib political parallels, when in fact hard reality necessitated someone's controlling the scanty resources.

The second pressing personnel problem was the lack of script writers. Some believed this could easily be solved, fallaciously reasoning that any writer (or even any individual) could be a scenarist, since all that was necessary was an idea. With this notion regnant, it is not surprising that the script shortage did not abate.

By the end of 1924, the term "scenario crisis" had made its debut, with 90 percent of submitted scripts being rejected.[22] This crisis, said the critics, was caused by only partially implemented centralization and poorly organized and inadequately paid script writers. The solution to the scenario crisis therefore would be: (1) to work out a common thematic plan for all cinema organizations; (2) to create a professional association for script writers in either the proposed ARK (the Association of Revolutionary Cinematography) or in Rabis (the Art Workers' Union); and (3) to increase rates of payment for script work.[23]

The last solution was surely an eminently practical one because the talented writer would not be attracted to cinema any other way. The other preferred solutions, especially the first, indicated that the "line" of *Cinema Gazette* was again veering toward more organization, not less. The individual initiative extolled earlier in the year, with regard to Goskino, did not, in the end, answer the demands of the day. Yet *who* was qualified enough to propose themes and organize the artistic councils of the various cinema companies?

The final personnel problem widely discussed in 1924 concerned the actor. (The troubling shortage of technical cadres, like projectionists, did not attract much concern except in *Cinema Week*.)[24] Although Dziga Vertov had summarily dismissed the actor as a participant in the postrevolutionary movie, most recognized that the actor (whether professional or nonprofessional) would continue to be an important factor in cinema.

The first question posed was: Is there something specific about the craft of a cinema actor, or could a theater actor easily work in the movies? Film critics early answered the latter part in the negative, saying that theater actors had no place in cinema, their acting being "theatrical," meaning "false." "Bolshevik" heroes —"steel-like, full-blooded, life-loving, strong people"— were expected to come "not from bourgeois theaters, but from the land."[25] That an actor playing a worker must be of proletarian stock, or better yet, actually *be* a worker was the beginning of the casting principle known as "typage." But because of the difficulty of fulfilling this ideal, production companies continued to draw upon the theater for acting talent.

The fundamental problem underlying all aspects of the labor issue in the cinema industry was the lack of training facilities. Lev Kuleshov, who had proved his devotion to film education through pedagogical activities both in GTK, the State Film Technical Institute (founded in 1919), and in his own collective, bluntly asserted:

All failures come from our immense "craft" free-and-easiness....

We do not know how to deal with the material of our craft; we do not know how, because we do not want to study; we do not know how, and consequently, are not acquainted with the formal side of cinematography....

In order to know how to show really interesting and expressive people, the organized movements of the masses, convincing shots, and finally to obtain correct development of the plot [*siuzhet*], it is essential to *know* and to *know how*. To know all the characteristics and peculiarities of cinematography, to know how to manage and to know how to obey.

For Kuleshov, the revolution could not be realized in cinema without attention to training.

But which sort of training should come first: technical or political education? Indicative of the waning interest in ideology, Kuleshov was convinced that the ideological side of films could be strengthened only *after* the technical side, after the achievement of professional mastery. Kuleshov's attitude toward prerevolutionary specialists, who were an obvious source of cinematographic knowledge, was a combination of caution and prophecy:

On the path of study and perfecting of cinema craft stand people who specialized in the old art. They are our enemies.... It is not necessary to listen to them, but it is necessary to learn the trade [from them].... If there is an exaggerated tendency on the side of formalism in youthful work; then one should not forget that, first, this is a temporary phenomenon, and, second, knowledge of the craft is essential for the resolution of the scripts we need. Otherwise we will come to the Western blind alley. There the cinematographic twilight has begun, here the dawn is breaking. We will conquer. The light comes from the East, the light of genuine mastery which casts off the aestheticism of artistry and which will learn to build the communist film of the future world of cinematography of the USSR.[26]

Kuleshov's statement reflected a not uncommon mixture (for a Russian) of resentment at backwardness and praise for the *virtues* of backwardness. But was it possible to take what one needed from the "old" specialists and reject the rest? The coexistence between those who wholeheartedly considered themselves Soviet, like Kuleshov, and the fellow travellers, like director Iakov Protazanov, recently returned from abroad, was often uneasy. Kuleshov was not the only young film activist who admired proficiency and professionalism, nor was he the only one who recognized the built-in dangers in co-opting the talents of politically neutral specialists. His point of view was, however, moderate when compared to others.

By far the sharpest attack on cinema specialists to this date appeared in a *Cinema Week* article by Albert Syrkin, a member of VAPP, the All-Russian Association of Proletarian Writers. Syrkin scoffed at those who expected to see truly "Soviet" films and were therefore naive enough to be amazed at all the "hastily-made nonsense, petty-bourgeois, philistine [and] narrowminded, loosely draped in red rags." This was not surprising considering the source of

"Soviet" films: "Who makes Soviet films? In 99 cases out of 100, a director reactionary to the core, dreaming about the past; a scenarist from the all-knowing youth; artists at best indifferently neutral."

Syrkin pointed to the debate in literary circles over fellow travellers and urged that such a debate begin in the film community. He did not deny that the technical expertise of specialists was vital, but that after the "debacle" of a film like *Aelita* (to be discussed below), leadership was clearly necessary:

> Give them ideological soil for work, say precisely and clearly what you need . . . and we, it seems at last, will have *Soviet cinematography*.
> Without this knowledge we will have empty, naked technique, at best with "neutral," but nearly always with ideologically harmful content.
> If we have mastered technique, it would be odd not to master ideology.[27]

That anyone could think the Soviets had mastered technique was an ominous sign.

Leningrad's *Cinema Week* was the most militant cinema publication (which lends piquancy to its absorption in March 1925 by *Cinema Gazette*, which then became *Cinema [Kino]*). It supported Syrkin in an editorial calling for political commissars in cinema in order to avoid further waste of money on films which were "neutral or worse." Every director needed a permanent political adviser, as in the Army. The editorial continued:

> This work seems to us many times more important and immediate than the resolution of the general problems of our film industry. *We do not need a cinema industry without ideological significance.*[28]

Directors, as might be expected, were less than enthusiastic about this. All publicly admitted a certain necessity for political guidance, but one "fellow traveller," director Cheslav Sabinskii, courageously and perceptively noted that having a political commissar on the premises during the actual shooting would be as absurd as having two conductors for an orchestra. Young directors like Abram Room who considered themselves truly "Soviet" assumed that *they* did not need political watchdogs and that the deployment of commissars would be restricted to the prerevolutionary directors.[29] This complex problem of the relationship between the old and new cadres continued to be a major controversy, but fortunately for the development of Soviet cinema in the silent period, the idea of political commissars for the studios was ignored for the time being.

Cinefication *(Kinofikatsia)*

Another sign of growing activity on the cinema front was that attention was at last turned to the countryside. It is hard to learn what was happening in the rural areas because as yet few cinema activists were much interested, especially true of those associated with *Cinema Week* (indicative of the cosmopolitanism of Leningrad). The Main Committee for Political Education (Glavpolit-prosvet) was the section of the Commissariat of Enlightenment vested with authority in the arts; not surprisingly, it was the first organization to turn attention to the countryside. Significantly, its interest was commercial, not ideological—a plan to sell the projector GOZ. The staggering cost of 640 rubles (25 percent down, 75 percent in five months) was admitted to be "rather high," but it was claimed the projectors could pay for themselves in three to six months.[30] Glavpolitprosvet's uncertainty as to the success of this scheme was evident in the questions asked in their market survey: Was it economically feasible to buy a projector? Were any projectionists available?

Critic Nikolai Lebedev energetically promoted sending movies to the countryside, not as entertainment or propaganda, but as an educational device, the most common attitude toward rural cinema. He therefore supported the newsreel and documentary as being "more valuable than newspapers" in a country with 70 percent illiteracy (an optimistic figure). Like Glavpolitprosvet, Lebedev hoped that such films could bring economic as well as political profit.[31] If fiction films were to be shown in rural areas, they had to be simple and direct, attacking the evils of contemporary Soviet life, of which Lebedev saw many:

> ... we need pictures which in vivid and sarcastic images will "flog" the plagues of our present; which will show primitively but dynamically, the figures of the NEPman, his wife and progeny, will show the bureaucrat and the Soviet fool [*sovdurak*], will show careerists and toadies, ... will show dozens of other deformed masks of our contemporary life.[32]

For the present, however, given the lack of Soviet production, Lebedev proposed re-editing imported detective and adventure films so that they would be suitable for peasants and workers.[33]

Lebedev had been a Party member since 1918, and his was an unusually tough political approach to cinema. But was it also the Party's attitude toward the function of cinema in Soviet society? The answer must be negative. The Party in 1924 was not monolithic, and interest in cinema was virtually nonexistent within higher Party circles. Lebedev was in fact a harsh critic of the Party's "free market" policies, like many other cinema activists.

Some of Lebedev's demands were less controversial than his views on the types of film suitable for rural areas. He wanted to increase the availability of the cinema to all areas of the country. His goal was that those in urban areas and in the armed forces should be able to see films once a week by 1930, and peasants about once a month—a modest and seemingly attainable aim.[34] The "film hunger" and "distribution disorder" had to be ended[35] to enable the expansion of the theater network. (The term "cinefication" was coined for this process.) In most cases the "theater" was a travelling projector *(peredvizhok)*. After cinefication and presumably after the development of the Soviet film industry, a "cultural-educational" program of films was to gradually replace the "bourgeois-entertainment" films on the program.[36]

This stultifying prescription for cinema was only to be visited on the peasants, not city dwellers. One should keep in mind that Lebedev really meant *educational* films; he was no friend of Dziga Vertov's radical nonfiction cinema. But despite the sober virtuousness of the project, cinefication's supporters had difficulty attracting financial aid from the government, and their dreams were not soon realized.

The Search for a Soviet Style: Realism

The year 1924 was pivotal in the development of the film industry. Considering the severe financial problems and organizational chaos, it is no surprise that the mental energy of cinema activists was devoted, as we have seen, to practical matters. Unlike the period from 1919 to 1923, when theoretical issues predominated, in 1924 there was almost no such interest. Nevertheless, the sole book which might be considered "purely" theoretical, prerevolutionary scenarist Al. Voznesenskii's *Art of the Screen (Iskusstvo ekrana)* significantly contributed to the formation of a Soviet cinema aesthetic, although it was on the surface somewhat arcane. Voznesenskii, like his predecessors, believed that cinema, due to its inherent realism, was the art of the future. But he sharply disagreed that montage was the basis of cinema. This was, in his opinion, the "illiterate mistake of the theatrical futurists." Montage was nothing more than the scenes in a play, therefore not original at all. The foundation of cinema, said Voznesenskii, was not form, but "man and only man."[37]

Voznesenskii sought to humanize cinema by rejecting the tendency toward formalism that he saw in the avant-garde and placing man, not montage, at the center of cinema. For the same reason, Voznesenskii was sharply critical of the propaganda film, although he was not opposed to "propaganda" in cinema as long as "the idea ... [was] dissolved in the artistic work like sugar in tea."[38] He was one of the first to express concern that the simple-minded sloganeering of the earliest revolutionary productions could not possibly attract the viewer. The screen writer, he said, should not "thrust his own idea on the viewer" but present it artistically enough to win him over.[39] But because Voznesenskii held the naive view that content and form cannot be separated in photography, he thought that ideology could be gracefully inserted in the film.[40]

Dziga Vertov and the cinema constructivists had a vision of Soviet style—the complete abolition of the fiction film with total rejection of art in cinema. Voznesenskii was offering a more man-centered approach—the actor and the story would have the central place, and *after* that, technique and propaganda.

Political leftists, represented by Vladimir Erofeev and Nikolai Lebedev (and *Cinema Gazette* as long as it was under their editorship, through 1924), were in an unenviable position. While they adamantly rejected what they thought of as "bourgeois" art, they recognized that Vertov's radical aesthetics were incomprehensible to the masses—and they were sincerely dedicated to the principle of bringing cinema to the people. More and more, such people were drawn to Voznesenskii's view of cinema.

Consequently, the earliest statement of a realistic aesthetic for Soviet cinema appeared in a *Cinema Gazette* editorial. In all areas of the arts, it said,

> ...the worker and worker-intellectual consumer demands *intelligibility, simplicity, logic, lifelikeness, orderliness, way of life* [*byt*]. The worker does not suffer...affectation, idiosyncrasy, mysticism. The world view of the working class, Marxism, is the most well-defined and harmonious of existing world views. Only one style, realism, corresponds most to this world view.[41]

What genre best corresponded to realism? For the time being it seemed that "contemporary revolutionary-detective stories full of heroism, struggles, the reality of the present day and of contemporary life" would be ideal. (The comedy-adventure *Little Red Devils* was touted as an example.)[42] Because of the ease with which the historical film could turn into a costume drama,[43] contemporary subjects were strongly preferred. Unfortunately for the development of Soviet cinema, ideas on the "realistic" treatment of contemporary life were peculiarly Soviet and, in the end, not very realistic.

Films

"Export" Films

Although activity in the film industry had greatly increased in 1924, very few movies were made. The film of the season was without a doubt prerevolutionary director Iakov Protazanov's first Soviet production, *Aelita*. Produced by Mezhrabpom, *Aelita* was promoted with unusual flair for the Soviets: advertising leaflets were dropped from airplanes, and a slick, Western-style program bragged about the 3,000 workers and 22,000 meters of film shot.[44] (Such extravagance would not long be a boasting matter.)

Aelita is remembered in film history for being the rare science fiction silent movie and for the constructivist sets and costumes designed by the well-known artist Aleksandra Ekster. There was nothing else innovative about it. Based on Aleksei Tolstoi's popular novel, *Aelita* is the tale of a Soviet engineer who during the Civil War builds a spaceship, travels to Mars, and becomes involved in a proletarian revolution. Obvious concessions to Soviet power in the film include a shot of women putting on shoes at a ball cut to peasant women putting on bast shoes, to name one example. Titles about the joys of building a revolution are tendentious and the ending is pious: dreams are fun (the adventure was, after all, only a dream), but Soviet citizens must remember the "real work" that lay ahead. Yet Soviet life seems so drab by comparison—there are hints in the film of food shortages—that we may easily accept that Soviet earthlings prefer fantasizing about Mars to thinking about "real work."

The appeal of *Aelita* is an unabashedly romantic one, with the very young, plumply sensuous, and scantily clad Iuliia Solntseva (a major film star and later director) in the title role of the Martian princess. Typical of prerevolutionary directors, Protazanov relied heavily on theatrical talent, and most of the principals—Solntseva, V. E. Kuindzhi, N. M. Tseretelli, Konstantin Eggert, and Igor Ilinskii—were theater actors. In short, *Aelita* was an old-fashioned entertainment movie using theater actors, exotic glamour, and a certain amount of bare flesh to good purpose.

Dissatisfaction with *Aelita* centered on its budget, but the polemics surrounding it indicate the attitude toward both "fellow travellers" like Protazanov and toward entertainment films. The charge of "commercialism" was directed not only at *Aelita* but at the films of Mezhrabpom in general.[45] Mezhrabpom was an important *independent* production company founded in 1921 with foreign capital; the name is an acronym for International Workers Aid.[46]

It was alleged that Mezhrabpom deliberately produced films to be "hits" (that is, financially successful) for *Western*, not Soviet, audiences. In other words, Mezhrabpom was accused of making what came to be known as the "export" film. The proof of this indictment was *Aelita*, but the brouhaha over *Aelita* was a two-pronged attack, directed not only against policies of a particular studio but also against "old" specialists working in Soviet cinema. At forty-three, Protazanov could not of course really be considered "old," but he already had a long history in the movies. From 1907 to 1917, he had directed eighty movies, so even considering the short length of these early films, he was an experienced director by any standards. Protazanov had been in self-imposed exile from 1920 to 1923, and his return to the Soviet Union was of great importance in providing his countrymen an example both of solid professionalism and dedication to the entertainment film.

The harsh criticism of *Aelita* may have caused Protazanov to reflect on the wisdom of his decision. Vladimir Erofeev called for making dozens of *Little Red Devils* rather than *Aelitas*, asserting that a story of love and intrigue on Mars made Soviet reality look prosaic in the extreme. The public, according to Erofeev, did not need "philistine dreams about bourgeois Mars . . . [since they] live on Soviet earth."[47] Another critic (identified as "N. L.," undoubtedly Nikolai Lebedev) felt that the film, although "technically well-enough done" was "pretentious." Lebedev pointedly noted that since Protazanov had been abroad during the Civil War, he did not understand its implications, and had therefore removed the ideological significance of Tolstoi's novel from the film. Significantly, Lebedev said that the film's chief fault was that it was "ideologically unprincipled."[48]

Erofeev and Lebedev were right in rejecting the putative revolutionary aspects of the movie. The Martian revolution in *Aelita* was staged for entertainment value alone. They were also right that Protazanov's film could not be faulted technically, for his films were always professionally finished. The *Aelita* affair was definitely a blow to Lev Kuleshov's hopes of cultivating an atmosphere of mastery first, ideology second. It was unfair to say, as it was said, that because Protazanov had made a technically literate movie in *Aelita*, the problems of backwardness had already been overcome. Protazanov's technical expertise had been hard earned prior to the Revolution and reflected absolutely nothing about the state of *Soviet* cinema. Nonetheless, the struggle between the advocates of ideology and those of technical preparedness had begun. And it was not the last time the charge of "commercialism" would be hurled at Mezhrabpom.

Despite the disapprobation in the cinema press, others reacted to *Aelita* more positively. *Cinema Gazette* printed large advertisements for *Aelita*, quoting from favorable reviews in newspapers like the Party's organ *Pravda* and the military's *Red Star (Krasnaia zvezda)*. Whether this was *Cinema Gazette*'s sense of fair play or their own commercial deviation is impossible to judge.[49]

Comedies

A more gifted film which received comparatively little notice was Lev Kuleshov's first full-length work, *The Extraordinary Adventures of Mr. West in the Land of the Bolsheviks (Neobychainye prikliucheniia mistera Vesta v strane bolshevikov)*. Kuleshov had directed Civil War agit-films which have not survived, but this was his first movie employing his specially trained collective. Vladimir Erofeev dryly noted that although *Mr. West* showed Kuleshov's mastery of American techniques and his collective's formidable acting ability, it was not a suitable demonstration of his talents.[50]

Erofeev displayed a singular lack of humor, for *Mr. West* is a hilarious satirical romp. Mr. West (P. Podobed), the president of the YMCA, fearfully comes to Soviet Russia with his trusty bodyguard, the cowboy Jeddy (Boris Barnet), to protect him from the savage Bolsheviks. Jeddy dresses in full cowboy regalia: wildly furry chaps, a ten-gallon hat, six-shooters. He rides shotgun on top of the car. West and Jeddy meet up with a gang of "former people" (down-and-out aristocrats and other déclassé elements) and out-and-out adventurers: the countess (Aleksandra Khokhlova) and her cagily sinister cohorts (Vsevolod Pudovkin and Sergei Komarov). The hoax is too implausible to bear repeating, but *Mr. West* is so high-spirited and good-natured that its narrative deficiencies make no difference. It pokes fun not only at American stereotypes, but also takes sly digs at the stock figures of agit-films.

The physicality of the jokes—Jeddy's hijacking a sled and walking tightrope between buildings (which nearly killed Barnet and later caused a rift between him and Kuleshov)—are reminiscent of American slapstick comedy, but the sharpness of the satire and the high level of the acting make *Mr. West* a classic in its genre. The movie introduced the most improbable film star of the decade, Kuleshov's gangly and eccentric wife, Aleksandra Khokhlova. Far from a traditional silent film heroine, she was nonetheless a brilliant actress.

Mr. West's zaniness quite unexpectedly fizzles out at the end; after all the villains come to justice, Mr. West tours the "true Soviet Russia" and sees the evidence of the great new life. Was Kuleshov forced to end the movie this way? Some reviewers euphemistically noted the "slow-down in tempo" as being unfortunate.[51] Ironically enough, considering his later association with Kuleshov on another "American" picture (*By the Law* [*Po zakonu*], 1926), the formalist critic Viktor Shklovskii openly criticized *Mr. West* for not being "Russian." Asking why *Mr. West* "emigrated," Shklovskii said: "... a real Russian picture is more interesting than Mr. West against the background of the Kremlin."[52] But *Cinema Week* reported that viewers liked the film *because* it was American in style, comments being that it was "witty, easy to watch... not a cine-opera."[53] Kuleshov wanted to entertain the viewers; he succeeded, but he continued to be attacked for his fresh "American" approach.

Mr. West did not get the attention it deserved as the first step toward a Soviet comedy; nor did the other major comedy of the year, *The Cigarette Girl from Mosselpro;* (*Papirosnitsa iz Mosselproma;* Iurii Zheliabuzhskii, director). *Cigarette Girl* was in fact criticized for *not* being a proper Soviet comedy, for lacking "class-consciousness" and being "typically sentimental."[54] This is significant because like *Mr. West*, *Cigarette Girl* is a genuinely funny film which satirizes NEP life and the making of movies. The cigarette girl (Iuliia Solntseva) is "discovered" by a film crew; the plot revolves around the competition of her various admirers for her attention. These are an American businessman, a bookkeeper (the popular comedian Igor Ilinskii), and a movie cameraman (N. M. Tseretelli).

At first the American is stereotyped in a friendly fashion: his huge amount of luggage causes the carriage to break down. Ilinskii (who like Solntseva and Tseretelli had been in *Aelita*) here played an idiot, his patented silent movie role. Much more amusing than Ilinskii's slapstick antics is the depiction of the shooting of the movie. The director is a dictator with megaphone, who imperiously shouts orders at the crew. They in turn abuse those pedestrians who dare to get in the way, but the passersby do not mind, for they are movie "maniacs," a common "psychosis" in NEP Russia.

The picture sours somewhat as the cigarette girl goes to work for the infatuated American businessman. Yet although the implications of this arrangement are less than savory, it is important to note that there is no moralizing. *The Cigarette Girl from Mosselprom* comes rather lamely to a traditional "happy ending," but despite the way it fizzles out, it is a decently made, if not dazzling, effort. Zheliabuzhskii, a director in the Protazanov mode, was another "old specialist," having had a varied career in the cinema since 1915.

Historical Films

In 1924, the Russians finally came out with a major historical-revolutionary film to counter the Georgian *Arsen Dzhordzhiashveli*—*Palace and Fortress* (*Dvorets i krepost'*; Aleksandr Ivanovskii, director), one of the first Soviet films to meet with international success. *Palace and Fortress* is the tale of a young officer, Beideman, who, disappointed in love, becomes a courier for the nineteenth-century radical democrat Aleksandr Herzen. Beideman is caught, imprisoned, and goes mad. Although the cruelty of the aristocracy toward their peasants and family is shown, it is for theatrical, not political, effect. A misbegotten love affair, not political conviction, causes Beideman (wonderfully played by the theater actor Evgenii Boronikhin) to become a revolutionary. A subplot which treats the ideologue of revolutionary terror Nechaev favorably weakens the focus. Yet almost despite itself, the film compels the viewer to suspend disbelief.

In the beginning *Palace and Fortress* is theatrical and dated, even for its time. But as Beideman descends into madness, the picture becomes realistic through the sheer power of Boronikhin's portrayal. It is one of the most memorable performances of the silent screen, a genuine tour de force. Cinematographically, however, the movie is ponderously static (caused in part by the frequent, unimaginative iris transitions). Aleksandr Ivanovskii's many years as director of the Zimin Opera Theater in Moscow[55] obviously influenced his style as the premiere director of Soviet "historical" films.

Palace and Fortress received an excellent press in *Cinema Week*, the "organ" of its producer, Sevzapkino; in contrast, the film was almost totally ignored in Moscow. There were some critical comments, on faults of detail or its expense, but the reviews were in general quite complimentary.[56] Interestingly enough, Politburo member Grigorii Zinovev was moved to write *Cinema Week* a letter complaining that Beideman was on the screen too much, which "irritated the nerves."[57] This then prompted a less enthusiastic review, which said the movie had succeeded neither as art nor as history.[58]

Nonfiction Films

In belligerent opposition to Ivanovskii's filmed "history" stood Dziga Vertov. Unfortunately his *Cinema Truth* series of documentaries, begun in 1922, was for the most part not available for viewing. Opposition to Vertov continued, not so much to *Cinema Truth*, as to his theories. Critics like Vladimir Erofeev, an ardent supporter of the nonfiction film, recognized that Vertov's movies were not factual enough to fit the category. Although Erofeev did not actually analyze the contradictions in Vertov's films and writings and opposed those who wanted to prevent Vertov from working, he did worry that such aesthetically radical experimentation might hamper the development of "real" newsreels.[59] It is difficult to know what the public reaction to *Cinema Truth* was, but *Cinema Gazette* (at this point consistently anti-Vertov) did publish a letter from one Polikarp Malakhov, Rostov-on-Don, who called for less "Lefitis" (*Lefovshchina*, referring to Maiakovskii's group) and more "simplicity" in *Cinema Truth*.[60]

The sharpest criticism against Vertov in 1924 came from Aleksandr Anoshchenko who warned that a new strain of bacteria was threatening the health of the cinema world. This was the *kinococcus*, a scathing pun on Vertov's Cinema-eyes (in Russian, *kinokoki* for the "bacillus"; *kinoki* for the Cinema-eyes). Anoshchenko saw Vertov's worship of the machine (that is, the camera) as the chief threat.[61] Even Grigorii Boltianskii, who was generally sympathetic to Vertov and his goals accused him of "fetishism" in his use of the camera.[62]

The *Cinema Truth* series laid the groundwork for Vertov's first feature-length film, *Cinema Eye* (*Kino-glaz*), subtitled "life unawares" (*zhizn' vrasplokh*), a favorite notion of Vertov's. With his usual flair for self-promotion, Vertov said of this film: "The first series of *Cinema Eye* is the first slap in the face of fiction cinematography and at the same time a lesson to the cowardly imitator who releases pictures 'without actors.'"[63] The picture was advertised as a "cinema-thing without script, without actors, without directors, without sets."[64]

Not unexpectedly, Vladimir Erofeev did not like it, feeling that it was not so much "a demonstration of life [*byt*]" as a "cinematographic chamber of curiosities [*kunstkamera*]."[65] This is not so much true of the first part of the film, which shows a cooperative and a young Pioneers' camp, as it is of the second and third. In the second part we see a Chinese magician, a fly landing on a table, a boy sniffing cocaine, a man killed in a bar, and a chillingly clinical scene in a mental institution. In the third part, the images are random: faces, children playing, a ferris wheel. There is a lot of trick photography throughout—the making of bread and its "unmaking," a diver going in and then "out" of the water, Tverskoi Boulevard on "its side"—along with some animation.

Erofeev was enough of a cineast to know that the film was beautifully shot and interestingly cut. But ideologically speaking, he found that "the absence of a script or even themes leaves the picture without thought." (The notion that Vertov worked without script or plan was a widespread one, which he encouraged, but it was not true.) Erofeev concluded that although Vertov had "able hands," he needed a "communist head."[66]

Cinema Eye as late as 1925 continued to provoke comment as part of a general analysis of Vertov's contribution to Soviet cinema. That Dziga Vertov's existence as a filmmaker could be justified by the quality of the critical response to his movies is not an overstatement. Khrisanf Khersonskii was at the beginning of his distinguished career as a Vertov critic. He wrote that Vertov approached the themes and material of *Cinema Eye* only as curiosities; in general, he found Vertov childishly dazzled by his virtuosity. Khersonskii felt Vertov knew how to organize his visual material, but that he was far from being a mature artist.[67]

The formalist critic and theorist Viktor Shklovskii also began to earn a place for himself as a Vertov adversary. Shklovskii charged that Vertov's group, the Cinema-eyes, did not grasp the essence of cinema:

> They [the Cinema-eyes] do not understand that cinema is the most abstract of all arts, close in its foundations to several methods of mathematics. Cinematography requires action, and meaningful movement just as literature requires the word. Cinematography needs a plot [*siuzhet*] just as a picture needs ideational significance. Without this, it is difficult to orient the viewer, to give a single defined direction to his glance.
>
> In the works of the Cinema-eyes, cinema art has not left for new ground, but has only narrowed the old. They work like a person with frozen fingers: they do not know how to take small objects and are forced to content themselves with work on secondary form.

To Shklovskii, Vertov did not understand the semantics of cinema and therefore could not make the necessary connection between things.[68] In his view Vertov, far from being an innovator, was in reality quite traditional. Khersonskii had reproached Vertov for his cavalier treatment of serious material, repeating what by now had become standard: Vertov is an excellent filmmaker, *but.* . . . Shklovskii's critique was fundamentally different and far deadlier; by positing plot and meaning as the law of cinema, he was saying that Vertov was *not* a competent director.

A. Kurs continued the "unmasking" of Vertov with a backhanded compliment: Vertov, despite his anti-art rhetoric, deserved the label "artist" more than did "many others," because an artist is a "constructor-organizer" of material. Kurs feared the extension of Vertov's anti-art ideas to cinema as a whole, since in his opinion they were false. It is important to note that Kurs, unlike other critics of Vertov, was an ardent supporter of nonfiction films and newsreels, but he did not consider Vertov to be fulfilling that need.[69] Although Vertov had long been rejected by the fiction-film community, now devotees of the nonfiction film rejected him and threw him into the "enemy" camp. Vertov had thus managed to alienate himself from two bases of support, and this would have important ramifications for his artistic future.[70]

While the year's films show some improvement over previous ones, the 1924 season was not a brilliant one, and the situation was still so unsettled that movies cannot be described as being part of trends. Yet films were beginning to be criticized, not as isolated works of art, but with reference to the problems of the film industry and society at large, as *Aelita, Cinema Eye,* and to a lesser extent *Mr. West* show. This development marked the beginning of a unique and often penetrating body of film criticism that went far beyond the ordinary "review."

All things considered, the cinema outlook still was not bright. *Cinema Week* was particularly discouraged at the seventh anniversary of the Revolution. The Party, complained an editorial, had not paid much attention to Soviet cinema (concerned as it was with pressing economic and political problems). It was hoped that there would be both financial and ideological support for cinema in the future.[71] Despite its intransigent left-wing political stance, *Cinema Week* printed two articles which began developing, albeit cautiously, a new line for the salvation of the ailing infant industry.

The first was by I. P. Trainin, the chairman of the Main Repertory Committee (Glavrepertkom), soon to achieve fame—or notoriety—as the chief spokesman for Sovkino, which would replace Goskino as the state cinema enterprise for the Russian Republic. This article was more ideological in tone than Trainin's later pronouncements, yet his predilection for the entertainment film was clearly discernible. Trainin stated that bourgeois films were successful with Soviet viewers because of their entertaining treatment of contemporary life; therefore, the Soviets needed to make some long, Western-style entertainment films to compete with the foreign.[72]

The second article, by the Commissar of Enlightenment, A. V. Lunacharskii, supported Trainin. Although Lunacharskii's theses were misleadingly titled "Revolutionary Ideology and Cinema" ("Revoliutsionnaia ideologiia i kino"), he emphatically rejected "narrow propaganda" in cinema. While agit-films could not be abandoned altogether, they should be short, and more importantly, entertaining. Lunacharskii favored the melodrama as the main genre for Soviet cinema because: "Our films should not be less fascinating or less attractive than [those of] the bourgeois."[73]

Since economic recovery from the Revolution and Civil War meant that cinema production was slowly becoming a reality, the film industry began to organize and plan accordingly. At this time a concept of Soviet cinema which was not in the least avant-garde nor particularly revolutionary, came to the fore, supported by influential individuals like Trainin and Lunacharskii. By the end of 1924, the battle lines were being drawn.

3

The New Course: Sovkino Policy and Industry Response (1925-26)

Late in 1924, the two bodies which would most influence Soviet cinema in the 1920s were created—ARK and Sovkino. The young, ambitious, and energetic members of the film community had many plans by the end of 1924. They wanted more effective organization of production and distribution; they wanted to raise the professional status of cinema workers; they wanted to publicize cinema. It was generally held that since little support could be expected from the upper echelons of the Party for these goals, a "lobby" for their interests was needed. Such was the impetus behind the formation of ARK (Association of Revolutionary Cinematography).

ARK was a professional society, and in Moscow everyone who counted as a member of the "new guard" belonged: directors, writers, actors, editors, administrators, journalists. According to Nikolai Lebedev, ARK's first chairman, a group of communist filmworkers connected at that time to the Proletkino studio and *Cinema Gazette* (of whom he, Vladimir Erofeev, Aleksandr Anoshchenko, Boris Martov, and Ivan Kobozev were the most important) decided in mid-1923 to form ARK. It was founded in February 1924 with thirty-four members, 60 percent of whom were communists, the rest being the "most active non-Party cinema workers." Among the charter members were directors Sergei Eisenstein, Lev Kuleshov, Boris Mikhin, Evgenii Ivanov-Barkov, and critic Khrisanf Khersonskii.[1] ARK's slogan was: "Cinema is the strongest weapon in the struggle for communist culture,"[2] but within the organization there were diverse views as to what constituted "communist culture." It is important to remember that ARK was emphatically *not* a "proletarian" culture group like VAPP, the Association of Proletarian Writers, with which ARK has often been compared.

The draft version of the ARK program differed somewhat from the final, public version. Both versions declared that ARK wanted to "work out and make known new forms of cinematographic culture which will answer the interests of proletarian ideology." Both versions called for the "elaboration of new methods of creative and organizational work in cinematography corresponding to the principles of the development of the socialist economy and culture." Both called for publicizing cinema through the creation of a complementary mass organization to be called ODSK (Society of Friends of Soviet Cinema) in order to win the attention of the Party and society.[3]

The major difference between the two versions of the program is worth noting. The draft stressed making professional connections abroad and studying technical developments and organizational methods of foreign firms, even to the point of sending members outside the USSR to achieve these ends. This emphasis on foreign contacts was markedly absent from the printed version, with the exception of a clause stating that ARK would establish ties with professional, scientific, and educational groups in the USSR and abroad.[4] As previously stated, there was a reaction in the cinema community against the self-flagellation of previous years and a patriotic attempt to build self-respect through self-reliance.

Also missing from the printed brochure were items whose absence is harder to explain, points about fighting the infiltration of bourgeois ideology and making films which would propagandize "revolutionary cinematography."[5] Perhaps these were deleted because there was no consensus of opinion within the diverse ranks of the young organization as to what revolutionary cinema should be. Perhaps the moderates in the organization dominated at this point. What ARKists had in common in these early years was their youth, talent, exuberance, and dedication to the creation of Soviet cinema. So by the end of 1924, ARK was set for action, and in 1925 it began publishing its journal, then known as *Cinema Journal ARK* (*Kino-zhurnal ARK*), soon to become a major force in film criticism.

The desire to galvanize Soviet cinema was also behind the replacement of Goskino with Sovkino. Goskino had proved ineffectual and had been the object of persistent though restrained attacks in *Cinema Gazette*. As mentioned above, the Mantsev Commission, a government-appointed body charged with studying the problems of cinema organization, had recommended the abolition of Goskino at the Thirteenth Party Congress in May 1924, but due to the protest of the cinema companies, the final decision was postponed until November of that year.[6] In December 1924, Goskino lost its distribution powers to the new organization, Sovkino, but continued to function as a production company.[7] Sovkino quickly asserted itself in a way that its predecessor had never been able to.

The Economic Situation

If ARK signaled the growing professionalism of the film community, the creation of Sovkino was in response to the severe economic and technical problems discussed in previous chapters—lack of film, equipment, electricity, and expertise—which affected two separate areas: the studios and the theaters. The first and most pressing problem for the studios was to produce raw film stock, in chronic shortage because importing it represented a serious drain on hard currency. But a very large capital base—which Vladimir Erofeev estimated at 10 million rubles—was needed to establish a film stock industry in the Soviet Union. And even if the money were available, the Soviets did not know the secret of making celluloid.[8]

A. A. Levitskii, one of the most experienced cameramen working, was scathing about conditions in the studios, labelling them "beneath any criticism." Since the cameraman of the twenties was in effect the technical director of the movie, Levitskii's comments carried considerable weight. He bemoaned the fact that Soviet films were forced to rely on natural light due to lack of lighting equipment and electricity, considering that in the West, artificial lighting was used even for outdoor shooting.[9] (Levitskii somewhat exaggerated the sophistication of Western movie making, perhaps deliberately, to dramatize his plight.)[10] What electrical equipment the Soviets did have was so outmoded that it squandered precious electricity. Furthermore, the lights in common use (Jupiters) were dangerous, throwing off burning cinders, as Kuleshov and others reported. According to one commentator, this problem would continue indefinitely, not only because the country was poor, but because there was a demonstrated reluctance on the part of foreign manufacturers to extend credit to Soviet importers.[11] In addition to the problem of antiquated lighting equipment, the supply of electricity was inadequate. The maximum amperage possible in Moscow was 2,000 amps, while the average American studio (according to the Hollywood veteran Leo Mur, who had recently returned to the Soviet Union) used 40-50,000 amps.[12] From the artistic as well as the technical standpoint, one cannot overestimate the importance of lighting in the making of the movie.

Critical deficiencies also existed in the laboratory. Film had to be developed and, again, we see that the lack of materials (high quality chemicals) and technical expertise (the ability to regulate temperature)[13] could be reduced to lack of money. One writer estimated that a minimum of 8 to 10 million rubles (10 million being more realistic) was necessary to modernize the studios. He worded his plea forcefully:

> Only when the film studios succeed in equipping themselves properly, are given necessary and sufficient working capital, when our primitive film laboratories are equipped with the newest machinery of the type of contemporary, foreign laboratories that will permit the film industry to save more than 100,000 rubles a year, only then, relying on a strong distribution apparatus, will we have a cheaper and better quality picture.[14]

Yet these pleas went unheeded by Party and government.

But if the above-mentioned problems were somehow miraculously overcome and a movie actually made, then showing it presented another challenge. One writer believed that there were only about ten well-equipped theaters in the whole country: "The remaining thousand have a poor little projector, a dirty counterfeit screen, and a third-rate projectionist."[15] A few grand theaters in Moscow contrasted sharply to this picture. The First Goskino Theater had an orchestra, a reading lounge in the foyer, and a kiosk selling film journals and books.[16] Other Moscow theaters, presumably commercial ones, with imaginative names like Fantomas and Magical Reveries (*Volshebnye grezy*), even had string quartets playing in their foyers.[17] But the Queen of the Moscow theaters, the Malaia Dmitrovka, had a seventeen-piece orchestra and got the best foreign films.[18] These theaters catered to "mixed" audiences (of workers, NEPmen, Party functionaries, etc.), and their ticket prices were high, ranging from 35 to 90 kopeks. At least one "proletarian" cinema, Labor (*Trud*), was reasonably modern, with a musical trio playing in the lobby and a good repertory of popular films like Mary Pickford's *Rosita*.[19]

In most other theaters, especially those in provincial towns, the experience of seeing a movie was quite different. Speeding the film up in order to pack more screenings into an evening was a common practice which prompted an amusing satirical article in *Cinema* (the former *Cinema Gazette*) about the "miracle" process of compressing the viewing and enabling a movie to be seen eleven times in one evening.[20] A correspondent from Rostov-on-Don bitterly claimed that even at the Proletkino theater (which presumably should cater to the worker) the movie was run so fast that it did not matter whether the viewer was literate or not—it was impossible to read the titles.[21] As for music, one would frequently hear, instead of the grand orchestra of the Malaia Dmitrovka, a "doleful melody from a single, broken-down piano."[22]

And of course the shortage of films greatly affected provincial theaters. A common complaint was that there were literally *no* movies; or less seriously, no hits or no Soviet movies. The Penza correspondent to *Cinema* reported for example that the town's two theaters had yet to show a Soviet film, while the newspaper's Kharkhov informant reported that popular films like *Aelita*, *Cinema Truth*, and *Commander Ivanov* had yet to be seen.[23] There was still no choice of pictures; provincial theaters took what they could get.[24]

The shortage of films was made worse by the fact that due to the many projectors in poor condition run by ill-qualified operators, a copy of a movie would only last for about 250 showings. Proper handling could increase this by about 30 percent.[25] The life of a print varied widely according to care; in some cases the film would be completely worn out in four to six weeks; in others, the film would be only 5 percent worn after two and one-half months.[26] There were thus sound economic reasons for giving attention to training projectionists.

The Birth of Sovkino

The cinema studios realized by the beginning of 1925 that the formation of Sovkino as a joint-stock company instead of a syndicate was a foregone conclusion, and even the radical *Cinema Week* at times seemed resigned to the inevitable. One editorial pointed out that perhaps Sovkino would succeed where Goskino had failed, and nationalize the industry, since the official nationalization in 1919, "as is well known," had been more in name than fact.[27]

Yet *Cinema Week* had not really changed its left-wing posture, repeatedly publishing articles by M. P. Efremov, the head of the Leningrad-based studio Sevzapkino, on the dangers of bureaucratic centralism (*glavkism*). Efremov urged that individual production companies be allowed to retain control over the distribution of their own films within the Soviet Union.[28] Another example of *Cinema Week*'s position occurred in a note appended to an article on the acquiescence of the Art Workers' Union (Rabis) to the establishment of Sovkino, the editors adding that this resolution had been passed despite the protest of *all* cinema organizations.[29] Yet another protest came from the head of the Leningrad Goskino studio, A. Khokhlovkin, who worried that Sovkino would become the "dictator" of the market, thereby hampering the work of existing organizations.[30]

By the beginning of March 1925, Sevzapkino's Efremov (who had been, incidentally, a Party member since 1914) had softened his position, explaining that he favored a gradual centralization. He proposed that 80 percent of Sovkino's income and 70 percent of the total rental from foreign films go to the production companies.[31] The rationale behind Efremov's change of heart was clarified in the same issue: he had been named vice-chairman of Sovkino, thereby removed from the ranks of the new organization's critics.[32]

Sovkino's chairman was K. M. Shvedchikov,[33] but it was the capable and energetic I. P. Trainin, the former chairman of the theatrical censorship organ, Glavrepertkom, who as a member of Sovkino's board became its leading spokesman. Trainin (an "Old Bolshevik" who had been in the Party since 1905) was a vigorous pragmatist who wanted to develop a sound commercial basis for Soviet cinema. He lost no time in presenting his views to the public at the Eighth Conference of Moscow Rabis, the Art Workers' Union.[34]

Trainin was in an unenviable position. His strategy was to broadcast the deplorable state of the film industry, buying time to institute reforms by warding off adverse criticism. The first problem Trainin faced was Soviet dependence on imports: 100 percent for raw materials; 85 percent for movies.[35] This reliance on foreign suppliers for raw materials explained the slow production rate for Soviet films, which in turn forced the continued importation of foreign movies. In addition, as explained above, theaters were in poor condition. There were not enough movies to satisfy demand, and taxes exacted a heavy burden. Although taxes had recently been reduced from 33 percent to 10 percent, theaters still had not had time to recover.[36]

Production organizations were also in a shaky financial position and had little capital behind them. Goskino's capital was 500,000 rubles; Sevzapkino, 250,000; Proletkino and Mezhrabpom together, 400,000. With the average cost of making a movie 50,000 rubles, Goskino estimated it would need capital of at least one million to stay solvent. Since Sovkino's founding capital was only one million, it obviously lacked the resources with which to bail out the production companies.[37] (But to put this in perspective, Trainin pointed out that *none* of the Western European film companies had the capital necessary to compete with the large-scale productions of American studios.)[38] Trainin saw the shortage of workers as being as critical to the crisis in Soviet cinema as the lack of money and hoped to double the current work force, bringing it to at least 10,000.[39]

Yet another problem for Sovkino, and therefore for the budding Soviet film industry, was what Trainin subtly termed "the struggle between organizations," which he believed to be a symptom of the "crisis of growth."[40] This statement deserves particular attention, as the first recognition of the dominant factor in the politics of the silent film industry: the fierce competition among film organizations resulting from the paucity of resources.

In making this remark, Trainin had VUFKU, the All-Ukrainian Photo-Cinema Administration, specifically in mind. VUFKU's independence remained a thorn in Sovkino's side. Because of VUFKU's constant wrangling over distribution first with Goskino and now Sovkino, major films of Russian production were a long time coming to the Ukraine (if ever) and vice-versa. VUFKU insisted on outright purchase of Russian films instead of combining a rental price with a percentage of the box-office, as was traditional. Trainin did not want to lose the opportunity of reaping the rewards of a possible Russian "hit" in the Ukraine.

Why did VUFKU deviate from ordinary practice, and more importantly, *how* could it get away with it? Trainin frankly admitted that VUFKU's view was that cinema affairs in the RSFSR were poorly managed; therefore, allowing its profit margin to be determined by the virtually nonexistent Russian distribution "system" was risky.[41] Conversely we may also assume that VUFKU did not want Sovkino to profit from its superior organization. It is worth noting that Trainin did not attempt to rebut this argument, and in fact pointed out that similar problems existed between Sovkino and each of the other non-Russian organizations.[42]

What did Sovkino propose to do? According to its mandate from the government, Sovkino had sole control over the import and export of materials and movies, and the distribution of *Russian* films in the country at large, as well as the organization and exploitation of theaters in the RSFSR.[43] Trainin hoped to extend Sovkino's charter to control distribution on an all-Union scale in order to prevent rifts such as that with VUFKU.[44]

What kinds of movies would Sovkino import? Trainin reminded the public that since the fledgling Sovkino had yet to make a foreign purchase, it was unfair to blame it for the unsuitable foreign films littering the Soviet market. While Trainin admitted that many of these movies were indeed "trash," he observed that since foreign films were made for *their* audiences, Soviet critics could not legitimately complain about "faulty" ideology. Thus neatly dispensing with ideology, Trainin promised to buy enough copies of foreign films in the future to ensure adequate distribution.[45] Soviet ambivalence toward foreign films persisted—leaders piously decried them, but the public loved them. For his part, Trainin was more than willing to serve the masses. As an incentive for the studios to swallow their misgivings and cooperate with his policies, Trainin promised that 75 percent of Sovkino's income from theaters would go to production.[46]

If one had suspected from Trainin's evasiveness on the question of foreign pictures that import policy under Sovkino would favor entertainment films, this suspicion would have been strengthened by his comments on the quality of Soviet films. He said bluntly: "In our productions, there is still nothing in which we can really take pride. We often see in them much publicistic, clamorous communism, but no art."[47] After such dull fare, of course the viewer enjoyed "bourgeois" films.[48]

Trainin saw two kinds of films dominating Soviet production: the agit-film (propaganda) and the fiction film. The agit-film he acerbically characterized as "... pretentious films in which the agitational side bulges, which abound in numerous intertitles [written frames of a silent film], often very revolutionary, but at the same time very boring."[49] Foreign "art" films were therefore even more popular by way of protest. What Soviet cinema needed was "truly" artistic films which would earn profits at home and abroad. Production of such films would require the cooperation of several studios but could be achieved without any major ideological sacrifices.[50]

Trainin had another proposal for improving the financial situation of production companies, this one involving acceptance of foreign capital or offers from foreign movie companies to come to the Soviet Union to make "Russian" films. Profits from these ventures would be divided with Sovkino but would require no Soviet outlays. The scheme would have the further advantage of bringing Russian workers into contact with their well-trained Western counterparts, and would even, Trainin claimed (perhaps a bit self-servingly), strike a blow at the "White" filmmakers active in the West who purported through sentimental Russian costume dramas to represent the "true" Russia.[51]

Trainin's report to the Art Workers' Union accurately outlined the course Sovkino would follow during the five years of its existence. He had astutely assessed conditions within the film industry, reducing all problems to the shortage of capital. Sovkino therefore needed to raise capital, which it would do by importing commercially successful foreign entertainment films. The profits from these films would be plowed back into Soviet production to make "exportable" movies, which of course translated to entertainment films on the order of their Western counterparts. The approach was a rational one but its ideological opportunism was bound to enrage both the political and artistic left wings of the cinema community. Trainin's policies and the opposition to them formed the basis for the conflicts of the rest of the decade.

The Attack against Sovkino

Events now began to transpire with bewildering speed. In 1924 there was virtually no Soviet cinema. In 1926 two of the greatest achievements of silent cinema came to the screen: Sergei Eisenstein's *Battleship Potemkin* (*Bronenosets Potemkin*) and Lev Kuleshov's *By the Law* (*Po zakonu*)—along with a number of near-great pictures. On the artistic side, there is no doubt that 1925-26 was a period of remarkable achievement, and the creative momentum would be sustained for two years more. Although some pessimism had dissipated,[52] the economic and ideological problems of the immediate postrevolutionary period still had not found solutions, and ominous rumblings could be heard.

The target for discontent was Sovkino, which had been allowed virtually no grace period. The earliest complaints appeared by mid-1925 in two articles by labor activist Boris Fillipov, the chairman of the Leningrad Union Council. His charge was that Sovkino was not treating workers' clubs fairly; that it sent films to the clubs only after they had played commercial theaters; that rental prices were too high; that Sovkino cared only for its profit margin.[53] (Fillipov later charged that Sovkino was in fact earning high profits from club rentals.)[54] These attacks were part of a general war on what came to be known as Sovkino's "price politics," that is, that film theaters everywhere suffered from the high prices Sovkino exacted for the "hits."[55] Sovkino rebutted these charges through vice-chairman M. P. Efremov, who produced figures showing that Sovkino had considerably reduced the average price per program.[56]

This minor skirmish foreshadowed what was to come. It is not surprising that the first major onslaught against Sovkino came from those connected with the Artistic Council on Cinema Affairs in Glavpolitprosvet, the Main Committee on Political Education in the Commissariat of Enlightenment, wherein most power over cultural affairs was vested. The Commissariat was not happy that Sovkino had escaped its control, and a number of articles making serious accusations appeared in Glavpolitprosvet's cinema journal *Soviet Cinema (Sovetskoe kino)*.

It was charged, for example, that there was no rationale behind the current organization, with its separation of production from rental and distribution. Sovkino allegedly set rental prices arbitrarily. Because it profited from its position as middleman, there was absolutely no way that Sovkino could have "the interests of Soviet cinema production" at heart. Glavpolitprosvet proposed a syndicate of all production companies under the Commissariat's control to facilitate ideological guidance.[57]

Cinefication

Glavpolitprosvet was potentially one of Sovkino's most powerful opponents. Although its attacks were as yet indirect, battlelines were being drawn. As mentioned in the preceding chapter, the project most favored by the Commissariat was the cinefication of the countryside, an issue noticeably absent from Trainin's litany of the ills of Soviet cinema. Since Sovkino never paid more than lip service to the goal of bringing movies to rural areas, cinefication served as a focal point for bureaucratic scuffles between Glavpolitprosvet's Artistic Council on Cinema Affairs and Sovkino. The Artistic Council began publishing *Soviet Cinema* in April 1925—and *Soviet Cinema* espoused the cause of rural cinema with fervor. (Not coincidentally, it was the dullest of all Soviet film publications and the one most removed from mainstream issues.)

The Artistic Council's first concern was to form a "mass" organization of film buffs and amateurs to complement the professional association ARK. A group somewhat fitting this description already existed, OSPK (Society of Builders of Proletarian Cinema). OSPK had been founded in September 1924 by representatives of studios, Party, and government, but seems to have been connected mainly with the studio Proletkino and the Leningrad newspaper *Cinema Week* (the only publication to report on its activities). Its membership reportedly was about 10,000, and its philosophy was that proletarian cinema should not be a "source of entertainment, enrichment, refined debauchery, and stupefication of the masses," but rather a "weapon of organization, education, enlightenment of the worker-peasant masses" in the struggle against the West for communism.[58]

OSPK, like other "proletarian" cultural organizations in the mid-twenties, was both ahead and behind the times. It revealed its political naiveté by denouncing bureaucrats, specialists (especially those with international connections), and movie theater managers just as the self-same were accruing power as part of the co-existence with fellow travellers and specialists which characterized NEP. OSPK was therefore doomed to failure. The Artistic

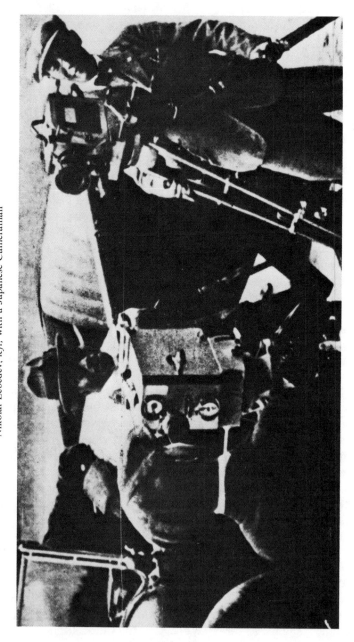

Nikolai Lebedev, *left*, with a Japanese Cameraman

Council rejected its continued existence due to its "narrowness";[59] ARK attacked it for not sufficiently supporting the cause of Soviet cinema in the provinces.[60]

The Artistic Council favored the replacement of OSPK with ODSK (Society of Friends of Soviet Cinema). ODSK would be a group backed by all Soviet cinematography, not just one production company. Therefore, in December 1924, Agitprop of the Party Central Committee (following the recommendations of ARK, the Orgbureau of Glavpolitprosvet, and most film organizations, *including OSPK*) organized ODSK.[61] With the founding of ODSK, ARK lost its short-lived independence, becoming an autonomous unit of ODSK. ARK's founder, Nikolai Lebedev, noted that the idea of creating another "proletarian" organization on the order of the Moscow Association of Proletarian Writers (MAPP) had been considered but rejected for two reasons: the failure of the self-proclaimed proletarian cinema company Proletkino, and the absence of proletarians working in the film industry. ODSK's communist membership would have to substitute for proletarianism.[62]

ODSK's theses were as follows: Cinema was the art most suitable for the masses because of its "visual clarity, simplicity, and general accessibility"; cinema should be a cultural instrument with suitable ideological content created by the working class and peasants to serve the working class; and "Soviet society, the Party, and the government *will give* [emphasis added; note future tense] cinema maximum attention, concern, and means." ODSK was also mandated to study viewers and issues and to involve itself actively in the cinefication campaign.[63] In addition, the organization was to "propagandize" Soviet cinema (in the sense of popularizing it and bringing its current plight the attention it deserved), sniff out bourgeois and petty-bourgeois heresies in cinema, and develop cinema as a tool in the building of Soviet society.[64] The history of ODSK is obscure. Judging by later criticism its operations were not very successful, but because it was infrequently mentioned in the cinema press and its archive was closed, ODSK's range of activity remains almost completely unknown.

The Artistic Council was now ready to begin the cinefication drive in earnest. No justification for the campaign was ever given—peasants were supposed to need and want cinema. Nor did the question of repertory stir controversy in the pages of *Soviet Cinema*, not surprising considering that its sponsor was the Commissariat of Enlightenment. (One should therefore be cautious about assuming that this nonchalance was shared by the cinema community at large.) According to *Soviet Cinema*, film in the countryside should promote communist aims and heroes.[65] Dramas were to be forbidden, with comedies the only permissible entertainment films.[66] One leader of the cinefication movement, A. Katsigras, did suggest, however, that peasant viewers might be studied to determine their preferences.[67]

Important as questions of repertory were, the major issue with which the Artistic Council dealt was still the mechanics of bringing cinema to the countryside—via stationary (permanent) or travelling projectors? Travelling projectors won out, one writer evasively noting that rural areas were "not developed enough" to sustain permanent systems,[68] although Glavpolitprosvet announced more forthrightly that the problem was electricity—there was none.[69] Travelling systems had their own generators but were quite expensive, an important drawback.[70]

The other film journals and organizations were only mildly interested in cinefication of the countryside. It occupied little space in either *Cinema Gazette/Cinema*, ARK's journal *ARK*, or *Soviet Screen* (*Sovetskii ekran*). Although ARK had a peasant section (which never seemed to do much), it took a "hands-off" approach, offering to supply nothing more to the campaign than ideological advice.[71] Of far greater concern to the independent journals than projectors or electricity[72] was the nature of the "mass" audience. As professional filmmakers, they were concerned about the undeniable lack of sophistication of the major Soviet social class, the peasant. A movie is a "language" with conventions that must be learned in order to follow the story; the typical peasant viewer was not conversant with cinematic conventions.

A few dreamers (or zealots) reported that peasant viewers were "serious and thoughtful,"[73] and that they enjoyed movies like *Drunkenness and Its Consequence* (*P'ianstvo i ego posledstvie*).[74] A more realistic assessment was that "the peasant and worker still look at cinema more as a means of entertainment or as a magic lantern, everyone knows, than as a 'serious thing.'"[75] For that reason it was suggested that films be simple and short, no more than four reels (about forty minutes).[76] Peasants had a hard time concentrating on the screen, and the typical Soviet feature film (six reels, sixty to seventy-five minutes) was too long for them to watch. Equally serious was the problem posed by the intertitles of the silent film in a country with an illiteracy rate estimated as high as 80 percent.[77] In most cases it was impossible to follow the film without reading the titles, and there was often no one in a village who could serve as narrator.

A. Katsigras, who was a serious and devoted proponent of rural cinema, wrote that when peasants were first exposed to movies they really did not see or understand the movie *at all*. The experience was nothing more than flickering lights and shadows. Even after repeated exposure to cinema, peasants still did not seem to understand movies as they were intended. For example, Katsigras reported that city audiences greatly enjoyed the joke in Razumnyi's 1924 Civil War adventure *Father Knysh's Gang* (*Banda Batki Knysha*) of a man carrying Nikolai Bukharin's *ABCs of Communism*, his wife an icon; then a bandit comes along and says "Hands up!" But peasants only laughed when they saw something they recognized; in that film, a horse harnessed to a waterwheel.[78]

Grigorii Boltianskii

Katsigras hoped this lack of comprehension could be overcome through simple, clear editing, and he proposed that workers accompanying travelling shows be able to explain the movies.[79] There was no opportunity to put these theories into practice, for by the end of 1925, half of Glavpolitprosvet's 655 travelling projectors stood idle from lack of films. This situation continued through 1926.[80]

Lacking the opportunity for concrete action, proponents of cinefication engaged in ever more detailed discussions about what kinds of films should be offered. The "hard liners," represented by Katsigras of Glavpolitprosvet or Grigorii Boltianskii, the head of Goskino's newsreel division, followed the path first set forth by Nikolai Lebedev on this subject. They held that rural cinema should be socially and politically uplifting, dealing with subjects like the struggle with "illicit liquor," "social role of the press and *sel'kor* [rural correspondent]," "significance of aviation," and so forth. Boltianskii cannily realized that the wonderment of the peasant regarding the "magical" moving picture could be exploited politically, but he did not know how to take advantage of this opportunity. He assumed that cinema fascinated peasants no matter what appeared on the screen, and therefore that Soviet life could be effectively promoted just by *showing* it, like giving "real healthy food."[81]

Another school of thought was that these uplifting films were too boring to win converts and that peasants did not want to see films about the country, preferring more exotic locales. One writer joked about the stereotypes of "rural" films:

> The priest and the *kulak* [rich peasant] hurt the *bedniak* [poor peasant]; the *bedniak* wants to wed his daughter forcibly to a man she does not love. The *kulak* sets the cooperative on fire. The *kulak* and the priest always appear with a bottle of moonshine in their hands.
> The teacher and the Komsomol member give a speech before a gathering.... As a result, everything ends happily: the *kulak* in prison, the priest discredited, the *bedniak* satisfied, the daughter marries her lover. [82]

Talented directors not surprisingly shied away from this "recipe" for the rural film, and since Sovkino saw no money to be made in the countryside, the quality of films shown there continued to be execrable.

By 1926 *Soviet Cinema* believed Sovkino to be the main enemy of the cinefication campaign. Katsigras, the major spokesman for rural cinema, had two accusations to level: (1) tariffs were too high, and (2) complete anarchy of distribution reigned. Production companies were still selling their own pictures despite Sovkino's putative distribution monopoly. Katsigras charged that Sovkino had "remained deaf" to Glavpolitprosvet's efforts to come to an understanding on these subjects. Sovkino policies helped neither the viewer nor the studio since neither production nor cinefication could possibly develop under such conditions. [83]

Soviet Cinema published a book-length indictment of Sovkino by V.N. Meshcheriakov (the deputy head of the Commissariat), M.S. Veremienko, and Katsigras with the ugly title *Cinema Ulcer (Kino-iazva)*. Sovkino was depicted therein as a reactionary force which refused to do business in the countryside, although profits were to be had. But instead of promoting Soviet production and printing more copies of films for distribution, Sovkino imported foreign "trash." Furthermore, it was charged that Sovkino had openly declared its enmity for cinefication, campaigning "ceaselessly" against rural cinema. Sovkino behaved like a merchant without "a grain" of political sense; its motto was: "To the pocket!" Meshcheriakov wrote: "This tactic is harmful to the Republic, to cinema affairs and should be radically changed." [84] As a counter-agent to Sovkino, he proposed the creation of an agency for rural cinema to be called Sel'kino.

If further proof of Sovkino's disdain for the rural viewer was needed, it was to be found in the kinds of films they sent to the provinces. Seventy-five percent of these prints were too old and worn to run; in any case, 70 percent of the pictures were judged unsuitable for peasant viewers. Copies in circulation varied from the original by as much as 300 meters (about one reel). [85]

Katsigras made charges in *Cinema Ulcer* which contradicted some of his colleagues' remarks. He said Sovkino was earning a good return in the countryside due to their 7 kopek per meter per month rate—but if that were so, and Sovkino administrators were the clever businessmen Meshcheriakov accused them of being, then why would Sovkino allow over half of the rural projectors to remain idle at any one time?

Although it was a well-known fact that prints had a short life due to improper handling, Katsigras alleged that Sovkino fabricated this to jack up the rental price. Sovkino said a copy lasted five months; Katsigras claimed it really lasted a year and proposed halving the rental price. Near the end of his diatribe, Katsigras did admit that Sovkino sustained significant losses on the few educational movies (*kul'turfil'my*) shown—as much as 50 to 100 percent of their usual share of the box office receipts[86]—which must tell us something about the popularity of such edifying fare. Yet despite its internal contradictions, *Cinema Ulcer* was an important tract. It set a polemical tone unheard since the days of Aleksei Gan and *Cinema-photo* and posited a scapegoat for all the ills of Soviet cinema—Sovkino.

Glavpolitprosvet was not Sovkino's only opponent. Talk of a syndicate of the studios resurfaced by the end of 1926 in other circles. In a number of unsigned articles, the newspaper *Cinema* supported *Cinema Ulcer*'s arguments against Sovkino.[87] Katsigras, who also wrote for *Cinema*, was absolutely tireless in the incessant repetition of his point of view. He even accused Sovkino of lying to *Pravda* about the number of travelling projectors it had.[88] This negative publicity had results: ARK and the Central Committee of the Art Workers' Union recommended the liquidation of Sovkino,[89] with the Supreme Council of the National Economy and the Commissariat of Enlightenment vying for control. In an ARK debate on the subject, all spoke to the necessity of union of rental and production— and therefore, against Sovkino.[90] From this point on there was no love lost between ARK and Sovkino.

Anti-Sovkino polemics aside, what little information there was in the cinema press about conditions in the countryside indicate that the situation was very bleak indeed. One issue of *Soviet Cinema* featured letters from rural areas and provincial towns which complained bitterly about lack of films, high prices, poor quality of the repertory, and the wretched physical condition of those few movies that finally arrived.[91] A. Katsigras admitted in a book devoted to the subject, *Cinema Work in the Countryside* (*Kino-rabota v derevne*), that the cinefication movement had not been very effective due to the problems of the travelling projectors. Because expenses were high but tickets low-priced (from 10 to 15 kopeks), the travelling cinemas were losing about 6 percent a month.[92] Katsigras proposed a graduated system of ticket prices based on ability to pay as a way of increasing receipts.[93]

Katsigras felt that projectionists needed to be political commissars and cinema propagandists as well as mechanically competent,[94] not an easily fulfilled order. He suggested that films begin with a short lecture during which the plot would be related, in addition to a more general discussion of the issues raised therein. During the film the projectionist should read the titles aloud, and afterwards conduct a discussion, keeping a diary of audience reaction.[95] Katsigras also suggested suitable films for rural audiences, among the well-known ones: *Potemkin, Stepan Khalturin, Palace and Fortress*, and *Death Bay*. Unsuitable films were: *The Bear's Wedding, The Devil's Wheel, The Cigarette Girl from Mosselprom, Aelita*, and *The Overcoat*.[96]

Others interested in cinefication were less confident than was Katsigras that they knew which films peasant viewers needed or wanted. Peasants were reported to be quite attentive to detail and disturbed by any departure from reality.[97] A successful film specifically intended for rural audiences, *Father* (*Otets*), prompted a thoughtful essay from an unlikely source, Viktor Shklovskii. Shklovskii wrote (and this was significant for future aesthetic debates): "The film *Father* is shot simply, elementarily, from one point of view, is edited from long pieces, and by this one may explain its reaching the peasant viewer." Shklovskii added, however, that it was "objectively good," pointing out that peasants, like everyone else, enjoyed an interesting, well-made movie.[98] Even Katsigras admitted that the informational function of cinema was best served in the context of the entertainment film,[99] since the educational film was hampered by the fact that peasants still were not literate enough to read titles.[100]

Because of the need to produce films especially for the peasant audience, there was further discussion of Meshcheriakov's proposal in *Cinema Ulcer* of organizing a joint-stock company to be called Sel'kino, a project supported by ARK, the Commissariat of Enlightenment, and the Cinema Commission of the Party Central Committee. Sel'kino would produce its own films but would utilize existing studios to do so. Sovkino's chairman, Shvedchikov, adamantly opposed this plan,[101] further fueling suspicions about Sovkino's attitude toward the countryside.

ODSK, the organization created for disseminating film to rural areas, oddly enough, stood apart from these debates. Because it was having financial difficulties, the only way it contributed to the campaign was to conduct studies of the viewer.[102] Although ODSK should have maintained a high profile in the cinefication controversy, there is little evidence of concrete action on its part.[103] It did, however, propose for the countryside a "serious" cinema above mere "empty satisfaction."[104] ODSK sternly opposed showing foreign films to peasants since they were tools of counterrevolution:

K.M. Shvedchikov

[They]... act upon the petty-bourgeois [*meshchanskie*] instincts... of the backward strata of workers and peasants. Moreover, such pictures might be an agitational aid in the hands of our enemies, rich peasants [*kulaks*], and other non-Soviet elements who know how or have the possibility of tying up relations and connections with the backward elements among workers.[105]

Foreign films catered to the unhealthy side of human instincts: "sadism, naked lewdness, depravity":

The foreign film without a moral, with a naked woman, a petty-bourgeois, with a eulogy of bourgeois, philistine well-being..., is supported on our screen by the administrator of the theater as the "product that sells."[106]

Although cinefication was a resounding failure, it did lead to a gradual restriction on the kinds of films that were seen as suitable for showing in the countryside. Not only were these films to be technically simpler than the typical film, as Shklovskii had reasoned, they were also to be realistic, moral, and "cultured." Viewer interest was an afterthought. It was asserted that organizing Soviet social opinion with the assistance of ODSK circles would show that the "taste" of the Soviet viewer was not vulgar, but "healthy" and cultured.[107] By the standards of the proponents of cinefication, it is indeed true that Sovkino was not fulfilling its "duty" toward the masses.

Foreign Films

Dislike of foreign films was not limited to supporters of the cinefication campaign. In fact, Sovkino's import-export policy was subjected to widespread attack at this time. The cornerstone of Sovkino's program for building a sound financial base for the film industry was the importation of foreign films. Although reasons for opposing foreign films varied, the pure "commercialism" of Sovkino's Trainin had no support among rank-and-file cinema workers.

Some critics voiced blanket opposition to foreign films, viewing their influx into the USSR since the beginning of NEP as a potential danger for the success of the revolution.[108] In these quarters, the slogan "Only Soviet pictures on the Soviet screen" began early,[109] it being seen as essential not to expose the proletariat to the pernicious influence of the imports.[110] For others, the concern was mainly economic. One writer claimed that it cost 20-50,000 rubles to buy a foreign film and only 15-45,000 to make a Soviet film. The drain of hard currency had to be stopped[111] in order to concentrate on Soviet production. (This position does not take into account Trainin's claim that a great deal more money could be made on foreign films, thus creating revenue for domestic production.)

Although the argument that foreign films were unsuitable for Soviet audiences continually cropped up,[112] the most important criticism always seemed to be that purchase of foreign films would mean fewer Soviet productions. Yet this viewpoint must not be regarded as oversimplification. A strongly worded statement appeared in the first issue of *Cinema Front* (*Kinofront, Cinema Journal ARK*'s new title as of April 1926) which is worth quoting in full for its combination of economic and ideological concerns:

> ...It is essential to view the means paid for foreign films by Sovkino as an irrational export of Soviet hard currency.
>
> In the interest of the Soviet government and Party, it is better to have one Soviet film than ten anti-Soviet....
>
> In what sense can we be proud that we have 700 travelling cinema projectors in the countryside, when these travelling projectors are served by unneeded and harmful rubbish.[113]

The years 1925-26 saw the beginnings of strong opposition to foreign films. At first such concerns were ideological rather than xenophobic. Formalist writer and critic Osip Brik, a consistent opponent of Sovkino import policies, charged that Sovkino catered to the tasks of the petty-bourgeoisie.[114] Films which were frequently cited to prove this point were Douglas Fairbanks's *Mark of Zorro* (which had "zero" social-educational value for the workers)[115] and *Thief of Baghdad* (which ran for 108 days at the Malaia Dmitrovka after a sophisticated advertising campaign).[116]

One may infer that the passions foreign films aroused attested to their popularity. Indeed, readers' letters appearing in the newspaper *Cinema* reflected high interest in foreign movies and the lives of their stars.[117] *Cinema* had no particular reason to propagandize foreign films; sudden cessation of readers' letters in mid-1926 may have been caused by undue interest in the subject. These letters expressed adoration of Mary Pickford, Doug Fairbanks, and the German star Harry Piel. Fairbanks's pictures *Mark of Zorro* and *Robin Hood* were especially popular judging by the glowing missives *Cinema* printed.[118]

Yet it was not only the negative ideological influence of foreign films that was worrisome. Another aspect of anti-foreign rhetoric concerned the technical influence, which was seen as being (too) strong. One writer warned that even technical methods were in fact politically biased and could not be accepted uncritically! Cinema techniques had to be developed and perfected for Soviet conditions, meaning primarily that they had to be economical. Emphasis should be placed on shooting in natural light and outdoors, since there was no money to waste on "capitalist" studios.[119]

Were foreign films viewed only as purveyors of alien culture or capitalist techniques? Osip Brik, while rejecting the "trash" that Sovkino imported (specifically mentioning the films of Fairbanks, Pickford, and Pola Negri), believed that foreign educational films were allowable.[120] But the prevailing view was that the "liquidation" of foreign films was an affair of the same order as the campaigns to liquidate illiteracy and patriarchalism in Soviet society.[121]

For this reason, the degree of influence of these films on the viewer was of major concern, because although the number of foreign films shown had been reduced (it was claimed that in March 1926 only 51 percent of the movies on Soviet screens were foreign),[122] their popularity had not waned. Most frequently the effect was seen as a harmful one; for example, a certain American film was believed to promote the "world-view of hooliganism," thus interfering with the government's current campaign against hooliganism.[123] Though in theory all ideological problems could be repaired by re-editing, the censorship was as clumsy as it was ubiquitous.[124] One critic dryly noted that "Los Angeles does not coordinate its production plans with Soviet political education," and lamented that the censor's scissors had become the symbol of the industry.[125]

Some opponents of the import policy were brazen enough to dispute the popularity of foreign films. An article in *Cinema* claimed that *The Station Master* and *Cross and Mauser* had been more popular than *Thief of Baghdad*, or that *Potemkin* had thrilled Soviet audiences more than *Robin Hood*.[126] As we have seen, letters from readers do not support this. The more realistic critics were interested in learning *why* Soviet viewers preferred foreign films, a common conclusion being that there were no attractive Soviet stars.[127] (This idea, which would become a refrain, was intimately connected with the urgent re-evaluation of the role of the actor and the hero in Soviet cinema, to be discussed in the next chapter.)

Knowledgeable observers knew, however, that the popularity of foreign pictures—and for "foreign" one could substitute "American"—was not just a Soviet problem. In France, one writer pointed out, 65 percent of films shown were American; in Germany, 60 percent.[128] A few years earlier Kuleshov had expressed the opinion that technical superiority made foreign films more desirable; now it was simply admitted that American movies, particularly the comedies of Charlie Chaplin, Buster Keaton, and Harold Lloyd, were wonderful entertainment.[129]

The American and other foreign movies that appealed most to Soviet audiences were those which "offered very dynamic material, often combining comic situations with improbable inventiveness, and in any case, with some kind of positive, life-loving tone."[130] As long as Soviet cinema was simple agitation and "nothing else," it could not hope to attract viewers, who naturally preferred "art" to naked propaganda.[131] This did not mean the abandonment of ideology in Soviet cinema, but it did mean recognition that agitation was not effective if it did not engage the attention of the public.

Therefore, at this point absolute rejection of foreign films was a rarity. It was instead agreed that while foreign films were undesirable from both ideological and economic points of view, because of the current shortage of films and Sovkino's revenue-generating plans, Soviet filmmakers should study these pictures to learn the secret of their perennial popularity. The goal was to make "true" Soviet pictures embodying these principles without sacrificing ideological content, thereby enabling the film industry to become independent of foreign films.[132] The slogan "The Soviet film on the Soviet screen," which began to appear frequently in *Cinema*,[133] may also be taken as a sign of awakening national pride. Many critics believed that Soviet directors were being unduly disparaged by "skeptics" and "cinema-Westerners" who felt the only films Soviets could make were "cultural-enlightenment films." According to this view, if Soviet feature films were not as popular as their Western counterparts, it was because they were not properly distributed and advertised, rarely appearing in commercial theaters.[134]

The needs of the domestic market aside, Soviets were to be encouraged to sell films for export. Soviet films had thus far not enjoyed financial success abroad, with the exception of the films of Mezhrabpom Rus', but what had been shown outside the USSR had been well received critically, including documentaries.[135] Whether the claim is true is not as important as the claim itself. Soviet cinema was sadly lacking in confidence, neglecting to make extra prints of movies to sell abroad in the belief that no one would buy them.[136] The drive against foreign films did indeed have an ideological side, but what mattered in the end was the fact that if limited resources were directed toward the purchase of foreign films, there was correspondingly less money for Soviet directors. Patient waiting for Sovkino policies to come to fruition was not a virtue of young directors eager to make films.

The Beginning of Group Strife

Sovkino was not the only organization in trouble, although on the surface, ARK's first year was passed peacefully discussing issues and organizing sections. A major practical activity had been sponsoring children's Sunday matinees at various Moscow theaters, a benign undertaking that nonetheless met with considerable bureaucratic resistance.[137] ARK's major achievement, however, was the regular publication of *ARK*, which added considerably to the level and quality of cinema discussions. *ARK* consistently condemned the work of Dziga Vertov but otherwise represented a variety of opinions on its pages. It appeared that despite its avowedly "revolutionary" orientation, the organization was still looking, as it were, for a political niche.[138]

But the group conflict which would characterize the film industry through the rest of the decade was beginning. A troubled spot for ARK in 1925 was its relationship with VAPP, the proletarian writers' association. If Western writers ever mention ARK (and this is rare), it is usually to say that it was a "tool" of VAPP.[139] This quite emphatically was not true; as we have seen, ARK had no proletarian cast. Yet because screen writers could belong to VAPP and ARK simultaneously, there was "infiltration," complicated by the fact that VAPP had its own cinema section, which aspired to leadership on the cinema front.

VAPP's attempts to influence ARK were fiercely resisted in Moscow. ARK was a Moscow-based organization (Leningrad ARK was not established until 1928), and two Muscovites in particular viewed VAPP as a threat to ARK. One of them noted in *Soviet Cinema* that not only was ARK's membership 60 percent Party, but equally as important, ARKists were actual cinema workers actively engaged in creative, practical work. The implication was that the VAPPists who were condemning the work of "specialists" in cinema were not actively working; cinema, this critic of VAPP declared, must be "Soviet," not "proletarian."[140] The other counterattack on VAPP, in *Cinema*, more explicitly stated that VAPP was overstepping its bounds in cinema. Cinema workers, not writers, it was argued, should assume the leadership role in the film industry and community; ARK and ODSK fulfilled this need.[141]

In the three months prior to the Leningrad newspaper *Cinema Week*'s dissolution in March 1925, it staunchly supported VAPP over ARK. VAPPists were concerned with the ideological deficiencies in cinema and had established their cinema section at *Cinema Week*'s suggestion, according to G. Lelevich, a member of the cinema section's board.[142] Lelevich and the other board members (Albert Syrkin, Dmitrii Furmanov, L. Grabar, Fedor Gladkov, and K. Minaev) launched a blistering attack on ARK and its guiding light, Nikolai Lebedev. They charged that while ARK had seemingly "revolutionary" meetings, its true colors could be seen in the movies ARKists made. Although there were a few honest communists in ARK, most of its members were "dubious fellow travellers." It might be necessary to "reconcile temporarily with cinema fellow travellers," but not to associate freely with them as ARK encouraged. Bourgeois elements, they declared, needed to be ousted from the cinema schools and replaced by proletarians, not coddled by ARK.[143]

Finally the VAPP cinema section went too far for even *Cinema Week*. Denouncing writers Viktor Shklovskii and Aleksei Tolstoi and directors Fedor Otsep, Dmitrii Bassalygo, and Cheslav Sabinskii (among others) for their "left words and right deeds," the cinema section declared that VAPP should take control of the studios.[144] *Cinema Week*'s editors demurred and printed a rebuttal from ARK which condemned VAPP's intrigues.[145] But VAPP got an important boost from Glavpolitprosvet's Artistic Council on Cinema Affairs which declared its work in cinema "necessary and useful."[146] Despite the threat from VAPP, ARK continued to maintain an independent position as a professional organization not allied with particular political currents.

The year 1926 was one of change and considerable cinematic achievements. Yet before the cinema industry could entrench itself and revel in its successes, it was being undermined, as evidenced by attacks on Sovkino and the acrimonious tone of film discussions. ARK was a barometer for these changes. The association was in a most precarious position, because it had as yet done nothing and adopted no platform. It did serve as the forum for the most interesting, active, and innovative segment of the film community, but even at this early date neutrality could be dangerous.

Recognizing this, as mentioned above, in 1926 ARK had changed its journal's title from *ARK* to *Cinema Front*. This militaristic terminology was not just a slogan, according to an editorial, but represented a "definite stage in the struggle and building of our Soviet cinematography." Capitalist encirclement called for new attitudes, especially for a "regime of economy" (to be discussed).[147] Not only was the tone of the reviews and other articles in *Cinema Front* considerably harsher, but blocks of slogans such as this one began to appear:

DIRECTORS, CAMERAMEN, ACTORS, SCENARISTS, FILM CRITICS, ALL SOVIET CINEMA WORKERS!
DO NOT FORGET ABOUT THE BASIC CONSUMER OF CINEMA, THE WORKER AND PEASANT!
REMEMBER THAT CINEMA SHOULD BE AN ACTIVE PARTICIPANT IN THE BUILDING OF SOCIALISM IN OUR COUNTRY![148]

Militarism had infected the organization. In July 1926 ARK began its first "reregistration," a euphemism for a purge. It lasted through December and when it was over, 196 members remained; eighty-three of these full members. The rest were on probation or were provisional (all new members were in the latter category). Those expelled for inactivity numbered 109; twenty-one had been purged for serious offenses, such as not adhering to the ideals of revolutionary cinematography or failing to understand the aims of ARK. At the end of the purge 40 percent of the pre-July membership was out; of those purged 35 percent were either Party or Komsomol members.[149] It was the first purge of the film industry.

A growing number of talented people were competing for resources that had not appreciably increased. One solution to this problem had been to cut down on the number of production organizations so as to better coordinate use of resources, hence the demise of Goskino, Sevzapkino, Proletkino, and Rus'. But at the same time that Sovkino had seemingly gathered more power (and because of this), ARK and most young filmmakers allied against it as a symbol of both excessive foreign ties and bourgeois interests that prevented the allocation of materials to less-established and younger directors[150] and the making and distribution of films for the Soviet masses. How Sovkino's policies and opposition to them affected aesthetic controversies and filmmaking in the critical years 1925-26 will be the subject of the next chapter.

Filmmaking and Films (1925-26)

The debate over Sovkino's path and dissatisfaction with ARK were not the only signs of internal strife in the film industry. Other rifts concerned the role of writers and actors in the filmmaking process. The Soviet film industry faced continuing shortages of personnel as well as material. Sovkino found the education of new cadres theoretically desirable but expensive, with no guarantee of a good return on the investment. It was prerevolutionary directors like Iakov Protazanov who were saleable abroad.[1]

The impression that Sovkino neglected cinema education was reinforced by the lack of success of GTK, the State Film Technical Institute, which had been established in 1919. A cartoon in *Soviet Screen* (the movie magazine most "popular" in style) depicted this well. Some old crones leaning on canes are shown leaving GTK saying, "Now that we have finished GTK we may at least die." A note explained that after six years no one had yet graduated from the institute.[2]

GTK did not have trouble attracting enrollment (nor did its counterpart in Leningrad, the Technical Institute of Screen Art), for interest in cinema was high among the populace, and cinema was seen as a glamorous occupation.[3] But GTK, like all Soviet cinema, suffered from lack of money. Sovkino reportedly planned to turn 20 percent of its income over to the school (after the pattern of the Ukrainian company VUFKU and the Odessa Cinema Technical Institute),[4] but for the moment courses were unplanned, teachers were unqualified, and there was no discernible connection between the school and production.[5] In addition, GTK did not train lesser technical workers like lab technicians and projectionists.[6]

Given this situation, the deployment of prerevolutionary directors was commonplace and therefore a cause for concern,[7] but the personnel problem that seemed most serious from 1925 to 1926 concerned the script writer. Because of the "regime of economy" campaign, the "scenario crisis" assumed center stage in cinema polemics. The discussion was a complex one that concerned both the preparation of the writer for his task and the nature of

Soviet cinema dramaturgy. It revealed growing divisiveness within the industry which would have important consequences for the future.

The Regime of Economy Campaign

The big debate of 1926 was the "regime of economy" campaign, part of a general effort to rationalize Soviet industry at large. At first the campaign was not specifically directed against Sovkino, although that would soon change. In response to the regime of economy, ways to rationalize film production were discussed, culminating in the growing conviction that the screenplay was the answer to all ills.

By spring 1926, claims were being advanced that Soviet films were abnormally expensive. One writer declared that the average Soviet film cost l00,000 rubles which in the West would result in a "grandiose" movie (the implication being that the Soviet product was less than "grandiose").[8] The reason behind the failure of Soviet production was its cottage industry (*kustar'*) nature. A curious feature of these polemics is that it is never clear against exactly whom the charge of cinema cottage industry-itis (*kustarnichestvo*) was directed. The term would imply the existence of small private studios, of which there were now none. (Goskino, Sevzapkino, and Proletkino were liquidated in March 1926 and transferred to Sovkino. Mezhrabpom acquired Rus' and a new name—Mezhrabpom Rus'.)[9] The best example of this sort of obfuscation was a note appended to an article in *Soviet Cinema* which was much more revealing than the article itself. The editors stated (1) that cinema *kustarnichestvo* was "harmful... and anti-industrial"; (2) that "insufficiently cultured" bureaucrats *(chinovniki)* held the power in cinema; (3) that centralization was "progressive," though thus far it had suffered from a "bureaucratic distortion"; and (4) that cinema *kustarnichestvo* was especially dangerous because it produced good films.[10]

Soviet Cinema inaugurated the issue of economy in cinema in March 1926. (It is important to remember that it was the only cinema journal connected with a government agency—the Artistic Council on Cinema Affairs in Glavpolitprosvet, the Main Committee on Political Education of the Commissariat of Enlightenment.) *Soviet Cinema* charged that the present organization (i.e., Sovkino) of the film industry was to blame for its slow development. Detailed knowledge about every aspect of film production (average number of scenes, their length, etc.) and full-scale planning would help overcome this. Sloganeering becoming ever more common, there was, of course, a new slogan: "Without stock-taking there is no plan; and without a plan it is impossible to organize production rationally."[11]

The waste in the industry was reflected in the fact that the cost of a meter of negative film could vary from 7 to 26 kopeks. This cost differential depended on the percentage of shot film which went unused and the length of the production schedule. Only 21 percent of the movies used more than 51 percent of the film shot; only 19 percent completed production in less than two months.[12] Another complaint was the frequent abandonment of the screenplay during shooting; Eisenstein was singled out in this regard for *Potemkin* (and it is true that he ignored the script by Nina Agadzhanova-Shutko, which led to a lawsuit over author's rights).[13] In response, the idea of an "iron scenario" which would be the basis of a concrete production plan was developed to avoid overruns.[14]

This was a striking change from earlier years when it was held that all the problems of Soviet cinema could be attributed to lack of money rather than to mismanagement of production. Gone were the days when an impressive advertising point for a film, as in the case of Protazanov's science fiction fantasy *Aelita*, would be how much it had cost. On the contrary, it was now asserted that the quality of a film was not related to its budget. The Civil War adventure *Little Red Devils* had, after all, been a cheap *and* popular film.[15] (Somewhat later, a big budget would have a decidedly negative impact on the reception of a movie.)

Sergei Tretiakov, the futurist poet and critic, was a cinema critic and script writer as well. He astutely characterized this debate over cost as a war between the "minimalists"—those who believed the Soviets could not afford to make expensive pictures—and the "maximalists"—presumably Shvedchikov, Trainin, and the rest of Sovkino "gang" of "bureaucrats" who believed the Soviets could not afford *not* to make expensive pictures which would be attractive to the foreign market. Tretiakov refused to ally himself with either side but concluded that Soviet directors must analyze their situation and learn to work within their limitations. His observation that their only "hard currency" was their considerable native talent was apt.[16]

Cinema also embraced the subject of economizing. Topics ranged from shortages of materials, to attacks on specific films for being wasteful and expensive, to problems of reorganization. Whereas earlier the very real lack of raw material had been recognized as a serious problem, now this attitude was labelled "defeatist." The organization (again, this meant Sovkino) was held up as the scapegoat; the solution was *increased* centralization.[17] Viktor Shklovskii, with his gift for the vivid image, attacked the supposedly prevailing "decentralization" (a term frequently used instead of *Soviet Cinema*'s "*kustarnichestvo*") this way: "Each [film studio] works for itself and in its own way. Everyday they receive wages for the discovery of America."[18] An ARK resolution was less colorful: " . . . from the general disorganization of the Soviet film industry as a whole, lack of economy and control, Soviet cinema production has been led to a grave crisis."[19]

Left, Iakov Protazanov, *upper right,* Vladimir Gardin,
lower right, Iurii Zheliabuzhskii

Viktor Shklovskii

ARK was just as critical of the cinema industry as was *Soviet Cinema.* One of the better *Cinema Front* editorials described the situation this way:

> In every corner of the studio, in every chemical drum of the laboratory, in every joiner's bench of an auxiliary shop, the little founder-master, the little Moscow merchant who has created things narrowly his, has reckoned on *his* studio, on *his* production, feels himself a Khanzhonkov, a Drankov [the famous prerevolutionary directors].

ARK demanded that the film industry turn away from the "little old master, little Moscow merchant" way of doing things, which led to thinking of movies in dozens, or even mere hundreds. Cinema had to be made an *industry* in order to survive.[20]

The regime of economy campaign could be furthered by applying the principles of NOT (Scientific Organization of Labor). NOT would also aid creativity, because art flourished within a framework of strict organization.[21] According to critic Ippolit Sokolov, "NOT in cinema production is economy of money, means, strength and time"—which would lead to a rigorous analysis of production costs.[22] An odd—if somewhat naive—interpretation of NOT was an effort to revitalize the shooting group by giving the director *more*, rather than fewer, assistants.[23]

But the most important means of implementing NOT became the script. "Scenario hunger," already a prominent feature of cinema polemics, hereafter became more acute as the script came to be seen as the organizational fundamental of the cinema. As one writer put it, the law of the studio should be: "Not one meter of film shot from an unreworked film script."[24] A screen writer as well as critic, Viktor Shklovskii not surprisingly agreed with this, but the terms in which he expressed it are enlightening:

> Of all the arts, cinema is the most mechanical. It demands knowledge and calculation.
>   The script should become the blueprint of the picture. The art director and director should study the significance of each frame.
>   For that reason, many cinema-magicians [Shklovskii's term for old-style directors] should become students.[25]

The term which came into currency for this kind of screenplay was the "iron scenario" (or in another version, the "steel scenario"). Ippolit Sokolov was one of the first to advocate it, charging that the director did not know how to prepare a shooting script from a scenario, reworking it on location, which was very expensive. Whereas in America 10 percent of the cost of a film was budgeted for script work, only 1 percent was devoted to the same purpose in the Soviet Union. Furthermore, Soviet directors worked without a shooting schedule. Sokolov optimistically believed that there were in fact few financial problems that the "iron scenario" could not solve.[26]

Opposition to the "iron scenario" came primarily from older directors who felt (according to one writer) that such a script would limit their creative scope. Supporters of the "iron scenario" insisted that far from hampering creativity, it would guarantee the artistic integrity of the work,[27] meaning the *writer's* work. In any case, the script was definitely seized upon as the way to fulfill the intensified demands for economy in the film industry.

The "Scenario Crisis"

While some deliberations over the screenplay were theoretical—how a play differed from a screenplay or which genres were peculiarly cinematographic—in general the debate was tied to the regime of economy, the immediate problem being how to get a larger percentage of usable scripts from poorly qualified writers. Many were eager to write scripts, but few understood the requirements.

From October 1, 1923 to October 1, 1924 Goskino received 365 scripts and accepted only twenty-six. Eighty-five percent of the total was labelled "completely unsuitable." The film censorship exacerbated the shortages, for its unpredictability caused a great deal of confusion. Because of restricted sources, it is difficult to reconstruct the operation of the censorship, but the Commissariat of Enlightenment held ideological and artistic control over film matters in two of its departments: Glavrepertkom (the Main Committee on

Repertory) and the Artistic Council on Cinema Affairs in Glavpolitprosvet (the Main Committee on Political Education). I. P. Trainin, who as former chairman of Glavrepertkom was an expert on its workings, caustically noted that "chaos and *kustarnichestvo*" reigned as far as ideological matters were concerned.[28]

Glavrepertkom had censorship control over foreign as well as domestic films but apparently was not consulted until *after* a foreign movie had been purchased, hardly an economically rational approach. It could then suppress the film (according to one source, it rejected from 10 to 15 percent of the foreign films)[29] or order its re-editing. In any case, no prints for distribution could be made until after the review process was finished. From experience, Trainin recognized the friction built into such an arrangement and hoped that Sovkino and Glavrepertkom could work cordially together on the approval of foreign films, since income from them was the key element in his plan to put the industry on a sound economic footing.[30]

The Artistic Council on Cinema Affairs in Glavpolitprosvet was the ideological adviser for Soviet production. Established in July 1924, it also devised production plans, suggested themes for production, and helped "rework" foreign films.[31] In its first months of existence, it had approved thirty-eight of eighty-five scripts submitted, although some only provisionally.[32]

To make censorship even more complicated, the film production companies also had an artistic advisory board (*khudsovet*). One writer indicated that the steps in the censorship process were as follows: the script went to the studio's advisory board first, then to the studio, then to the Artistic Council on Cinema Affairs in Glavpolitprosvet. Any of these groups could disapprove a script. Furthermore a great deal of the production could have been carried out before the script was turned over to the Artistic Council. The separation of censorship (euphemistically referred to as "ideological leadership") from production was a serious problem.[33] In addition, there was already some concern that the Artistic Council was not sufficiently playing the political watchdog.[34] The question of which of the three bodies would review the finished film long remained unresolved and bitterly disputed.

Thus, the uncertain operation of the censorship (rather than its harshness) added to the persistent shortage of screenplays. Concern over the quality of scripts meant criticizing the banality of the recurring stereotypes in Soviet cinema (the absence of real people and vivid images), rather than looking for ideological deficiencies.[35] A startling exception to this was an article in *Cinema Week* in which A. Seifer declared that " . . . the poor lighting of a shot is a one-quarter misfortune, artistic carelessness, a half-misfortune; [but] foul ideology—is counter revolution."[36]

Interest in solving script problems through "rationalization" was growing. Without taking either talent or the nature of creativity into consideration, it was believed that rationalization could by itself foster interesting and lively scripts. There were several plans for achieving this streamlining of the untidy creative process. One came from the scenarist and critic Valentin Turkin. Raising both quality and quantity of scripts could not, in his opinion, be achieved without a literary group (*litotdel*), which would organize work in conjunction with the producer and director.[37] (The place of the individual writer in his plan was not made clear.)

Another version came from the Lef poet and script writer Sergei Tretiakov, and considering his connections, it is not surprising that he sought to "industrialize" script production through an "assembly line." First there would be a sketch of the plot (libretto); then the details would be filled in by the *bytovoi* sector (experts on Soviet life); next, the scenarist proper would write the script; after which a shooting script would be drawn up.[38]

It was, in fact, very popular to apply factory terminology to directors and scenarists. Filmmaker Nikolai Anoshchenko wrote: "The scenarist is an engineer-constructor, but the director is a production engineer."[39] Such statements obscured the growing conflict between director and writer; it was frequently said that it was difficult to attract good writers to cinema work because they lost control over the screenplay to the director. Although some believed that the director should have a hand in the script,[40] others saw the director as a dictator who could and did pervert or even destroy the ideological content of the screenplay.[41]

Another factor contributing to the clash of egos was the authorship law, which, as mentioned above, regarded the scenarist and not the director as the "author" of a movie. This became a matter of debate early in 1925, and *Cinema Gazette* published a cartoon with all the "pretenders [to the throne]" gathered around in threatening postures.[42] The Cinema Section of the Central Committee of the Art Workers' Union recommended that the director get only 25 percent of film royalties.[43] Yet even this favoritism toward scenarists (which reveals a fundamental misunderstanding of the art of the cinema) did not convince literati to work in film. Despite the movement toward establishing the script as the basis for rational film production, it was difficult to get capable writers to give up their creative independence for work that was truly collective in nature.

So, by 1926, the regime of economy campaign had definitely focussed attention on the script, but the shortages continued. As discussed earlier, one remedy for script starvation was to hold scenario competitions. A Goskino-sponsored contest in 1923 had produced 104 entrants of which not one received a "first."[44] Even considerable sums of money[45] did not seem to bring in higher quality work. Osip Brik reported on a Glavpolitprosvet competition which yielded 256 scripts, all of which were rejected, leading him to conclude that amateurs could not write screenplays and that these contests were a waste of time and money.[46] Film professionals slowly began to realize that the regime of economy campaign could be exploited to work in their favor.

Sergei Tretiakov also used the regime of economy to oppose screenplay competitions,[47] again a sign of the growing sense of professionalism within the film industry. He predicted that it would soon be recognized that amateurs had no place in the film world.[48] Viktor Shklovskii felt amateurs foolishly tended toward exotic subjects concerning "Spaniards, tsarist officers, counts, and ichthyosauri."[49]

Waste occurred not only in connection with the scenario competitions but also with scripts that had been accepted by the censorship and then not used by the studio. In 1924-25, 55 percent of the scripts submitted to the censorship had been approved, but only 66 percent of these were used. The situation had not changed much in 1925-26: 63 percent of the scripts were passed; only 68 percent of these were used. M. S. Veremienko, a prominent opponent of Sovkino, blamed this on the "weak political preparation of writers [that so few were passed] and directors [that so few scripts were used]."[50]

Critic Ippolit Sokolov offered even more dismal figures, based on the large numbers of unsolicited scripts. He wrote that in 1926 only 30 percent of the scripts sent to the studios were accepted (up from a low of 5 percent the year before), and that Glavpolitprosvet then rejected about 53 percent of these.[51] Significantly higher figures appeared elsewhere. The typical explanation for the low acceptance rate was that scripts were written by "accidental people" who knew nothing about cinema and submitted "politically illiterate" scripts which were "coarsely agitational, poster-like [*plakatnyi*] and tendentious," a popular theme being the fate of the peasant girl who comes to town.[52]

Ippolit Sokolov was emerging as a major theorist on the scenario, and in an important contribution to an issue of *Cinema* devoted to this subject, he drew some guidelines to alleviate the "crisis." The basic principle a script writer should keep in mind was economy. Soviet scripts were typically overflowing with dramatis personae, sets, and costumes. The script should be "dialectical" (employing the dramatic principle of contrasts) and "photogenic" (cinematographic, not literary). Sokolov limited amateur participation to the submission of the libretto (story line), leaving the real work to the professional. Because he felt that production and the script had to be inextricably connected, he proposed that the script writer also work as assistant director.[53]

With the increasing attention paid to the script as a factor in the regime of economy campaign, the ideological dimension became more important. Near the end of 1926, *Cinema Front* devoted most of an issue to questions of ideology. The editorial declared that there were still no "good, Soviet scripts," which it defined this way:

> What does good mean: artistically literate, written with account taken of our requirements and possibilities, with retreat from cliché, without superfluous inventiveness and so forth; that is, a script on which one might base a picture.
> What does Soviet mean: that which reflects the ideas, mood, experience, and struggle of the working class for its own power, for its own structure, for its own culture, counting on the continuation of revolutionary activity on the cultural front.[54]

The search for a Soviet style in cinema was central to cinema debates from this point on.

Sokolov also treated the subject in this issue of *Cinema Front*. There was, he said, new material for Soviet cinema but "some harmful and unnecessary deviations" such as "stunts [*triukizm*], circus attractions, curiosities, horrors, ... pathology plus 'physiology'" persisted along with a return to bourgeois subjects under the guise of "the decay of Europe," or "the degeneration of the bourgeoisie." The last two he connected to an unhealthy preoccupation with violence and sex.[55] When writers attempted to deal with Soviet reality, clichés and "naive" portrayals predominated. Yet at the same time Sokolov could propose the creation "of a whole gallery of types: the communist, Komsomol member, Pioneer, worker, etc."[56] But how could these new "types" free Soviet cinema from the clichéd dullness to which it was subject?

Sokolov's "new path" in the search for a Soviet style was articulated in his essay "Where Is Soviet Cinema Going?" ("Kuda idet sovetskoe kino?"). For the new Soviet cinema, Sokolov favored epics and dramas, with the former taking precedence. He wrote:

> The epic is a monumental, heroic, and classic genre; the hero is the masses. The drama is an intimate, lyrical, and romantic genre; the hero is the individual.
> Heroics, monumentalism, classicism are the large style of our epoch. Psychologism and intimacy are the small style of our epoch.[57]

In Sokolov's book *Cinema Screenplay* (*Kino-stsenarii*) he further developed his theory of Soviet cinema dramaturgy. While he continued to insist, as before, that "decadent naturalism" had to be rejected in favor of "psychological realism and monumental classicism," he also rejected the crude agit-film. He wrote:

> We have already passed the stage of "agitation in art"; we are going toward "agitation by means of art." We need to renounce completely the naive-tendentious methods of '19 and '20.[58]

He accurately identified the weaknesses of Soviet films as their boring subject matter and poor dramatic construction—"instead of 'living people,' there are schema and empty spaces."[59] Therefore, an improved screenplay could do two things—serve as the organizational basis for production and make films more entertaining, a quality sorely lacking in Soviet cinema. Sokolov's "psychologism and intimacy" might satisfy the demand for an interesting Soviet film, but could "heroics, monumentalism, classicism?" Unfortunately, as we shall see, it was the latter rather than the former characteristics that became the basis of the new Soviet realism.

The Actor

The heat of the screenplay debate came in part from the perceived need to strengthen the position of the writer vis-à-vis the director, as the one who could best bring color and interest to a cinema dominated by clichés. In some respects, the debate surrounding the actor had a similar basis. As discussed in the preceding chapter, Soviet audiences found Western stars like Douglas Fairbanks and Mary Pickford much more attractive and appealing than Soviet actors. (One *Cinema* reader wrote that after seeing Doug Fairbanks in one of his swashbuckling roles, he felt himself relaxed and renewed, able to attack his daily work with vigor.)[60] Some critics believed that Soviet cinema should learn from the West and create its own "stars."

This suggestion met with strong opposition from the cinema "left," and for once the political left (critics of NEP like Nikolai Lebedev, founder of ARK) and the artistic left (avant-gardists like director Dziga Vertov) were united. Acting was early viewed in Soviet film theory as one of the areas in which cinema could and must distinguish itself from theater; the use of "stars" from the theater like Moskvin (*Polikushka*) or Leonidov (*Wings of a Serf*) was definitely to be scorned.[61] In this view, theatrical acting and the cult of actors were bourgeois and decadent, the most extreme reaction being, of course, Dziga Vertov's total rejection of the actor and the acted film. Variations on the theme included Eisenstein's use of both professionals and nonprofessionals ("types") in the acted "mass" movie, or Kuleshov's careful training of his actor-model (*akter-naturshchik*). Until Pudovkin made *Mother* (*Mat'*), however, "revolutionary" directors did not use theatrical actors, that being the hallmark of bourgeois directors like Iakov Protazanov.

The "old" directors were in general practical men who did not aspire to "art" and were hostile to what they viewed as the intellectualization of cinema. Cheslav Sabinskii, who had worked in cinema since 1908 (directing since 1912), felt Kuleshov's actor-model denigrated the actor, who should be not a "model" (to Sabinskii this meant a "thing"), but a co-creator with the director.[62]

Yet a counterbalance to Sabinskii's argument came from another traditional director who also relied heavily on theater actors, Iurii Tarich. Tarich, who himself had been an actor (albeit in the theater), was now fiercely protective of the powers of the director. Actors' salaries consumed about 50 percent of the budget for a movie, and Tarich attacked them as money-

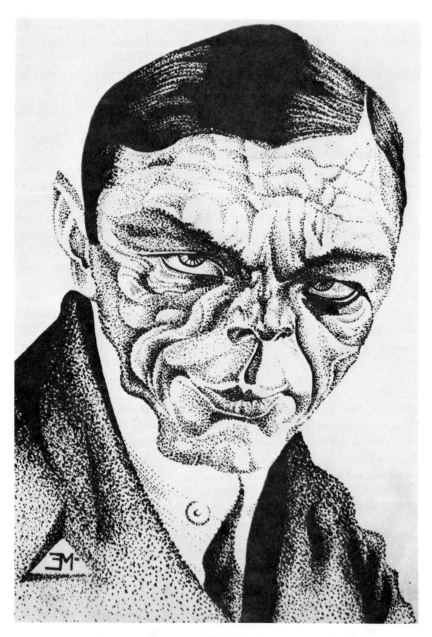

Iurii Tarich

grubbers. Actors, he claimed, had no loyalty to the studio, considering themselves free agents unless they tripled their previous salary from film to film. They felt themselves so completely the masters of the situation that they even dared to dictate conditions to the director. Neither, he charged, did they have any loyalty to the building of Soviet cinema which was, after all, "an affair closely concerning them." Tarich called for actors to become socially active (*akter-obshchestvennik*) in order to raise the artistic quality of Soviet cinema.[63]

The hostility between director and actor was even more evident in the "debate" between the actress Olga Tretiakova and director Leo Mur. Tretiakova was a popular cinema actress (*Commander Ivanov*) who was actively engaged in trying to raise the esteem in which her profession was held. She was also the secretary of the actors' subsection of ARK, which had been established to publicize the plight of actors.[64] Tretiakova demanded that writers create good roles for actors and urged directors to discuss the roles with them.[65] Mur was amused by Tretiakova's taking at face value a remark he had made about the "dictatorship" of the director,[66] but she was probably not far wrong in assuming that he meant it. Actors were still fighting to have their hours and pay regularized or even to get a copy of the script![67]

In the early twenties it was impossible to find a consensus on the role of the actor in the movie, and difficult to delineate clearly defined groups of "right" or "left." That even a director like Tarich, whose work was intimately connected to "established" (that is, theater) actors, could be so hostile toward them is evidence of the competitiveness of the industry rank-and-file. But more than competition was at work here; we see a fundamental difference in the attitude toward cinema as an art.

In the jargon of 1925, to be on the artistic "left" meant to reject actors like Vertov or to use "types" like Eisenstein (a more moderate view). To be on the "right" meant to use theater actors. Kuleshov's concept of the actor-model, which dominated the acting courses at GTK, the state film school, was somewhere in between, and in the opinion of the excellent critic Ippolit Sokolov, it trained the actor to be a real artist.

The Kuleshov "theory" was an early form of method acting, based on the development of the body through ordinary gymnastics and more philosophically sophisticated exercises like Delsartism and reflexology. The first year of the actor's course at GTK was 50 percent gymnastics and 35 percent Delsart movements. Sokolov approved this as conforming to the demands of the regime of economy, for "all principles, methods, and plans for the upbringing of the cinema actor should be constructed on the laws of NOT [Scientific Organization of Labor] and reflexology."[68] It seems that the origins of this "system" lay not so much in the director's desire to gain control over the actor as it did in the mania for rationalization characteristic of early Soviet society.

To those closely connected with the concept of the actor-model, it most emphatically did not mean an untrained person off the streets, mere clay for the director. But the more common, vulgarized version of the actor-model held that he was simply a "type." One observer, who believed he was defending the notion of the actor-model wrote: "Working with actor-models, with *simple people* [emphasis added] . . . was very easy and pleasant . . . ."[69] Kuleshov must have been appalled to see his well-trained actors identified with "simple people."

Actors outside the Kuleshov collective and GTK regarded the notion of the actor-model with varying degrees of hostility. Their claim that the method was a denigration of acting (and therefore, of man) was important in the politics of Soviet film theory. People, not things, should be the focal point of a movie; if the actor was "material" for a film, he also had to be a "master." Actors did not categorically reject the gymnastics, Dalcrose rhythmics, or Delsartism of Kuleshov, but they wanted emphasis on psychology, practical experience, and makeup as well.[70]

Actors also resented "typage," stereotyping by physical characteristics in order to get "realism." This practice was a deviant variant of Kuleshov's actor-model and came to mean the selection of nonprofessionals who "looked the type." Since typage was Eisenstein's preferred casting method (although he did use professional actors), it was erroneously believed abroad that Soviet directors *never* used professional actors. Exaggerated though this was, typage began to be taken so literally that it could be attacked on economic grounds; good-humored criticism of some directors' devotion to typage was conveyed in a cartoon showing production being stopped so that an actor could grow a real beard.[71] Typage in another sense meant role-stereotypes; a problem here was that "negative" types like nobles or tsarist officers were in general more attractive physically than "positive" types like workers or revolutionaries.[72] In short, actors had a right to be dissatisfied, and they lobbied for more prestige and respect at a time when the avant-garde and the "revolutionary" were being critically re-examined, much enhancing their chances of success.

Significantly, supporters of the acted film tended also to be supporters of realism in cinema. Scenarist Valentin Turkin, like the theorist Voznesenskii before him, believed that the superiority of cinema over theater lay in its greater realism[73] and that acting distinguished cinema as an art. For Turkin, true cinema acting should be simple and straightforward, qualities he did not see in Kuleshov's work, which he found just as theatrical as that of the avant-garde theater director Meierkhold.[74] Turkin believed theater was theater, even if it was "left-wing." He described cinema acting this way:

> On the screen it is necessary not to "imitate," not to "play," but to do convincingly, to "work"; not to "imitate" a running person, but really to run; not to "imitate" a fight, but really to fight, really to be adroit and strong. . . . [75]

Lev Kuleshov

Yet was this not more or less Kuleshov's theory of the actor-model, which emphasized physical exercise? Turkin himself admitted that the reason for the popularity of the actor-models was that they underplayed instead of the overplaying which was the bane of the silent screen.[76]

But there was one real difference between Turkin and Kuleshov. Like Kuleshov, Turkin rejected physical beauty, but unlike the great director he sought *moral* beauty; he wanted "... a new hero, cheerful and courageous, physically strong and agile; characteristic actors who would be able to play the worker, peasant, laboring intellectual [*intelligent*], Party member, Komsomol member."[77] Kuleshov's collective of eccentrics hardly fulfilled these requirements.

Turkin, like many others, saw the actor-model as a director's robot, not creating but repeating actions at the director's command.[78] He regretted that this mechanical and anti-humanistic system had been enthroned at the film school GTK as the only acting method.[79] But Turkin's views hardly formed a system. How did one teach "underacting?" The "expressive movement" methods of Delsart and Dalcrose appealed to those bent on increasing the labor force, because they seemed a rational approach to the problem of training cadres.

Ironically, just as the actor was being installed as the basis of Soviet cinema, there was also a resurgence of support for Dziga Vertov and the nonacted feature film in 1926. Many politically minded cinema activists recognized the acted film had proven a poor propaganda vehicle while coarse agit-films simply alienated the viewer.[80] High-minded revolutionaries had to face the fact that Soviet fiction films like *The Bear's Wedding*, *Miss Mend*, or *Case of the Three Million* were as bourgeois as they were popular. For these reasons, it seemed essential to support Vertov as a force against the creeping decadence of Soviet cinema. Therefore, although Vertov still had powerful detractors, for the first time he also enjoyed a measure of support in the film community.

Vertov had toned down his rhetoric since his 1923 *Lef* essay "Cinema-eyes: Coup." He wrote that he had passed from his *Cinema Truth* newsreels (directed against "red-detective" films like *Little Red Devils*) to the *Cinema Eye* period which was:

> ... not a cinema picture, not a group of cinema workers, not some kind of tendency in art (left or right) but a gradually spreading movement of the influence of acts against the influence of invention.[81]

Vertov wrote another seminal theoretical essay to express his principles. Simply titled "Cinema-eye" ("Kino glaz"), it appeared in a Proletkul't collection.[82] Though not as radical (and entertaining) as his *Lef* essay, it is central to an understanding of Vertov. In "Cinema-eye," Vertov explained the genesis of his ideas on cinema. He had seen from his experience with showing peasants movies that they did not understand fiction films, since they could neither read the titles nor follow the action. He claimed peasants had asked him to show them "life" because theirs was so limited. Theater or film drama could not fulfill this desire, because in Vertov's opinion, drama is not basic to the human experience, art being a mere surrogate for life. A movie with actors, a director, and a script is only art and therefore inherently incapable of addressing the elemental needs of the masses.

Vertov's own *Cinema Truth* series was in his mind the first indication of a new path for cinema, one that was factual and *collective*, one based not on literature but on living material. No more did he boast of manipulating time and space through montage, the line closest to the spirit of the old Vertov being that "cinema drama is the opium of the people."[83] Vertov still fervently believed that Soviet cinema was serving the interests of NEPmen rather than those of the working classes. He pledged to eschew experimentalism in the future the better to serve the proletariat in the struggle against "businessmen and specialists."[84] He was making his peace with the political left—those opposed to NEP—and now some were willing to listen.

Yet this period proved to be Vertov's swan song, for the plotted movie with a hero was definitely on the ascendant. Aside from political and aesthetic reasons for putting "life-loving" Soviet heroes on the screen, it cannot be denied that Soviet viewers loved movie stars as much as did their Western counterparts. Vertov could not long pretend to be satisfying the demands of the masses; the poor box office returns of his films belied his grandiose claims.

The Virtues of Realism

The debates over the scenario crisis and the acted film were converging on the same point, an interest in injecting realism into the Soviet film. Realism found supporters of different backgrounds. Sovkino's Trainin, for example, no friend of the Soviet avant-garde, favored realism in cinema, but realism of a particular sort. The issue was how Soviet realism was to be defined since no one at this point supported the "unrelieved" propaganda film, although few supported the avant-garde. Sovkino's alternative was to make Western-style entertainment movies. The other alternative was as yet almost inchoate, the precursor of the aesthetic theory known as Soviet Socialist Realism.

Traces of this concept were first found in the discussion of the superiority of cinema over theater.[85] It was sometimes part of the debate over cinema acting, as we have just seen with Turkin's "new" hero. Although no serious cinema critic any longer predicted the imminent demise of the theater, everyone claimed with monotonous regularity that the superiority of cinema over theater lay in its realism. Abram Room, a gifted young director and independent-minded critic, summarized the major arguments succinctly:

> Theater is first of all transformation, illusion, ideas, the play of unreality, conventionality, stylization.
> Cinema is primarily realism, life, way of life [*byt*], "concreteness," justifiable conduct, the rational gesture. Theater is "to show"; cinema is "to be."[86]

The prevailing concept of cinema realism was becoming more and more simplistic. Director Leo Mur felt that the intrinsic realism of cinema lay in its rejection of symbolism, writing: "Cinema, in distinction from the other arts, does not have, (and by its nature) will never have prepared, conventional symbols...."[87] Furthermore, material for cinema was seen to be more "typical," more "authentic" than that for theater. Cinema shows; theater describes.[88]

Valentin Turkin concurred, as we would have expected from his views on the actor. Cinema, he wrote, "freed" theater from its "rude conventions"; its techniques were altogether more "convincing."[89] Furthermore, "cinema is the enemy of the false and approximate" and "sheds new light" on things—literally (he jocularly noted) and figuratively. Cinema realism was revelation, showing man "the 'wealth' of his natural expression and the techniques of his movement."[90]

Turkin was careful to point out, however, that cinema realism was not vulgar naturalism. The artistic style of conventional realism (by which he apparently meant "naturalism") was boring and irrelevant to cinema. The styles suitable for Soviet realism he ambiguously termed the gay and the tragic, neo-romantic, neo-realistic, and expressionist.[91] These styles awaited further development,[92] but to some extent were reflected in the movies of 1925-26.

The Films

Revolutionary Films: Strike *and* Potemkin

Although none of the practical and artistic problems of Soviet cinema were near resolution, the situation had improved enough for the pent-up creative energy of the past eight years to explode. Critical debates over specific movies were very closely related to abstract questions of style. The major film of 1925 was *Strike* (*Stachka*) produced by the Proletkul't theater collective, Tisse on camera, according to its advertisements. *Strike* is no longer considered a product of the Proletkul't, but rather that of the most remarkable figure of Soviet cinema, Sergei Eisenstein. This was his first film, although he had been active previously in the Proletkul't theater. *Strike* unleashed a veritable furor of comment and controversy, centering on the role of the individual in the fiction film, a question that had been implicit in the polemics over both the actor and the popularity of foreign films. The issue now became explicit, and Dziga Vertov had a worthy rival in Eisenstein, the inventor of a new kind of fiction film.

The critical reception of the film was generally enthusiastic. Unlike other sensations of the past, which now seem merely quaint, *Strike* still dazzles the viewer with its bizarre combination of agit-film stereotypes and avant-garde techniques. It concerns the struggle of the workers during a strike, their betrayal to the police, and their slaughter. *Strike* lacks a traditional plot and the only "hero" is the masses, the workers. The drama of the movie is found in its mass action and violence, in addition to the stunningly original photography and shot composition (which some film historians see as being strongly constructivist in influence). Eisenstein used the typical silent film editing device of parallel cutting (between the decadence of the wealthy owners and the poverty of the workers, for example) to make a moral and political point, but he also tried a new technique—symbolic cutting—which he termed "montage of attractions." In this film the most famous example of montage of attractions is a cattle slaughterhouse sequence cut with the troops firing on the strikers; cattle are not really being killed during the events of the movie, of course—the purpose is to express moral judgment on the soldiers. Although we may scoff at the depth of such "intellect," Eisenstein's "intellectual cinema" would prove a key issue in the subsequent debate on formalism in cinema.

One of the most unreservedly enthusiastic reviews of *Strike* appeared in *Soviet Screen*. The writer applauded both the "dialectics" of the work and the obviously strong influence of constructivism as indicating that at last a new form, a new path had been found for Soviet cinema.[93] A later review praised *Strike* for extolling class consciousness and internationalism, for being absolutely unlike a Western film.[94] Nikolai Lebedev was also excited—"By its content, this is the first strictly working class picture"—and he predicted its success with the workers.[95] *ARK* studiously ignored the potentially explosive issue of its avant-garde form and analyzed the movie only on the basis of its content.[96] *Soviet Cinema* recognized its originality and "healthy direction" but refrained from suggesting that *Strike* be taken as a prototype, asking why had it not shown the organizational work of the Party in connection with the strike.[97]

An outright enemy of *Strike* was Dziga Vertov, who declared that the movie was only a "reform" of the fiction film; he clearly felt threatened by a genius which rivalled his own. *Cinema* published his article with a disclaimer that Vertov had used the space not to criticize *Strike* but to reiterate his "unserious and superficial" positions.[98] Eisenstein rose with relish to Vertov's challenge. Like Vertov, he was a genuine personality and his own best publicist. His writing was dense with a phraseology he doubtless connected with "materialism"; Eisenstein was prodigiously well read (a legend among his peers) and a man of genuine culture, but he, like most other directors, knew little about Marxism. He personally felt that *Strike* was "October in cinema" because "*revolutionary form is the product of the correctly found technical means of the concretization of the new view and approach to things and phenomena.*"[99]

He scoffed at comparing *Strike* to Vertov's work, and he denied any Vertovian influence. Eisenstein proudly declared that *Strike* was a work of art (in contrast to Vertov's persistent denials of artistic merit in his own films). Eisenstein charged that Vertov's work was mere "impressionism"; in *Cinema Eye*, Vertov had simply "run after things as they are," without making the all-important socially conscious connections. Eisenstein continued:

> The "Cinema-eye" is not only a symbol of seeing but also a symbol of contemplation. We do not need to *contemplate*, but to act.
> We do not need a "Cinema-eye," but a "Cinema-fist."[100]

Strike, a true "cinema fist," could not and did not fail to shake Soviet critics out of their doldrums. In this sense it marks a turning point in Soviet film criticism. The long-hoped-for future had arrived. But considering some of the concerns we have already seen exhibited, such as the needs of the Soviet mass audience and its ability to understand films, *Strike* was also bound to disquiet. A difficult film to watch, *Strike* was the catalyst for the beginning of serious debate over the place of the hero in Soviet cinema.

ARK placed opponents of the film into two groups. The first admired the effort but did not see *Strike* as a truly revolutionary film; the second was the decadent "back to Pushkin" camp, which favored classical literature for subject matter in cinema and the Moscow Art Theater style of acting and directing. ARK declared that a measure of agitation in Soviet films was necessary, for there could be no such thing as non-Party art in the USSR.[101]

Sovkino's I. P. Trainin, his eyes always shrewdly trained on the market, was an opponent of *Strike* who did not fit neatly into either of ARK's categories. He criticized the absence of a hero in *Strike* as the cause of the film's lack of drama. Everyone, including workers, he said, liked romantic tales with human interest. While an overabundance of characters was not required to hold his attention, stories of contemporary life were necessary to help the viewer understand "socialist morals and ethics." Although Trainin admitted that there were many "purely cinematographic, interesting achievements" in *Strike*, he insisted its stereotypes could not win over an audience's heart.[102] Later Trainin flatly stated that the film was not successful with the viewers, playing only thirty-seven days in Moscow while even a "commonplace" film like *Stepan Khalturin* had a fifty-two-day run and earned more money. *Strike* was, according to Trainin, more "dogmatic" than "dialectic."[103] (The one concrete report of audience response to *Strike* that I have seen supports Trainin. When shown in Red Army clubs at the time, it held attention for a mere twenty-five minutes before restlessness and chattering began.)[104]

Eisenstein's immense talent, while apparent in *Strike*, came to fruition in his second film, *Potemkin*, arguably the most brilliant achievement of silent cinema. Of the several outstanding movies of 1926, *Battleship Potemkin* immediately attracted the most attention. Viewers (as opposed to critics) may have received it indifferently, but it was *not* an unsung masterpiece at the time of its first release, as the Commissar of Enlightenment Anatolii Lunacharskii later tried to suggest for political purposes. As befits a work with claims to greatness, there was a vociferous reaction to *Potemkin* in the press, both in praise and criticism.

It is superfluous to detail the events of *Potemkin*, one of the best known and most analyzed films in cinema history, except to point out that it concerns mutiny at sea and the support of the people of Odessa for the sailors. The hero is the battleship itself. For most present-day critics, *Potemkin* stands as the vindication and purest example of the "Russian" technique of rhythmic montage (especially in the Odessa steps sequence); for many, it is the perfectly constructed movie. The combination of Eisenstein's instinct for dynamics and dramatic construction (even without a traditional hero) and his brilliant cameraman Eduard Tisse's pictorial sense (the dimly lit foggy harbor scene was technically "impossible" until Tisse dared to do it) won the film its justly enduring fame.

Soviet film critics on the whole were a gifted and perceptive, if politically partisan, group; they could not and did not fail to notice that *Potemkin* was even more of an event than *Strike* had been. Their lack of critical consensus indicates both the originality and controversial nature of this powerful work, considering the new trends in cinema politics. If the film of the future was to have both a plot and a hero, then how was *Potemkin*, which had these only in highly unorthodox form, to be judged?

ARK came out wholeheartedly in favor of *Potemkin*, as seen in this *ARK* editorial:

> This is a victory for Soviet cinematography; for Kuleshov and Vertov who paved the way; for ARK which praised *Strike*. Long live *Potemkin*, the greatest achievement of cinematography in the USSR.[105]

ARK's sense of community was both touching and naive, for most assuredly Vertov wanted no credit for *Potemkin*, and as it happens, neither did Kuleshov. Very enthusiastic reviews came from Viktor Shklovskii and Ippolit Sokolov, the latter of whom, in a rare tribute to a cameraman, praised cinematographer Eduard Tisse, as well as director Eisenstein.[106]

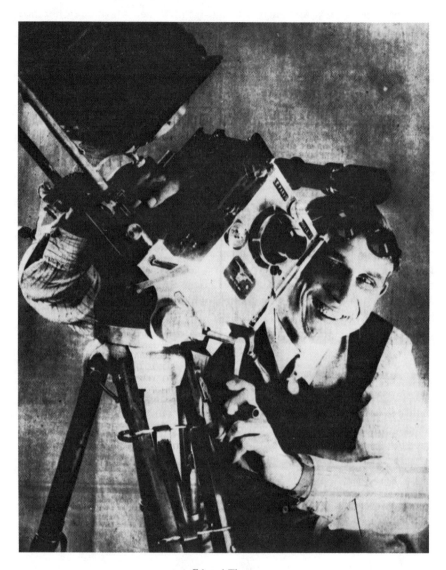

Eduard Tisse

Negative criticism came from constructivist Aleksei Gan (now seldom heard in cinema debates) who thought the film "poor,"[107] and from some pedants in ARK who criticized its historical inaccuracies.[108] It was Khrisanf Khersonskii, however, who offered the most penetrating review from the point of view of the era's cultural politics. He recognized that although the work of Eisenstein was different from that of Vertov in many ways, they were alike in one critical way—they lacked a central character, and therefore, human interest. He wrote: "*Potemkin* was made with a wonderful head [meaning, it is intellectual], but somewhere inside it is cold."[109] Director Abram Room concurred in an ARK discussion.[110]

In view of the increasing, sometimes misguided but genuine, concern for the opinion of the viewer, this was a valid criticism. *Potemkin* was a brilliant film, but for whom? For cineasts or for the ordinary filmgoer? As always, it is difficult to gauge viewer response, because few polls were taken. ARK kept records of some screenings for workers which were followed by discussions; the results were mixed. In one, the film was seen to be confusing and hard to follow because of the rapidity of the cutting;[111] in another, the reaction was extremely enthusiastic because of the revolutionary fervor generated by the movie.[112] But Viktor Shklovskii reported that several readers wrote letters to *Cinema* complaining about the newspaper's promoting *Potemkin* over *The Bear's Wedding*,[113] a traditional and very popular melodrama to be discussed below.

The most surprising critic of *Potemkin* was the founder of Russian montage theory, Lev Kuleshov, who thought that Eisenstein, though gifted, lacked technical mastery. He declared Eisenstein's montage, even in *Potemkin*, weak.[114] In order to understand this seeming anomaly, we must examine the state of montage theory in the mid-twenties.

Today, Eisenstein and montage theory are inextricably linked. In 1926 this was not the case, because Eisenstein was far busier making films than writing about them. (It was only later, after the disruption of his career, that he seriously turned to theory and criticism.) Actually, Kuleshov's theory of montage as linkage, of each shot as a word in a sentence, was quite different from Eisenstein's notion of montage as collision, as conflict, as opposition, out of which an idea "grew." Kuleshov therefore found Eisenstein's montage obtrusive and superficial.[115]

Nor was Eisenstein's montage supported by a new theorist on the subject, Sergei Timoshenko, who in his book *The Art of the Cinema: Film Editing* (*Iskusstvo kino: Montazh fil'ma*) took up where Vertov had left off. Timoshenko saw montage as the defining principle of cinema. His explanation for the superiority of cinema over theater had profound political implications: cinema is more "comfortable" for the viewer because it relieves him of choice. The theater viewer is confronted by a range of choices on which to focus his eyes; in cinema the choice is made through editing. For this reason, cinema is also a more complete art since the director is in *full* command. Timoshenko wrote: "Cinema shows: *when, what, where*, and *how long* one needs to look at one or another occurrence or thing in order to receive the appropriate feeling." Furthermore, cinema is less taxing because the viewer need only to *look* (not to look and listen); the emphasis of a film should therefore be: "the organization of the viewer's attention, the direction of this along the necessary path."

Timoshenko constantly repeated that the importance of montage was as a means of *controlling* the viewer, bluntly phrasing it the "forcible attraction of the viewer's attention."[116] The director needs to decide what emotions he hopes to arouse and how to achieve them. The "steel scenario" (Timoshenko's version of the "iron scenario" popularized in the screenplay debates) was the ideal vehicle for allowing the director to "establish and retain control over events." The "steel scenario" was in fact to be so rigid that the critic should be able to write a review from this without ever seeing the film, negating the visual experience of moviegoing.

Kuleshov had analyzed Eisenstein's work as being *too* manipulative. It is doubly ironic that Timoshenko, a seeming proponent of manipulative editing, also chided Eisenstein for his "conscious rape of the viewer's emotions." Timoshenko claimed that his refined definition of montage theory meant that montage should not be the end, but only the means of relaying content.[117] The controversy over *Potemkin* was over, but that over Eisenstein and his methods was just beginning.

Other Revolutionary Films

Revolutionary heroism not surprisingly was the topic of yet a third major film in 1925-26. Unlike Eisenstein's maiden efforts, this one was not the least bit controversial; everyone agreed that it was a masterpiece and just the example Soviet cinema needed. It was Pudovkin's *Mother* (1926), a loose adaptation of Maksim Gorkii's famous novel. *Mother* was Pudovkin's first feature film[118] and a very good one indeed, although its niche in the Soviet pantheon of precursors to Socialist Realism unfortunately overshadows Pudovkin's later masterpieces, *The End of Saint Petersburg* (*Konets Sankt-Peterburga*) and *The Heir of Genghis Khan* (*Potomok Chingiz-khana*).

The first Soviet production of the Gorkii novel had been made in 1919 by Aleksandr Razumnyi. Razumnyi's version is much truer to Gorkii but very inferior cinema. Recalling the serious material shortages of 1919, it is understandable that the quality of the film and lighting was very poor. In fact the release of this film had been held up until 1922 due to lack of positive stock on which to make prints; in the interim, part of the film was lost, and it was never shown in its entirety.[119]

Vsevolod Pudovkin

Considering what we have seen of the evolution of Soviet film aesthetics over the five years up to 1926, it is not surprising that Pudovkin's *Mother* was popular among critics. The film was revolutionary in spirit, had a plot (of a mother's and son's rise to revolutionary consciousness and their work in the revolutionary underground), and featured a strong cast led by Nikolai Batalov (a boyishly handsome and exuberant actor who was surely the epitome of a Soviet hero) and Vera Baranovskaia, both theater veterans. (Baranovskaia emigrated in 1928, but so central is her Pelageia Vlasova to Soviet cinema mythology that her name has not been expunged from the record.) Viewers loved *Mother* for the same reasons as the critics; it is important to keep in mind that behind the polemics against avant-garde and intellectual cinema lay a genuine desire to bring films closer to the the viewer.

Reviews of *Mother* were almost monotonously enthusiastic. Characteristic praise of the film was that it was "living human drama" which fearlessly employed the actor.[120] Viktor Shklovskii coined the term "psychological montage" for the editing style of the new master, Pudovkin.[121] This is misleading because it refers not to montage, but to the kind of *drama* Pudovkin preferred. He too used "associative montage" or symbolic cutting (his ice-flow scene in *Mother* symbolizes hope) like Eisenstein or Vertov, but he did not accept Eisenstein's idea of montage as "collision" or Vertov's of montage as manipulation. Khrisanf Khersonskii noted that *Mother*'s dramatic strength was one reason for its popularity with the "unsophisticated masses."[122] *Mother* was easily the single most successful film thus far in terms of satisfying the demand for a traditional, narrative film with revolutionary content.

Not all films with revolutionary themes were masterpieces, of course. There were three less successful (and more typical) examples in 1926: *Death Bay* (*Bukhta smerti*), *Wind* (*Veter*), and *The Tripol Tragedy* (*Tripol'skaia tragediia*). Yet Abram Room's *Death Bay*, while inferior to *Potemkin* or *Mother*, was also a critical success for its handling of revolutionary material. It is a story of a simple man, a ship's mechanic, who resolutely tries to avoid politics and works for the Whites even after his son has gone over to the Reds. Eventually, he sees the right in the Red cause and is responsible for the sinking of his own battleship.

Despite some superfluous violence which drew negative comment, *Death Bay* is not an engrossing film. The only time it comes to life is due to the superlative acting of Nikolai Okhlopkov (the famous theater director) in a small and irrelevant card-game scene on board ship.[123] Room, a great admirer of Okhlopkov, apparently wanted to use his considerable talents in the movie but was unsure how to integrate this segment.

Reviews were good, but not exceptionally enthusiastic, with the exception of one "I. S.," probably Ippolit Sokolov, who found the film a "great event." It was counted most successful on the ideological level, but there was concern expressed over the violence of the ending.[124] As for the reception accorded this film by the laboring masses, the "vast majority" at a workers' club screening liked it.[125]

Another "middling" film of the revolutionary genre was *Wind*, directed by L. Sheffer. The similarities between this film and *Death Bay* are noticeable; Abram Room and actor N. Saltykov (a sailor in *Death Bay*) wrote the script, and Saltykov played the lead, Vasilii Guliavin, a cavalry regiment commander during the Civil War. Guliavin falls in love with a vicious but seductive *atamanka* (female Cossack leader). The movie starts slowly, wending through the revolution, using the device of parallel cutting to contrast between rich and poor under the tsarist regime; a few documentary shots are interspersed. But when Guliavin meets the *atamanka* the tempo picks up. The movie is quite violent, with a strongly sexual undercurrent. The *atamanka* loves to kill, personally executing captured Whites (cleverly shown by her pointed gun in closeup). Yet her "temper" only serves to make her more attractive to her lover; he smiles adoringly as she smashes a vase, to name but one example.

The staff officer from headquarters, an intellectual-looking man, repeatedly warns Guliavin against trusting the Cossacks, particularly the *atamanka*. Realizing that she has an enemy, she brutally murders him; we see him lying on the cellar floor in a pool of blood, shot in the head. At last Guliavin comes to his senses; his hours of remorse before his lover's execution are well done: his pacing, the ticking clock, the memory of his loving indulgence of her rages. He falls on his knees before the assembled company saying: "Forgive me. I sold a brother for a woman." It ends with the Reds vigorously riding off to war. The film was regarded as being a modest but entertaining effort guaranteed to succeed with the viewers, a fair evaluation.[126]

The third film of the war-and-violence type was the Ukrainian *The Tripol Tragedy*, a VUFKU film directed by Aleksandr Anoshchenko (whom we should remember for his "hard-line" attacks against "left" art). The "plot" is nothing more than the depiction of an orgy of murder in the Ukrainian village of Tripol during the Civil War; it is a vehicle to proselytize against Ukrainian nationalism, for the villains are Cossacks, not the typical counterrevolutionary Whites. *The Tripol Tragedy* is a ludicrous, interminable stream of violence, shootings, hangings, lootings, fires. The Cossacks beat up old ladies and even bury soldiers alive and dance on their graves (an unintentional parody of the beloved "Russian" dance scene which was de rigueur in most Soviet films of the period). The ridiculous gives way to the unexpectedly realistic—a closeup of a girl's face as she is being raped. The editing is frequently hard to follow, and the film suffers from its skeletal plot: a young woman inexplicably falls in love with the bestial *ataman* (Cossack leader) but kills him before falling victim to the Cossacks herself.

The relentless gore of this film aroused much negative commentary. One reviewer pointed out that showing "atrocities" on the screen, even if "historically accurate," was not suitable for youth. Furthermore, after a while excessive bloodshed lost its effectiveness. *Death Bay* was commended by comparison for its restrained use of violence, but "... in *The Tripol Tragedy*, although 'blood' floods the whole film, the viewer receives it as theatrical window dressing. He does not believe in the realism of the atrocities shown."[127]

The "American" Films of Kuleshov

If revolutionary movies were often unsuccessful, it was nonetheless difficult for Soviet filmmakers to work in other genres without encountering obstacles, as the case of Lev Kuleshov shows. The movie most negatively received in 1925 was Lev Kuleshov's *Death Ray* (*Luch smerti*). Viewers disliked it intensely,[128] and the critics reacted the same way. There has been a tendency, in connection with artists like Kuleshov whose subsequent careers were blighted, to dismiss every word of criticism against them. *Death Ray*, however, is a genuinely bad movie, a wildly disjointed tale of international conspiracy. The violence and intrigue should have made for a good adventure but failed miserably.

Kuleshov defensively said that he regarded it only as an experiment in using a variety of film techniques and as a "bridge" to truly "dramatic-social" productions.[129] Unfortunately, it is difficult to watch, unless one has a surpassing interest in seeing an encyclopedia of cinema techniques. There is a multitude of unusual shots, lighting effects, and double exposures, some of which are effective (for example, Kuleshov "echoes" sound through closeups of tiptoeing feet or a ringing doorbell), but most of which are not. There are many scenes with the athletic shenanigans Kuleshov loved, and although he makes impious use of the favorite stereotypes of Soviet cinema—a police chief chews on a rose, and the nephew of a capitalist wears a monocle—nothing is effectively integrated.

Some critics regarded this effort indulgently, as a last youthful fling. Everybody knew Kuleshov could work; "... he should show that he knows how to create."[130] Most were much harsher, asking, as did An. Skachko, "for whom was this picture created?" since there was "absolutely nothing for the worker-peasant" in it. Skachko came to the point: "Of course it is impossible to negate the necessity of work on form, but our communist relationship to art is such that we subordinate form to content and not the opposite." Significantly, financial considerations also entered into this evaluation, Skachko dourly noting that the Soviets were too poverty-stricken to be wasting money on a film like *Death Ray*.[131]

The most negative assessment came from Nikolai Lebedev. If enemies of cinema needed a movie to illustrate and confirm their theories, he said, then

Death Ray would be it: "what poverty of content, thought, and fantasy" to come from eight months of work. The charges that Lebedev hurled at the film—"narrow technicism" and "blind alley of neo-aestheticism"—[132] were new and alien to cinema discussion, but it was not the last time they would be directed at Kuleshov.

With this movie Kuleshov earned an opponent even more formidable than Nikolai Lebedev in the person of Sovkino's I. P. Trainin. Trainin not only attacked Kuleshov's alleged emphasis on form over content, but flatly stated that his "dynamics" were both "artificial [and] idle."[133] Kuleshov thus had the distinction of earning the scorn of two cinema activists who could not have been more different: Lebedev, the opponent of NEP, and Trainin, author of the "commercial deviation" in Soviet cinema. Kuleshov was never again free from the stigma of formalism.

Kuleshov was no luckier with his next film *By the Law,* a sadly neglected masterpiece of silent film art. As *Potemkin* was a historic film in world cinema so was *By the Law* a historic film in Soviet cinema, for it marked a real turning point, the start of a creeping intolerance in the film community that was reflected in a new brand of "criticism." It was also the beginning of the end of Kuleshov's career.

By the Law's script was adapted by Viktor Shklovskii from Jack London's story, "The Unexpected," a stark tale of greed, murder, and retribution among gold miners in the Klondike. In an argument at the beginning of the film Dennin (Vladimir Fogel) kills two of his partners; the surviving pair, Hans (Sergei Komarov) and his wife Edith (Aleksandra Khokhlova) subdue the killer, bring him to "trial," and execute him. This simple plot is the basis for a brutally vivid psychological drama completely bereft of sentimentality. Kuleshov's mastery of technique in this film is absolute. Every device is employed for maximum impact, and his use of closeups and cutting on detail give an aura of realism to a very spare and economical set.

Kuleshov's shots are unusually long, totally different from what is associated with "Russian" montage, but suited to the dramatic tension of his story. The subtlety of Khokhlova's portrayal of the neurotic Edith is beautifully heightened through closeups. Kuleshov was beginning to understand that the art of the movie actor is playing in closeup (and not full figure, as the Kuleshov acting method with its emphasis on gymnastics would suggest). Konstantin Kuznetsov's camerawork is also outstanding. The action is set in a violent rainstorm; the characters are minuscule against the horizon, battered by the wind. The final scene after the "sentencing"—Edith and Hans struggling up a hill pushing Dennin along to be hanged (all in silhouette)—is unforgettable. A shot of Dennin's swinging feet and the executioners' horrified faces provides the only catharsis.

Aleksandra Khokhlova in an Unkind Caricature

This uncompromising film called forth a storm of abuse—and a little courageous praise. Even before its release at the end of 1926, rumors were buzzing. Scenarist Shklovskii was worried and wrote about the "shortcomings" in the script (meaning its American source) and that perhaps showing prolonged preparations for an execution was "sadistic."[134] Kuleshov saw fit to point out that the film dealt with the British, "the most inhumane of people."[135] This timid (and absurd) rationalizing did not help.

The mildest of the negative reviews came from the pen of Mikhail Levidov, and his reasons for disliking the film revealed much about the current direction of Soviet film criticism. For him the *uncompromising realism* of the film was the basis for its unacceptability. Kuleshov, he wrote, had not transformed life but "... [made] only life from life," not the kind of realism Soviets needed.[136] Feofan Shipulinskii (who was incidentally an "Old Bolshevik") shared Levidov's opinion, but his prescription was drastic. He called for the physical destruction of the picture, not merely because it was "lacking" in ideology, but also because it "irritated" the nerves. The lesson of this film was that Soviet cinema should show "joyful emotions," not "horror."[137]

More frightening than Shipulinskii's ignorant opinion, because it was not provoked by insensitivity to art, was the denunciation in *Cinema Front* by Viktor Pertsov, an attack which revealed how profoundly he understood Kuleshov's genius. Pertsov wrote that *By the Law*'s stark vision was evidence of the director's alienation from Soviet society, and that the film's chief fault was its "total unity." Its self-sufficient, "completely organic world of images and emotions" could not be surgically corrected by re-editing, for as Pertsov said: "To divide the screen world of Kuleshov into 'technique' and 'ideology' is impossible with any scissors." Pertsov also indicted *By the Law* for not guiding the viewer to moral judgment, due to the fact that it lacked a "social key" and was "hermetically sealed." Pertsov did not believe that Kuleshov was a lost cause,[138] but it was disquieting that a critic could recognize the true artistry of the film and reject it on those very grounds.

An equally chilling review, by the pseudonymous Arsen, appeared in the same issue of *Cinema Front* as Pertsov's. Arsen not only rejected as Christian the symbolism he saw in the execution scene (a valid reading), but more significantly he also rejected Kuleshov's "anarcho-individualistic" attitude toward the law, which he saw as undermining the class struggle. While Kuleshov had had undeniable impact on Soviet cinema, now dependence on him was potentially crippling:

> For the Soviet fiction film, Kuleshov is a trampoline, without which you will not jump, but from which it is absolutely necessary to push off; if you do not push off, there will be no jump.[139]

ARK's publishing of these two strongly negative reviews did indeed indicate its "line" on the matter. The association recognized the quality of *By the Law* in its discussion but the resolution passed asserted that:

> ...the theme of the picture *By the Law* is alien to our viewer in script and essence...; considering the instances of pathology and hysteria [in the film], it is a sick phenomenon in our cinematography which harmfully affects our Soviet screen.[140]

This published statement did not, however, reflect the heated debate in ARK. The public form of the resolution, harsh as it is, was actually *softened*; after a hard-fought battle, the word "mysticism" was removed.

At heart of the controversy in ARK was that *By the Law* was neither contemporary nor Soviet. Its scenarist Shklovskii protested that Kuleshov *was* making a "Soviet" film, *The Female Journalist (Zhurnalistka*, released as *Your Acquaintance [Vasha znakomaia]*; the unhappy fate of this film will be discussed later). Shklovskii pointed out the extreme economy with which *By the Law* was made (total cost, 18,000 rubles) and wanted to know why expensive blockbusters like *The Bear's Wedding (Medvezh'ia svad'ba)* or *The Decembrists (Dekabristy)*, not yet released but costing over 300,000 rubles, were not being similarly denounced.[141] As a matter of fact, these pictures would come in for criticism, but Shklovskii was right that the venom was lacking. As lesser works of art, they did not represent the threat to the new ideal of Soviet Realism that *By the Law* did.

A. Kurs twice supported Kuleshov and the movie in the press, declaring it a "work of art," but then Kurs was the scriptwriter on Kuleshov's next project, *The Female Journalist*. Kurs rightly feared for Kuleshov's future, seeing the director's position as being like that of "Dennin between Hans and Edith."[142] The bitterness of the debate over *By the Law* revealed that the days were quickly passing when an "experimental" work, however brilliant, could come to the screen without vicious denunciation.

FEKS

There was another collective that consistently deviated from the norm of the revolutionary film, FEKS (Workshop of the Eccentric Actor). As discussed above, in 1921 FEKS had been a theater group and part of the vociferous artistic left. In 1924, the collective had made a short film comedy *The Adventures of Oktiabrina (Pokhozhdeniia Oktiabriny)*,[143] and now with Grigorii Kozintsev and Leonid Trauberg as co-directors, Andrei Moskvin on camera, and Evgenii Enei (a Hungarian communist) as art director, they formed a team which would produce some remarkable and distinctive silent films. FEKS released two full-length films in the spring of 1926.

Grigorii Kozintsev and Leonid Trauberg,
with FEKS Pins on Their Lapels

The first was *The Devil's Wheel* (*Chertovo koleso*), the story of a naive young sailor from the *Aurora*, Vania (Petr Sobolevskii), being sucked into the underworld by his girlfriend Valia (Liudmila Semenova). FEKS' wonderful villain Sergei Gerasimov played the sinister "Question Man," who also tries to draw Vania into a life of crime. The script was written by the literary critic Adrian Piotrovskii, soon to become artistic head of the Leningrad studio.

The plot is that of a conventional entertainment film, conforming to FEKS' stated aim of bringing art to the people. But as the term "eccentrism" implies, the film was not quite as simple as its plot suggests. The very locations in the movie call to mind FEKS' fascination (as expressed in *Eccentrism*) with the music hall, circus, and carnival. The "devil's wheel" of the title is a carnival ferris wheel which symbolizes the attraction of novelty for the naive Vania. The distortion of reality in *The Devil's Wheel*—shots from odd angles, bizarre cuts, figures blurred by the camera lens, whirling images—are wearisome to the eye but artistically justifiable. *The Devil's Wheel* is technically interesting, but even with bomb throwing and banditry tossed in for effect, it is not dramatically compelling.

Ippolit Sokolov wrote a measured analysis of the film, laying most of the blame on the weaknesses of Piotrovskii's script. Sokolov thought Kozintsev and Trauberg too heavily influenced by the experimentalism of Kuleshov's *Death Ray* and Eisenstein's *Strike* but admired their "sharp feeling for life, great inventiveness, and good taste." Sokolov judged the movie negatively, but thought it at the same time one "of the most technically brilliant pictures of the last two to three years."[144] Other reviews were lukewarm, although former FEKS member Sergei Iutkevich found it a "strong and good work" and a "victory of romanticism and eccentrism."[145]

The second FEKS film of 1926 was better realized and wonderfully strange. This was *The Overcoat* (*Shinel'*), a poetic adaptation of Gogol's stories "The Overcoat" and "Nevskii Prospekt." *The Overcoat* was remarkably true to the flavor of the originals without strict adherence to their plots and without excessive titles (exciting the literary critic Boris Eikhenbaum to believe that perhaps there was hope for literary adaptations in cinema).[146] Kozintsev's and Trauberg's love for the grotesque and the distorted were perfectly suited to the subject, the tale of a poor bureaucrat whose new coat—his only desire in life—is stolen shortly after he obtains it.

Akakii Akakievich is always shot small in relation to the objects around him—to the coachman, to the tailor, to everything in Petersburg. He is so dehumanized that at first we cannot even pity such a miserable creature. By the end, Andrei Kostrichkin's remarkable performance succeeds, without mannerism or cliché, in making us believe in his humanity. The theft of the overcoat is very stylized and exceedingly well done; the shock of hands coming over the wall and the shadows falling on the victim are vivid.

Sokolov, however, also rejected this film, although as with *The Devil's Wheel,* he admired it technically, particularly Moskvin's camerawork and lighting. But Sokolov said that ordinary people did not like it:

> It has had very little commercial success and a very bad press. The reason for the failure is that the classical subject of Gogol's "The Overcoat" was not psychologically modernized and was not socially emphasized.[147]

Indeed, one may well believe that it was not a movie to appeal to the masses. *Soviet Cinema* concurred, saying that it was boring and "left the viewers cold."[148] As consolation, at least *The Overcoat* was an inexpensive mistake.[149]

Literary Adaptations

The literary adaptation in fact continued to be a popular genre, but was usually not as adventurous as *The Overcoat*. The film *The Collegiate Registrar* (*Kollezhskii registrator*; Iurii Zheliabuzhskii, director) is an adaptation of Pushkin's tale "The Station Master" ("Stantsionnyi smotritel'"); the difference in titles caused unending confusion. It was a much more typical example than *The Overcoat* of the problems inherent in translating literature for the screen. Pushkin's subtle short story of a simple man whose daughter becomes a rich young officer's mistress is transformed into a tear-jerking and hair-tearing melodrama thanks to the overacting of the inimitable Ivan Moskvin and the primitive cutting and camerawork.

The movie was not well received, its perversion of Pushkin generally recognized. Khrisanf Khersonskii credited both the script (by Valentin Turkin and Fedor Otsep) and Moskvin's acting for turning a "tragedy" into a "petty-bourgeois [*meshchanskaia*] melodrama." Khersonskii ironically noted that Moskvin was so theatrical that he seemed to have been directing himself. Only in a few instances does the movie become visually interesting (for example, the closeups in the sledding scene), and Khersonskii was right in lamenting the "operatic, picturesque, and solidly false" in this and other movies set in the past.[150] The literary critic P. S. Kogan concluded from this movie that cinema was incapable of preserving the essence of literary art.[151] In any case, it was hardly, as its advertisements claimed, "the picture the whole world has been waiting for."[152]

Historical Films

The principle of translating classics for the screen was an accepted one, but in practice the results were almost never satisfactory. Another example of such a shortfall in expectations was the historical film, desirable in theory but not in practice. A typical "historical" movie was *Stepan Khalturin* by the director Aleksandr Ivanovskii (*Palace and Fortress*). *Stepan Khalturin* is based on the true incident of the worker who went from labor organizer to People's Will terrorist and set the bomb in the Winter Palace in 1880. This promising revolutionary story held dramatic interest but also was fraught with the danger of political misinterpretation, given the disinclination of the Bolsheviks to identify themselves with the People's Will. Unfortunately, Ivanovskii brought neither good drama nor sound politics to the film.

Stepan Khalturin is very banally executed and the tempo quite slow. The motivation for Khalturin's activities is never clear, as a penetrating review in *Cinema* charged.[153] Political considerations aside, this makes the movie weak dramatically, for the screen action lacks a rationale. An extraordinarily absurd subplot is inserted to lend "romantic" interest to the dismally boring proceedings: an engineer is falsely implicated in the bomb scheme; his wife, trying to save him, falls into the clutches of the lascivious prosecutor Strelnikov. This could not fail to attract unfavorable attention; one reviewer sarcastically noted that it must have been this incident, rather than political considerations, that prompted Khalturin to kill Strelnikov.[154]

There are a few interesting touches. Ivanovskii fortunately did not miss the obvious opportunity for drama that the bomb afforded (there is cutting back and forth from the burning fuse to the emperor, slowly leaving the room). But the view that the movie was not very good technically is justified.[155] As an example, a scene with parallel action is edited to seem factual when it is only fantasy (Strelnikov's describing to the engineer's wife what will happen to her husband if she does not submit)— not an "illegal" practice, but a dubious one.

Just as *The Overcoat* was an extraordinary version of the literary adaptation, so was *Wings of a Serf* (*Kryl'ia kholopa*) an extraordinary example of the historical genre. This visually memorable fantasy-drama of life in the days of Ivan the Terrible is the best of its kind made in the silent period, but it was indifferently received domestically and is virtually unknown today. *Wings of a Serf* was the work of some very talented people: Iurii Tarich as director, the by-now ubiquitous Viktor Shklovskii as scriptwriter, Esfir Shub as editor, and theater star L. Leonidov as Ivan.

The plot is simple enough: a young serf invents a flying machine à la Icarus and is defeated in the end by court politics (particularly by the insatiable sexual appetite of the tsaritsa) and the machinations of the Church. Shklovskii had high hopes for the film. He wanted to avoid the trivial details of the typical historical extravaganza to get below the surface, believing that the historical film could answer both "political requirements" and the hunger of viewers for the "exotic."[156] He rejected the preoccupation with quaintness he saw in historical melodramas, writing that it was necessary to do away with an "aesthetic perception of antiquity."[157]

On these terms *Wings of a Serf* was a marvelous success. Despite the clichéd ring of the plot, it was neither a ponderous recreation of historical details nor a sentimental story of oppression. Rather it was a bold interpretation of what Tarich and Shklovskii saw as the spirit of the times (and one wonders whether the contemporary Soviet director Andrei Tarkovskii was familiar with *Wings of a Serf* when he made *Andrei Rublev*). As with the best of the silent films, images linger in the mind, starkly beautiful and compelling: a low shot of horses galloping up a snow drift, Ivan the Terrible's terrorist *oprichniki* marauding, the brooding visage of Leonidov's Ivan, the shadow of the boy flying. The photography is superb, both in shot composition and variety of technique. Shub's editing is equally effective in building the tension of the inevitable tragedy.

At first the reviews were not very critical although *Wings of a Serf* was regarded as being a commercial film with excessive love, adventure, and bloodshed.[158] Leonidov was criticized for being too theatrical and for not looking enough like Ivan![159]—which latter criticism shows that Shklovskii's ideas on historical films were a bit elevated for his confrères. An extremely damaging reinterpretation of *Wings of a Serf* lay ahead, to be discussed in the next chapter.

Historical films never satisfied. Most critics found them superficial at best,[160] yet interest in such movies continued, undoubtedly prompted in part by political considerations, but also because the public apparently enjoyed melodramas like *Stepan Khalturin*.[161] Directors, however, were not particularly eager to dramatize specific historical events, because there were too many pitfalls with too little dramatic license allowed. To help overcome such reluctance, a group of Marxist historical consultants was suggested,[162] but it is not clear from the sources whether this proposal was ever effected in the twenties.

Non-Russian Cinema

Historical and literary films were not the only troubled genres. Films made in or about the other Soviet republics were desirable in principle, but in practice less so. Non-Russian cinema, with the exception of Ukrainian, has been little discussed both because the activity was extremely limited, and because it was definitely not part of mainstream cinema culture. A few of the best non-Russian films did receive distribution in the RSFSR, however. In some cases, like *Abrek Zaur*, this was not even a completely non-Russian film but a Goskino production with a "mixed" cast and crew: I. Bei-Abei, script; Boris Mikhen, director; Esfir Shub, editor.

Abrek Zaur concerns a Caucasian mountaineer Zaur, who after killing a Russian becomes an *abrek*, a member of one of the anti-Russian gangs which roamed the Caucasus in the nineteenth century. It is an action-packed Georgian Robin Hood story, with Zaur repeatedly coming close to capture but always escaping in the end. The original version was ten reels, but even at half the length the picture is very dull, with no shot variation and little of visual interest. The director did not comprehend that a movie needs more than action to entertain. But because it was a matter of policy to promote non-Russian cinema, the reviews were not as bad as *Abrek Zaur* deserved.[163]

Honor (*Namus*), billed as the "first Armenian fiction film," was a better effort than *Abrek Zaur*. It was a co-production of the Georgian studio Goskinprom Gruzii and Armenkino, with Amo Bek-Nazarov (who later became famous) directing. *Honor* is a traditional romance of thwarted young lovers and a forced marriage. After the marriage, the "jilted" suitor Seiran taunts the husband Rustam by alleging prior intimacy with Susanna. As "proof" Seiran says Susanna has a birthmark on her breast (but the viewer knows he saw this years before when as a child her dress had been torn during an earthquake). Rustam accordingly kills Susanna to save his honor in a well-made scene which builds suspense through cutting and titles. In remorse Seiran kills himself. *Honor*, though every bit the stereotypical silent film, is at times touching (as in the wedding scene when one can see the tears behind Susanna's veil). Khrisanf Khersonskii was *Honor*'s champion and reviewed it warmly for both *Cinema* and *Cinema Front*.[164]

Ivan Perestiani's next film after the phenomenally popular *Little Red Devils* was *Three Lives* (*Tri zhizni*), a two-part screen adaptation of a novel by G. Tseretelli about a love triangle in late nineteenth-century Georgia, a common plot in the movies of the non-Russian republics. *Three Lives* stars the queen of the Georgian silent screen, Nata Vachnadze, as Esma, a young hatmaker and daughter of a prostitute who marries a wealthy, but self-made, man. Her happiness is short-lived, however, for she is lusted after and murdered by the scion of a noble family.

All this happens in the first part; in the second half, contrary to expectations of a protracted vengeance carried out by the bereaved husband, we watch the murderer living it up in Tbilisi, the Georgian capital, while the widower turns into a slovenly drunk. The killer finally goes on trial but is released due to the seductive wiles of his cousin. At last, Esma's husband is goaded into action. Aided by an escaped killer he has befriended, he murders the villain, after which he sits dolefully writing "Esma" in blood. *Three Lives* might have been an interesting twist on the vengeance motif, except that the characters are uninteresting and poorly developed. There is no justification for the great length of the film, and it entirely lacks the flair which made *Little Red Devils* a standout. *Abrek Zaur*, *Honor*, and *Three Lives* were definitely more old-fashioned than the best filmmaking in either Russia or the Ukraine, but escaped the sharp criticism that similar Russian or Ukrainian films would have received.

Fridrikh Ermler

Contemporary Films

The growing clamor for the contemporary (*bytovoi*) film produced one success at the end of 1926, *Katka the Apple Seller* (*Kat'ka bumazhnii ranet*). The film's talented director, Fridrikh Ermler (a Party member who formerly worked for the secret police, the Cheka), joined the ranks of the prominent young filmmakers. *Katka the Apple Seller* also marked the beginning of yet another particularly fortunate screen collaboration, this one between Ermler and the actor Fedor Nikitin. Their work together in the next few years was truly outstanding.

Katka (Veronika Buzhinskaia) is a country girl who comes to the city to earn money for her family by selling "paper reinette" apples (*bumazhnii ranet*). She becomes involved with a hooligan and petty criminal Semka (Valerii Solovtsov) and has a child by him. Katka realizes her mistake, breaks with Semka, and tries to raise the child alone. She finds a nanny for the baby in the person of a homeless bum, Vadka (Nikitin). A parallel story concerns the relationship of Katka's former lover and Verka, a shopgirl who bootlegs perfume. Eventually Semka and Verka come to justice after several nefarious deeds; from this ordeal Vadka becomes a "real" man and joins Katka working in a factory.

Even this brief summary shows that *Katka the Apple Seller* reveals a great
deal about the problems of NEP life, particularly its crime, poverty, and
unemployment. The technique of parallel relationships is a classic one in silent
cinema; usually one pair is very "good," the other obviously "bad." But in this
film Katka (the most positive character) and Vadka are quite an odd couple.
Vadka is spineless, terrified of the thug Semka, and content to live off a woman.
He is so incompetent that he cannot even commit suicide properly. This little
twist elevates the movie to much more than a hackneyed moral tale and reveals
Ermler's innate talent for movie making. *Katka the Apple Seller* is a technically
competent film displaying a keen sense of drama and local color and well-
defined characters.[165] It showed that Soviet cinema had yet another director of
promise.

"Bourgeois" Films

All of the films discussed so far were either "revolutionary" or presented some
kind of moral about power relations, showed the status of the poor, attacked
old customs, or portrayed the conditions of contemporary life. Better loved by
Soviet viewers were films which made not the slightest pretense to be "new" in
either form or content. They were honored by the majority of critics in the
cinema press with the label "bourgeois."

The most interesting of these, *The Bear's Wedding* (1926) we have already
seen mentioned in the cinema debates as a costly, but popular, film. Grigorii
Grebner and Anatolii Lunacharskii adapted Lunacharskii's play (based on a
story by Prosper Mérimée) to the screen. Since it was yet another glaring
example of the commercial "line" of the studio Mezhrabpom Rus',[166] *The
Bear's Wedding* was an odd effort indeed for the Commissar of Enlightenment
to be associated with.

Konstantin Eggert both directed and starred as Count Shemet, cursed by
his insane mother's traumatic experience with a bear to have seizures during
which he himself becomes a "bear" on the kill. Eggert's direction of the movie is
as odd as the plot. The whole film is unsettling. The titles are too long; there are
interminable shots of irrelevant action; the cutting is uneven. The heroine is
unsuitably comic, spasmodically jumping around, smearing ink on her face,
knocking things over. For some reason the somber, doomed count falls in love
with this girl and decides to marry her.

Yet, from the wedding scene to the end (the last third of the movie), it is
almost as though there were a different director. Eggert suddenly gained
control of the material. The wild celebration of the wedding becomes a sinister
and completely appropriate metaphor for the madness in the household:
madness both apparent (the mother) and hidden (the count). The climax of this
nightmare is the bride's violent death in her wedding bed, a gruesome, sexually

Anatolii Lunacharskii, with "Tip Top"

charged scene brilliantly executed by Eggert. There is a striking shot of her maimed body in the foreground as the "bear," coming to his senses, realizes what he has done. The moving closeups of his face as he flees the scene on his horse are also extremely effective. The victim's sister eventually kills him, and the cursed castle is engulfed in flames.

In reference to the controversy over *By the Law*, Viktor Shklovskii had asked why this picture was not abused. In fact it was, one critic sneering that he could sniff the "Gold Series" (referring to a series of prerevolutionary blockbusters) in this film.[167] Sokolov also criticized it mildly, but at least one *viewer* thought it a "colossal victory on the cinema front."[168] Later, *The Bear's Wedding* was the object of persistent attack as an *expensive* as well as ideologically useless film, but the only way to explain why it suffered less than *By the Law* is that it was far less powerful as a work of art.

Another Mezhrabpom "bourgeois" film was the three-part adventure serial *Miss Mend*, based on Marietta Shaginian's novel by the same name. (The adventure serial, so popular in Western silent cinema, was rare in Soviet cinema.) Sometime screenwriter Fedor Otsep and actor Boris Barnet (the cowboy from Kuleshov's *Mister West*) co-directed. Barnet, Vladimir Fogel (from the Kuleshov collective), and Igor Ilinskii (Protazanov's favorite comedian) starred as the heroes. The plot is totally inane, positing an international conspiracy against Soviet Russia as the motivation for the action. There are killings, body snatchings, barroom brawls, fights on ship, cliff-hanging endings. The adventures of the third part take place in the Soviet Union and provide interesting glimpses of real life, including the continuing problem of homeless children (*bezprizorniki*). This picture came in for criticism due to its lighthearted subject matter. One reviewer counted it merely "naive and stupid,"[169] but Khrisanf Khersonskii was harsher, asserting that its antics promoted "hooliganism."[170] Moreover, the advertising campaign for *Miss Mend* was sophisticated, provoking charges of commercialism from ARK.[171] (Many critics alleged these "bourgeois" films to be better advertised and circulated than revolutionary classics like *Potemkin* or *Mother*, and from what I saw, they were.)

"Bourgeois" entertainment pictures were the veteran director Iakov Protazanov's speciality, and of his three movies in 1925-26—*His Call* (*Ego prizyv*), *Tailor from Torzhok* (*Zakroishchik iz Torzhka*), and *Case of the Three Million* (*Protsess o trekh millionakh*)—the latter two were indubitably of this type. But it was the exception, *His Call* (1925), that redeemed Protazanov from the *Aelita* debacle of 1924 and earned him some long-lasting good will.

His Call is an enjoyable melodrama with irreproachable subject matter. In the last days of the Revolution, a factory owner and his son Andrei (played by Protazanov's favorite dramatic actor, Anatolii Ktorov) hide some of their fortune before they emigrate. At first their life abroad is lavish (shown in some well-constructed cafe scenes) and is contrasted to the hardships of Soviet life (for example, a shot of school children wearing coats in the classroom due to lack of heat). But after five years, life has become difficult for the pair; Andrei, remembering the money left behind in Russia, decides to return. He immediately finds an accomplice, the obligatory *kulak* (rich peasant). A young working girl, Katia, is living with her grandmother in Andrei's former house, so he begins to woo her. (As an added fillip, we know, although she does not, that he killed her father during the Revolution.)

Katia falls in love with Andrei, but to no avail—desperate for his gold, he murders her grandmother and beats her up before coming to an appropriate end (shot in the back). Now Katia has to be rehabilitated. She hesitates to join the Party when it "calls" her because she does not feel worthy after her sordid love affair; the religious symbolism of Lenin as the savior of this "fallen woman" is blatant indeed.

The movie has historical interest as well as entertainment and propaganda value, for it is connected with the "call" for increased Party membership after Lenin's death. It is also a "contemporary" movie which shows details of everyday life, like the excitement over the new electrical generator in the village or the feelings of anxiety engendered by Lenin's demise. The search for contemporary life on the screen was a much-desired goal; here, it was entertaining as well as politically uplifting. *His Call* was reported to be a great success[172] and is one of the best examples of propaganda content smoothly incorporated in the ordinary fiction film.

Protazanov's second effort in 1925 was certainly his least fortunate Soviet silent. More typical in subject matter than *His Call, Tailor from Torzhok* is an unsophisticated but popular comedy about the state lottery, starring the Soviet favorite Igor Ilinskii, a rather limited comedian of the slapstick school. The plot consists of Ilinskii's shenanigans in trying to retrieve his winning lottery ticket and avoid marrying his landlady. Social commentary is poorly integrated in the plot: Ilinskii's true love is a slavey for her bullying shopkeeper relative, who relies on such reprehensible exploitation, of course, because he cannot otherwise compete with the cooperative. The *profkom* (union committee) helps the girl. The other dose of ideology in the film is an extraneous shot of a kite with the slogan "Religion is the opium of the people" emblazoned on it. Yet only later, in connection with the sustained assault on all aspects of Soviet cinema, was this movie retroactively criticized as being deficient in social purpose.

Protazanov made another popular comedy, *Case of the Three Million*, a screen adaptation of the Italian writer Notari's story, "The Three Thieves." One of the thieves is a "common" thief, Tapioca (Igor Ilinskii); one is a "gentleman" thief, Cascarillia (Anatolii Ktorov); the third "thief" is a banker. The banker sells his country house to the Church for three million so that he can take advantage of famine in the provinces by investing in speculative ventures. The gentleman thief learns this by intercepting a note to the banker's wife Nora (Olga Zhizneva, who plays her role in panting "vamp" style). Nora hardly seems alarmed when the thief shows up in her boudoir; in fact, she is titillated by the idea of having a criminal for a lover.

Cascarillia, aided by Nora, successfully makes off with the three million. By chance, Tapioca was trying to rob the mansion at the same time, and he is captured. He becomes a public hero because no one can figure out what he did with the loot. In the only cinematographic scene in the movie, Cascarillia dramatically appears at the trial with the money, which he throws all over the courtroom to reassert his hegemony as prince of thieves.[173] There is a chaotic fight among those at the trial to grab a part of the cash.

Four of these five movies (the exception being *His Call*) were made purely for entertainment value and include an absolute minimum of social content; indeed, one has to be imaginative to see *any*. They could have been made anywhere; nothing distinguishes them as Soviet films.

Another example of the work of prerevolutionary directors was the worst picture of 1925, *Cross and Mauser (Krest' i mauzer)*, directed by Vladimir Gardin. Both an "anti-religious" and "international revolutionary-conspiracy" film, *Cross and Mauser* featured one of the beloved villains of the day, Naum Rogozhin, as a Catholic "vicar" (garbed more like a bishop) with evil designs against humanity in general and the Soviets in particular.

This relentlessly mean-spirited and repellent movie uses every anti-clerical cliché imaginable in a cynically sensational way. The emphasis is on perverted sexual pleasure (Viktor Shklovskii slyly noted that the filmmaker satisfied the viewer's desire to know the "inner secrets of monasteries").[174] Priests read pornography; beatings are orgiastic; a pogrom is played for thrills, with a sensual lust for brutality. There is plenty of violence (including murders and fires as well as ordinary fights), some nudity (bare-breasted beauties swimming), and an illicit pregnancy (the father is a priest). Priests are all heavily made-up and have sharply filed fingernails, in stark contrast to the healthy, masculine Soviet hero. The movie making is old-fashioned and dull; for example, some backgrounds are completely blank, with the result that the actors look disembodied. *Cross and Mauser* did not, however, arouse the negative response that it should have, considering the concern over increasing violence and "pornography" in Soviet films, because of its perfectly correct line on religion. It is an example of how certain directors could "use" Soviet themes in a blatantly opportunistic fashion, thus escaping just censure.

Nonfiction Films

Very different from these bourgeois melodramas were the nonacted films of Dziga Vertov, still the only major Soviet director to make feature-length "documentaries." After *Strike*, the other film sensation of 1925 was Vertov's, and the legacy was as mixed as that of Eisenstein.

Vertov produced his twenty-first number of *Cinema Truth*, titled *Leninist* (*Leninskaia*), in 1925 in honor of the first anniversary of the leader's death. While its more traditional construction (compared to his previous films) was seen as a step in the right direction, *Leninist Cinema Truth* was not met with much enthusiasm.[175] There was no doubt that Vertov meant this to be a sincere tribute to Lenin, but the film suffered from his typical problems. It lacks a sense of geographic reality; shots seemed to be (and probably were) made in different locations, then edited together as if "real." The result is that the unsophisticated viewer would be more confused than manipulated. One particularly unfortunate juxtaposition of shots is a cut without explanation from Lenin to a pile of starved corpses. Vertov continued his limited experiments in animation with graphs showing Lenin's state of health, or a humorous bit with a cartoon capitalist rejoicing at Lenin's death. The movie has great historical interest, but it strikes one today, as it did the critics then, as lacking focus.

Renewed attention to Vertov in 1926 was prompted by the sensation caused by his new film *Stride, Soviet!* (*Shagai, Sovet!*). *Stride, Soviet!* is a collage of scenes from the days of the Revolution to the then-present day. After opening shots illustrating the wonders of modern factories, the film jumps back in time to demonstrate what had to be overcome: disaster, hunger, disease, and death. Gradually the Soviet way dominates, and the film focusses on electrification, education, health, cooperatives. But Vertov shows the contradictions of NEP culture as well; along with the aforementioned successes, banditry, speculation, poverty, and hooliganism are also depicted. The final title of the film is: "From NEP Russia will come Soviet Russia."

This theme struck a chord among the many who were sincerely disenchanted with NEP as well as among those supporters of the educational film *(kul'turfil'm)* who realized that although Vertov may not have been their ideal, he was the only prominent filmmaker dedicated to the nonfiction movie. One of these advocates of the educational film, K. I. Shutko, enthusiastically wrote that *Stride, Soviet!* was a "step forward" toward a film of a higher order than fiction.[176] Another new Vertov supporter was Izmail Urazov, who endorsed the film for its "facts" and "life" and also for responding to new demands of the times, saying it was a "heroic chronicle of our days."[177]

Yet one should not assume from the praise *Stride, Soviet!* received that Vertov was now taken into the bosom of the film community. Viktor Shklovskii was unwavering in his opposition to Vertov's work. In one of his most famous cinema essays, "*Where Is Dziga Vertov Striding?*" ("*Kuda shagaet Dziga Vertov?*"), Shklovskii made some serious accusations indeed. First, he charged that Vertov had not even shot most of the material in the film, which was certainly contrary to the director's vaunted allegiance to "cinema truth." Furthermore, no facts were given to orient the material. Because of this, the appearance of Mussolini in the film, for example, lost all significance; many may not even have realized who he was (Shklovskii was quite right). Through his faulty methodology, said Shklovskii, Vertov was not helping the idea of documentary cinema; he was, on the contrary, hurting it.[178] The well-known editor Esfir Shub, who would soon pioneer her own form of nonfiction film, also protested against what she termed the "fabrication of facts" in Vertov.[179] It would not be long before the charges against Vertov became much more serious.

The films of 1925-26 revealed for the first time a strong and varied body of work that was as good as the critical and theoretical side of Soviet cinema. Movies and criticism now became entwined: the movies for better or worse reflected the climate of opinion, and critics were able to see the concrete results of their theories. The creative momentum of Soviet filmmakers, so long stifled for lack of experience and material, pushed forward long after internal strife forced a decline in the quality of criticism.

Whether these films served the "interests" of the Soviet viewer was another question, one which most critics were inclined to answer in the negative although the best among them, like Shklovskii, Sokolov, and Khersonskii, were not much concerned with what viewers liked or needed. While this perception that Soviet films were removed from the needs of Soviet viewers was not necessarily wrong, it did intensify the pressure within the film community to "rationalize" the artistic aspects of cinema in the same way that production was being "rationalized."

Soviet cinema was approaching its Armageddon even as it was in full flower, and the heterogeneity of purpose within the cinema community became increasingly pronounced. From this point on, aesthetic issues concerning scripts and plots, heroes and actors, would become as politicized as the filmmakers were polarized. But from 1927 to March 1928, personal rivalries were temporarily subordinated to a concentrated attack on Sovkino.

5

Sovkino under Fire (1927-28)

The period 1925-26 is traditionally known as the "flowering" of Soviet silent cinema, and in many ways it was. Yet the cinematic achievements of these years did not stem the growing tide of discontent with Sovkino's "politics." There was no "withering away" of the commercial line. In 1927 Sovkino became the focal point for the discord within the cinema community, and a full-fledged battle for control of film production began.

The Economy

The "regime of economy" campaign discussed in chapter 4 continued into 1927, for despite the artistic and political successes of the previous year (as exemplified by *Potemkin* and *Mother*), the material crisis remained severe. The Party was still little concerned about alleviating the financial problems of the film industry. According to Sovkino chairman K. M. Shvedchikov, the film stock shortage was so serious that it held up the release of completed films and prevented the distribution of films from the other republics to the RSFSR.[1]

As a response to the regime of economy, Sovkino's Moscow studio had cut its personnel by 23 percent (resulting in a 27 percent reduction in salaries since March 1926) and cut other overhead by 37 percent.[2] These economies amounted to only 30,000 rubles, however, which would not put a dent into Sovkino's 1926-27 deficit of nearly 1.25 million rubles (which sum had supposedly accrued as the result of expenditures for development). Moreover, Sovkino projected a deficit of 3.5 million rubles for the 1927-28 season, nearly 60 percent of which was intended to finance the construction of new studios.[3] Since cinema was self-supporting, how Sovkino's deficit would be covered was a matter of growing concern to the cinema community.

Because of the extreme fiscal shortfall seen for the coming months, the urge to centralize, rationalize, and plan became even stronger. Soviet cinema was expected to grow from "cottage" (*kustar'*) production to an "industry," but it still lacked a sound capital base.[4] In addition, it was believed that Soviet filmmakers were poorer planners than their Western counterparts, resulting in wasted money and time. It was said that while the Germans could make a film in fourteen days, it took Soviet directors one year.[5] Considering this obsession with economizing, it is significant that in 1927 there was a trial of sixteen filmworkers who had been connected with the now defunct Proletkino and Goskino studios for economic crimes, to wit, the misuse of large advances paid for certain films. A number of the "Sixteen" received prison sentences in May; the most prominent of these was I. N. Bursak, the former chairman of Proletkino, who got one year.[6] The example of the Trial of the Sixteen intensified the unease among filmworkers.

Another sign of the unmitigated penury of the industry was the virtual abandonment of the cinefication campaign on the very eve of collectivization. It was possible to argue quite convincingly that increase in revenues must depend on the spread of the distribution network,[7] but even Glavpolitprosvet's most stalwart advocates of cinefication, Katsigras and Barshak, admitted defeat. The travelling projectors were in disrepair, more often than not operating at a deficit, and ODSK (the Society of Friends of Soviet Cinema) had not succeeded in earning support either among its supposed constituency in the countryside or from Sovkino.[8] There was widespread agreement that cinefication had failed from lack of means and because Sovkino had not been willing to fund the project.[9]

Ideology

The economic problems of the film industry would have been difficult enough to surmount without the aggravation of the ideological element, which for the first time was becoming quite pronounced. While increased attention to ideology may well have been a reflection of the power struggle within the Party,[10] it was as yet impossible to see direct evidence of this in the cinema press. Filmmakers were "political" only in an abstract sense, and they had little idea, most of them, of the significance of what was happening in the country at large. Sergei Eisenstein, that quintessentially "political" of directors, could not show his *commissioned* tenth anniversary film *October* (*Oktiabr'*) until 1928, because he was naive enough to make *Trotskii* the hero of his movie. *October* was ruthlessly re-edited.

Another source of intensified political and ideological concerns originated from *within* the film industry. Given that there was so little money for production, it was widely believed that Sovkino's distribution of funds should be carefully scrutinized. At this time of political crisis in the Party and intensified economic pressure within the film community, the tone and content of cinema polemics significantly changed. Discussion of issues gave way to a far-reaching criticism of organizations, principally the production companies

Sovkino and Mezhrabpom Rus'. It was this debate which decided the fate of the Soviet film industry at the end of the decade.

An excellent summary of these concerns appeared early in 1927 in an article in the VAPP journal *On Literary Guard* (*Na literaturnom postu*) by V. Solskii titled "Cinema Tasks and Cinema Dangers" ("Kino-zadachi i kino-opasnosti"). Solskii illustrated well the complexity of the issues facing cinema. A member of VAPP—that is, a supporter of "proletarianism" and realism in literature—Solskii was at the same time an artistic advisor to Sovkino (and in 1929, the center of a scandal when he fled the country for "health" reasons). The first problem Solskii examined was that of the so-called export films, using Tarich's 1926 film on the reign of Ivan the Terrible, *Wings of a Serf*, as his example. According to Solskii, *Wings of a Serf*'s success abroad could only be explained by its compatibility with bourgeois ideology. After all, a Latvian right-wing newspaper had warmly praised the movie for being apolitical.[11] What had led, asked Solskii, to the situation where movies like this could be made and exported?

First Solskii blamed the lack of qualified scenarists; few trained writers (for cinema or otherwise) were producing scenarios. Of those who were, fewer still were drawing on proletarian literature for ideas and sources. The second culprit was the plethora of unsuitable directors.[12] Poorly prepared writers and "fellow traveller" directors were behind the production of decadent and petty-bourgeois Soviet films.

The prime example of the decadence of Soviet cinema, according to Solskii, was Kuleshov's *By the Law*, more dangerous than most petty-bourgeois films because of its high level of artistry.[13] The petty-bourgeois (*meshchanskii*)—as opposed to decadent—character of Soviet films was exemplified by three films discussed in the previous chapter, Ermler's *Katka the Apple Seller*, Protazanov's *Case of the Three Million*, and Otsep's and Barnet's *Miss Mend*, as well as by Abram Room's *Third Meshchanskaia Street* (*Tret'ia Meshchanskaia*).

Solskii thought this trend toward petty-bourgeois films would continue to dominate Soviet cinema, pointing to films currently in production as proof.[14] He dismissed Sovkino's claim that it was serving the public, asserting that the array of decadent and petty-bourgeois pictures had *not* had commercial success, whereas revolutionary films like *Potemkin* and *Mother* had. (Solskii thought Mezhrabpom Rus', the producer of *Mother*, guilty of the same commercial orientation as Sovkino but on a smaller scale.)[15]

Decadence and "petty-bourgeoisism" were the "right-wing" deviations which Solskii noted in Soviet cinema. The "left-wing" deviation to be fought was Dziga Vertov, whose sin was his theory that cinema should concern itself with life as it is, thereby rejecting actors, directors, and scripts. Working without actors could sometimes give good results as Eisenstein had proven,

Solskii argued, but working without a script could *never* yield good results. In Solskii's opinion, the praise heaped upon Vertov's latest film, *One-Sixth of the World* (*Shestaia chast' mira*) proved the press's total disdain for the public (the film played only four or five days in Moscow). If *One-Sixth of the World* had had ideological value, viewer response would not have mattered so much, but the film had erred mightily in not concentrating on the problems of industrialization. Moreover, Vertov's Cinema-eye collective was especially dangerous because of its monopolistic pretensions and pseudo-revolutionary phraseology.[16] Finally, Solskii struck a parting blow against the cinema press for not guarding the interests of the film industry vigilantly enough.[17] His conclusion was that in this period of the expansion of the industry, ideology had to become a matter of vital concern.[18]

Solskii succinctly presented the issues that would engage the attention and task the ingenuity of cinema activists up to the beginning of the First All-Union Party Conference on Cinema Affairs in March 1928. The wrong types of films were being made; the studios and the press were culpable; somehow the conflicting demands of ideology and the need to make a profit must be reconciled. Attention to ideology could not have come at a more unfortunate time for Soviet cinema, because although it had reached artistic maturity, it was still crippled by poverty and thus unable to develop fully. Since there was no sign of increased state aid to cinema to alleviate the financial crisis, Sovkino persisted making "export" films to raise hard currency, the production of which devoured its meager budget. With few funds remaining for the efforts of younger and less established filmmakers, Sovkino unwittingly created a pool of underemployed perennial malcontents ready to do battle with the monopoly regardless of the long-term consequences. The struggle with Sovkino (and to a lesser extent with Mezhrabpom Rus') was therefore at the heart of cinema polemics from 1927 to spring 1928, and the particulars of this debate are critical for understanding the future.

Sovkino

As Solskii's article had indicated, the central point of the attack against Sovkino was to be its "export" films, which were seen as being bourgeois (or petty-bourgeois), "decadent," far too expensive, and tailored for European interests and tastes. Sovkino did not deny these charges, justifying them in terms of economic necessity and catering to viewers' preferences.

Ten expensive features (or "hits" [*boeviki*]) were on Sovkino's production schedule for 1927-28. Sovkino stated that while it would economize in making these films, their number could not be appreciably altered, for it would be harmful both financially and politically (politically because it would further alienate the Soviet viewer from Soviet productions).[19] Yet as a sop to the demands of society (*sotsial'nyi zakaz*), Sovkino's production plan included films about revolution, industrialization, and the fight against private elements (*chastniki*) and rich peasants (*kulaks*).[20]

The Artistic Section of Glavpolitprosvet believed Sovkino was not acting in good faith, pointing out that all its so-called historical films could easily become tales of intrigue and adventure.[21] ARK also dismissed as unreliable any thematic plan that Sovkino might release, *Cinema Front* publishing a copy of the 1926-27 plan, crossing out with large "Xs" the films Sovkino had *not* made. To an extract of a Sovkino protocol about plans for yet more export films was added this cutting editorial note: "With com(mercial) greetings, comrades!"[22]

In addition to producing films for export, Sovkino still imported foreign pictures as part of its income-generating scheme. Foreign films were estimated at about 70 percent of the movies actually shown (although figures could be juggled to show a more equitable balance between Soviet and foreign films). But despite the continued predominance of foreign films on Soviet screens, they received much less attention from critics than in the past.[23] Polemical energies were rather exclusively focussed on Soviet production.

The term *inostranshchina* (a virtually untranslatable pejorative—the domination of things foreign) was therefore not used now to attack foreign films but to emphasize that their distribution in the USSR had led to the production of Soviet-made "foreign" films.[24] An editorial in *Soviet Screen* said that while the journal was not calling for a return to agit-films, it did insist that it be easily discernible whether a picture was Soviet or not. Commercial success, therefore, should not be the ultimate goal of Soviet cinema.[25] (Yet *Cinema Front*, which espoused essentially the same view, attacked Sovkino for not having been successful *enough* in penetrating the American market!)[26]

Concern over *inostranschina* was broader than fears for its effect on the Soviet viewer; many warned that the Soviet Union was represented to the world only by means of such "pseudo-Soviet" pictures. With the exception of *Potemkin*, a genuinely revolutionary film received with acclamation by startled European and American cineasts, Soviet exports consisted of "bears' weddings" (referring to Eggert's *The Bear's Wedding* which had also enjoyed success abroad) and a "huge quantity of 'Eastern' exotic pictures." The danger of retitling existed: *Third Meshchanskaia Street* was shown abroad as *Bed and Sofa*; *Minaret of Death* as *Harem from Bukhara*.[27] (*Minaret of Death* had been suppressed in the USSR, but Sovkino exported it as the "latest Soviet hit.") Worse yet was what could happen through re-editing: Eisenstein claimed that in Germany *Potemkin* had been shown with the tarpaulin execution scene moved from *before* the mutiny to *after*, drastically changing both the motivation and the moral of the story.

Little sympathy was expressed for Sovkino's alleged poverty. *Cinema Front* asserted in an editorial that 50 percent of Sovkino's budget went to twelve big export films (only 18 percent of its sixty-five proposed titles): "These figures do not speak but shout."[28] By spring 1927 the term "commercial deviation" began to be applied to Sovkino. *Cinema* announced that "the imperialist struggle between the Soviet and foreign film has only just ended, to be replaced by a desperate civil war inside Soviet cinematography."[29] The term "civil war" was particularly appropriate for what was happening in the film industry.

Few were disinterested enough to foresee what lay ahead, but some did try to resolve the contradictions between the demands of ideology and profit. For example, an editorial in *Soviet Screen* entitled "Ideology and the Box Office" ("Ideologiia i kassa") stated that the demands being placed upon Soviet directors to make class-conscious films with a good box office were almost intolerable.[30] That the "left" was getting carried away in its emphasis on ideology was typified by a remark made in a worker-correspondents' (*rabkor*) discussion of Protazanov's new Civil War film, *The Forty-first* (*Sorok pervyi*): "Every camel participating in a Soviet film should carry a little piece of ideology at the end of its tail." *Soviet Screen* urged that ideology be regarded in a broader light and that an effort be made to educate the public to like the right kinds of films.[31] As Soviet filmmakers were painfully aware, just as a box office success without sufficient ideological content would be attacked by an increasingly vociferous opposition, so was it also increasingly harder to find financial support for either tendentious *or* experimental material, because neither type was profitable.

The fact is that everybody expected a film to be profitable, not just Sovkino administrators. Therefore, pains were taken to persuade Sovkino that "Soviet" films (as opposed to the bourgeois films of Soviet production) spoke the ruble language too.[32] If an ideologically correct film were not commercially successful, then blame should be laid (according to this line of reasoning) on the director, cameraman, script writer, and actors, *not* on the content. Although no one wanted agit-films or tired, "socially conscious" themes, directors should not fear the "sharpest problems of the *present day*. Our slogan: 'Give us a class-oriented and profitable film!'"[33]

Rather than attempt a positive solution to this extraordinarily difficult demand filmmakers found it easier to attack Sovkino. An example of the drive to find a scapegoat was an article by O. Beskin in *Soviet Cinema*. Beskin charged that Sovkino *itself* (rather than the theaters) had changed the title of *Third Meshchanskaia Street* to *Ménage à trois* (*Liubov' v troem*, a more descriptive title) for domestic circulation and to *Bed and Sofa* for the foreign market. Sovkino, wrote Beskin, had long demonstrated its proclivities for "adultery" and the exotic and was in fact hard put to produce a good Soviet film. If such a film were accidentally made,[34] it quickly faded into oblivion because of Sovkino's incompetent distribution and rental politics.

Since the loss of independence of Rus', Goskino, and Proletkino in 1926, the only two production companies operating in the Russian Republic (with the exception of Gosvoenkino, which did not produce films of note) were Sovkino and Mezhrabpom Rus'. Mezhrabpom had never been exempt from criticism;[35] Beskin in fact thought it more corrupt than Sovkino. From his point of view, everything the studio had turned out (with the exception of Pudovkin's *Mother* and Protazanov's *The Forty-first*) had been a bourgeois export product. Protazanov's maligned *The Man from the Restaurant* (*Chelovek iz restorana*) illustrated Mezhrabpom's apparent belief that the Soviet audience "loves women and the beautiful life, just as in Europe." Boris Barnet's Mezhrabpom film *Girl with a Hat Box* (*Devushka s korobkoi*) was a so-called "contemporary life" (*bytovoi*) film "straight from Paris." Other examples Beskin gave were Mezhrabpom's *Case of the Three Million, The Bear's Wedding, Miss Mend,* and *Aelita.* Its historical blockbuster, *Poet and Tsar,* was "dismal anti-social, anti-cultural hackwork."

Beskin suggested that:

> It is essential to compel the monopolist-distributors...to subsidize more broadly the production of really Soviet pictures.
>
> If the old slogan was: "The Soviet picture on the Soviet screen," then the slogan of the present day should be: "The Soviet screen for the Soviet picture, and not for pseudo-Soviet experimentation made under foreign influence."[36]

Although Beskin was not Mezhrabpom's only critic,[37] Sovkino definitely occupied center stage in the vilification campaign against producers. Yet the movies Sovkino produced were not the sole grounds for the assault. As frequently mentioned, its distribution policies were seen to favor big city theaters. Given Sovkino's profit motive, this was undoubtedly a valid perception but to a certain extent it reflected the power struggle between Sovkino and the Commissariat of Enlightenment for the control of theaters. As early as 1926, "proletarian" newspapers in the provinces began criticizing Sovkino for being more interested in petty-bourgeois big city viewers than workers.[38] Although the desires of the working class were usually ignored in cinema debates, almost everybody believed that Sovkino catered to the first-run theaters in Moscow and Leningrad.[39]

The Commissariat's cinema journal, *Soviet Cinema,* continued to hold Sovkino responsible for the failure of the "cinefication of the countryside" movement that had occupied so much attention in 1925 and urged the transfer of all movie theaters to ONO (the Commissariat's Section of People's Education).[40] M.P. Efremov of Sovkino was allowed to respond to these charges. He asserted that distribution *had* improved in the provinces although he admitted that the travelling projectors were usually inoperable after two years (which lent credibility to the arguments of his opponents that Sovkino was not interested in their maintenance). The crux of Efremov's defense was that Katsigras and the entire Glavpolitprosvet crowd clamoring for cinefication were out of touch with reality concerning Sovkino's financial situation. Sovkino was not financially able, he argued, to do any more than the little it did.

Katsigras rebutted this by questioning the whereabouts of over 1,500 missing projectors. He also criticized Sovkino for losing, by its own admission, one million rubles on worn-out film while at the same time refusing an outlay of 3-4,000 rubles to train projectionists. Katsigras insisted that this was a foolish economy,[41] and this time logic was on his side.

Interestingly enough, despite the severe censure of Sovkino in *Soviet Screen*, that journal was opposed to the transfer of theaters to ONO, which indicates not only that public dissent was still possible at this late date, but also shows how the political position of the Commissariat of Enlightenment had eroded. *Soviet Screen* admitted that while "it would be ideal to free Sovkino from dependence on the cinema/theater box office," because cinema "needs greater means which *the government may not now give cinematography* [emphasis added]," this was a financial impossibility. Therefore, control of theaters must fall under the production companies (that is, to Sovkino) in order to hasten the development of Soviet cinema. Stronger *Party* leadership should prevent any tendency Sovkino would have toward pure commercialism with regard to the theaters, but more *government* control was not desirable.[42] Sovkino's chairman Shvedchikov promised improved distribution if Sovkino continued to control all theaters and pledged a return of 75 percent of the profits to local cinema interests.[43]

The only major gathering called to criticize Sovkino before the 1928 Party Conference on Cinema Affairs was the October 1927 "debate" organized by the Society of Friends of Soviet Cinema (ODSK) and the Young Communist League (Komsomol). The debate format allowed ample opportunity for Sovkino's self-defense, which was undertaken by P. A. Bliakhin, I. P. Trainin no longer maintaining the high profile of the previous two years. Bliakhin began Sovkino's case by charting the seemingly impressive growth (in percentages) of the theaters for which Sovkino was responsible. He declared that although it was impossible to cease importing foreign films completely (due to the demand caused by Sovkino's diligence in expanding the distribution network), in 1926-27 foreign films were only 32 percent of the total, down from 79 percent in March 1925. If some of these movies were not ideologically suitable, this was the censorship's responsibility, not Sovkino's. Bliakhin defended Sovkino's production and pointed proudly to the success of Soviet movies abroad. Perhaps a few Mezhrabpom productions had been counterrevolutionary, but none of Sovkino's were.[44]

The Komsomol's Kostrov scorned Bliakhin's attempt to divert blame to other organizations and charged him with juggling figures. Kostrov said that 70 to 80 percent of the films actually on the screen were foreign. Meshcheriakov, deputy head of the Comissariat of Enlightenment and a long-time foe of Sovkino, sneered that Bliakhin had admitted everything, begging: "Condemn me, righteous judge, flog me, brothers! We are guilty of everything; we have a commercial deviation." Laughter followed Meshcheriakov's query as to whether anyone had heard satisfaction expressed with Sovkino. "Stern" words were the kindest Sovkino could hope for. It made no difference to Meshcheriakov that Bliakhin himself was an old revolutionary for he was, paraphrasing Lenin, "a chauffeur who does not drive where he should." Meshcheriakov's quip was greeted with more laughter.[45]

Sovkino's M. P. Efremov gave a speech explaining the apparent failure of the cinefication campaign by recounting the costs involved. Furthermore, he said that if the program *had* been successful, Soviet production could not have made enough films to supply the countryside (200 films a year would be needed). When Efremov pointed out that there were now 1,200 travelling projectors, he was sarcastically interrupted with the question: "How many work?" to which he responded: "They all work."[46]

Trainin took the floor to defend Tarich's *Wings of a Serf* against Solskii's charges in *On Literary Guard* of counterrevolution. Trainin, although he may have been an opportunist and a "commercial deviant," proved himself a man of artistic integrity when cornered. He insisted that contemporaneity and political probity were not necessarily bedfellows and admitted to being "confused" about the new standards: "When they say, *there* is a workers' film, and *there* is a peasants' film, I really don't understand this very well. A film is either good—or bad."[47] But castigating Sovkino was the order of the day. Some condemned the "adventure trash" allegedly dominating the screen, particularly the films of the German star Harry Piel (referred to in inimitable Russian fashion as the *Garri Pilevshchina*); it was asserted (falsely) that no one, not even youth, liked his films.[48] Specific films were attacked, particularly Room's *Third Meshchanskaia Street* and a new object of abuse, *Mr. Lloyd's Voyage* (*Reis mistera Lloida*).[49] Poet Vladimir Maiakovskii lambasted Sovkino's attitude toward scenarists (he had had unhappy experiences in this regard), while another speaker deplored cinema's isolation from current problems in society.[50]

Sovkino's Bliakhin closed the conference with a half-hearted recantation, saying that poor organization (and the ineffectual censorship) had been responsible for Sovkino's slogan: "Ten percent ideology and 90 percent commerce."[51] Just a few weeks later, Bliakhin completely repudiated this slogan:

Ninety percent commerce—10 percent ideology? There are no such percentages! Soviet cinematography is obligated to search for commerce in new Soviet thematics, in ideology. It should help the Party and Soviet power conduct the cultural revolution in the reconstruction of life [*byt*], in socialist construction.[52]

The ODSK/Komsomol debate correctly foreshadowed future trends in many respects. *Cinema*, still a voice for moderation, labelled the conference a part of the "left deviation" in cinema for its narrow definition of "commercialism" as synonymous with support of the entertainment film. If the leftists were allowed to expel non-Party directors and produce only political or scientific films, then, said *Cinema*, "within a year, we would not have any cinematography, and the 'left' deviation would seem ten times more dangerous than all the mistakes of Sovkino." Cinema *did* have a political function, which should be fulfilled through artistic means, cinema never having been intended to serve as a school for politics.[53] As these statements indicate, there was no unanimity in the film community about the future course.

The dilemma was a formidable one. Many filmmakers and activists had good reason to oppose Sovkino on genuine principles—aesthetic, financial, and political. But at the same time, a few were perspicacious enough to realize that Sovkino, for all its faults, was led by relatively cultured and intelligent people. Sovkino also was the only organization with enough power to head off the leftist hotheads who wanted to replace the "art" in cinema with "industry." Aesthetic principles and artistic freedom were in jeopardy, as were the interests of the Soviet viewer.

Those who claimed that audiences did not like Sovkino's "petty-bourgeois" films were either hypocritical or naive. As A. Kurs phrased it: "The viewer does not search for life as it is in cinema, but for life as he wants it."[54] People then as now went to the movies for pleasure and relaxation. Noting the success of *Case of the Three Million*, Kurs added resignedly: "I do not argue with the viewer. The viewer is always right."[55] However much one might wish, as Kurs did, for the success of Vertov and the nonacted film with the masses, "workers vote with their tickets" and voted against Vertov.[56]

Even more vivid proof of the inherent "philistinism" of the Soviet viewer was a letter that Khrisanf Khersonskii said Cinema Press (Kinopechat'), the cinema publishing company (and publisher of *Soviet Screen*), had received from a young girl:

It's boring, comrade editor, in a country busy with the replacement of the plough with the tractor, where peasants [*muzhiki*] and cooks run the government, where lovers of the electric light bulb don't understand the tales of Baghdad. It's boring, and I'm tired of life. Life has become loathesome. I want to forget myself. I want romance. For that reason I love Harry [Piel] and Doug [Fairbanks] and Conrad [Veidt].[57]

It is clear that this poor girl was infected with a disease epidemic in the USSR of the twenties—"cinema psychosis"—and to the left it indicated the total bankruptcy of the New Economic Policy. But the epitome of the creeping decadence of NEP society in the minds of leftist critics was Abram Room's great film *Third Meshchanskaia Street* (*Bed and Sofa* in American release) which figured heavily in the attacks against Sovkino and also served as the basis for an onslaught on the hard-preserved apoliticism of the professional association ARK.

Third Meshchanskaia Street and the Attack on ARK

There were three films in 1927 which seemed especially pathological to the leftists: *His Highness's Female Soloist* (*Solistka ego velichestva*), the already mentioned *Mr. Lloyd's Voyage,* and *Third Meshchanskaia Street.* Because the last film was so outstanding, it received the most intensive scrutiny. The young director was Abram Room (*Death Bay*), whom we have seen several times as an advocate of realistic, acted cinema; Viktor Shklovskii was the scenarist.

   Third Meshchanskania Street is a model of realism, the story of Liudmila (Liudmila Semenova), a lazy, unawakened *meshchanka* (petty-bourgeois woman) who putters dreamily about her cluttered apartment on Third Meshchanskaia Street (the choice of address is deliberate). She is apparently a film buff and has a cover from *Soviet Screen* tacked on the wall. Her stifling life is changed due to the Moscow housing shortage, for her self-centered but good-natured husband (Nikolai Batalov) invites a friend (Vladimir Fogel) who cannot find a room in Moscow to come live with them. When her husband goes away on a business trip, Liudmila responds to the lodger's advances, and her husband finds on his return that it is now he who has to sleep on the sofa. But Liudmila's dreams of true romance are shattered as it becomes clear that the men value their friendship more than they do her. She is pregnant and the two "fathers" (for she does not know whose child it is) join forces to bully her into having an abortion. In the end she resists them and leaves for an unknown fate, but one which is at least hers, like the baby.

   Third Meshchanskaia Street remains vivid, fresh, and powerful because of its matter-of-fact treatment of this "shocking" material, the excellent acting and characterization, and the almost palpable physicality of the movie. It *is* Moscow in the twenties. The movie was warmly welcomed in ARK and *Cinema Front,* one *Cinema Front* review calling it the "first film of Soviet contemporary life that is successfully executed from beginning to end."[58]

   The resolution ARK passed on the film in January 1927 was extremely favorable; *Third Meshchanskaia Street* was applauded for its realism, for its contemporary theme, for its superb use of detail, for its technique, acting, and economy of production. The sole criticism—an accurate one—was that the rebirth of the heroine was "insufficiently" developed, but in all:

> The picture *Third Meshchanskaia Street* successfully refutes the existing opinion about the "uncinematographic nature" of Soviet life and the impossibility of creating an interesting fiction picture on a foundation of everyday life.

The resolution went on to congratulate the film for treating an important social problem in a "soft [meaning, non-propagandistic], artistic, and consistently Soviet" way and concluded: "The artistic virtues of the picture permit its recognition as one of the most successful of Soviet production."[59]

ARK would soon discover it had made a grievous "error" of interpretation, for the association was alone with the producer Sovkino in support of *Third Meshchanskaia Street*, an undesirable position which left it dangerously exposed to attack.[60] Two perfectly coordinated denunciations of the film appeared on January 29, 1927, in *Soviet Screen* (which apparently did not appreciate Liudmila's patronage) and *Cinema*. The former criticized the sympathetic portrayal of an "undeveloped" woman and her "cultured" husbands as being yet another example of Sovkino's box office politics.[61] *Cinema*'s review was by *Soviet Screen*'s editor N. Iakovlev, who termed the movie "psycho-pathological," writing: "... Room does not resolve either *in a Soviet way or in a revolutionary way* even a small part of this theme about a ménage à trois." According to Iakovlev, the function of Soviet cinema was "actively to build the new way of life—socialism," not to coddle misfits like those depicted in *Third Meshchanskaia Street*.[62]

Later it was charged that the movie had not been made economically, since 38 percent of the film shot had not been used (in fact, this is a quite reasonable proportion of excess film). Room should have used a "precise" script (a dig at Shklovskii who was already in trouble), and why, it was asked, was the film released nearly three months after the editing had been completed?[63] (There may have been no positive stock on which to print it.) At the last moment, there apparently was concern that the storm over the movie would frighten directors away from contemporary topics, for it suddenly subsided. Osip Brik, for example, said that mistakes like this were useful—showing as they did the importance of making absolutely clear moral judgments in films.[64]

Nonetheless, anti-ARK forces used the occasion to full advantage. The first attack against ARK's support of the movie appeared anonymously in March in the theater journal *New Spectator* (*Novyi zritel'*) and pointedly noted ARK's approval of the film's ambiguous ending.[65] This was followed shortly by a smug article announcing the December 1926 ARK purge. *New Spectator* thought more purging in order to cure ARK's "soft" handling of social questions.[66]

The use of the word "soft" ("soft, artistic, and consistently Soviet") in the ARK resolution on *Third Meshchanskaia Street* must have been forever regretted by the one who first used it, for ARK's opponents would not let the issue die. N. Iakovlev, quoting from that part of the resolution, said that ARK had gone over to the right if it supported the view that cinema's purpose was to pose problems and not to solve them. Art, said Iakovlev, should not be concerned with "'life as it is' but with '*life as it should be*.'... Otherwise art will not serve the interests of the proletariat, will not fulfill its social function...." ("Life as it should be" would become an intrinsic component of the doctrine of Socialist Realism.)

But Iakovlev did not find ARK's stand at all surprising, since it was:

> an organization consisting to a significant degree of those mostly déclassé cinema-specialists who especially strongly are subject to the influence of petty-bourgeois philistinism [*meshchanstvo*].
>
> The danger harmful for Soviet cinema in the ARK theory of the "soft" posing of the hard questions of our present is intensified because the Association of Revolutionary Cinematography preaches it using revolutionary phraseology.[67]

New Spectator echoed Iakovlev's criticism of ARK's membership. Because of the "old specialists" dominating ARK, its work could never really be "revolutionary" or "politically active." Old specialists accounted for the "pessimism" and "passivity" with which ARK had greeted the Trial of the Sixteen, and its passivity was further reflected in the pages of *Cinema Front*, a journal as tranquil, claimed this writer, as *Red Virgin Soil* (*Krasnaia nov'*) or *New World* (*Novyi mir*) (two of the more moderate literary journals).[68]

ARK could not fail to answer charges as serious as these and came to its defense in a letter to *Cinema* signed by its chairman Iukov and film directors Eisenstein and Vasilev, among others. They asserted that the intensity of the ARK discussion over *Third Meshchanskaia Street* prior to the resolution showed ARKists were *not* apolitical, and if there had been errors of interpretation, they were not irreparable. *Cinema*'s editorial response was something of a non sequitur, indicating that there was more to this furor than ARK's opinion about a single film. It echoed Iakovlev's charges about "specialists" by stating that 77 percent of ARK's membership came from the "free professions" while the others were bureaucrats. It was this liberal social background that had led ARK to defy "mass" opinion as expressed by "workers, Red Army gatherings and the local press" that Room's film was alien and "déclassé."[69] It is quite clear that ARK's hapless proclamation on *Third Meshchanskaia Street* provided an excuse for the political left to draw ARK into the society-wide campaign against specialists that was part of the attack on the right wing of the Party known as the "cultural revolution."

ARK, as we recall, had become an autonomous section of ODSK (the Society of Friends of Soviet Cinema, the shadowy "mass" cinema organization) in 1925 when the latter had been founded. Now for the first time friction between ARK and ODSK surfaced, and ARK's autonomy was in jeopardy. ODSK had taken a more suitable line on *Third Meshchanskaia Street,* urging Room to study Soviet life (and speculating whether Liudmila might not be a prostitute in disguise).[70] *Soviet Screen*'s Iakovlev suggested that ODSK police ARK more closely.[71] (ODSK's Barshak, however, indicated general support for ARK's work.)[72]

ARK began very cautiously to defend its independence. Khrisanf Khersonskii admitted that ARK was politically weak and needed to set new goals, but that it was nonetheless a vital and necessary organization "on the cinema front." A single labor union could not take over ARK's centralizing role because the industry's many professions would necessitate the creation of *several* unions; also, because of cinema's high unemployment rate, many filmworkers would not be eligible for union membership. If labor unions could not replace ARK, then ODSK, which was not connected to production at all,[73] was an even less suitable substitute.

An unbridled attack against ODSK came from the VAPPist Vladimir Kirshon, now also a member of ARK. Care should be taken, he said, to evaluate ODSK separately from ARK to see its "generally wrong course." ODSK's line might be called "ideological connivance" (*popustitel'stvo*). Kirshon cautioned that anyone who thought ARK should be liquidated should look at the "extremely reactionary comments of the formalist Shklovskii against ARK in order to understand for whom the closing of ARK will be the most necessary and most pleasant."[74] According to Kirshon, ODSK persisted in duplicating the work of other organizations (like organizing a laboratory, for example) when it really needed to attend to the political and ideological demands of the "cultural revolution".[75] In an ARK meeting, Kirshon noted that ARK had "serious ideological disagreements with ODSK," but these were not spelled out.[76]

In this way ARKists tried to counterattack ODSK. That done, ARK felt the need to retrench by adopting a significantly harder line apparent in *Cinema Front* as early as mid-1927. An example of the new militancy was an article by M. Nikanorov on "cinema psychosis" and the season of petty-bourgeois films, which ended: "We will strive for new conquests and victories on the cinema front. ARK should steadfastly stand on cinema-guard."[77] Bold-faced slogans began adorning *Cinema Front*'s pages; for example: "THEY SAY THAT IDEOLOGICALLY CONSISTENT PICTURES ARE UNPROFITABLE. A LIE!"[78] or: "SOMEONE IS BEGINNING TO SAY THAT THE POLITICAL ENLIGHTENMENT TASKS OF CINEMA ARE TASKS OF THE SECOND ORDER. A FURIOUS REBUFF TO THE REAC-TIONARIES!"[79]

ARK's new "hard line" was closely connected with the phenomenon of the "cultural revolution," part of the attack on the "soft [moderate] line" in culture. There was an end to toleration of "fellow travellers" and bourgeois specialists; in the literary sphere, the proletarianism of RAPP, the Russian Association of Proletarian Writers (the former VAPP), became predominant. Although the cultural revolution is not considered to have started until spring 1928, this term began appearing in *Cinema Front* in late 1927, and it provided a perfect rationale for the war against Sovkino.[80] One of the major complaints against the state cinema enterprise had always been its alleged preference for old specialists and fellow travellers like director Iakov Protazanov (*Case of the Three Million*).

Under the circumstances, it was impossible for ARK to avoid strongly supporting the cultural revolution,[81] and so it did, at the same time stepping up its attacks against Sovkino. First ARK chairman K. Iukov denied Sovkino's claim of financial shakiness,[82] and the VAPPist Solskii denounced Sovkino's "purely commercial politics" as not even serving the goals of commerce. According to Solskii, Trainin's philosophy of "ideology in small doses" had to be vigorously rejected because there was a definite (and *positive*) connection between ideological and artistic levels. Soviet cinema would be able to surpass Western cinema only when it no longer made Western-style pictures. At home, he contended without deigning to offer proof, Western and Western-style films were not commercially successful. Abroad, even second-rate revolutionary films like *Wind* did very well because they were uniquely Soviet products. Solskii concluded by saying: "The struggle against the incorrect politics of Sovkino is a struggle for Soviet cinematography."[83]

These public pronouncements more or less matched what was happening inside ARK. At the end of October 1927, the general session of ARK formally denounced Sovkino, and the board upheld this a month later. It condemned Sovkino's "commercial films" as "historical" pictures not based on Soviet material and designed for export. Soviet cinema would not reflect proletarian ideology until Sovkino had renounced its "bureaucratism." ARK proposed to assist in the reconstruction of Soviet cinema through the following measures: it would organize writers, study script problems and have "public" readings of scripts to determine their suitability, reorganize its journal *Cinema Front*, "bring flexibility and eradication of the bureaucracy to the studios," and deal with any other ills of production.[84]

ARK was at last forced by the political climate to define a course of action. In October, through its chairman Iukov, ARK began a self-criticism campaign in preparation for the coming Party conference. According to Iukov, ARK's shortcomings were that it had not properly dealt with "principles" and "artistic questions"; ARK's own "principles" (whatever they were) had not been "carried through" in ARK's work; and ARK's members were active neither in circles of "lower" cinema workers nor influential with the "bosses" (*verkhushki*). ARK had to shed its tendency toward "academism" (professionalism) and fight two major foes: the "pessimism" in its ranks and the hostility of the "leaders of cinematography" toward it. ARK promised to overcome its weaknesses through better political preparation.[85]

ARK was a professional society in the best sense of the term, and the diversity of its membership presented an almost insurmountable obstacle to such "reforms" being achieved. By 1927 a majority of ARKists belonged to the Communist Party, but as always its ranks included directors of various artistic and political persuasions, VAPPists, Sovkino administrators, Glavpolitprosvet workers, literally everybody whose name has appeared on these pages.[86] For these reasons, the "new course" caused much internal strife, and ARK's adversaries never accepted the association as a stalwart force for the cultural revolution. It is true that those against whom the cultural revolution was aimed formed ARK's most active segment, so peaceful coexistence between the radical supporters of the cultural revolution and ARK was shortlived. By the beginning of 1928, ARK was accused of "nihilism" for allegedly approving the poor cinema distribution network. Since Sovkino films were too bad to be seen, Sovkino's distribution politics were irrelevant.[87]

Although the struggle for dominance of Soviet cinema was not yet over, it was clear by 1927 that neither ARK nor Sovkino would emerge victorious. Near the end of the year, an editorial in *Soviet Screen* urged caution. Friction among competing groups was to be expected, but current antagonisms threatened to destroy the film community. Despite these words of wisdom, *Soviet Screen* still dismissed ARK sarcastically as the organization "which has pretensions to the leadership of cinematography and which has put, in the given case, its 'revolutionary' stamp on this big *basic mistake* of A. Room [referring to *Third Meshchanskaia Street*, still a hot issue]." Yet the extreme radicalism of the ODSK/Komsomol debate was likewise rejected as "absurdity." The film community could not afford to indulge in ideological hairsplitting when practical matters needed attending to:

> In a time when cinema production finds itself on the ascent, when we do not have enough people, when among cinema specialists there are many desiring to create by artistic inspiration but *not to work* according to a plan, it is impossible to unleash demagogical tempers. Otherwise, under the noise of "ideological" conversations, we will have even worse production than up to now.

Soviet Screen looked with confidence to the upcoming Party conference to decide the course of action which would lead Soviet cinema out of its blind alley.[88]

Preparations for the Conference

Despite *Soviet Screen*'s admonitions, "ideological conversations" did not cease in the first ten weeks of 1928, the weeks leading to the conference. ARK's new line bought it some breathing space, and the debate was once again directed solely against Sovkino. Just as V. Solskii had written an article in 1927 which forecast major problems, so he inaugurated 1928 with another such article in *On Literary Guard*, this one titled "Some Results of the Cinema Discussion" ("Nekotorye itogi kino-diskussii"). Although Solskii concentrated on lambasting Sovkino, he first took great care to distinguish his position from that of the "left or so-called opposition" by saying that unlike the Commissariat of Enlightenment's Meshcheriakov (a political leftist), he believed cinema theaters should be under the control of Sovkino, and that unlike Vertov and the "formalists" (artistic leftists), he supported the fiction film.[89]

The first point is yet another indication of the erosion of the Commissariat of Enlightenment's control over cinema affairs (which corresponded to its weakness in all its spheres of influence, becoming more pronounced as the cultural revolution progressed). Solskii not only believed the principle of a centralized state cinema enterprise more desirable than expanding the Commissariat's control over cinema, he also labelled Glavpolitprosvet members part of the left opposition (by implication, connected to Trotskii). But Sovkino was still the main focus of his wrath.

Solskii derided Sovkino's chairman, Shvedchikov, for saying that criticism of the organization was hampering the work of socialist construction. Solskii reminded Shvedchikov that since Sovkino was "not the Communist Party," it was certainly not above criticism. Solskii's contempt for the Commissariat could not therefore be construed as support of Sovkino; Solskii's own litany of complaints actually differed very little from that of the Commissariat.[90]

Solskii in fact expanded the arguments against Sovkino's commercial line that he had already advanced. He claimed, as he had before, that contrary to Sovkino's assertions, the most profitable films both at home and abroad were revolutionary ones. His new idea was that Sovkino's concentration on export films was courting financial disaster, Solskii quoting Shvedchikov himself as having said that Soviet film export would continue to fall from year to year. Quite unaccountably (to Solskii, at any rate), Sovkino ignored this prediction from its own chairman, allocating the bulk of its 1928 budget to "apolitical historical hits."[91] While Shvedchikov claimed that cinema was in a "blind alley" because of its poverty, Solskii preferred to look at the present troubles as a "crisis of growth," which could be overcome by concentration on the mass market.[92]

Solskii's article was an excellent distillation of the prevailing case against Sovkino. What was most significant was the way he connected ideological deficiencies with *unprofitability*, for Sovkino's strength had always been its appearance of economic rationality. Other Sovkino opponents increasingly tried to discredit Sovkino on commercial grounds. One of the freshest and most interesting of the rash of polemical books and pamphlets that appeared just prior to the cinema conference was S. Krylov's *Cinema instead of Vodka (Kino vmesto vodki)*, which tried to show how Sovkino's policies had corrupted the entire film industry. Krylov declared that it was clear that petty-bourgeois (*meshchanskie*) films about adultery ruled the screen, naming *Third Meshchanskaia Street* and Kuleshov's latest effort *Your Acquaintance* as prime examples.[93] He admitted that cinema was in an unenviable position due to the twin pressures of ideology and finances. (Finagling the money to import the necessary film stock was still a major obstacle to increasing production.) Because of this—and here Krylov was at one with Solskii and many others—it was not concern with commerce that was so bad, but the fact that the financial plan was an "unhealthy" one not based on the mass market (80 percent of the profit was slated to come from commercial theaters). If Sovkino continued to serve commercial urban theaters, then the production of ideologically unsuitable films was a given.[94]

Concentration on the commercial market was also behind the excessive importation of foreign films. According to a report Shvedchikov gave to the Presidium of the Central Committee of the Art Workers' Union (Rabis) in 1927, Sovkino's profits had come almost exclusively from foreign films. Another time Shvedchikov claimed (and this is all on Krylov's authority) that with one million rubles one could either buy fifty foreign pictures or make ten Soviet, the former being preferable from the point of view of projected income.[95] Krylov also attacked scenarists and critics for being Sovkino lackeys. He quoted Ippolit Sokolov as having said that: "Half the workers of the Sovkino studio [including himself]—are [also in] the cinema press." According to Krylov, these "monopolists" were "very adept at creating simultaneously such a stifling atmosphere of nepotism and intrigue" that it prevented "real" writers like the proletarian authors Ivanov, Leonov, Gladkov, Fadeev, and "many others" from working in cinema.[96] (Despite Krylov's assertions, dual loyalties, although common, did not seem to discourage attacks on Sovkino from those thus "compromised.")

On the other hand, Krylov realized that "naked agit-films" would not redress the ideological deficiencies of Soviet cinema. He proposed as alternatives: broadening the distribution network to working-class and rural areas; removing foreign films from distribution; and "abolition of all elements of *monopolistic putrescence* in the cinema production apparatus."[97] He confirmed that neglect of rural and working-class areas continued, with more than 80 percent of the districts (*volosti*) of the Russian Republic without projectors, although "many had electricity."

As mentioned earlier, good Soviet and foreign films were very late reaching provincial screens (if such regions were lucky enough to have screens), and by then the physical quality of the film had significantly deteriorated. Krylov blamed the failure of the cinefication program on the fact that less than one-third of the travelling projectors were still in operation. As a result, disappointed movie-loving peasants had been heard abusing Soviet power. With these conditions, it was obvious why cinema had not yet succeeded in replacing vodka as either a source of entertainment or *income* in the Soviet Union. The income from vodka was 500 million rubles; from cinema, 22 million.[98] Comparing the state's income from vodka to that from cinema was not an aberration introduced by this writer. Stalin himself had averred that cinema would be better able to win the Party's monetary and moral support if it could provide the state as much revenue as the vodka monopoly.[99]

Krylov's was the single most effective and sustained attack on Sovkino policies in the immediate preconference period, but both *Cinema Front* and *Soviet Cinema* also pursued an aggressively anti-Sovkino course. In *Cinema Front*, Vladimir Kirshon laughed at all the "noise" Shvedchikov was making about the "cinema opposition" and stated that opposition to Sovkino was the position of the Party[100] (this could not be substantiated through other sources). *Cinema Front* was, however, more moderate: Sovkino's "line" was errant, but correctable.[101]

Soviet Cinema challenged both Sovkino's production costs and censorship record (only 68 percent of its scripts had been passed—with alterations).[102] Another article spoke of Sovkino administrators as "slaves of adultery, slaves of the double bed" who were wallowing in the "swamp of petty-bourgeois philistinism [*meshchanstvo*]."[103] G. Arustanov argued that while Sovkino's poor finances had resulted from its own rental politics, the *Party* and public opinion had not played a constructive role, *the government failing to provide enough capital* to develop the industry properly.[104] *Soviet Cinema*'s editors added a disclaimer to this article, but it was too late—*Soviet Cinema* published only one more issue, as did *Cinema Front*. The demise of these two journals at the beginning of 1928, for reasons more to do with their attacks on the Party's lack of activity on the cinema front than their anti-Sovkino stance, seriously impoverished the arena of film criticism and further demonstrated the precarious position of both ARK and the Commissariat of Enlightenment in film affairs.

Sovkino's leaders had from the very beginning exhibited a fighting spirit, and they continued to do battle with their enemies. In 1928 Sovkino issued a short history of its operations. Among the achievements listed therein were lowered rental prices and an increased fund of both foreign and Soviet films (with Soviet outnumbering foreign for the first time). Sovkino also tried to prove its role in developing rural and club theaters and in expanding exports, and pointed with pride to its exemplary Party composition: 28 percent of its staff were Party/Komsomol members. If Sovkino had not made enough "strikingly political" films, this was because the talents of Soviet filmworkers were unsuited to such movies. If equipment were in disrepair, this could be attributed to lack of qualified workers and money to import parts from abroad. On the whole, however, the polemic consisted not of excuses but of statistics testifying to the steady improvement on the cinema front during Sovkino's tenure.[105]

The last major offensive on Sovkino's behalf, *Cinema on the Cultural Front (Kino na kul'turnom fronte)*, came from the pen of I. P. Trainin, who had issued the first statement of Sovkino philosophy a long three years earlier. The language Trainin used is misleading at first glance; when one reads about "the cultural problems of our epoch," it simply does not sound like Trainin. But like any good politician, he was co-opting the jargon of the hour—in this case that of the cultural revolution.

Trainin believed that Sovkino's opposition, in trying to "industrialize" cinema production, had forgotten that cinema is an art. Particularly erroneous was the "regime of economy" ideal of the "iron scenario" which totally ignored the fundamental contributions of directors and actors. Cinema needed a strong and efficient industrial base, but that did not necessitate the perversion of the creative process.[106] The dispute over utilitarianism and ideology in cinema had also been misguided. It was superficial to say that *Wings of a Serf* did not deal with meaningful problems because it was not set in the present. Recently, the demand for strong ideological content had all too often been taken to mean "the exclusive preparation of agit-films." But agit-films were not effective propaganda; on the contrary, wrote Trainin, the stronger the artistic content, the more effectively would the political point be made.[107]

What was Trainin's dream for Soviet cinema? He condemned absolutely the notion of workers' and peasants' films. While he did not, he said, believe in slavishly following the demands of the viewers, it must be recognized that peasants and workers had no desire to be restricted to dull fare. He asserted that costume dramas like *The Decembrists* and *Poet and Tsar* had enjoyed a "colossal box office" among workers as well as with the petty-bourgeoisie. The proletariat went to the movies for hard-earned relaxation.[108]

What were Trainin's guidelines for satisfying audience preference? Films needed "strong emotions, adventures, and perhaps violence" because "a dry and conventional approach to the problems of life [byt] has frequently turned the viewer (as in the case of the reader) to things and ideas alien to us ...." A correct understanding of the central position of the individual in cinema was also important.[109] Soviet cinema should reflect the complexity of Soviet life as had *Third Meshchanskaia Street*; Trainin observed that even communists were not immune to domestic problems.[110] Although here and there he promised support for the educational film and newsreel, he was a firm believer in the fiction film.[111]

Trainin was politically astute enough to realize that he could not avoid self-defense altogether. If Sovkino had perhaps not done as well as it should have, this was due to the "disruption" in leadership and the "absence" of scripts. "Comrades" did not realize how complicated the script situation was, how scripts needed to be tailored to certain directors' skills or the time of year in which production would take place. Poverty as always was the decisive factor.

Trainin further complained that the polemics were beginning to resemble an Inquisition.[112] He too could point his finger to enemies—one category (borrowing from Lenin's terminology) was the "infantile" left communists; the other was the formalists. Both stood to gain from the demise of Sovkino but masked their true interests in revolutionary phrases, labelling anyone opposed to their "ideology of the machine petty-bourgeois [*meshchanskaia*]." But it had been demonstrated again and again that the empty screen dynamics they proposed only alienated the Soviet viewer.[113]

On the question of Sovkino's so-called "export" films and the "commercial deviation," Trainin categorically denied that the organization gave this primary consideration. He pointed out, however, that in his opinion, the decision on which films were to be produced should consider artistic merit and ability to hold attention (*zanimatel'nost'*) more than ideology.[114] In the course of *Cinema on the Cultural Front*, Trainin constantly obfuscated—he would intone phrases conciliatory to the hard-liners, then almost immediately contradict or weaken them.

This tactic is particularly evident in his concluding remarks. Although Trainin urged that cinema participate wholeheartedly in the cultural revolution, promoting the positive attributes of Soviet life, he insisted that agitation should be like a "sugar pill" and that "the cinema art of our epoch should reflect the worldview of the working class but not be confined only to dry factual exposition of naturalistic life [*byt*]." He promised that Sovkino would make stronger efforts to ensure the ideological content of each film, but he asserted his allegiance to *art* in cinema so often that it effectively undermined anything positive he had to say about propaganda.[115]

Despite the conciliatory tone and the obvious awareness of a changed political atmosphere that Trainin demonstrated in *Cinema on the Cultural Front*, he emerged unrepentant. Much of his stance is admirable, most of all his unwavering support of cinema as art or entertainment and his total rejection of agitation. There was a welcome note of good sense in his emphasis on how bureaucratic rivalry and technical backwardness hampered cinema. He may also be applauded for defending the desires of the ordinary viewer.

But Trainin did *not* discuss the central cause of the extreme antagonism toward Sovkino. This was that Sovkino had chosen to allocate most of its admittedly scarce resources to a few established directors for large-budget films. Sovkino administrators could quote all the figures they wanted to show that the numbers of Soviet films in circulation now surpassed foreign,[116] but what mattered was what aspiring directors *thought*. True or not (and I believe it was true), many filmmakers saw themselves deliberately slighted by Sovkino in favor of a policy directed toward the foreign market. In a debate sponsored by *Worker's Gazette* (*Rabochaia gazeta*), Trainin reluctantly addressed this question by saying that "the necessary amount of film [stock]" could not be imported to allow more directors to make movies.[117]

The vice-chairman of Sovkino, M. P. Efremov, offered a defense of the Sovkino line that was much more cautious and conciliatory than Trainin's. He chose to focus on the increase in Soviet production and on how Sovkino had lowered rental prices. Like Trainin, Efremov remained faithful to the fiction film but with an impossible qualification. He thought Soviet films should and could be 100 percent ideological and 100 percent commercial! In his opinion, the main solution to the quandary of Soviet cinema would be to produce film stock domestically. He naively asserted that Soviet cinema could then develop freely,[118] a judgment which ignored the changed political climate.

Over the past three years, cinema society had become quite polarized; moderation, like most everything else, was in short supply. An important exception to this was the Commissar of Enlightenment, A. V. Lunacharskii, who still attempted a middle course, best expressed in *Cinema in the West and at Home* (*Kino na zapade i u nas*). Lunacharskii recognized that cinema was in crisis and noted with satisfaction the new attention the Party was paying to cultural problems as evidenced by the approaching cinema conference. He saw as the most pressing questions the scenario crisis (which he felt resulted from cinema's lack of prestige among writers and the confusion over the censorship), the shortage of workers, the relationship between cinema and society, problems of genre, and "economic-organizational" questions.[119] Lunacharskii did not automatically place art above ideology, as had Trainin, but he was troubled by the near-impossibility of reconciling fundamentally contradictory factors (that is, art and ideology) which he felt should carry equal weight.[120] In his capacity as the authority on Lenin's views on film, Lunacharskii in fact claimed that Vladimir Ilich thought the entertainment or fiction film "more important" than any other type of film propaganda.[121]

Lunacharskii deplored "commercial" films, whether cheap and vulgar or well made and expensive (the latter were almost exclusively American). He admitted with amazing frankness that if Soviet films were indeed more popular these days with the public (as was frequently claimed by Sovkino's opponents), it was because "rubbish" was all the Soviets could afford to import![122]

Lunacharskii admitted, moreover, that the best Soviet films, like *Mother* and *Potemkin*, had yet to show a profit.[123]

In *Cinema in the West and at Home*, Lunacharskii was scarcely critical of Sovkino. Indeed, in an essay on the crisis in Soviet cinema, he was even sympathetic. Although himself no friend of "commercialism," Lunacharskii thought Sovkino's chieftain Shvedchikov under such pressure to raise money to provide a material base for industry that he had no choice but to pursue a commercial line. Lunacharskii elsewhere asserted that if importation of foreign films was halted, there would not be enough films available to satisfy the domestic demand.[124]

Lunacharskii did not, however, speak for the Party. An important indication of the Party's position was the preconference booklet published by its Leningrad district (*oblast'*) committee. The committee was neither as cognizant of the complexity of issues as was Lunacharskii nor as stridently anti-Sovkino as were many other commentators. Although Sovkino was not even mentioned in the committee's recommendations, they reflected the attitudes which Sovkino most feared—the need to study the "problems of socialist construction and the basic slogans of Party-Soviet politics in cinema"; a war against films which were "vulgar" representations of social problems or otherwise catered to the viewer; a call for "interesting" themes like "workers' life" and "industrial motifs"; and more emphasis on educational films and newsreels. The committee demanded "societal control" over all areas of cinema work.[125]

By the end of 1927, some important changes had taken place in the nature of cinema polemics. Most discussions centered on Sovkino, and to a lesser extent on Mezhrabpom, for "commercial deviation." Although Sovkino had not had much chance to develop its policies, its practice of buying foreign films to finance established directors discouraged many in the film community, since it neither provided the extra funds for production nor appreciably increased distribution. The "scenario crisis" worsened, due to intensified ideological demands resulting from revulsion against Sovkino politics, from competition for limited resources, and from political pressures of which the cinema community was only dimly aware.

With the dissipation of revolutionary enthusiasm, the divisions within the "community" were becoming pronounced, with director against actor, director against scenarist, the studio against the director, censorship against the studio. New names drifted into the cinema press, names connected with the attack on ARK and the re-evaluation of artistic standards in cinema. The kind of film demanded in reaction to stereotyping threatened to become an even more tedious cliché; after the *Third Meshchanskaia Street* debacle, it became clear that "realism" was to have a different meaning in the Soviet context.[126] The last attempt to support the nonfiction film as an art form had failed, and this, coupled with the rise of traditional acted forms of cinema, spelled the end to experimentation. The problems were real, the concerns, genuine, but freedom to resolve these issues imaginatively was rapidly dissipating.

Yet there were occasional light notes in the midst of the deadly seriousness. Cinema humorist and scenarist Vadim Shershenevich (better known as an imaginist poet) wrote a "cinema dictionary" in which he lampooned the burning polemical issues of the day as follows:

> MONTAGE: the art of carelessly cutting and carving. To edit a foreign film is to render it unprofitable.
>
> DIRECTOR: distinguishable from God, who would make a world from chaos,... the director makes chaos from everything.
>
> SCENARIO: dirty paper put on a table.
>
> TYPAGE: the devil only knows what this means![127]

6

The Crisis in Production (1927-28)

In 1927-28, the internecine strife went on without end. As *Soviet Screen* had feared, the "ideological conversations," although mild at this point compared to what was to come, threw the industry into disarray. Production was indeed hampered.

The Scenario Crisis

Particularly burdened were script writers, for as more and more films were abused in the press, so the procedure of writing and reviewing scripts came under urgent scrutiny. Writers for cinema were in an uncomfortable and unenviable position, subject to a bewildering array of intimidating directives that could only aggravate the scenario "famine" which had been an intrinsic part of Soviet cinema since its inception.

The script shortage therefore continued, one writer estimating that 200-360 scripts a year were needed for the 100-120 pictures of which Soviet production was capable (allowing for the rejection factor). At present cadres could churn out only sixty "good" scenarios a year.[1] Adding to the confusion, scripts paid for and accepted by the studios were still often rejected by the censorship and for unaccountable reasons some scripts accepted by both studios and censorship were still not used! In 1926, according to P. A. Bliakhin, fifty-four scripts were thus wasted (down from seventy-nine the year before), but at an average of 1,000 rubles per script, this was a considerable sum for the money-conscious industry.[2] The conflicting artistic and ideological standards of the censorship and the studios continued to aggravate one of cinema's built-in problems.

Studios still relied on the much criticized competitions, but whereas in the early years these had been for complete scripts, now they merely called for a story outline (libretto). *Soviet Screen* announced a contest in 1927 with a 1,000-ruble first prize from Sovkino and two 500-ruble second prizes from Mezhrabpom Rus' and Gosvoenkino. It is important to note that the only restriction was that the theme had to be postrevolutionary.[3]

Nonetheless, despite the continued use of scenario competitions, support for more professionalism in script work was definitely on the ascent. A *Soviet Screen* editorial argued that the screenplay problem would continue as long as it was held that any writer was qualified to write a movie script.[4] Ippolit Sokolov said that of the 800 scenarios Sovkino had received in the past six to seven months, not one had been "grammatical" in cinematographic terms.[5] Yet some "highly qualified" comrades (meaning Party members), like Boris Gusman (*The Captain's Daughter* [*Kapitanskaia dochka*]) and A. Kurs (*The Female Journalist*), had also written ideologically questionable scripts.[6] One prominent example which went discreetly unmentioned was that of the Commissar of Enlightenment, A. V. Lunacharskii, who had contributed the scenario to two highly criticized pictures: *The Bear's Wedding* and *Poison*.

Another as yet unresolved issue contributing to the scenario crisis was the "profession's" lack of prestige. Viktor Pertsov revived the old argument that good writers would not be attracted to cinema as long as they received neither credit nor adequate compensation for their efforts. He noted that studios were adept at economizing on script fees;[7] Viktor Shklovskii concurred, saying that there always seemed to be money for building studios—obliquely referring to Sovkino's ambitious construction project—but not for writers.[8] Abram Room stated, like Sokolov before him, that only 1 percent of a film's budget was spent on the script, and that script writers were not even given passes to enter the studios.[9] Another complaint was that writers lost artistic control over their scripts to directors. Pertsov described this very colorfully: "The writer-scenarist gives the director a blood transfusion. This transfusion should be valued as a heroic act."[10] The well-known "proletarian" novelist Fedor Gladkov complained that there was no art in film writing, that it was "just cut-and-paste, just production."[11]

Gladkov may have thought that there was too much "production" in movie writing for a "real" writer to be bothered with, but another—very persuasive—point of view was that the writer would earn more esteem and do better work by being more closely connected to *actual* production, not merely to the preparations for production. As it was now, according to this viewpoint, the writer was trapped between the warring factions of the director and the studio's artistic advisory board (*khudbiuro*). The scenarist should ally with the director[12] if he wanted increased authority.

The scenarist was now accepted as a key figure in the filmmaking process because since the 1926 "regime of economy" campaign in cinema, the script had been regarded as the basis for economical and well-planned production. The quality of the scenario was given ultimate responsibility for the quality of the picture.[13] Ippolit Sokolov enthusiastically promoted the importance of the screenplay, his slogan being: "To the regime of economy through the script." In his opinion, a well-written script (one that took filmic requirements under consideration) could cut wasted film from the current 400-600 percent to about 100 percent. Writers could assist the budget-cutting drive by reducing the numbers of sets required 33-50 percent, as well as by avoiding expensive mass scenes and superfluous characters, since actors' salaries consumed 25 percent of the cinema production budget.[14]

But what troubled script writers more than issues of art, prestige, fees, or rationality in production was the question of themes. At the beginning of 1927, *Cinema* decided that the scenario crisis was caused by the lack of contemporary themes.[15] At the end of the year, *Soviet Screen* declared that there was no dearth of themes.[16] What had happened in the interim?

By the late twenties there was a genuine crisis in Soviet cinema. Social critics, film critics, and the most important critics of all, the viewers, were extremely dissatisfied. That they were dissatisfied for different reasons made the crisis virtually insoluable. There were two basic approaches to the problem of viewer dissatisfaction. One was simple resignation—an admission that viewers liked the happy endings of American films and went to the movies for relaxation. The other was that it was the duty of the critics to *educate* the viewers.[17] But consensus on what they should be educated to like was hard to find.

There was agreement, however, that Soviet cinema was riddled with clichés, one hit film inviting a dozen mediocre copies. If an "Eastern" film were a success, movies set in the Orient flooded the market; after a historical hit, a rash of costume dramas appeared.[18] Ippolit Sokolov jokingly predicted (but it was soon to become no joke) that a spate of tractor movies would follow Eisenstein's *The General Line* (*General'naia liniia*, released after much difficulty in 1929 as *The Old and the New* [*Staroe i novoe*]) and that after *Third Meshchanskaia Street*, with its descriptive title, *Ménage à Trois,* there would be ménages of two, four, and five on the Soviet screen. He ridiculed the array of Soviet stereotypes:

> Generals always take bribes, rich peasants [*kulaks*] set fire to cooperatives, poor peasants [*bedniaks*] support cooperatives, NEPmen always have angora cats, "White" soldiers dance in prison, etc. ... Is it possible that this is "life as it is?" No, this is simply nonsense—this is lack of talent. This harmful business discredits Soviet pictures in the eyes of the mass viewers.

Sokolov ended on a strangely prophetic note: "Illusions in cinema production are harmful and cost very dearly."[19] The new illusion (and this may not have been what Sokolov had in mind) was that thematic production plans would be the industry's panacea. The increased centralization of the studios allowed for the early coordination (in theory) of such a plan, although it required the creation of yet another administrative department.[20]

If there was agreement that clichés had to be purged from Soviet films, there was also consensus that Soviet films should be about Soviet life. Thematic plans were seen to be especially useful, to show writers which aspects of Soviet life called for filmic treatment. The scenarists' workshop in Sovkino met several times to discuss this issue. P. A. Bliakhin claimed that one writer (mercifully unnamed) had answered his question: "Why don't writers know our way of life?" with a shrug and the offhand answer: "I don't want to know. It's boring, drab." How could aversion to Soviet life on the part of scenarists be overcome?

The suggestion that writers should go to the country to study the people (*narod*) was rebuffed on grounds of incipient populism. Bliakhin intimated that writers were taking their cues from the press: "We need real, living people, not walking clichés, not talking slogans from the newspapers."[21] *Soviet Screen*'s critic "Arsen" agreed that

> the core of our scenario crisis is that our Soviet artist to a certain degree still does not realize the essence of our way of life, the complex process of the birth of high culture, our transfer to a higher degree of social, and following this of industrial, organization.[22]

It is likely that the blistering cinema debates *did* encourage screen writers to scour the press for clues on the correct approach to the great problems of the day or to take refuge in hackneyed themes. That results were not particularly artistic *or* entertaining is indisputable, but would the indeterminate new path be any better?

It was rare that any critic would intimate what that new road should be (although negative examples were abundant), but one ominous suggestion, which could not have quieted writers' growing apprehensions, came from Viktor Pertsov:

> From the director of the Soviet "way of life" [*bytovoi*] film, we must require, not moralizing, but the kind of "fable" that adds fuel to the fire in the struggle for the new way of life.
> The more the film sets "one part of the population against another" in the plan of life, the better.[23]

Sovkino also managed to come up with some suggestions for subjects. For workers' pictures these were:

> the union of town with country, rationalization of production, socialist insurance (sanitariums, resorts, spas), public nutrition and institutions which emancipate the female worker.

And for peasant films:

farm laborers in the Soviet countryside and the struggle with rich peasants [*kulaks*], resettlement, the organizing of handicraft workers to involve them in the course of socialist construction, agricultural cooperation, electrification of the countryside, the struggle for collective forms of agriculture.[24]

The caveat was that these movies were to be "artistic" and "interesting" as well![25]

This conception of the Soviet contemporary film was unfortunately put into practice and dominated Soviet cinema for many years. Another desirable, but less easily defined, genre was the comedy, the perennial sore spot of Soviet cinema. Critics agreed that successful comedy was important (because viewers liked it)—but nonexistent in Soviet production.[26] In response to a *Cinema* survey, Osip Brik made a startling but accurate observation which succinctly explained the problem of comedy in the Soviet context: "Comedy without laughter is impossible. It is difficult to make Soviet comedy because we don't know what to laugh at."[27] Ippolit Sokolov echoed this when he wrote: "Laughter is a *weapon of the class struggle*. [To know] at whom and how to laugh is the main thing."

Could a comic script possibly be infused with ideology and still be funny? Could a comic hero be "positive?" Western experience indicated that it was *not* possible, for Western comic stars were idiotic types (and Sokolov quite rightly considered the Soviet favorite Igor Ilinskii very Western). Sokolov, however, proposed a constellation of new comic types drawn from Soviet life: "the comic Komsomol member, comic Red Army soldier, comic college students, and so on."[28] Such ludicrous suggestions not surprisingly bore no results, but considering the frequency with which they were made, it is small wonder that Soviet scenarists were paralyzed.

As always, most attention was devoted to the kinds of films to be discouraged. According to Vladimir Kirshon, "pseudo-revolutionary" films were more harmful than bourgeois comedies like *The Cigarette Girl from Mosselprom*. Life in Soviet films should be really proletarian, not reflected in a "distorted mirror."[29] Another genre to be avoided was the pseudo-national film, especially those dealing with the Asian nationalities. Films frequently mentioned unfavorably in this regard were *Minaret of Death*, *Road to Damascus* (*Put' v Damask*), and *The Female Muslim* (*Musul'manka*). By all accounts, these films suffered not from being too dull, but from exoticness and lack of realism.[30] Most of all to be avoided were historical films, which were deplored as the "bread and butter" of the industry. This aversion to historical films was not only prompted by the criticism heaped on the great *Wings of a Serf* but also by the reception of the elaborate, expensive, and dull costume dramas, *Poet and Tsar* and *The Decembrists*.[31]

N. Lukhmanov, *New Spectator*'s cinema critic, saw a "historical sickness" infecting the film industry, caused by the slogan "Back to the classics." This idea was useful to a limited extent in cultural work if it helped the proletariat surpass the bourgeoisie by mastering bourgeois culture, but Lukhmanov thought it worth pointing out that "old cinema specialists" supported this slogan because it bolstered their position—a "provocation" which it was "essential to nip in the bud."[32] Indeed, both the historical film and the literary adaptation had seemed a safe refuge for writers (and directors) who were either cautious or unimaginative or uncompromising or politically aware enough to recognize the dangers inherent in using contemporary themes. For the next several years, until the revival of traditionalism in the early thirties, even this haven was gone.

No one knew what themes or genres could be safely tackled. And with the exception of Osip Brik, no one evinced much sympathy for the terrifying plight of the script writer. The scenarist should not carry the "ideological burden" alone, he wrote, but should seek safety in numbers, in writers' workshops which would serve as a new form of mutual responsibility.[33] Because the script was the first step in the making of the film, writers definitely bore the brunt of the new political demands. It is no wonder then that writers did not want to work in cinema and that the "scenario crisis" worsened. This reluctance would soon have a marked effect on both the quantity and quality of production.

The Acted versus the Nonacted Film

The year 1927 was the twilight of real cinema debate, and not coincidentally, also a period marked by the evolution of a new style in the arts, Socialist Realism. Its definition emerged in part in the debate over the scenario crisis, and its rise helps explain why the question of acted versus nonacted (not necessarily nonfiction) cinema continued to stir so much controversy. Although we have seen that in 1926 there was a surge of support for films of Dziga Vertov in reaction to the perceived domination of "bourgeois" films on the Soviet screen, in 1927 the anti-Vertov offensive was resumed with fury.

Vertov had released another film in 1926 after *Stride, Soviet!—One-Sixth of the World.* This film is more innovative in style than *Stride, Soviet!,* with heavy use of the split screen and fast motion, but it has considerably less unity and impact than does its predecessor. It begins by showing the decadence of the West—colonial exploitation of Negroes and weapons making, for example— but most of the film is an amalgam of images of Soviet industry, with a few scenes on the superstition and way of life of the non-Russian nationalities.

One-Sixth of the World was welcomed with adulation from ARK and ODSK, a fact perhaps not unrelated to Vertov's having announced with characteristic audacity that to be against his new movie was to be against Soviet power.[34] Vertov also declared that the film proved the "full victory of the *factory of facts* over the factory of the grimace" (his quaint term for acting). It was also a "record of revolutionary principle [*ideinost'*]" which every Soviet from 10 to 100 should see.[35]

Vertov's admirer Izmail Urazov announced that it was a "pathetic symphony" and "pathos in action." Urazov enthusiastically declared: "You forget about the facts and vote for Vertov, for the slogans of his film. . . . "[36] In a different article, Urazov attempted to use some of the new rhetoric of cinema politics by pointing out that not the least of *One-Sixth of the World*'s virtues was its economy. Vertov, he wrote, planned to use the excess film shot in future movies.[37]

Sovkino, however, directly challenged this claim of Vertov's frugality. In a letter to the editors of *Cinema Front* that was never published, Sovkino charged that the film cost 130,000 rubles when it was budgeted at 30-40,000. If Vertov refused to submit a plan for his next movie, *Man with a Movie Camera* (*Chelovek s kinoapparatom*), he could consider himself relieved of his responsibilities.[38] (This is apparently the reason that *One-Sixth of the World* was Vertov's last work for Goskino/Sovkino; *Man with a Movie Camera* was produced by VUFKU.)

Viktor Shklovskii criticized the movie for being a series of anecdotes, poorly situated in space, so freighted with symbolism and literary titles that it actually had more in common with the fiction film than with the nonfiction film.[39] Shklovskii's expose of Vertov's so-called "objectivity" was excellent cinema criticism, but an essay by Vladimir Korolevich, a staunch advocate of the professional film actor, was politically more relevant. He wrote:

Many have argued about: "where Dziga Vertov is striding" [referring to the titles of Shklovskii's and Urazov's articles about *Stride, Soviet!*, discussed above]. With *One-Sixth of the World* Vertov has shown where. From the bare facts of the newsreel to manufactured "pathos." This means virtuoso montage and the dictatorship of the scissors.

For Korolevich, Vertov's rejection of the actor and the script indicated how divorced he was from the desires of the ordinary viewer despite his claims to be representing them. Korolevich claimed the danger was that Vertov's followers, not as capable as he, were leading cinema into a blind alley.[40] (One Vertov supporter refuted Korolevich's arguments, however, by saying that audiences watched *One-Sixth of the World* with unflagging interest even though there was no intermission.)[41]

Despite the controversy, *One-Sixth of the World* was the first full-length documentary to play Moscow's premiere theater, the Malaia Dmitrovka.[42] The small groundswell of support for Vertov was not, however, to be the trend of the future, although it did reinforce both the call for "contemporary" films and the rejection of historical "relics."[43] The advocates of acted cinema, despite this challenge, held their position of hegemony.

The resumption of the anti-Vertov offensive began with a withering denunciation of Vertov and his work by Ippolit Sokolov, an assault which was much more damaging to the director than Shklovskii's "Where is Dziga Vertov Striding?" Sokolov based his lengthy attack on *One-Sixth of the World*, charging that the film was neither art nor fact:

> *One-Sixth of the World* is the *confusion of the methods of artistic and scientific cinematography.... In the picture, factual material is changed into artistic material.... The deformation of facts was done by montage....*

Sokolov criticized Vertov (as had Shklovskii) for using facts as symbols and for dealing with geographical contrasts more than with key issues. He also criticized Vertov's editing as a simplistic changing of shots with the "psychological rhythm" of an art film. For Sokolov, Vertov's montage was: *"ultra-American, ragged, often cut to the utmost."* He believed—and this is a fair evaluation—that the motivation behind Vertov's editing was the fundamentally uncinematographic one of making way for the titles.

Vertov's manipulative editing was not all Sokolov had on his mind. Perhaps prompted by Sovkino's letter to *Cinema* on Vertov's profligacy, Sokolov combined his artistic critique with an investigation of Vertov's fiscal prudence. In these days of economy-mindedness, the combination was deadly. Sokolov charged that the shooting of *One-Sixth of the World* had been "accidental, without a precise plan," resulting in 26,000 meters of film shot for a 1,140-meter film. Furthermore, said Sokolov, Vertov had gone on ten costly, cross-country expeditions in the course of production and for what?—to shoot closeups of men's legs and dogs in the tundra. This, in Sokolov's opinion, was taking pursuit of the "truth" too far.

One-Sixth of the World's contract had been for eight months and 80,000 rubles. Vertov had worked on it nineteen months, spending 130,000 rubles. (Vertov himself admitted this, attributing the overruns to "chaos," unnamed financial problems, and difficulties caused by the reorganization of the film industry.) Despite such serious shortcomings, Sokolov alleged that *One-Sixth of the World* had enjoyed an "unhealthy" and overblown press campaign which deceived the viewers, through the authority of the critics, into thinking it was a worthwhile film. Sokolov even speculated whether Vertov may have brought some pressure to bear to effect this response, for he noted that during the ARK discussion of the film, Vertov supporters had attempted to influence the proceedings by "packing" the hall.[44] ARK had, however, resisted; its resolution criticized the film for ideological omissions and for its "lyrical" and "individualistic" style.[45]

It is interesting that Sokolov saved for his coup de grace the fact that *One-Sixth of the World* had been unprofitable; one gets the idea that a healthy profit would have gone a long way toward the expiation of its sins. But where the average picture grossed 12-13,000 rubles in its first five to six days, *One-Sixth of the World* earned only 8,500 rubles in a six-day period which had included two holidays. Yet despite this thoroughgoing critique, Sokolov concluded on a charitable note, saying that Vertov was a better filmmaker than *One-Sixth of the World* indicated and that "although Vertov has been fired from the studio he, of course, should work, and of course, will work."[46] It was—and this is significant—the first time that any critic found it necessary to make such assurances, yet another sign of the darkening horizon on the cinema front.

Vertov responded sharply in *Cinema Front* two issues later. First, he reiterated Izmail Urazov's claim that the 26,000 meters would make six more films. Then he launched a personal attack on Sokolov:

> The unwillingness, or rather, *inability* of I. Sokolov to understand the structure of *One-Sixth of the World* should not call forth surprise; it is by no means necessary for a specialist in the study of the lace on Mary Pickford's pantaloons to understand anything about the process of constructing the nonacted film.

(This barb, referring to Sokolov's unabashed admiration for American movies and their stars, was especially venomous considering the extreme disfavor into which foreign films had fallen.) Vertov pleaded with the "friends" of the nonfiction film to deny Sokolov, an adherent of *acted cinema*, any critical credibility.[47]

Sokolov responded immediately, but his reply was not published in *Cinema Front* until almost two months later. This delay may have been caused by an investigation of Sokolov's new charges against Vertov, by some kind of political maneuvering in Vertov's favor, or by a reluctance to publicize the views of a "specialist on Mary Pickford's pantaloons." Whatever the cause, Sokolov supplied additional financial data with which to damn Vertov. *One-Sixth of the World* had cost 100 rubles per meter compared to 25-30 rubles per meter for the typical fiction feature film. For that reason, Sokolov suggested that it be nicknamed *The Decembrists* (an expensive costume drama, to be discussed) of the nonfiction film.

But Sokolov had even more damaging evidence. He said that Vertov had lifted material from other films: the nonfiction movies *October in Life* (*Oktiabr' v bytu*, Dubrovskii), *Kazakstan* (Stepanov), *Around Europe* (*Po Evrope*, Lebedev), and even from the fiction film *With Iron and Blood* (*Zhelezom i krov'iu*, Karin).[48] This accusation was confirmed in part by Lebedev, who wrote that Vertov had indeed used his material—and without his permission![49]

Furthermore, some of what had not been plagiarized had been *staged* (for example, the fox-trot scene), which was absolutely contrary to Vertov's stated principles. Sokolov concluded: "*One-Sixth of the World* is not a superlative example of the nonacted film, but a poor example of fiction cinema." There were many true nonfiction films to be emulated, films which were good and had been made quickly and cheaply. For Sokolov, the Vertov tragedy demonstrated the pitfalls of "unhealthy eclecticism."[50] With this review, Vertov was thoroughly and irreparably discredited.

After it, no supporter of nonfiction film could safely back Vertov. The controversy over the nonfiction/nonacted film was further complicated by its Lef connection. The "Left Front" of the arts once again entered the arena of cinema polemics, this time through its journal *New Lef* (*Novyi Lef*), which was published from 1927 to 1928. Although Lefists supported the "fixation of facts" in cinema as they did in the other arts,[51] this no longer implied support for Vertov. Lef critic Osip Brik had long been, like Vertov, an opponent of foreign films and entertainment in cinema, but in an essay which appeared in *Cinema*, Brik left no doubt that Lef had abandoned Vertov. Vertov's mistake, wrote Brik, had been in forsaking the newsreel, which was specific and realistic, in favor of an intrinsically misguided attempt to create a new genre. The feature film and the newsreel were totally different genres, the techniques of which could not and should not be mixed.[52]

Brik's essay was the best expression of Lef's point of view on the nonacted film,[53] but the Lef symposium in which Brik, Viktor Pertsov, Sergei Tretiakov, Esfir Shub, Viktor Shklovskii, and others participated should not be overlooked. The attitude of most Lefists, like Brik and Pertsov, was that while the nonacted film was preferable, the fiction film also had its place. Lefists wanted to combat the misuse of the nonfiction form and the low esteem in which it was held (for which they considered Sovkino primarily responsible).[54] The Lef discussion, although interesting, was couched in terms too obtuse to attract much attention, and the fact that Lef was also under fire in ARK for "formalism" tended to erode further whatever influence or authority Lef might have had in the film world.[55] Indeed, considering the configurations of the cultural politics of the late twenties, Lef's support of the nonfiction film must be considered detrimental.

Support for newsreels and educational films did come from more "respectable" sources, like the publicist Grigorii Boltianskii and the journals *Soviet Screen* and *Soviet Cinema*,[56] but the issue consumed less and less energy and space as time went on. The revolutionary ideal of the nonfiction film as a viable alternative to the entertainment film was quite dead. Far more central to the theoretical debates was how to save the entertainment film from stagnation through increased emphasis on strong dramatic roles for trained cinema actors. If there was money to spare, only then was it agreed that nonfiction films should be made, but the fiction film had won the battle for hegemony. The question was what kind of actor was best suited to Soviet cinema, no longer whether there should be actors at all.

Abram Room, the unhappy director of *Third Meshchanskaia Street*, made the strongest theoretical statement supporting the concept of acted cinema, saying that "without the actor," there is "no cinematography." Although the newsreel or nonacted film had its place, its predominance was simply impossible, because "real" cinematography was the acted film.[57] For this reason the entertainment film naturally and easily dominated the nonfiction film: most talented people wanted to make them, and most viewers wanted to see them.

In March 1927, ARK devoted an entire issue of *Cinema Front* to the actor in Soviet cinema. The lead-off editorial declared that Soviet cinema needed both "stars" and a "firm cadre of cinema actors," but that if theater actors were seriously interested in cinema, they might be given some roles. The call for "stars" did not, however, mean the use of big theatrical names to ensure box office success.[58] It was believed that theater actors received extraordinary salaries—75 rubles a day to Tseretelli (a favorite of the "bourgeois" director Protazanov), for example.[59] Such observations tended only to obscure the contradictory elements of the question. Were there actually too few actors or was not the problem really that roles were poorly written? Should film acting be the exclusive domain of professional film actors? Some theater stars, like Ivan Moskvin or Mikhail Chekhov, were poor movie actors (although popular with audiences), but most of the best movie actors had also come from the theater: Baranovskaia, Batalov, Tseretelli, Ilinskii, to name only a few.[60] Purging theater actors from cinema could only aggravate the shortage of actors.

Clearly, actors continued to trouble the critics of the day. How could it be explained that the few genuine Soviet "stars," like Ilinskii and Moskvin, were still not as popular as Western stars? One answer offered was that these actors were too "bourgeois" to play the lower-class heroes of Soviet cinema well; another explanation, advanced earlier, was that due to the purported "dictatorship" of the director, actors were not even privy to the script and therefore could not bring their creative energy to the development of their roles.[61] Yet another explanation was that directors were always searching for new faces, so that experienced and popular actresses like Vera Baranovskaia (the mother in *Mother*), Iuliia Solntseva (*Aelita*, *The Cigarette Girl from Mosselprom*), and Aleksandra Khokhlova (Kuleshov's leading lady) were without work.[62] One must remember, however, that unemployment among cinema actors, whether "names" or not,[63] was high. Given this situation, why the numbers of cinema actors needed to be increased at all is an interesting question for which there is no easy answer.

Increasing the cadres was nonetheless perceived a necessity, to be achieved through renewed emphasis on training, particularly method acting.[64] Although enthusiastically supported and undoubtedly well intentioned, these systems failed to take into account that the majority of film critics was now *against* the mechanization of acting.[65] Rationalizing the process was desirable only insofar as it was not dehumanizing. Indeed, to a large degree, emphasis on the actor was in direct response to the "coldness" of the montage theory of cinema (that is, that the fundamental artistic principle of cinema is editing). Technically able directors, like Fridrikh Ermler, began saying that it was the actor, not the frame, that "made" the film. Directors needed to concentrate on training and developing three or four main characters to produce a cheaper and more interesting film than the "mass" movie.[66]

While Abram Room agreed that directors bore some responsibility for the neglect of actors in Soviet cinema, he also indicted Sovkino for false economizing in this area. (Room claimed that Nikolai Batalov had had to work at the Moscow Art Theater at the same time he was filming *Third Meshchanskaia Street* for monetary reasons, belying the oft-repeated view that theater stars commanded ridiculously high fees.) Lev Kuleshov also believed the problem lay in Sovkino's attitude toward actors, writing: "The commercial pursuit of beauties and names is none other than hidden pornography or psycho-pathology for which there is absolutely no place in Soviet cinematography."[67] (Kuleshov reported in his memoirs that he was offered work as a director only if he forsook his wife, the actress Khokhlova, who was no beauty.) Other suggestions for improving the lot of actors included giving them more prominent credits in the film and more attention in reviews.[68]

But the debate over the actor skirted what seems (especially in retrospect) the central reason for the viewers' unhappiness with Soviet films—the lack of a meaningful and interesting hero. Poor roles, rather than bad acting, were the culprit, so the concentration on the actor, if not exactly misdirected, was skewed. One critic, however, did boldly announce that the reason for the success of American films lay in their sure creation of believable heroes. People needed to be depicted in their daily life, not just on the barricades.[69]

The Films

Major changes were afoot. Cinema debates were no longer abstract but intimately connected with specific movies, most of which received *negative* (rather than favorable or mixed) reviews. In addition, critics were at last coming under scrutiny, with some justice—too often critics referred to a film's being "good" or "bad" without any indication of their criteria for evaluation.[70]

Because every film became the object of close analysis, and because directors sought guidelines for future work from reviews, efforts were made to evaluate Soviet reviewing practices more stringently. Ippolit Sokolov, one of the best critics, felt that his kind in general did not know much about movies or take them seriously, which explained why many critics hid behind pseudonyms.[71] Mikhail Levidov, another able critic, preferred an interesting explanation for the alleged weakness of Soviet film criticism: it was not that critics were always wrong, but that they were sometimes right for the wrong reasons, merely following the whims of the public. In addition, Levidov repeated the time-honored charge made against professional criticism, that critics write to be read by other critics and tend to play God.[72] Director Sergei Iutkevich called for an end to the "dictatorship of *personal taste, superficiality of analysis, biting, but not far-sighted, feuilletonism*" in Soviet criticism, for which he urged a Marxist approach be substituted.[73] Soviet film critics were not yet adept at formulistic reviews written in pseudo-Marxist jargon, but reviewers began to try harder to inject social and political criteria into their work.

Historical Films

Historical films, particularly costume dramas, came under heavy critical fire in 1927. We have already seen Tarich's excellent melodrama set in the reign of Ivan the Terrible, *Wings of a Serf*, attacked as a counterrevolutionary film by the VAPPist Solskii.[74] The historical films of 1927 (*Poet and Tsar*, *The Decembrists*, and *His Highness's Female Soloist*) now came under fire for being apolitical, for costing too much, and for not appealing to the viewers.[75]

The long-recognized propensity of the historical film to degenerate into a "bourgeois" costume drama was perfectly realized in *The Decembrists*. Another in the series of historical films by the director Aleksandr Ivanovskii and the historian-scenarist P. Shchegolev (*Palace and Fortress*, *Stepan Khalturin*), *The Decembrists* played into the hands of critics of the historical genre. A ponderous melodrama which reveals little about the unsuccessful Decembrist uprising of 1825, *The Decembrists* focusses instead on the love affair between Ivan Annenkov and Pauline Geueble. Its anti-tsarist touches are quite unsophisticated. The Grand Duke Konstantin Pavlovich is depicted as a "typical" warmongering Romanov (why, even as a boy, the lad was a militarist—he loved to play with toy soldiers!). As another example, his morganatic wife sees herself as an empress complete with crown whenever she looks in a mirror.

The rebels themselves do not come off much better; they are portrayed as a frivolous bunch of aristocrats who stand idly by as a peasant girl is being beaten. Clearly the purpose of the film was to show the glamorous lives of these people, not to depict the drama of the event. (The "battle" scene on the square in Petersburg is laughably unrealistic, crowds of people motionlessly watching.) The whole picture is constructed on crude parallels: Annenkov's attempted suicide cut to a court ball; the execution of the rebels contrasted with fireworks. *The Decembrists* is altogether a superficial and boring movie.

The critic Arsen charged that the film was not "artistic," historically accurate (lacking some of the most important Decembrists), or economical (even though the sets and costumes were to be reused in *Poet and Tsar*).[76] Others agreed that not only was *The Decembrists* not the kind of historical film needed, it brought back "unpleasant memories of the 'psychological' fairy-tale plays of the time of [the prerevolutionary directors] Ermolev and Drankov."[77]

Poet and Tsar offers an even more vivid example of the trap of the historical film. The prerevolutionary veteran Vladimir Gardin directed this look at the last days of Pushkin's life with the help of Evgenii Cherviakov as co-writer, co-director, and star. The movie posits a Nicholas I-Bulgarin conspiracy theory against Pushkin for which the great poet and his purportedly simple country ways are no match. Pushkin is characterized as having had a great distaste for court life (at a masquerade ball, for example, he sees the revelers as real animals), submitting himself to it only for the sake of his frivolous wife. Although the duel scene is well cut to achieve maximum drama, it takes a very long time to get there, and afterwards, one fears that Pushkin will never expire but go on posturing and sighing.

Perhaps because of Pushkin's immortal stature among Russians, *Poet and Tsar* provoked more protest than had *The Decembrists*, although it is not a worse film. P. Neznamov noted quite correctly that the picture is slow and static with such uncinematographic scenes as Pushkin wandering around "reading" his poems (which would have been bad enough in a *sound* film, let alone a silent).[78] Pushkin specialists were even marshalled to denounce the movie.[79] Mikhail Shneider thought *Poet and Tsar* should be held up to directors as a negative example, for "in Soviet cinema, it is necessary to make a picture with living and concrete content...." Nevertheless, the film was a commercial success, and this had to be rationalized. Shneider believed that its success resulted less from the film's general "vulgarity," than from the public's fascination with death and violence. Pandering to such base instincts, said Shneider, was a "crime against the viewer, against society, against cinematography."[80]

The third heavily censured "historical" film was *His Highness's Female Soloist* (*Solistka ego velichestva*), which is no longer extant. Despite the scanty and necessarily secondhand information concerning it, *His Highness's Female Soloist* was subjected to such abuse that it must at least be mentioned here. Set in 1904-05, but apparently only peripherally concerned with the strife of those years, the film centered instead on the jealous rivalries of a prima ballerina and mistress of a Grand Duke, Matilda Plesinskaia (clearly Kseshinskaia, the one-time mistress of Nicholas II), toward younger dancers.[81] Mikhail Shneider thought that this film, *The Decembrists*, *Katerina Izmailova*, and *Victory of a Woman* (*Pobeda zhenshchiny*) constituted a "whole front" of movies catering to the bourgeois tastes for the sensational. It is easy to imagine from the plot of *His Highness's Female Soloist* that this could be true. Shneider wrote:

> What is easier: to build Soviet industrial cinema or to work in cliché; to obtain knowledge and culture or to make petty-bourgeois [*meshchanskie*] meters of film for our own market and the international market?
>
>   The profitability of the Gold Series might cost us very dearly. A gamble on the commercial director might turn out to be a gamble against Soviet cinematography.[82]

Shneider was expressing an honest concern shared by many in this time of disillusionment with the course the Revolution had taken.

Two other examples of the genre were not as notorious as the films just discussed but exhibit the general weakness of the Soviet historical film: *The Skotinins* (*Gospoda Skotininy*) and *S.V.D.* (*Soiuz Velikogo Dela*, Union of the Great Cause). *The Skotinins*, based on a comedy by Fonvizin, was Grigorii Roshal's first film (in the sound period he became a director of some repute). It is set in the eighteenth century during the Pugachev rebellion and underscores the coarse brutality of the gentry toward each other as well as toward their peasants. Any humor in Fonvizin's original has been lost. *The Skotinins* differs from *The Decembrists* and *Poet and Tsar* in that upper-class life is more sordid than glamorous. Even so, the film was too poorly made to be well received. Both Mikhail Shneider and ARK saw it as technically backward, badly and unevenly edited, and insufficiently informed about the period.[83]

S.V.D. was not successful either but holds more interest because of the talent of its directors, Grigorii Kozintsev and Leonid Trauberg of FEKS. *S.V.D.* also concerns the Decembrist rebellion, in particular the 1825 uprising of the Chernigov regiment, and focusses on the plan of an adventurer, Medoks (Sergei Gerasimov), to betray it. The movie survives only in fragments; therefore, a plot which was by all accounts confusing becomes even harder to follow. *S.V.D.* has many memorable scenes, all eerily unrealistic: a band marching toward the artillery on ice, its drummer beating incessantly; shadows and silhouettes of the perpetrators of violence. As always in the work of the FEKS collective, technique predominates: angle shots, fast motion, blurring of the screen to show confusion.

The critical response was fairly consistent. P. Neznamov noted that the film's evident deficiencies did not prevent recognition that "*the cinematographic thing* [veshch'] *is wonderfully done*," but that it should have concentrated on people, not things.[84] Mikhail Shneider thought the film a work of art but saw an "internal emptiness," feeling that the "social significance of the picture is smudged" because the historical material merely served as a vehicle for aesthetic exercises.[85] In truth, the film is *not* dramaturgically interesting, due to the lack of both plot and strong characterization.

Ippolit Sokolov was much more enthusiastic, although he found the script by Iurii Tynianov and Iuliian Oksman "weak" with poor characterizations. Sokolov nonetheless saw a perfect harmony of style and subject matter in this film and declared *S. V. D.* "one of the best Soviet pictures" and the filmmakers "real artists, great masters, and courageous innovators who created their own manner and style."[86] Despite certain lapses in courage and judgment, Sokolov genuinely loved cinema and appreciated attempts to explore the possibilities of the medium, even if they were not completely successful. His generous views were not, however, always representative of Soviet critical opinion and were not in this case.

Contemporary Films

We have already seen how vigorously the greatest Soviet silent film of contemporary life, *Third Meshchanskaia Street,* was demolished by enraged "public opinion." Concomitant with the growing disenchantment among the political left with NEP was a growing distaste for honest representation of the many unpleasant contradictions in Soviet society. This made work on contemporary, "everyday" themes increasingly difficult for Soviet directors. Some films of this type were unfavorably re-evaluated; Ermler's 1926 *Katka the Apple Seller,* for example, now became an "alien" representation of Soviet life because like *Third Meshchanskaia Street* it did not resolve problems and, according to its critics, depicted "stereotyped" characters (who actually were far from stereotyped).[87]

Nothing could approach the scorn heaped on *Third Meshchanskaia Street,* but the prolific "bourgeois" director Iakov Protazanov's *The Man from the Restaurant* (*Chelovek iz restorana*), a Mezhrabpom production with a nearly contemporary time frame starring the famous theater actor Mikhail Chekhov, was also much criticized.[88] Chekhov plays a poor waiter whose daughter must drop out of school to play the violin in the restaurant. There she attracts the attentions of a wealthy industrialist, but the waiter, despite his servile attitude, saves his daughter's virtue through the power of his moral outrage.

The movie concentrates on the gluttony, wastefulness, and petty cruelty of the waning days of tsarism (1916-17). The purity of the waiter's daughter is contrasted to the corruption, born of necessity, of the women around her. Yet none of the old waiter's personal tragedies really shake him into hatred of the capitalist system until it begins to taint his beloved daughter; on the eve of the Revolution, this "little man" is seething with rage.

Protazanov honestly tried to evoke the rise to social consciousness of a downtrodden member of prerevolutionary society. But the character is too humble and ingratiating for the story to work dramatically; this weakness is accentuated by Chekhov's mannered melodramatic style and exaggeratedly mournful expressions. He calls forth only pity, not empathy. The critics reacted to this film with fatigued annoyance, failing to recognize that Protazanov had tried something above and beyond his typical entertaining, but shallow, production. Sokolov labelled it a "naive, liberal-humanitarian" picture directed at the petty-bourgeois audience for the purpose of making money. Shneider also saw the film as a planned "hit," in his view, "the most reactionary form of cinema work." Both critics found *The Man from the Restaurant* fundamentally uncinematographic and panned Chekhov's acting."[89]

Another film of more-or-less contemporary life was Evgenii Ivanov-Barkov's *Poison (Iad)* based on Commissar of Enlightenment Anatolii Lunacharskii's play with the screenplay by Lunacharskii and Ivanov-Barkov. The plot concerns a vamp who seduces a young man into becoming a member of a spy circle; he very nearly is persuaded to kill his father, *Poison* is quite a bad movie, which uses the overworked silent screen device of sharply contrasting characters (here, debauched riffraff and wholesome Komsomol members) in a most banal way.

There are, however, a few well-made scenes, such as the fight in the bar with cutting to different parts of the body to emphasize action, or (the best) a chilling shot of the coquette's smile turning sour, after which the closeup slowly blurs. But the story lacks emotional underpinnings: why would the boy so readily agree to kill his father? Why does the seductress suddenly confess the nefarious plan? Although *Poison* was condemned as false "formal eclecticism," Lunacharskii was absolved of blame, it being revealed that the script had been reworked several times. The Commissar had allegedly pronounced it "boring" before production, but Sovkino went ahead with it, seeing "undoubted commercial value" in *Poison*.[90]

Criticism of the above films was justified, but there were two good films in this category which met the same fate. These were *Your Acquaintance* (sometimes known by its production title of *The Female Journalist*) and *Peasant Women of Riazan (Baby riazanskie)*. Lev Kuleshov had hoped *Your Acquaintance* would rehabilitate his sagging reputation after the disaster of *By the Law* by demonstrating that he could make a "Soviet" film. Only one reel survives, but judging from this fragment, it seems to have been a powerful film with a physicality absent from Kuleshov's earlier work. It is the story of a reporter (Aleksandra Khokhlova) whose affair with a married man costs her her job. There is a wonderful scene of the woman slowly walking around her office touching objects as though trying to imprint them on her memory; if this is any indication of the quality of the rest of the film, it was one of Khokhlova's finest performances. *Your Acquaintance* was reviled as an "apology for adultery" and apparently had a very limited release.

At the end of 1927 a very different, but equally reviled, film was released. A steamy melodrama of a young woman who marries into a rich peasant family, set during the World War I-Civil War period, *Peasant Women of Riazan* was directed by prerevolutionary Russia's first woman director, Olga Preobrazhenskaia.[91] After her husband goes to war, Anna (R. Puzhnaia) is raped by her father-in-law and has a baby therefrom. When her husband returns and rejects her, she drowns herself in the river. Contrasted to this traditional couple is the young husband's strong-willed and modern sister, Vasilisa (Emma Tsesarskaia), who defies parental authority and village opprobrium to live openly with her lover, a poor peasant.

Peasant Women of Riazan is miraculously saved from triteness by its beautiful photography and rich details (like the scenes of threshing or peasant women gossiping). Preobrazhenskaia's technique is deft and subtle; the rape scene is shown, for example, by a blurring of the screen and some suggestive cutting. The acting is consistently believable, and Puzhnaia is especially good in the challenging role of Anna; even her suicide is dramatically controlled.

Despite the fact that *Peasant Women of Riazan* fulfilled several of the demands for Soviet pictures—combining peasant material, an interesting plot, and strong characters—it was nonetheless controversial and provided the basis for a very lively ARK debate. Although *Peasant Women of Riazan* was commended for its technical achievements and its rural subject matter, it was also criticized for not showing "the difference between the old and new countryside," for few references to Soviet power, and for completely ignoring the Civil War. Opponents of the film claimed it was "sugary" and unrealistic and that the father-in-law should have been punished.[92] What was the tenor of the discussion that had led to the adoption of these resolutions?

Some spoke in favor of the movie. A "voice" protested from the floor, in answer to the criticism about the absence of the Civil War in the picture, that *Peasant Women from Riazan* was not, after all, about the Civil War. Another speaker asked why 100 percent was demanded from everybody all the time, asserting that this movie had realized its modest aims, which should suffice. ODSK's Barshak said that picayune criticism was irrelevant in the end, because peasants would like it (and producing a film for the rural population had been a long-desired but heretofore unachieved goal of Soviet cinema).

But a horde of unfamiliar names attacked the movie, even criticizing the "positive" character Vasilisa for not being positive *enough,* the clothing for being too white, the use of closeups on old people (instead of young ones).[93] The press was quite critical, P. Neznamov calling it a "partyless and inter-class" film, a kind of ethnographic museum.[94] *Soviet Cinema* bemoaned its melodrama and inability to show class differentiation in the countryside.[95]

Peasant Women from Riazan was a perfect example of quite a good and entertaining film being criticized just as harshly as those which were boring and poorly made.

Revolutionary / Civil War Films

Since 1927 was the tenth anniversary of the October Revolution, a number of films had been commissioned to commemorate the event. Eisenstein's *October* was not released until 1928, due either to technical difficulties, as he claimed, or to the political problems that others have surmised.[96] But Pudovkin's *The End of St. Petersburg* (*Konets Sankt-Peterburga*) and Barnet's *Moscow in October* (*Moskva v Oktiabre*) did manage after herculean labors—Soviet directors always seemed to have trouble meeting deadlines—to come to the screen in November 1927.

The End of St. Petersburg is one of Pudovkin's best and most original films, technically quite superior to the better-known *Mother*. As in most of the great silent films, what is memorable is visual and independent of plot, theme, or characters. Once again, Pudovkin uses a single hero, this time a young peasant who becomes a revolutionary. But unlike *Mother*'s Pavel, the hero of *The End of St. Petersburg* is abstract and unnamed, "Anyman" who participated in the days of the Revolution. Cameraman Anatolii Golovnia time and again achieved superior shot composition, reflecting the charged atmosphere of the Revolution through the excitement and unexpectedness of his technique. Yet given the dominant critical criteria of the day, the film could not, objectively speaking, meet with the same adulation as had *Mother*.

Oddly enough, Mikhail Levidov greeted this innovative film as a "simple thing" (which it emphatically is not) that showed Pudovkin dutifully trodding the path of artistic realism which had begun with Tolstoi (as opposed to the Dostoevskii-Meierkhold-Eisenstein route). His commentary bore so little relation to *The End of St. Petersburg* it was as though Levidov were writing another review of *Mother*. Pudovkin was *not* a "Russian realist." He had strong realistic tendencies, but he loved symbolism and formal technique. Significantly, Levidov also used this "review" to bolster the acted film, writing:

> There is no argument. It is necessary to fight against the acted feature film, *if it is bad*, but on the other hand, more important is the acted film with a plot [*siuzhet*] and a hero *if it is good*. *The End of St. Petersburg* showed this.[97]

But the movie did *not* show this; its hero is as impersonal as the battleship Potemkin, and the only plot is the Revolution. The studied irrelevance of this "review" to the movie at hand (a rarity even at this late date) indicates that it was really intended as a polemical article on aesthetics.

Only Khrisanf Khersonskii dared express what a departure from *Mother, The End of St. Petersburg* was. He found the unity of script and characterizations faulty and aptly characterized the film as "beautiful fragments." He believed the lyricism was too abstract and the romanticism too elevated to reach the viewer. This is the film's strength from an artistic point of view, but its weakness if one judges cinema as a mass art. Khersonskii chose the latter interpretation, because "*the tasks and aims* of the director *are found not on the screen but in the viewing hall.*"[98]

Even more than *The End of St. Petersburg*, Boris Barnet's *Moscow in October* was a disappointment, although a departure from the much-criticized serial *Miss Mend* and light comedy *Girl with a Hat Box* (to be discussed). This "staged history," a recreation of the Revolution in Moscow, succeeded only in being boring and confusing. It features one of the most tedious examples of parallel action imaginable: telephone operators mix up lines on the switchboard, enabling the Bolsheviks to learn the Provisional Government's plans. The attack on the military school is so unconvincing that it is laughable. Barnet had attempted a mass film without any of the skill necessary to make a crowd more than an aimlessly milling mob. *Moscow in October* was harshly and justifiably criticized.[99]

Civil War pictures continued to be popular although there was still concern over excessive bloodshed on the screen.[100] The best of these came from the versatile Iakov Protazanov—*The Forty-first*. Based on a short story, *The Forty-first* is the tale of a Bolshevik sharpshooter, Mariutka (Ada Voitsik), and a White officer stranded on a desert island. They fall in love, but as a White cruiser approaches to rescue them, Mariutka remembers her political duty and kills her lover, her forty-first victim. Protazanov was far too experienced to fail with a plot like this, and *The Forty-first* is probably the most enjoyable film of the decade. Up to the capture of the White lieutenant, the action is somewhat slow, including an overlong trek across the desert replete with the obligatory wind storm. But after that, the tempestuous love affair between the refined officer and the pretty, earthy girl proves a winning formula.

The movie received a mixed response. The Society of Friends of Soviet Cinema (ODSK) reviewed it favorably on the whole. Khrisanf Khersonskii admitted that the film was neither boring nor one-dimensional (a common problem with Civil War pictures) but thought the director's attitude toward the material "unclear."[101] It is true that the viewer does not know whether to regard the end as the girl's victory as a Bolshevik or her defeat as a human being (but one suspects the latter).

The critic Arsen as usual was not inclined to be charitable. He found the picture "socially primitive" with too-traditional characterizations. Because of its subject, good production, and acting, Arsen thought it a likely success with the public, a very offensive and "dangerous" state of affairs. He wrote: "The acceptance of *The Forty-first* is the acceptance of Western adventure literature (and cinema) which historically fulfill the same reactionary role as the slogan 'art for art's sake.'"[102] Arsen (and P. Neznamov) epitomized the new cadres infiltrating the ranks of the established film critics; they could be characterized by their skill at sniffing out heresy. Yet what Arsen said about *The Forty-first* was quite true. Protazanov *was* interested in the story, not in ideology. The morality of the final scene *is* ambiguous. As someone remarked in the ODSK discussion, *The Forty-first* showed that Bolsheviks and Whites had one thing in common—they were human beings.[103]

Two Days (*Dva dnia*), a Ukrainian (VUFKU) production directed by Georgii Stabovoi, is a considerably less effective, rather old-fashioned, and much more typical Civil War story. It begins with the wealthy citizens of a Ukrainian town fleeing to escape the approaching Red Army. An old caretaker hides his employers' young son, who has accidentally been left behind in the panic. When the Reds come, the loyal retainer learns to his chagrin that his son Andrei is a Bolshevik, for he is outraged by their looting and uncouth behavior. On the second day, the Whites return; Andrei's unit has retreated, but he was ordered to stay. The callous little master informs on the son, who then is captured and executed. His grief-stricken father, servility vanished, burns the mansion, trapping all occupants, to avenge his son's death. On the third day, the father is found dead on the road out of town, whether from suicide or a broken heart, we do not know. This hackneyed treatment of a tired subject did not arouse much notice.

Comedies

The year 1927 saw three major attempts at comedy: *Girl with a Hat Box*, *Mary Pickford's Kiss*, and *Mr. Lloyd's Voyage*. The first of these, Boris Barnet's *Girl with a Hat Box* was scripted by Valentin Turkin and Vadim Shershenevich and starred the pretty and popular Anna Sten (who later emigrated and failed to make it big in Hollywood) as Natasha and Vladimir Fogel (from the Kuleshov collective) as her "fictitious" husband. It is a slight but charming comedy of the annoyances of NEP life (they marry so he can get a room in overcrowded Moscow), and like Protazanov's *Tailor from Torzhok*, it attests to the popularity of the state lottery. After a series of silly adventures, *Girl with a Hat Box* ends happily with the young couple in love and the winners of 25,000 rubles to ensure their love will last. With the possible exception of the time-honored Russian institution of the "fictitious" marriage, which may have struck Western viewers as bizarre, there is nothing particularly Soviet about it.

The reviewer "Iakov Lev," who was probably *Soviet Screen*'s editor N. Iakovlev, found this a "typical" Mezhrabpom production which made even *Third Meshchanskaia Street* look admirable by comparison. Like all

Mezhrabpom films (in his view), it was well made and deliberately "neutral" in order to avoid political mistakes. Although Iakovlev asserted that the film was in "coarse taste" and not very funny, he nonetheless conciliatorily added that Barnet had done well enough with his modest aims, not being out, after all, "to discover America."[104] (This sudden softening may indicated that Iakovlev was torn between following the correct "line" and being fair to the modest little film.)

A much more amazing venture into Soviet comedy was *Mary Pickford's Kiss (Potselui Meri Pikford),* directed by Sergei Komarov (formerly of the Kuleshov collective) and written in collaboration with Vadim Shershenevich. The film is about the epidemic of movie-madness which had struck the USSR in the mid-twenties. It stars Igor Ilinskii as Goga Palkin, a theater ticket-taker in love with a girl who will reciprocate his affection only if he is famous. Goga happens in on a film studio where Mary Pickford and Douglas Fairbanks are visiting as part of their July 1926 tour of Moscow, and his antics lead to his being introduced to them as "the Soviet Harry Piel [the popular German actor]." As the cameras whir, Mary bestows a kiss on Goga, thus convincing his reluctant girlfriend and a horde of adoring females that he is a Valentino-style sex symbol. The joke is strained to a full six reels but, in general, *Mary Pickford's Kiss* very cleverly incorporates actual Fairbanks-Pickford footage shot during their trip to the USSR. The couple did not make this movie, nor did Pickford kiss Ilinskii at any time; *Mary Pickford's Kiss* is another demonstration of the powers of editing. Some scenes are actual newsreel clips recording the hysteria of the Muscovites seeing their idols in the flesh; others satirize this: screaming women tear Goga's clothes after he has been sanctified by The Kiss. Cameras are everywhere, even mounted on a telephone, and when Goga wipes The Kiss off, everybody faints. This clever little satire was undoubtedly popular, but immediately became an object of scorn and was named with monotonous regularity in lists of "decadent" films.[105]

The final comedy to be discussed here is Mikhail Verner's *Mr. Lloyd's Voyage,* which became synonymous with "commercialism" in cinema. Access to this film was denied, and it is difficult to determine the plot from the reviews. According to *Soviet Fiction Films (Sovetskie khudozhestvennye fil'my),* it was based on Dmitrii Smollin's play *Ivan Kozyr and Tatiana Russkikh.* The plot concerned a voyage to Russia and the triangle among the master of the vessel, Mr. Lloyd; Ivan Kozyr, a White-guardist secretly returning home; and Tatiana, a maid who had been living abroad with her employers.[106] Khrisanf Khersonskii lambasted it for its vulgarity and cardboard characters, for its "sadism and hysteria." He declared that it was another failure on the path to Soviet comedy, being a film *"without living people, without sincere gaiety, without irony, and without style."*[107] This was a mild review compared with later comments, and there was a plagiarism scandal concerning the movie which prompted a letter from eight Moscow directors: Boris Barnet, Vsevolod Pudovkin, Fedor Otsep, Leonid Obolenskii, Verner (the director of *Mr. Lloyd's Voyage*), Iurii Raizman, and Nikolai Okhlopkov, denouncing the "baiting" in the cinema press. (The editors of the offending *Cinema* responded that the press must maintain vigilance against such blatant philistinism in cinema.)[108]

Nonfiction Films

The nonfiction film had a new star in 1927, just when support for the genre was on the wane after the Dziga Vertov scandal discussed above. Film editor Esfir Shub pioneered a new kind of documentary, called "compilation" documentary because it is fashioned not from original material, but from material already shot. (One might have quipped that Dziga Vertov was also a compilation documentarist.) Shub was a gifted and experienced editor who had cut many important films (like Tarich's *Wings of a Serf*). She put her talents to good use in her own films, which she constructed from old newsreels and photographs.

Her first such effort, *The Fall of the Romanov Dynasty* (*Padenie dinastii romanovykh*), is her best, a splendid example of the compilation documentary. Although Shub's material has intrinsic pictorial interest, it is her eye and flair for drama that makes this film a work of art *and* an important historical document. The film is a panorama of Russian life before the Revolution, showing the landowners' wealth, rural poverty, court functions, Church processionals, the Constituent Assembly (*Duma*) in action, World War I, and the February Revolution. The contradictions and absurdities are there; the horror is there; the people are there: Nicholas II, Pavel Miliukov, Aleksandr Kerenskii, and V.I. Lenin. The titles and editing express the director's viewpoint, to be sure, but a good documentary need not be objective if it is honest and straightforward.

New Lef championed Shub and *The Fall of the Romanov Dynasty*. Osip Brik acclaimed it for its creativity, even seeing it as striking a heavy "blow" against the studio-made fiction film.[109] Lev Kuleshov and Mikhail Shneider also admired it, and *Soviet Cinema* reported that it was popular with the viewers and earning money.[110] *The Fall of the Romanov Dynasty* is the rare example of how interesting uncompromised realism could be.

Shub's tenth anniversary documentary *The Great Way* (*Velikii put'*) was not as successful, lacking the inherent drama of the decline of a world and a revolution in the making. *The Great Way* is a paean to Soviet power and development, much of it visually boring, with excessively long titles, several quoting from Communist International reports. Some shots are unconnected in time and space, a favorite technique of Dziga Vertov. Parts of *The Great*

Way are historically significant: the funerals of Lenin and the twenty-six Baku commissars and Trotskii leading the Red Army, for example. Parts are moving: the degradation of "former people" (déclassé elements) with desperate faces standing on the street selling their belongings, and children shivering in skimpy coats. But *The Great Way* is not of the same caliber as *The Fall of the Romanov Dynasty.*

Viktor Shklovskii commented on the inferior interest and pictorial poverty of this Soviet-shot material, as did Sergei Tretiakov.[111] (In this regard, one must remember that the film stock shortages in the early years of Soviet power were severe, and the newsreel was not a cinema priority after the Civil War.) P. A. Bliakhin reviewed it enthusiastically,[112] but it had to be counted as just another disappointing "jubilee" film.

The crisis in Soviet cinema deepened in 1927. As we have seen, the range of cinema debates was becoming increasingly narrow and repetitive due to the new emphasis on ideology and the bitterness of the rivalries within the industry. The coming of the "cultural revolution" was a particularly ominous portent, not only for Sovkino, as was fully to be expected, but also for ARK. ARK would not become a vociferously hard-line proletarian organization like the Russian Association of Proletarian Writers (RAPP) and so did not benefit even temporarily from the policy of class warfare on the cultural front. It only half-heartedly adopted a "proletarian" stance, thereby serving as a bridge between two cultural "lines."

But perhaps more than did anything else, the films of the season exemplified the pervasive malaise that accompanied the decline of revolutionary dreams. They were a dull lot, even the commissioned anniversary films (with the noteworthy exception of *The End of St. Petersburg*). Two of the best films of the year, *Third Meshchanskaia Street* and *Peasant Women of Riazan*, were trying to show contemporary life on the screen, but they were attacked for being "too" realistic and therefore bourgeois. The other "big" pictures, like *Poet and Tsar* and *The Decembrists,* were expensive and irrelevant. It was not only impossible to make a film that satisfied everybody; it was becoming more difficult to make a film which satisfied *anybody*. At this point there was definite disillusionment in the film world, and the future did not look more promising.

7

The Party Conference and the Attempt to Restructure (1928-29)

In a very real way, the First All-Union Party Conference on Cinema Affairs, held in March 1928, marked the end of an era. After it, the issues which had provoked genuine—if obstreperous—debate ossified into formulae. The conference was wide-ranging, covering many aspects of cinema (the minutes running to over 450 typeset pages), but in the main, the conference may be viewed as the climax of the attack on Sovkino. Two major speeches—one by the Party's representative, A. I. Krinitskii, the head of Agitprop, and the other by Sovkino's chairman, K. M. Shvedchikov—were followed by lengthy discussion, after which the original speaker was allowed time for rebuttal and summation.

Krinitskii's general line was that Sovkino was responsible for the fact that Soviet cinema was neither socially responsible nor on a sound financial basis. (He admitted, however, that cinema had not been supported by the Party and society up to this point.)[1] Krinitskii argued that cinema was inaccessible to the average viewer, both physically (in the sense of too few theaters) and thematically. Like S. M. Krylov in the preconference polemic *Cinema instead of Vodka*, Krinitskii noted that the state's income from vodka far outweighed that from cinema and that expenditures for entertainment were low priority in the worker/peasant budget. Krinitskii and his supporters came up with explanations for this lack of interest in cinema in addition to the fundamental one of its relative inaccessibility. One suggestion was that widespread illiteracy hampered the reception of cinema since most Soviet films were unintelligible without the intertitles; another, more curious, idea was that free screenings had lowered cinema's prestige in rural areas.[2]

An important part of the debate following Krinitskii's speech concerned the question of peasant films. The discord on this point revealed a serious rift *inside* the Commissariat of Enlightenment. V. N. Meshcheriakov, the Commissariat's deputy head, lashed out at Commissar Lunacharskii for "wavering" on the question of peasant films. S.M. Krylov also attacked the

Commissar for trying to find a mean between the "petty-bourgeois commercial line" and the "worker-peasant line."[3]

Aside from the issue of cinema for the masses, the question of commercial abuses, specifically relating to the cost of certain films, frequently came up in the rather free-wheeling discussion following Krinitskii's speech. Vladimir Kirshon pointed out that *The Decembrists* had cost 340,000 rubles, while Ermler's *The Parisian Cobbler* (to be discussed), a film of far more value to society, had cost only 40,000.[4] Sovkino was further charged with poor distribution politics for not promoting Eisenstein's *Strike* and *Potemkin* properly.[5] Sovkino's import and export policies were also attacked. Import policy had of course been a longstanding grievance, but it was now stressed that Sovkino pushed the export of the wrong kind of Soviet film.[6]

Sovkino's Shvedchikov and Trainin were then allowed to rebut Krinitskii's speech and the many hostile remarks which had followed. Just as the critics offered nothing new, so were Trainin's arguments all too familiar. He once again blamed unreasonably high expectations for the furor and cited extreme financial difficulties, coupled with confusion over the censorship, as the explanation for Sovkino's inability to satisfy social requirements. Trainin repudiated the campaign to make the script the organizational basis of cinema, pointing out that good scripts do not good directors make, and that many heavily criticized movies like *Mr. Lloyd's Voyage*, *The Road to Damascus*, and *Your Acquaintance* had in fact been written by Party members.[7] In contrast to Trainin, Shvedchikov was vapid and conciliatory, protesting that Sovkino had good intentions but needed practical advice, money, and better-trained cadres in order to improve its performance and meet the expectations of society.[8]

Krinitskii, in his closing remarks, admitted that Party members had indeed been involved in ideologically questionable cinema projects. He also agreed that the masses enjoyed such unacceptable films. But because of this, sound organization and a responsible economic policy were all the more important[9]—a clear rebuff to Trainin's pragmatism. Now it was Shvedchikov's turn, and he, not surprisingly, concentrated on the economic problems of Soviet cinema. Shvedchikov claimed that Sovkino had not benefitted financially in 1926 when it absorbed Sevzapkino, Proletkino, and Goskino, for whatever capital these organizations had possessed had already been dissipated. He asserted that Soviet films were expensive to produce in comparison with those in the West, operating as Soviet producers were under a twin burden of unusually stiff taxes and complete reliance on imported material. The censorship further hampered both the production of Soviet films and Sovkino's import policy, and Shvedchikov implied that it was getting more stringent. His only concrete suggestion was to recommend the formation of a joint-stock company to solve the problem of insufficient capital.[10]

Shvedchikov's speech provoked a flurry of complaints, most of which can be divided into two groups—economic and ideological. On the economic side, comments were directed against the cottage industry (*kustar'*) nature of film production (the terminology was a holdover from the 1926 "regime of economy" campaign); the high cost of certain films (including Eisenstein's *October*); the predominance of foreign films (even in workers' clubs), which represented a drain on hard currency; Sovkino's export policies; the failure of cinefication; poor conditions in proletarian theaters; and the problem of unemployment among film cadres.[11] On the ideological side, there were the familiar allegations that in Sovkino's production plans, "bourgeois" films took precedence over those that were truly Soviet.[12] Shvedchikov's summary was weak,[13] and it is clear that Trainin and others usually spoke for Sovkino because Shvedchikov was not a gifted polemicist. In any case, the conference was so blatantly stacked against Sovkino that no amount of brilliant rhetoric could have saved it.

Although Krinitskii's and Shvedchikov's speeches represented the major part of the conference, two secondary addresses indicated future trends in cinema polemics. One, by K. A. Maltsev of the Society of Friends of Soviet Cinema (ODSK), called for the liquidation of ARK for having become an alleged tool of the proletarian writers group, VAPP.[14] This was followed by a sharp exchange between Maltsev and the VAPPist Vladimir Kirshon. Kirshon charged that Maltsev's talk of liquidating ARK was tantamount to rejecting the ideal of revolutionary cinematography. Maltsev, however, was not intimidated and asserted that since ARK had never wanted to be a "section" of VAPP, its liquidation would be for the best.[15] We have seen evidence of VAPP's "designs" on ARK as early as 1925 (in the pages of the long-defunct *Cinema Week*), and it is true that VAPPists like Kirshon and Solskii were active in ARK in particular and in cinema affairs in general. But one cannot support Maltsev's contention of a VAPP takeover of ARK on the basis of available sources. ARK drew closer to VAPP (in its RAPP guise) but never adopted its proletarian ideology.

The second address, by N. I. Smirnov, concerned an area which would be important through the rest of 1928: the press and film criticism. Major changes were taking place. ARK's journal *Cinema Front* and Glavpolitprosvet's *Soviet Cinema* had been liquidated, yet another indication of the weakened position of these two organizations. The newspaper *Cinema* had become an organ of ODSK. *Soviet Screen* was attacked for not devoting enough attention to the problems of the countryside. The theater/cinema publishing company Teakinopechat' was accused of printing too many popular biographies of film stars, particularly Western ones. Finally, Smirnov charged that the cadre of film critics was insufficiently communist, only two of thirty-three being Party members.[16]

The resolutions adopted at the end of the conference were in sharp contrast to its rambling and often obscure debates. Despite the fact that organizational wrangling had been behind most of the disputes brought to the floor, there was no mention of Sovkino and only one (unfavorable) reference to the Commissariat of Enlightenment in the resolutions. Given as reasons for the alleged failure of Soviet cinema were: insufficient political leadership both from the studio administrations *and* from the Party; poorly prepared cadres; foreign dependence; the extreme penury which had led to a preoccupation with business matters (instead of ideology); and the purported alienation of films and filmworkers from the masses.

Since cinema was slated to become an important propaganda weapon in the cultural revolution's struggle with the bourgeoisie, these weaknesses had to be overcome. Cinema during the cultural revolution was to be primarily fictional (although more support was promised the educational film), contemporary, and in a form easily "understood by the millions." But who would make these desired films?

Politically reliable cadres were necessary but lacking, since petty-bourgeois infiltration of the cultural front had been especially successful. Cinema therefore was exhorted to follow the example of literature and "proletarianize" by establishing closer ties with proletarian writers and with the masses, thus ending its elitist isolationism.

These primarily ideological concerns did not mean, however, that the economic difficulties of Soviet cinema could be ignored, and especially not if cinema revenues were to replace those from the vodka monopoly. The perpetual financial bind could be overcome, according to the conference's resolutions, through the "forced development" of the distribution network, the increase of exports, the curtailing of imports, and the end of the harmful notion that there was a contradiction between ideology and commerce. Furthermore, Soviet cinema had to become a true *industry* and manufacture its own equipment.[17]

Thus concluded the Party conference on cinema. Its end also marked the end of the debate over Sovkino. Although Sovkino would not be reorganized into Soiuzkino until 1930, this was a foregone conclusion, and after the conference, the emphasis in cinema polemics was markedly on the social and political characteristics of films, not organizational issues. What is more interesting than the substance of the conference (which was quite predictable, given the events of 1927) was the *tone.* Discussions were more often than not oblique; gone were the specific and hard-hitting accusations of the past—replaced by a jargon, which though frequently abusive, bore little relation to reality. This was the style of Soviet film criticism from this point on.

The film community had gotten what it thought it wanted—Sovkino's power was destroyed. The attention of the Party and "society" was at last turned to cinema affairs, but the Party's sudden solicitousness turned out to be not quite what cinema activists had bargained for. The cultural revolution had begun in earnest.

After the Conference

To a slight degree, the immediate postconference period saw a continuation of previous concerns. Not long after the conference, S. Kosior wrote an article for *Revolution and Culture* (*Revoliutsiia i kul'tura*) which summarized and reinforced the conference's resolutions, indicating that the economic problems of the film industry were still at least as important as ideological ones. He noted that while Sovkino had been irrevocably condemned, it was nonetheless necessary to remember that cinema was:

> not only a tool of cultural and political influence of the proletarian government on the masses, but together with this, a mighty and important state commercial enterprise. A purely cultural approach to cinema would be incorrect.

Cinema should not only be profitable, according to Kosior, it should be profitable enough to allow the government to cease the production of vodka. Important in this process would be the increasing film distribution network, especially in the countryside, and the strengthening of cinema cadres. Most critical, cinema equipment, especially film stock, had to be Soviet-made; this by itself would greatly ease fiscal problems.[18]

Concern was also expressed in *Soviet Screen* that as a result of the conference's lambasting Sovkino's "commercial deviation," economizing in cinema production would be considered irrelevant. On the contrary, insisted an editorial, this was not a "vulgar" question, for: "As yet, we do not have such unrestricted means that we might not interest ourselves in how much this or that picture costs." Expensive costumes, sets, and props were an easy-to-spot source of fiscal abuse, the article went on, but more or less ignored thus far were the cost overruns caused by the well-publicized inability of Soviet directors to keep to a production schedule. The disorganization of directors wreaked havoc on production plans; lost time was expensive, and films were always late. It was estimated that cinema production could be increased by 20 to 30 percent, if schedules were adhered to more closely.[19] As another facet of the push for greater economy, *Soviet Screen* approved the drastic restriction of foreign films that had been proposed at the conference. In answer to one reader's question about the absence of Chaplin movies on the Soviet screen, its editors solemnly reminded him of the hard currency needed to buy good foreign films. Viewers had to be prepared to make personal sacrifices (such as going without Chaplin) for their country's welfare.[20]

Although "commercialism" per se was thus not totally condemned, the aftermath of the conference revealed how thoroughly Sovkino and its policies had been defeated. One vivid indication was the purge of objectionable films from distribution, precisely those films which were the foundation of Sovkino's profit plans. The first notice of the purge appeared in May 1928, when the theatrical censorship organ, Glavrepertkom, removed eighteen films from distribution. Five of these were Soviet, the best known being the "Eastern" films *Minaret of Death* and *Eyes of Andozia* (*Glaza Andozii*) and also Isaak Babel's *The Planets* (*Bluzhdaiushchie zvezdy*). *Cinema* wrote:

> The pictures have been taken from the screen because they idealize the pathological and decadent mood of the decaying bourgeoisie; popularize covert prostitution and debauchery, the romance of naked stunts [*triukizm*] and criminal activity; lead to the propagation of bourgeois morals and mysticism.[21]

The network of Red Army clubs also purged their film library of those movies which were allegedly old-fashioned in content and technically backward. These included: *Commander Ivanov, The Extraordinary Adventures of Mr. West in the Land of the Bolsheviks, Mr. Lloyd's Voyage, His Highness's Female Soloist, Road to Damascus,* and *Eyes of Andozia,* among others.[22]

But the major "trash" removal occurred in November 1928. As reported in *Cinema,* about 300 foreign and twenty-six Soviet pictures were pulled from distribution, including all pictures of the ever popular German star Harry Piel. Concern was expressed in *Cinema* that some dark and "deaf" corners of the Soviet Union might have escaped the inquisition.[23]

This was a gloomy time for Sovkino. In July 1928 it held hearings on its proposed production plan for 1928-29; the meeting was well attended by watchdogs with unfamiliar names.[24] This plan (at least as it was published) was a depressing document which proved how absolutely Sovkino had been forced to capitulate. The plan announced that since Sovkino was now working according to the dictates of the Party conference, films would be about "new socialist social relations, the struggle against survivals of the past, the enlightenment of the masses, economic and political problems, achievements of culture, class illumination of history, the organization of leisure," and other such lively topics. Sovkino pleaded guilty to not having properly reflected international, domestic, political-economic, and anti-religious themes in its previous plans. Sovkino also promised to purge incompetent directors and support younger ones, to educate cadres, and to prepare better scripts.[25]

The State of Film Criticism

As indicated in chapter 5, the attack against Sovkino and Mezhrabpom and specific films of their production had dominated cinema polemics for about a year. Now a period of enforced "self-criticism" began, and the evaluation of Soviet film criticism and the cinema press became a central issue, a searching examination of critics preceding the actual use of the term "self-criticism" (*samokritika*).

Some of the first attacks against Soviet film critics came during the course of a survey of cinema workers on literature and cinema, organized by the proletarian writers' journal *On Literary Guard*. Soviet film critics had won many enemies, and it is interesting that *cameramen* were especially caustic in these interviews. The dean of Soviet cameramen, A. A. Levitskii, saw Soviet film criticism dominated by egotistical literati who "... criticize everything and everyone." Eisenstein's cinematographer, Eduard Tisse, wrote in his turn that most film critics knew nothing about cinema.[26]

A major article by R. Pikel on Soviet film criticism appeared in *Revolution and Culture*. Pikel believed that up to this point cinema discussion had been too exclusively economic in its focus, because "on the cinema front, we have very nearly no Marxist criticism." The absence of absolute standards for film criticism had led to a glowing review of the "trite and philistine picture" *Mary Pickford's Kiss* in *Worker's Gazette*, praise which was widely echoed in the general press.

To Pikel, cinema critics had definitely shunned their responsibilities to society. As an example, they had failed to fight the influence of Harry Piel, whom Pikel characterized as a "fashionable adulterer" whose films were a combination of "criminal wiliness, idealization of banditry, and an apotheosis of apacheism [*apashestvo*]." ARK had also demonstrated its "tailism" in its support of *Third Meshchanskaia Street* as had *Soviet Screen* in its "little noise" (*shumik*) over Vertov's *One-Sixth of the World*, a film of "doubtful" social value. Pikel allowed criticism its creative side, but among cinema critics he found many "accidental people," who were renegades from other, more legitimate types of literary work. Pikel asserted that cinema was like the Klondike Gold Rush (a veiled reference to Kuleshov's infamous *By the Law*) in the unsavory types it attracted. Though not always as colorfully, the cinema press came under frequent attacks of this type for allegedly serving the interests of the petty-bourgeoisie.[27]

The second major exposition of the state of Soviet film criticism was a report to ARK by VAPP dramatist Vladimir Kirshon. Kirshon believed the quality of film criticism was much lower than that of literary criticism. Because cinema critics had to protect their mass audience from the effects of "anti-proletarian" ideology in films, it was therefore essential to raise the level of criticism. Kirshon thought the reviews in the non-cinema press, although lacking in artistic merit, were "much more useful" than the reviews of "professional specialists." (His apparently contradictory call at the beginning of the article for *more* specialists seemed not to worry him.)

Kirshon was particularly critical of *Soviet Screen* for earning money from advertisements for suspect movies and for lavishing attention on foreign film stars. Kirshon charged that 75 percent of the so-called reviews in *Soviet Screen* were in fact "advertisements" and darkly alluded to those dangerous (but mercifully unnamed) reviewers who cloaked their "banal" thoughts in revolutionary garb. (*Soviet Screen* was indeed the Soviet film journal which had most resembled a "pulp" movie magazine until about this time, when its tone changed and it became concerned with educational films.)

Kirshon dismissed the newspaper *Cinema* as being characterless—which meant that it had managed thus far to preserve its catholicity. He also attacked the cinema publishing company Teakinopechat' for its production of "light" literature like biographies of Western film stars. According to Kirshon, Teakinopechat' had tried to defend itself by citing financial considerations, but he sternly admonished that " ... it is impossible to trade in ideology." Kirshon suggested that film criticism needed the guidance of the Party and that the cadres of film reviewers should be improved by collective rather than individual reviewing.[28]

Cinema devoted much attention to the state of film criticism. One editorial urged that cinema critics begin writing in simple language for the *viewer*, not for other critics. If audiences were educated to like the proper films, cinema could find its way out of its "blind alley" (*tupik*). *Cinema* noted that ARK was studying ways to increase attention given to cinema in the general press, and that the Association of Theater-Cinema-Music Critics was worried about the formalist "deviation" in cinema epitomized by *The Poetics of Cinema*[29] (an important collection of essays edited by the formalist critic Boris Eikhenbaum, to be discussed in the next chapter).

Although there was scattered resistance to the increasingly harsh tone of Soviet film criticism,[30] the climate of opinion was in favor of biting self-criticism. By May 1928, *Cinema* urged that the cinema community join the society-wide orgy of self-criticism. Sovkino had apparently written to *Cinema*'s editors asking them to cool their attacks, which prompted a sharp response:

> This fear of criticism, this fear of public-mindedness, seems to us to indicate how Sovkino workers understood and learned nothing, either from the conclusions of the Party conference or from the latest decision of the Party Central Committee on the question of self-criticism.[31]

Later articles in 1928 reaffirmed *Cinema*'s dedication (in theory) to the principles of self-criticism.[32]

The involvement of the cinema community in the nationwide self-criticism campaign was inevitable, for the time had passed when any segment of society could remain unaware of, and isolated from, politics. *Cinema* at least retained a sense of humor. A wry cartoon entitled "Self-criticism" ("Samokritika") had three frames: a man impaled on his own pen, another cutting himself with scissors, a third under a microscope.[33]

Still, all said, the cinema press was loath to criticize itself, and the self-criticism campaign did not have much vigor. The single exception was the shadowy affair of Teakinopechat', the cinema publishing house. Sniping against the books it printed continued—it was accused of producing "anti-Soviet hobby horses and Soviet cabbage."[34] But the behind-the-scenes action must have been much more serious than these seemingly minor jibes, for in April 1929, V. P. Uspenskii, editor-in-chief of *Soviet Screen* (replacing N. Iakovlev) and the recently ousted head of Teakinopechat', committed suicide, the first politically connected suicide in the film industry. (Actor Vladimir Fogel's suicide two months later followed a long struggle with depression and was unconnected with this affair.)

Uspenskii's obituaries in both *Cinema* and his own journal *Soviet Screen* were remarkably similar. He was seen as an individualist "of great personal strength in the petty-bourgeois sense of the word." The drive and initiative that had been useful to him in the days of the Revolution—Uspenskii was an "Old Bolshevik"—now were a definite liability. It was clearly implied that his death was *beneficial* both to himself and to society, an extraordinarily revealing statement about the harshness of the times.[35] (But one should keep in mind in view of future developments that his loyalty to the regime and good faith in his policies were not questioned.)

Almost immediately following Uspenskii's suicide, *Soviet Screen* changed its format to a stridently political line fervently devoted to the educational film.[36] This did not prevent it from being abruptly reorganized in November 1929 as *Cinema and Life* (*Kino i zhizn'*), with a change of personnel so sweeping that it amounted to a purge. The official purge of Teakinopechat', which had published *Soviet Screen*, was not announced until the beginning of 1930 and continued at least through mid-year. The reasons given for the purge were "commercial deviation" and the wasting of paper on harmful material,[37] but like so much in these years, the true story must remain a mystery until relevant sources are made more freely available.

The Cadres

Film critics and the press were not the only objects of scrutiny in the postconference period. Due to the resolution on the importance of training new cadres (which was, not coincidentally, a key element in the society-wide cultural revolution), there was now a stronger interest in the personnel question than at any time since the early part of the decade. At first, this concern seemed directed at answering real problems dealing not only with creative workers, but also with technical personnel like projectionists. (In addition to short film life from mishandling, some serious theater fires had also been attributed to unqualified projectionists.)[38] GTK, the State Cinema Technical Institute, at last received long-needed attention. The Society of Friends of Soviet Cinema (ODSK) reported in August 1928 that GTK was hampered by lack of material or moral support from either Sovkino or the Commissariat of Enlightenment. Its teaching staff was weak; its graduates unemployable. Ignoring the Party conference's resolution on the necessity of training new cadres, Sovkino still refused to extend cooperation to the school.

Despite the lip service paid to training, the sudden interest in "cadres" was in actuality a front for the purge of the film industry. The truth of this became evident in the debate about the social composition of GTK. One speaker at an ARK discussion on the subject said the student body was not "proletarian" enough, although another pointed out that its political composition was 45 percent Party/Komsomol, an unusually large percentage. (We may therefore infer that the Party members at GTK were *not* of proletarian background.) Sovkino's Shvedchikov was allegedly balking at shouldering more of the financial burden of GTK, because he disagreed with the principle of using social origin as an entrance criterion for GTK (one of the hallmarks of the cultural revolution). Reorganization and additional funds (400,000 rubles) were urged.[39] In September 1928, a note in *Cinema* referred to a purge of seventy students from GTK, so that its social composition was now 49 percent workers and peasants but still 45 percent Party/Komsomol.[40] Shortly thereafter, an article appeared which criticized the Party composition of the first-year students; out of eighty-two, only four were Party/Komsomol, which may indicate that Party/Komsomol membership was inversely proportional to worker/peasant origin.[41]

The demand for new cadres was bolstered by a new and unsavory scandal in the cinema community: the charge of widespread nepotism in the studios. At first this mainly involved actors (although some wondered what qualifications Lili Brik had for co-directing *The Glass Eye* [*Stekliannyi glaz*] other than being critic Osip Brik's wife).[42] It was asserted that under the guise of "typage"—the use of nonprofessional "types" which Eisenstein had popularized but which was used in some degree by many Soviet directors—friends and relatives of the director were being cast. The Art Workers' Union central mediation (Tsentroposredrabis) conducted an investigation of Boris Barnet's *The House on Trubnaia Square* (*Dom na Trubnoi*) and removed all actors who were not "qualified."[43] Nepotism roused particularly strong reactions because unemployment among cinema actors was considered severe, about 300 being registered on the jobless rolls.[44]

The question of "nepotism" or "protectionism" in the hiring of cinema actors and other personnel revealed a definite rift between Moscow and Leningrad film directors. The Leningrad cinema community maintained a degree of artistic independence that became quite marked by 1930 (not that it was so great in absolute terms, but that Moscow had sunk so low). The first indication of antagonism on the part of Leningraders to trends in Moscow came when some Leningrad directors published an "open letter" on the subject of film actors in the Leningrad newspaper *Cinema.*

The letter allegedly denigrated the importance of the professional cinema actor, but from the abridged version published in Moscow *Cinema* (there was *no* connection between the two papers), I surmise that it really took issue with the definition of "qualified" and who determined it. It said that the majority of people the Art Workers' Union (Rabis) considered "qualified" were in actuality "technically illiterate" and "significantly harder to work with than someone just off the street." Among those signing were Aleksandr Ivanovskii (*Stepan Khalturin, The Decembrists*), Grigorii Kozintsev and Leonid Trauberg (*The Overcoat, S.V.D.*), P. P. Petrov-Bytov, Adrian Piotrovskii (the critic and scenarist who was artistic head of the Leningrad studio), the prerevolutionary director Cheslav Sabinskii, S. A. Timoshenko (author of *The Art of the Cinema: Film Editing*), Evgenii Cherviakov (*Poet and Tsar*), and Fridrikh Ermler (*Katka the Apple Seller*).[45] All the directors in the group employed professional actors; some of them even used actors in a traditional way.

In Moscow, director Abram Room was the lone defender of the statement, but only insofar as it protested the charges of "nepotism" and "protectionism" as being thinly disguised harassment of directors.[46] *Cinema* continued its attack but admitted that the Leningrad directors were right in saying that there was confusion over how a "qualified" actor was defined. For example, Moscow Rabis did not consider theater actors "qualified" to work in the movies and could charge a director with "protectionism" for using them.[47]

ARK held a meeting to discuss the letter. Abram Room continued to defend it reservedly, but others indulged in an orgy of hyperbole, calling it "anti-social," "reactionary," "harmful," "against the conference." ARK resolved that the Leningrad directors did not have enough information to support their position. Qualified film actors had been important in the development of Soviet cinema, it said, and "unarguably" there had been protectionism and nepotism on the part of directors. This could be overcome only by increasing the qualifications of cinema workers through the "liquidation" of private cinema schools and training courses (I cannot say how widespread this private element was unless it referred to the "collectives" of directors like Kuleshov and Kozintsev and Trauberg) and through improved self-criticism.[48]

Following the affair of the Leningrad directors, there was a "social court" on the related question of "typage," the use of nonprofessional "actors" in cinema. The concept was roundly condemned. What is clear, however, was that the controversy over typage was a mere excuse for a continuation of the insidious effort to erode the authority of the director in the filmmaking process. An Art Workers' Union mediator (Posredrabis) said that typage had arisen from the director's inability to work with the actor. Therefore, directors who persisted in defending—and "fetishizing"—typage were acting in their own self-interest. Valentin Turkin proposed that the so-called actors' crisis be recognized for what it was: a *directors'* crisis.

Another way to interpret the controversy over typage would be as part of the persistent campaign to put the hero (and therefore the actor) back into cinema. At the "court" one speaker said that only a "literate film actor" could bring the "living person to the screen."[49] To a certain extent this is a valid point, but the fact is that the letter of the Leningrad directors and the struggle against "nepotism" in cinema marked the beginning of open season on directors, rather than a constructive attempt to better the lot of actors.[50] The debate over the actor and the scenario had always contained an element of resentment against the power of the director, which at this time became pronounced.

For this reason, the position of the script writer vis-à-vis the director was now as vital as that of the actor. RAPP (the Russian Association of Proletarian Writers, VAPP's new name) vigorously promoted the scenarist's importance so that, as a writers' organization, it could wield more influence in ARK. V. Sutyrin, in *On Literary Guard*, bluntly stated that since the writer was the author of the film, directors should not be allowed to tamper with the screenplay.[51] As long as directorial hegemony held sway, said Sutyrin, the "scenario crisis" would persist. In other words the "scenario crisis," like the actors' crisis, was really a *directors'* crisis.

Sutyrin was writing in direct rebuttal to S. A. Timoshenko's latest book, *What the Cinema Director Should Know* (*Chto dolzhen znat' kino-rezhisser*). What the cinema director should know, according to Timoshenko, was how to protect his position against the "pretensions" of the scenarist to control the script.[52] Of course, as we have seen, the putative "dictatorship of the director" was not the only reason for writers' reluctance to work in cinema.[53] The censorship was another unwelcome taskmaster; Khrisanf Khersonskii said that "a fact long well-known to all [is] that writers should write two scenarios, one for GRK [Glavrepertkom] and the other for the director."[54] So while the director was by no means a complete villain,[55] for political reasons having to do with the power struggle within the industry, it was expedient to exaggerate his authority and influence in order to have a scapegoat for the ills of Soviet cinema.

Soviet Cinema in Crisis

By the end of 1928, one can observe the beginnings of an articulated "crisis theory" of Soviet cinema. Ippolit Sokolov led off with an article in *Cinema* entitled "The Reasons for the Latest Failures" ("Prichiny poslednikh neudach"). The "reasons" however could be reduced to one: experimentalism. Sokolov singled out Viktor Shklovskii as a proponent of the "leftist infantile sickness" of innovation, and wrote: "We need genuine mastery, but not naive, so-called 'inventiveness'...." Because of filmmakers like Shklovskii (and director Tarich, for Sokolov was attacking their new movie *The Captain's Daughter*), Soviet cinema was characterized by films which were like "prison sentences" to watch.[56] Since access to see *The Captain's Daughter* was forbidden, I cannot say whether it may be judged experimental, but two other films that Sokolov condemned in this article which I did see, Boris Barnet's *The House on Trubnaia Square* and Protazanov's *The White Eagle (Belyi orel)*, were definitely not.

G. Lenobl responded sharply and courageously to Sokolov by writing that progress in cinema was impossible without experimentation, and that artists, like everyone else, have the right to make mistakes.[57] Although this was the only published indication that anyone perceived the danger inherent in Sokolov's view, others were offended by his definition of the "crisis." Arsen believed that while there *was* a crisis, its cause was that technical mastery had outstripped the maturation of thematic content.[58] In an ARRK debate (in September 1928 the Association of Revolutionary Cinematography became the Association of *Workers* of Revolutionary Cinematography), P. A. Bliakhin of the censorship organ, Glavrepertkom, claimed that the production schedule was too taxing for the abilities and training of the cadres, thus fueling the crisis. The Sovkino-ites (*Sovkinovtsy*) Rafes, Trainin, and Grinfeld preferred to label the situation not a crisis but "growing pains."[59]

The Offensive Resumed

The future was uncertain. That changes were in the offing was clear, but what would the new path be like? The acted fiction film was to be the basis for Soviet film production, yet both "experimental" and "bourgeois" feature films had been rejected. What was left? The themes proposed in Sovkino's production plan were subjects better treated in nonfiction, nonacted films; Sergei Tretiakov thought so, too.[60] This contradiction was inconvenient to resolve and so was ignored. Although there *was* some new interest in the educational film (*kul'turfil'm*),[61] the nonacted feature film had had its reputation hopelessly tarnished by its connection with artistic leftists like Dziga Vertov, Sergei Tretiakov, and the Lef group.

Boris Barnet

Could the apparently irreconcilable be reconciled? If cinema had to concern itself with prosaic economic subjects, especially industrialization, did this mean it must become mired in mere *facts*? As N. Lukhmanov noted in *Soviet Screen*, the ideal was to show life, not as it is, but as it "should be."[62] Ideology, not the "recording of facts" that Tretiakov supported, was to be the philosophical underpinning of the new "realism." K. Iukov, ARRK's chairman, wrote at the end of 1928 that cinema was at last *"recognized as the most essential and most important means of artistic propaganda in the hands of the Party."*[63]

The year 1928 had indeed marked a watershed in Soviet cinema history. Sovkino was brought to heel, and although occasional signs of life were apparent in those quarters, the organization seemed humbled, turning out production plans for countless dull films. But by 1929, the corpse had revived.

Although Sovkino did engage in a little self-criticism in 1929,[64] it preferred to find a new scapegoat. This time it was not the economic situation—which clearly would have been impolitic in the midst of the industrialization campaign—but "insufficiently cultured" cinema workers (or in Trainin's version, "accidental" directors) who were to blame.[65] In other ways, too, Sovkino began to reassert itself. It claimed to be interested in fulfilling the Party's demands to find the "new heroes, the new romantics" of the times, but it stubbornly resisted the demand for more educational films as being detrimental to the industry's profit margin.[66] Sovkino's M. P. Efremov actually managed to get an article printed in *Cinema and Culture* (*Kino i kul'tura*, a short-lived new journal) which "proved" that Sovkino had increased the rural cinema network. (The editors appended a disclaimer.)[67]

Immediately after the Party conference, criticism against Sovkino had abated, and polemical energy was directed toward other quarters, notably against the press and the power of critics and directors. By 1929, however, Sovkino found itself once again under fire. It was criticized for its 4 million-ruble deficit in particular[68] and for its economic policy in general. How could Sovkino win, condemned as it was for being too concerned with the "fat purse" on the one hand, and for not making enough money on the other![69]

Sovkino was now attacked not only for the films it did make, but also for the films it did not make. The Cinema-Radio Section of the new arts administration in the Commissariat of Enlightenment (Glaviskusstvo, of which Glavrepertkom became another section), rejected 50 percent of Sovkino's proposed scripts, resulting in a sharp decline in production. Glaviskusstvo also charged that Sovkino had fulfilled less than half its production plan.[70] In answer, Rafes, the head of Sovkino's artistic department, demanded some guidelines from the censorship,[71] since the decrease in production could be attributed to fears engendered by the "unhealthy" atmosphere.[72] The decline in production continued as Rafes had warned it would. It was a fearsome time to try to second-guess the capricious censorship. A movie that was acceptable one day might end a career the next.

The continuation of the attack against ARK is not as easy to trace as that against Sovkino, since ARK had been effectively muzzled through the loss of its journal *Cinema Front*. ARK's liquidation had been called for at the cinema conference in March 1928, so its sudden name change to Association of Workers of Revolutionary Cinematography must be regarded as another sign of its own state of siege. By 1929, in the brief lull between the self-criticism campaign and the purges, this had become apparent. ARRK was in serious trouble and began to construct a haphazard line of defense.

To begin, ARRK outlined its past accomplishments to the Photo-Cinema Section of Rabis, the Art Workers' Union—a clear-cut political rationalization which did not reflect ARK's one great achievement: offering a forum for meaningful debate on cinema issues. The statement included instead: fighting the "reactionary" Union of Cinema Activists (the only time I saw mention of such a union) in 1924-25; "carrying out the initiatives" of ODSK in 1925-26 (in connection with cinefication?); preparing for the Party conference; and re-establishing itself as an independent organization in 1928-29 (the first indication that ARRK was no longer part of ODSK).[73]

ARRK had always been plagued by its lack of a platform. The implication of the organization's name change, which added the very important word "workers," was that ARRK was now to function as a labor union. It was easy to criticize ARRK on these grounds,[74] because its membership was not drawn from rank-and-file cinema workers but from artists, critics, and administrators, making it a professional society instead. Furthermore, ARRK's uneasy existence was complicated by the now marked infiltration from RAPP.[75] Its fate therefore became linked to a certain extent with RAPP's, and in the middle of the purges of 1930, ARRK and RAPP issued a joint communique urging a more thorough look at the "alien" elements in ARRK.[76]

The Commissariat of Enlightenment's authority in cinema affairs had also been challenged at the conference, even from one of its sectors, Glavpolitprosvet. The disappearance of *Soviet Cinema* makes the course of the Commissariat in cinema affairs (up to its abolition in 1929) almost impossible to reconstruct; familiar names like Katsigras and Meshcheriakov left the scene at this time. Although Commissar Lunacharskii was himself directly attacked at the conference, this was more an indication of the Commissariat's losing battle on a much higher political level than a rejection of Lunacharskii's own views on cinema, since he favored the traditional narratives coming into vogue.

The upshot was that independents and iconoclasts everywhere were being subdued. Yet one symbol of independence remained—the production company Mezhrabpom Rus'; its durability may perhaps have been ensured by its foreign backers, the International Workers' Aid. As we have seen, Mezhrabpom had been a symbol of the "bourgeois export film" ever since *Aelita* (1924), even though it had also produced Pudovkin's immortal *Mother*. In 1926, when Goskino, Proletkino, and Sevzapkino were transferred to Sovkino, Mezhrabpom had absorbed the private studio Rus', a prerevolutionary survival, to become "Mezhrabpom Rus'." Attacks against Mezhrabpom Rus' had been steady in the ensuing two years,[77] but at the Party conference, it was scarcely mentioned. Was this because all energy was concentrated on Sovkino, or because Mezhrabpom still had an untouchable power base?

Whatever the answer (and available sources are insufficient for resolution of this question), by September 1928 (just as ARK became ARRK), Mezhrabpom's protected status had changed, along with the company's name. The studio was now Mezhrabpom-fil'm, since the "Rus'" was seen as an alien prerevolutionary survival of " 'private' initiative." The elimination of "Rus' " meant that "private capital" had been "destroyed" (which we may assume signifies an "appropriation").[78] K. I. Shutko wrote that while Mezhrabpom-fil'm should maintain its ties with the international workers' movement (and presumably, with its capital), it needed to become "100 percent Soviet."[79] This "reorganization" was apparently not unsuccessful, for as early as December 1928, Mezhrabpom-fil'm was accused in *Cinema* of standing "between workers and film," of being "politically illiterate," and of causing "the crisis in cinematography."[80] This final bastion of independence was under siege.

In 1929, *Soviet Screen* singled out Mezhrabpom for its "vulgar" artistic standards (as exemplified by *Miss Mend* and *The White Eagle*) and for not having a "revolutionary face."[81] Mezhrabpom's chairman, B. Malkin, made an excellent, if unheeded, response to the many attacks. Why, he queried, did Mezhrabpom's bad films constitute their so-called "line," and not their good ones, like Pudovkin's *Mother* or *The End of St. Petersburg* and Protazanov's *The Forty-first* and *Don Diego and Pelageia*? Malkin said he was open to constructive criticism, but not to demagoguery. *Cinema*'s editors responded that Mezhrabpom's productions endangered Soviet cinema even more than the "dullness" of Sovkino's, citing Protazanov's *The White Eagle* and Kuleshov's suppressed *The Gay Canary* (*Veselaia kanareika*) as examples.[82] But despite all this, Mezhrabpom managed to avoid dissolution until 1936.

The Films

Considering the obsession of film critics with self-criticism or the search for scapegoats as a substitute for self-criticism in this period up to the purges of June 1929, it is not surprising that comparatively little attention was paid to new films. There was no cause-célèbre, either in a positive or negative sense.

The great Ukrainian director Aleksandr Dovzhenko made his late-blooming appearance with his first major work, *Zvenigora*, but that notable exception aside, the movies were the products of familiar names like Eisenstein, Pudovkin, Protazanov, Ermler, and Vertov.

Revolutionary Films

Eisenstein's troubled tenth-anniversary film *October* finally made its debut in March 1928. *Potemkin* and *October* are Eisenstein's best known silent films, and much has been written about the latter, both by its director and by others.[83] In many ways, it is the most fully conceived and executed example of Eisenstein's "intellectual montage," in that through juxtaposition of objects and shots, he hoped to express ideas on, and pass judgments about, Kerenskii and the Provisional Government in a film language.

October is much more contrived and heavy-handed than *Potemkin*. Although some of its scenes are among the most brilliant in Eisenstein's oeuvre, such as that of the girl and the dead horse slowly falling off the drawbridge,[84] *October* lacks the rhythm and dramatic intensity that make *Potemkin* a masterpiece. *October* (based on John Reed's *Ten Days That Shook the World*) was intended to be a filmed recreation of the Bolshevik coup in Petrograd, on the same order as Boris Barnet's unsuccessful *Moscow in October*. The restrictions of filmed history are very severe; in the hands of a moderately capable director like Barnet, these limitations proved disastrous. Eisenstein, however, produced an arresting, though erratic, film.[85]

A major flaw is that unlike *Potemkin*, *October* lacks human interest. The most developed character (or caricature, depending on one's point of view) is Aleksandr Kerenskii (N. Popov), whose mannerisms are remarkably true to life (judging from newsreel footage in Shub's *The Fall of the Romanov Dynasty*). On the other hand, while the worker Nikandrov, who played Lenin, bore a striking resemblance to the leader, he revealed nothing of his personal magnetism. Nikandrov's weakness in the role became quite an issue, and Lenin's widow, N. K. Krupskaia, took strong exception to the portrayal (as well as to Kerenskii's too-frequent appearances on the screen). Krupskaia's observations on *October* were penetrating: while she praised Eisenstein's sentiments, she believed that his symbolism, particularly the series of shots of gods and idols, was unintelligible to the masses.[86]

In Moscow and Leningrad, critical reaction was mixed. The typical response was reluctant approval coupled with condemnation of the film's obsession with "things." Documentarist Esfir Shub thought it demonstrated the futility of staging "facts,"[87] and according to *Cinema*, in some (undisclosed) circles criticism was even harsher, the film being charged with "aestheticism" and "formalism." *Cinema* absolutely denied these accusations and staunchly supported *October* for its "enormous social-political significance."[88] In the provinces, reviews were reported to be extremely enthusiastic, beginning or ending (according to one ironic report) with the words: "*October* is a new, grandiose victory. All workers, all Party and Komsomol members should see *October*; it is October in cinema, a holiday of Soviet cinematography."[89]

At least some of these very serious charges of formalism and aestheticism came, oddly enough, from Lefists Osip Brik and Viktor Pertsov and the formalist Viktor Shklovskii. Their comments, though hard, were intelligent and just. Pertsov feared that Eisenstein, who now hoped to film Marx's *Kapital* (a project which was never realized), had totally repudiated man in cinema and was headed for pure "thingism" (*veshchizm*).[90] Indeed, *October* could by itself validate the need to discuss the place of actors and heroes in Soviet cinema, for it showed how removed the Soviet avant-garde was from the preferences of ordinary viewers. The Soviet Union was seen as too poor to pay for the luxury of pure art, no matter how great the artist.

The other major revolutionary film of 1928 was Iakov Protazanov's *The White Eagle*. It too was criticized, but for reasons quite different from *October*. Protazanov was incapable of making a film that could be charged with formalism, but he continued in his unsensational way to mature as an artist and to attempt films which departed from his successful comedies *Tailor from Torzhok* or *Case of the Three Million*. *The White Eagle* has the further distinction of being the only surviving screen performances of the famous theater actor V. Kachalov and the avant-garde theater director Vsevolod Meierkhold. It is a screen adaptation of a story by Leonid Andreev about a governor of an industrial province who orders soldiers to fire on a street demonstration in 1905. The dead include three children; for this brave deed, the governor (Kachalov) receives the Order of the White Eagle. He cannot, however, live with his bad conscience. The concentration on his internal conflict is the movie's strength (from the artistic viewpoint) and its weakness (from the emerging Soviet viewpoint).

The White Eagle was the most ambitious film Protazanov had thus far attempted; unfortunately, in many parts it is sadly derivative. His strike scene draws so heavily from *Potemkin* that it even plagiarizes the device of stone lions "roaring," but Protazanov was not a technical virtuoso like Eisenstein. Nor was he adept at social criticism; he still relied on the tired use of parallelisms, contrasting a banquet, for example, with conditions in prison. But perhaps more than any other Soviet director he excelled in creating human interest and in commanding strong performances from actors. Kachalov turned in a complex and subtle portrayal of the tormented governor, shunned even by society women for his crime of killing children (although Meierkhold fared less well as the stiff-faced imperial satrap). There is a psychologically interesting subplot about a governess (Anna Sten) who wants to assassinate the

Esfir Shub

governor but cannot bring herself to murder in spite of a just cause. *The White Eagle* was, as we have already seen, criticized as a "typical" Mezhrabpom production, especially for its "psychologism" and its sympathetic portrayal of the class enemy. Indeed, it was *not* clear where Protazanov's loyalties lay—and as in *The Forty-first*, that seems to be the way he wanted it.

Comedies

Turning back to the genre in which he excelled—comedy—Protazanov had an unqualified success in his best silent movie, *Don Diego and Pelageia*, a marvelous satire on Soviet bureaucratism. As mentioned earlier, critics had long hoped for good Soviet comedies, but they were seldom executed successfully. Good comedy depends on a satirical element difficult to achieve in a society where it was hard to know, from year to year (as Osip Brik said, apparently seriously), what could be safely laughed at. It is lucky, however, that Protazanov felt Soviet bureaucratism could be spoofed.

"Don Diego" (A. Bykov in an excellent performance) is a village station master, a silly fop who dreams of himself as the hero of a romantic Spanish novel. His peasant neighbors love surreptitiously to watch him act out his fantasies (to their unending amusement). Don Diego is also a petty martinet, ordering the arrest of an aged peasant woman, Pelageia Demina (the wonderful Maria Bliumental-Tamarina), for crossing the railroad tracks against the warning sign. For her offense, Pelageia is sentenced to *three months* in prison before being rescued by two young Komsomol members with the help of the local Party secretary.

Don Diego and Pelageia presents a humorous but scathing picture of Soviet provincial life; it is much more effective social commentary as a comedy than it would have been as a heavy-handed melodrama. Peasants are portrayed as having a minimal understanding of Soviet life and its ideals: they use newspapers for wastepaper, roll cigarettes from a court order. The guard escorting Pelageia is just a peasant lad who can hardly wait to take his boots off (being unused to wearing shoes). The court is equally absurd, run precisely by the letter of the law, no matter the mitigating circumstances. Misha and Natasha, the two youths who decide to help Pelageia's forlorn husband retrieve his spouse, find themselves stymied by insolent secretaries reading novels instead of working (although they snap to attention when the boss comes in).

Protazanov slyly poked fun at Soviet conference mania by having the ridiculous trial of Pelageia occur simultaneously with a conference on the evils of bureaucratism. The self-same idlers who will not help Misha and Natasha are more adept at talking about Marxist stages of development than putting theory into practice—yet they conclude that there is no "bureaucratic deviation." When the youths finally reach the Party secretary, they get results:

all the lazy officials are fired, and Pelageia is freed at last. (Although the Party does have a heart, this leaves the impression that it is not exactly in control of bureaucrat abuses.) Protazanov's comic touch in this picture was deft and sustained, holding true even when the too-good-to-be-true Komsomol members come to the rescue.

Don Diego and Pelageia was more or less well received as a "step forward" in the making of Soviet comedy.[91] ARK had learned enough by now to be cautious, and its resolution on the film stated that although *Don Diego and Pelageia* was funny, the Party's role in fighting bureaucratism had not been shown clearly enough. A. Aravskii, writing in *Cinema Front*, found it hard to believe that the movie's representative of that great evil, bureaucratism, should be the "theatrical, comically stupid, eccentrically narrow-minded" station master. But despite its unsuitably "vaudevillian" tone, *Don Diego and Pelageia* was a "great event" for Soviet comedy.[92]

Another comedy on the evils of Soviet bureaucratism was Aleksei Popov's *Two Friends, a Model, and a Girlfriend* (*Dva druga, model', i podruga*). This is much less successful than *Don Diego and Pelageia* but pleasant enough. Two boys invent a box-making machine which they, along with the "girlfriend" (Olga Tretiakova), take to town to patent. They are pursued by a capitalist-saboteur and his thugs. The youths build a makeshift boat to carry them down the river to town, where after several adventures, à la Huckleberry Finn, they of course meet with success. The comedy seems directed at children, although the director threw in a love triangle to capture adult interest—during the course of the trip, the "girlfriend" switches boyfriends. This modest effort could scarcely arouse either ill-will or strong praise: it was seen as technically impoverished, but with the type of humor the working class would enjoy.[93]

An altogether different matter was Boris Barnet's tiresome *The House on Trubnaia Square*. We have already seen that his cast had been purged for nepotism, which had doubtless hampered its production. That the film was in deep trouble was also indicated by the number of well-known writers brought in in a vain attempt to salvage the script: B. Zorich, A. Mariengof, Vadim Shershenevich, Viktor Shklovskii, and N. Erdman. *The House on Trubnaia Square* is a comedy about a country girl, Parasha, who comes to Moscow looking for her uncle and tries to adjust to petty-bourgeois city life. Typical of the film's humor are interminable scenes of Parasha asking directions which succeed only in seeming even longer than they are. She eventually goes to work for a barber's wife as a maid; the barber (Vladimir Fogel) had broken dishes as he washed them in order to avoid the task. Parasha joins the union, a clumsy insertion. Next it is mistakenly broadcast that Parasha has been elected to the Moscow City Soviet, and the barber's wife plans a large party in honor of this occasion for her unsavory NEPmen friends. Parasha loses her job over the mixup but gets her man (only after he assures her that he is a union member).

Iakov Protazanov

The most socially revealing part of the film is the vignette about the union's amateur theatrical because it shows the boorish behavior and naiveté of the crowd (Parasha actually jumps on the stage and tries to halt the action, believing it to be real). The only cinematographically interesting portion is the opening scene: Parasha is nearly struck by a tram trying to rescue her pet goose. The scene ends in a freeze frame with the driver jumping out of the tram in alarm, followed by a flashback to Parasha's arrival in Moscow. Not until the scene is completed do we know both girl and goose are free.

ARRK rightly judged this "comedy" most unsuccessful, Mikhail Shneider saying that the script was (dramaturgically) "absolutely illiterate."[94] K.

Feldman noted that Barnet's *Girl with a Hat Box* had not been successful either (and he could have mentioned the adventure-serial *Miss Mend*, as well). Although Feldman paid lip service to the right of directors to make mistakes, the implication was that Barnet had already used up his quota of goodwill.[95]

Non-Russian Cinema

The Ukrainian film trust VUFKU and Sovkino had at last managed to reconcile their differences, thus allowing an exchange of films between the two republics. Because of this improvement in relations Aleksandr Dovzhenko's first important film, *Zvenigora*, showed in Moscow less than a month after its Kiev premiere, and a new star was born. Dovzhenko had made two films before this—his 1926 short comedy, *Love Berries* (*Iagodka liubvi*), and the 1927 international-adventure conspiracy, *Diplomatic Pouch* (*Sumka dip-kur'era*)[96]—but neither gave any hint that Dovzhenko would prove himself one of the greatest and most original artists of the silent screen. (So distinctive is his later style that it has been said with justice that one can recognize a Dovzhenko movie almost from the first shot.)

Love Berries is a slight farce of a woman trying to get a barber, "the father of her child," to marry her. He refuses. The catch is that not only is he not the father of the baby, she is not the mother, either. The film is traditionally shot and not very funny. Dovzhenko's second effort, *Diplomatic Pouch*, less traditional and much more successful, is about the English waylaying Soviet diplomatic couriers headed for Leningrad. One is killed; the other manages to transfer the pouch to an English communist sympathizer who in turn hands it over to his nephew, a sailor bound for Leningrad. Dovzhenko dressed up this ordinary spy fare with an out-of-focus, kaleidoscope sequence of the wounded courier's delirium and with such techniques as distorted closeups. His fascination with the rhythms of the boat engine's pistons was undoubtedly influenced by Eisenstein's *Potemkin*. *Diplomatic Pouch* showed Dovzhenko to be a maturing and capable director but nothing more. (The movie received a not-too-favorable review which compared it to the much-maligned *Mr. Lloyd's Voyage*.)[97]

On the basis of *Love Berries* and *Diplomatic Pouch*, no one was prepared for *Zvenigora*; Dovzhenko came into his own as an artist when his subject was the Ukraine that he so dearly loved. *Zvenigora* was well subtitled a "cinema poem," for it is lyrical and plotless (and the intertitles are in verse)—a fable of wealth hidden beneath the Ukrainian soil and an old man's dream of finding treasure and meeting legendary heroes. The first part is an amazing succession of fantastic images: enemies falling out of trees; a candle-carrying monk materializing from the earth, then disappearing in a puff of smoke; a Cossack without a nose. The focus is often deliberately uncertain. By Dovzhenko's standards, the second part is realistic. It shows the idyllic life of a Ukrainian village rudely interrupted by the Germans in World War I. But this too is interspersed with snatches of folklore (girls floating wreaths down a river) and the grandfather's dreams, utilizing techniques like the double exposure. The fanciful old man has two grandsons: Timosh, a revolutionary sympathizer, and Pavlo, a brigand and anarchist, and the theme of divided family loyalties is treated in Dovzhenko's whimsical and nonmoralizing style.

Even today, one scarcely knows what to say after seeing *Zvenigora*. According to Eisenstein's assistant Grigorii Aleksandrov (later a director in his own right), Sovkino's chieftain Shvedchikov was so flabbergasted by this movie that he invited several well-known directors, including Eisenstein and Pudovkin, to view the film in order to tell him what he should think. When they enthusiastically hailed it as a masterpiece, he agreed to its distribution in the Russian Republic.[98] The stunned reaction to this film is relayed by another wonderful anecdote. Viktor Pertsov's review of the movie in *New Lef* was followed by a note saying Pertsov had first submitted the review to *Cinema*. It was returned to him with the explanation that *Cinema* could not make up its mind on *Zvenigora*'s merits—and therefore would not print any review— before appealing to the workers' judgment. *New Lef* found this caution excessive and rather amusing.

Happily, Pertsov's critique was published despite *Cinema*'s reservations, for it is brief, elegant, and penetrating. He observed that *Zvenigora* was a "thing sudden, unexpected, unforeseen," discussing it as the manifestation of a startlingly primitive consciousness (in its confusion of fact and fiction, of time and space) that somehow seemed to penetrate reality. In terms of the cultural politics of the period, it is worth noting that Pertsov saw as a shortcoming what present-day critics would regard as a virtue: the fact that despite Dovzhenko's attempt to bring the contemporary world into the movie, the totally fantastic "plot" was artistically so unified that one might say the film was "outside the social focus." Yet Pertsov still felt able to close by "celebrat[ing] the inventive risk of the director Dovzhenko," for only in risk taking could cinema develop.[99]

No other work of non-Russian Soviet cinema could approach the vision of *Zvenigora*. But the Georgian director Nikolai Shengelaia's first film, *Eliso*, was good in its modest way. A historical drama, *Eliso* shows the tsarist authorities' forced resettlement of a village in the 1860s so that the Cossacks could use it as a military camp. The scenario was by Shengelaia and Sergei Tretiakov.

There are two secondary sources of dramatic conflict within the larger drama of the resettlement: one is the romance of the young Christian hero with Eliso, the daughter of the Muslim village chief. The other is that a collaborator from the village assists the Russians in enforcing the eviction. Despite the efforts of the hero to get the Russian general to change his mind, the villagers are expelled in a strikingly shot night trek. Eliso returns to the village and sets fire to it (thus disobeying her father's orders not to resist), but she does refuse to leave her tribe for her lover. *Eliso* is a romantic film without a happy ending: the village is not saved; the lovers do not break with tradition. It ends with a shot of the villagers wending their way across the valley toward their new home.

The director had strong pictorial and dramatic instincts and good control over the silent film techniques of closeups and rhythmic editing; Eliso's stealthy return to the village is beautifully done, only shadows showing the course of the action. Shengelaia also showed a sense of humor rare in Soviet melodrama, turning a swordfight into a hilarious parody of a Fairbanks swashbuckler. The hero battles Russians in the general's office from under a table, then with his back against a door, holding off dozens of attackers on both sides. (One literal-minded ARK commentator took the scene seriously and criticized it for being unrealistic.)

This entertaining film provoked a very partisan debate in ARK. Several speakers found it a good example for Georgian filmmakers to follow, chiefly for its lack of conventional romanticism, and when one Paushkin criticized it for being historically inaccurate, he was interrupted by whistles and shouts. There was some debate over whether *Eliso* could fulfill the "demands of society" (*sotsial'nyi zakaz*) since it was neither contemporary nor concerned with class relations. Yet Mikhail Shneider's view of the film as "fresh and talented," despite its limitations, prevailed. Director Shengelaia showed himself politically adept at parrying criticism, although his demeanor was modest and self-deprecating.[100]

A much less satisfying example of non-Russian cinema came from the Armenian director Amo Bek-Nazarov. *Khaz-push* (a term for beggars), is an anti-imperialist historical drama about the struggle of peasants in Persia in 1891 against the English tobacco monopoly. Since the monopoly makes it impossible for the peasants to sell their tobacco, they cannot pay their Turkish overlords, leading to dire results. The Russians in *Khaz-push* are portrayed as *saviors* of the natives, a striking departure from the usual depiction in Soviet silent films of tsarist Russia as a villain. The obligatory love interest concerns a woman stolen for her beauty; her husband, in his despair, joins the mob (the *khaz-pushy*). The attempt to rebel against the merchants ends badly, and the hero is killed. Vitalii Zhemchuzhnyi praised the film for being neither "marmalade" for the petty-bourgeois viewer nor another "naive agit-film," but Izmail Urazov was much more accurate when he labelled it "tasteless" and "boring."[101] *Khaz-push* is quite simply a bad film with a confused dramatic line, stereotyped characters, and banal technique.

Contemporary Films

Because of the trend in cinema debates favoring contemporaneity, films on Soviet life (*bytovoi*) were considered more essential than ever before. This was the genre in which Fridrikh Ermler, the only major director who was both a proletarian and a Party member, continued to work exclusively. His film *The Parisian Cobbler* (*Parizhskii sapozhnik*), with Fedor Nikitin in the title role of the deaf-mute shoemaker, showed that it was possible to make a film about contemporary problems that was more than a simplistic morality play. The plot line is melodramatic: a village girl, Katia (Veronika Buzhinskaia), becomes pregnant. Her boyfriend Andrei (Valerii Solovtsov), refuses to marry her and wants her to get an abortion. Because he gets no help from his Komsomol leader, he is convinced by some hoodlums that the best way out of the dilemma is for Katia to be gang-raped (which could cause a miscarriage). The cobbler, who is in love with the girl, has been watching this sad tale unfold from the sidelines and rescues her in the final explosive scene, during which one of the hooligans is killed. The Komsomol leader arrives belatedly, wiping his glasses in consternation. The final title reads: "Who is to blame?"

The Parisian Cobbler is a most interesting commentary on Komsomol youth and their morals. The boyfriend Andrei, also a member of the organization, is portrayed as being more troubled than intrinsically bad. The only response the Komsomol leader (*starosta*) gives his plea for help is to proffer a book, *The Problems of Sex in Russian Literature*—a symbol of the inefficacy of intellectual solutions to problems. (The *starosta*, moreover, looks effete and is surrounded by books, reinforcing the basic anti-intellectualism of the film.) As had *Third Meshchanskaia Street*, Katia's story illustrates the return of traditional morality; free love and abortions are no longer to be condoned. *The Parisian Cobbler* is beautifully filmed, especially its scenes of village life: a gathering of youths by the flickering campfires in the moonlight, naked boys swimming in a pond. The unorthodox treatment of orthodox subject matter and the choice of a deaf-mute as a hero (Nikitin handled the difficult role well) proved another cinematic victory for Ermler.

This did not mean that Ermler, despite his impeccable credentials as proletarian, Party member, and former Chekist, eluded the problems other directors faced. In an ARK discussion, the picture was criticized for not giving answers and being open-ended, like *Third Meshchanskaia Street*. It was also condemned for dwelling too much on the landscape, which smacked of "aestheticism."[102] The Society of Friends of Soviet Cinema (ODSK) received *The Parisian Cobbler* the same way (even to the point of using *exactly* the same words).[103] But as a whole, reviews were favorable, especially one by Mikhail Shneider, who labelled it as important a landmark for the "Komsomol film" as *Potemkin* had been for the "battleship movie."[104]

Ermler's most troubled production was *The House in the Snowdrifts* (*Dom v sugrobakh*), which was completed before *The Parisian Cobbler* but not released until after it. The extant portions of this film are too fragmentary to have much impact, but it is a story of how three families try to adjust to the Revolution and the new life. A secondary theme is the place of art in the new society, for Fedor Nikitin again plays an anti-hero, this time a down-and-out classical pianist who cannot cope with his poverty after the Revolution. He is utterly degraded, driven to stealing wood and killing a pet parrot for food, before he realizes that there is hope for him in Soviet society after all.

This movie was treated in the press with unusual caution. K. Feldman noted that there were unspecified "difficulties" concerning it and that it was only showing in second-run theaters.[105] ARK's discussion of the film was more enlightening. The script by B. Leonidov, ostensibly based on Evgenii Zamiatin's story "The Cave" ("Peshchera"), had been attacked both in *Cinema Front* and in the artistic section of Sovkino. Ermler then allegedly had become alarmed that the film might be "counterrevolutionary," due to its concentration on the intelligentsia, and it underwent extensive reworking. The question of whether Ermler was satisfied with the finished product was also open to debate (Esfir Shub claimed that he in fact liked it *better* than *The Parisian Cobbler*). Whether the extremely delayed release was with or without Ermler's approval was also questioned.[106] This controversy may have been sparked by filmmakers' dawning awareness that control over their own work was passing out of their hands, but too little of the offending film survives to make an accurate judgment.

Sergei Iutkevich, the one-time associate of Grigorii Kozintsev and Leonid Trauberg in FEKS and more recently assistant director to Abram Room, made his directorial debut (according to the credits, in association with ARK) in a contemporary film on an industrial theme, *Lace* (*Kruzheva*). *Lace* concerns the personal problems of youths working in a lace-making factory and the campaign against hooliganism and drunkenness. It focusses on the efforts of one young rowdy to reform—his earnest desires hampered by the narrow-mindedness of intellectual-looking Komsomol leaders.

Like Ermler's *The Parisian Cobbler*, *Lace* represents an unmistakable attack on the Komsomol, the youth organization associated both with the beleaguered "left" wing of the Party and with the drive for cultural revolution. In the end, the protagonist is rehabilitated, the local Komsomol cell is purged of its lazy and cowardly members, and a youth club replaces the saloon as the center of local entertainment. *Lace* is an interesting attempt at treating a politically acceptable story line in a formally innovative way. Iutkevich was technically very gifted, and the beauty of the movie greatly overshadows the content. There is much "thingism" (*veshchizm*) in the film, especially evidenced by the fascination with machinery or equipment (as in the factory or gym scenes), which emphasizes the form and rhythm of machines, not what they produce.

The Sunday outing sequence is especially well done. A lyrical paean to nature is suddenly and rudely interrupted by the appearance of gross bourgeois families and young toughs. Their drunkenness is shown through split images and weaving closeups. In the case just cited, Iutkevich's technique enhances his content, but through most of *Lace* it is purely formal; his unorthodox use of horizontals—a low horizon shot of a train moving across the screen, its image reflected in the water—reveals his pictorial talents but has nothing to do with the story. The plot is satisfactorily developed, the acting is acceptable, but the images dominate.

There was a favorable review of *Lace* in *Cinema*,[107] but Khrisanf Khersonskii was too good a critic to miss the overriding "aestheticism" of the movie, even though it nominally concerned factory life. Khersonskii noted both the influence of French impressionism and what he termed the "eccentric deviation" of *Strike* or *The Devil's Wheel* in the film.[108] *Lace* was a profoundly formalist exercise, but its formalism was virtually ignored because of its impeccable subject matter.

A fourth movie of contemporary life was Grigorii Roshal's *The Salamander* (*Salamandra*), script by Commissar of Enlightenment A. V. Lunacharskii and his sometime collaborator Grigorii Grebner. The film is a fictionalized version of the tragedy of the Austrian Lamarckian biologist Paul Kammerer, and was co-produced by Mezhrabpom-fil'm and the German studio Prometheusfilm. *The Salamander* was better than Roshal's very bad previous effort, *The Skotinins*, but like *The Skotinins* it abounds with clichés, such as aristocratic men wearing lipstick. Yet the reworking of the Kammerer story is revealing, considering later Soviet developments.

Kammerer hoped to prove through his experiments on salamanders that, contrary to accepted biological theory, acquired characteristics could be inherited. In a highly publicized scandal, it was revealed that the salamanders had been injected with ink to produce spots, and Kammerer committed suicide. The case has continued to stir interest, some orthodox scientists believing that Kammerer was honest, that his results could be explained by mutation, and that the undeniably fraudulent experiment was the work of a saboteur.

The Salamander adheres to the sabotage theory, offering a conspiracy of the Catholic Church and noblemen against both scientific innovation and communism. (The scientist at one point in the film is accused of being a Bolshevik.) He becomes destitute, loses his beautiful wife to the decadent baron leading the cabal, and attempts to commit suicide in a ridiculously unbelievable scene. He does not die and is taken by a Russian student to the land where scientific achievement is really appreciated, the Soviet Union (so read the titles). Commissar Lunacharskii appears as himself, an instrument in bringing the scientist to sanctuary.

The Salamander was regarded as being one more "soft" treatment of a revolutionary theme, because it did not properly reveal the inner workings of bourgeois society. From the point of view of the audience, a more significant (and justifiable) charge was that the movie was slow.[109] *The Salamander* was yet another failure of a Lunacharskii script, joining his disgraced films *The Bear's Wedding* and *Poison*.

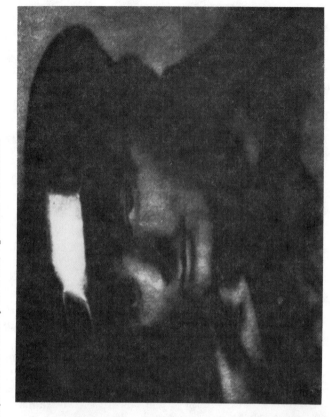

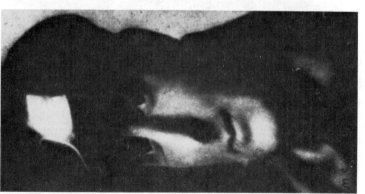

Dziga Vertov, *left*, after *One-Sixth of the World*, *right*, after *The Eleventh*

Nonfiction Films

In contrast to these romanticized versions of life stood Dziga Vertov's first film for the Ukrainian studio VUFKU, which he had joined after his ouster from Sovkino. This was *The Eleventh* (*Odinnadtsatyi*), in honor of the eleventh year of Soviet power. It is a strange amalgam of various industrial scenes with interludes of smiling faces intended to show mass support for the building of Soviet society. There are many superimposed or split-screen images and a number of fast camera shots. The general response was puzzlement. One critic wrote that it was a film "without a backbone";[110] Osip Brik criticized its lack of unity and focus, seeing it as an example of insufficient preproduction preparation.[111] The film was not widely shown and again illustrated how far removed Vertov's ideas were from Soviet cinema reality.[112]

The season was not an illustrious one, but due to the pessimism that had settled over the industry, it seemed worse than it actually was. After all, *October*, *Don Diego and Pelageia*, *The Parisian Cobbler*, and *Zvenigora* had graced the screen. Nonetheless, the conference and its aftermath, the self-criticism campaign and the attack on directors, had *not* rejuvenated cinema society into fighting shape. On the contrary, it was more enervated than ever before. The situation looked hopeless: all films were "bad," and artistic concerns were fading into the background of the coming struggle. It was a hard time to be making movies, it is true, but the tendency toward abstraction, the "coldness," in these movies indicates that there was truth to the fear that Soviet cinema was in a "blind alley." The problem of how to get out of the alley was about to be resolved.

8

The Purge Years and the Struggle against Formalism (1929-34)

By the end of 1929, the cultural revolution was in full swing and the cinema industry was approaching the paralysis in production which would characterize the next three years. The first to be purged were the studio administrations. Since much energy had been expended during the past several years calling for the downfall of Sovkino (and to a lesser extent, of Mezhrabpom-fil'm), this was not surprising. The public sentiment behind the purges was best expressed in "The Most Important Question" ("Vazhneishii vopros"), an articulation in *Soviet Screen* of the crisis theory of Soviet cinema that had emerged by the end of 1928. It read in part:

> Crisis in the laboratory. Crisis in film stock. Crisis in scenarios. Crisis in directorship. Crisis in artistic and ideological leadership.
> A factory needs oil; cinematography, people. Not dross [*shlak*], not an accidental "service person," but real people from cinematography.
> Who is causing the crisis? We need to answer the question directly—*people*.
> ... a bad doctor might slaughter dozens of different people. A harmful film "slaughters" millions. Cinematography is the strongest narcotic. It must be entrusted to the most responsible people.
> It is necessary to educate responsible people.[1]

It might have been added: "And it is necessary to rid ourselves of irresponsible people."

The purge of the film industry began on June 11, 1929 with an invitation to filmworkers to supply information to the Workers' and Peasants' Inspection (RKI) until the first of September to aid in its "inspection" of the studios.[2] By the beginning of August, it was announced that Sovkino had been purged, with no precise information as to the extent. (It is nearly impossible to get concrete information on any stage of the purges.)[3] By the end of 1929, both the Belorussian cinema enterprise Belgoskino and the Ukrainian VUFKU had also been purged.[4] *Cinema* urged that Mezhrabpom be purged as well (which did not occur until late 1930).[5] Mezhrabpom continued to present a problem; the source of its strength and its seeming ability to resist "restructuring" may have lain, as suggested above, in its foreign ties. These did not, however, forestall a violent attack against Mezhrabpom chairman Aleinikov and other administrators for their "foreign" ideology and their support of the unhappy Kuleshov.[6]

It was not until spring 1930 that the purges were in full swing. On May 10, 1930 an editorial in *Cinema* announced a forthcoming "purge and check-up of the bureaucracy [*apparat*] of the basic cinema organization" due to the failure of the self-criticism campaign.[7] This "basic organization" was, of course, Sovkino, liquidated after five and one-half years of troubled existence. In keeping with the secrecy of the purge period, Sovkino disappeared without fanfare, and on June 30, 1930 Soiuzkino, described as the "former" Sovkino, was first mentioned in the press (although according to archival sources, Soiuzkino existed as early as May 22, 1930).[8] The new organization promised to refrain from Sovkino's "politics."[9]

One Comrade Riutin, apparently a member of the Soiuzkino board of directors, promised that cinema would purge itself of "old bureaucrats" (*chinovniki*) and establish stronger ties with proletarian writers to enable cinema to participate actively in the class struggle.[10] By the beginning of 1932, this language was considerably stronger. The Soiuzkino information bulletin promised:

> a struggle with egalitarianism and lack of personal responsibility, not only in the area of technology, but also in the creative sphere, the elimination of elitism, lack of principles, apoliticism, and eclecticism in creative work; a struggle for the high quality-art-mass film which satisfies the basic demands of the proletarian collective farm mass viewer.[11]

These were mighty goals. Soiuzkino's activities are little known, but by autumn 1930, it was already under attack, first from Mezhrabpom. Mezhrabpom accused Soiuzkino of following Sovkino's "line" in hoarding film stock. (The editors of *Cinema* demanded a response from Soiuzkino, but reminded Mezhrabpom that conservation of film was vital, one of the few indications of how serious the film stock shortage was now that funds were being diverted to the industrialization campaign.)[12] In addition, Soiuzkino was criticized for being so out of touch with film politics that it had recommended already suppressed films like *The Tripol Tragedy* to the Red Army.[13] These charges led to a purge of Soiuzkino in November 1930, after less than six months of operation. (Included in this purge were Mezhrabpom and the Photo-Chemical Trust.)[14] One effect of the shakeup was that a Party hack with absolutely no cinema experience, B. Z. Shumiatskii, was named by the Supreme Council of the National Economy (Vesenkha) to the chairmanship of

Soiuzkino.[15] Former Sovkino chairman K. M. Shvedchikov hung on as Shumiatskii's lieutenant, but I. P. Trainin and M. P. Efremov at this time left the cinema scene.

Heading Soiuzkino was not an enviable assignment, for the intensity of the purges increased. *Cinema* called for "public" participation in suggesting new victims in order to establish "worker control" over the industry.[16] This challenge was taken up, and Soiuzkino was subjected to relentless, anonymous attack in the cinema press. Charges were identical to those that had been levelled at Sovkino—"harmful" scripts, wasted money.[17] Soiuzkino also allegedly harbored "opportunists" and "alien elements" who were conspiring against Soviet cinema.[18] Through 1930 the studio was in a constant state of purge, but by 1931, the "housecleaning" was complete enough to allow the full attention of "society," as it was termed, to be turned to other parts of the cinema front.

The Purges of ARRK and ODSK

The purge of all sectors of the film industry had begun in June 1929, but studio administrations were most easily purged because they were centralized and enjoyed little support within the film community. The years of controversy found their bitter fruition at this point. The purge of ARRK was begun in February 1930 to flush out those who were not making films "for the millions," thereby failing to meet the requirements of the cultural revolution.[19] Leningrad ARRK (LenARRK), which harbored a nest of "bourgeois, reactionary-realist elements," was purged in April 1930,[20] yet by August, it was accused of a "reactionary" defense of both formalism and petty-bourgeois "reactionaries and theoreticians" like the Kozintsev-Trauberg collective FEKS and Adrian Piotrovskii.[21] The April purge must therefore be judged unsuccessful.

The same could be said of the purge of ARRK. Despite the purge, ARRK was accused of not hearing "the voices of the laboring masses,"[22] and in October 1930, a vicious new campaign was launched. ARRK was said to be in "the hands of deceivers [*ochkotirateli*] and do-nothings," controlled by "contagious-flashy opportunists" who understood neither the aims of the Party nor the needs of Soviet cinema.[23] These charges were countered by critic Vladimir Kirshon, ARRK chairman K. Iukov, and director Vsevolod Pudovkin, who in a rare burst of courage denounced the attacks as "unprincipled" and "demagogic."[24] ARRK shortly thereafter tried to prove its "fighting spirit" with statements such as: "We will strengthen the affairs of the cultural revolution and Soviet cinema. We will beat the merciless class enemy!" ARRK also claimed that, contrary to accusations, it opposed "opportunists."[25]

This weak defense was soon breached. In late 1930, there was a long article in *Cinema and Life* (the former *Soviet Screen*) on ARRK's "political nearsightedness," "opportunistic deviations in practical work," its "petty-bourgeois" principles about "free creation," and its generally apolitical stance. "Where," it was asked, "is the struggle with formalism, with vulgar materialism, with Lef and other deviations and bourgeois influences in cinema?" Leningrad ARRK was seen as a sanctuary for the leading formalists, those "agents of bourgeois art." Both ARRK and ODSK were exhorted to follow the proletarian writers' organization RAPP's example in conducting "serious" discussions. ARRK was ordered to stop supporting directors "uncritically."[26]

ARRK was purged again in late November-early December 1930. Luckily, *Cinema* reported on the activity of this purge council in some detail, a virtually unknown occurrence. Victims were questioned about the "political problems of the day," and witnesses were brought forth to tell tales. Most such "evidence" was seemingly irrelevant. For example, one witness reported that director-critic Leo Mur and one Barskoi, a director of children's movies, had not kept their promise to write an article for a children's encyclopedia! This account noted that if all "politically weak" members of ARRK were purged, ARRK would have no members left. Those who escaped the purge were therefore far from vindicated—they were now subject to "re-education." The report concluded with the first list of those ousted, in alphabetical order, but only going through the "V's," the third letter of the Cyrillic alphabet. The rest was never published.[27] This second purge of ARRK was temporarily halted at the end of January 1931, with 40 percent (of 428 members) expelled. Of the 259 remaining, 28 percent were Party/Komsomol members.[28]

ARRK's stubbornly independent stance was broken in another way in 1931. There was a rigid restructuring that prohibited membership in more than one section, to prevent members from working independently. Some members protested this as harmful and unnecessary, but the response was that since specialization was the order of the day, cinema could not be an exception.[29]

By October 1931, rumblings once again appeared in the press about how ARRK was not fulfilling its societal obligations.[30] In 1932, ARRK, seen as being remiss in fighting formalism,[31] was eventually accused by a *Cinema* "brigade" of being allied with the many formalists formerly in its ranks, including scenarist Viktor Shklovskii, critic Mikhail Shneider, and director Olga Preobrazhenskaia (*Peasant Women of Riazan*). ARRK's head K. Iukov was charged with not admitting mistakes unless forced to.[32] By the end of 1932, ARRK's situation was most precarious, yet somehow it managed to survive the liquidation of the proletarian writers' association RAPP, with which it had indubitably become more closely tied since the 1928 Party Conference on Cinema Affairs.[33]

ARRK enjoyed a breathing space until September 1933. At this point it was sometimes referred to as RosARRK (presumably for "Russian"), sometimes simply as ARRK. The mutinous LenARRK had been demoted to a Leningrad "bureau" of ARRK. The new accusation was that ARRK had no influence and was silent on the problems of the day.[34] (This was undoubtedly true, since the purpose of the purge presumably had been to erode ARRK's influence.) ARRK was periodically sniped at through spring 1934, primarily for its inactivity but also for supporting director Abram Room in his latest scandal (the first being the *Third Meshchanskaia Street* affair).[35] ARRK silently expired in fact sometime in 1934 but was not formally liquidated until 1935 at the First All-Union Conference of Creative Workers.[36]

ARRK had long since ceased to offer even a forum for discussion. Its members had tried to master the rhetoric of the cultural revolution by talking about the "struggle for communist culture," the "raising of the cultural level of the broad worker and peasant masses," and about the struggle with "naked" formalism or the "mystical, symbolist, decadent, pathological and pornographic deviations" characterizing Soviet cinema,[37] but they were never very convincing. The artistic sensibility and culture which ARRKists had always shared counted for nothing in the "cultural revolution."

ARRK had outlived its time, and its end was inevitable, especially since independent organizations were being eliminated in all sectors of society as being incompatible with the new socialist order. But it is interesting that even in the end, ARRK was unable and unwilling to ally itself with the only other cinema organization that, for all its failings, supported and understood cinema as an art—Sovkino. It is instructive to look at this situation in more detail.

The bitterness of the Sovkino-ARRK dispute was revealed on the very eve of the purges in a debate over the "place of the writer in cinema." It quickly degenerated into a quarrel which revealed the magnitude of the gulf between the two groups. M. Rafes, the head of Sovkino's artistic council (*khudsovet*), violently denounced directors and their collectives for their constant bickering and power-mongering, both among themselves and with the studio administration. Rafes's outburst was an angry one, but his words had the ring of truth. He was speaking of Kozintsev and Trauberg in particular when he said: "They struggle for film stock, for territory, they struggle for everything." But it was clear from the context that he meant his remarks to apply to *all* directors.

The deep divisions in the film community were further revealed by the wrangling over who best fulfilled the Party's "demand" (*zakaz*). Rafes seemed to be trying to pull the ARRKists together to form a common front with Sovkino. Sergei Tretiakov and V. Sutyrin, to whom Rafes addressed his pleas, contemptuously refused his offer of a truce. Tretiakov reminded Rafes that "you are still not Soviet cinematography," and that "we work as we choose." Sutyrin told Rafes that the sterile and bureaucratic Sovkino production plan could "go to the devil." Sutyrin and Osip Brik agreed that Sovkino had so mechanically interpreted the "demands of society" (*sotsial'nyi zakaz*) that it could not possibly fulfill them. Brik added that after working in a studio for over two years, he believed it impossible for any reasonable person to survive there.[38]

What this exchange illustrates is the tragic inability to compromise which had characterized the film community since its inception. Tretiakov, Sutyrin, and Brik were right: the Sovkino thematic production plan (*templan*) was a perversion both of art and entertainment and could not be executed. Sovkino, on the verge of being liquidated, had devised it out of desperation. Rafes felt that because of the common danger all cinema workers faced, Sovkino had a right to expect cooperation, especially from directors and writers. The hoped-for alliance did not materialize, however, and the stalemate was never constructively resolved.

The path of the Society of Friends of Soviet Cinema (ODSK) was not as rocky as that of Sovkino and ARRK. Because ODSK had never even begun to fulfill its mandate as purveyor of cinema to the countryside, it had not accrued any threatening influence. Consequently, although Grigorii Boltianskii had criticized it a year earlier for being "old-fashioned,"[39] ODSK was overlooked as a candidate for purging until March 1931 when reorganization was seen as a way of strengthening its connections with the masses.[40] But by June, nothing had happened, except that ODSK was accused of only having 33 percent workers and 9 percent peasants in its ranks.[41] Sometime around the beginning of September 1931, ODSK became ODSFK, the "F" presumably standing for "photo" (*foto*). The only notice of this change was on the masthead of *Cinema*, the ODSK (and now ODSFK) organ.[42] The quiet fate of ODSK indicates how thoroughly the cinefication question had been forgotten; even *Cinema* never publicized its activities (if indeed there were any). One ODSK member was reported as having asked quite seriously whose journal *Cinema* was.[43]

The Attack on Directors and Critics: Formalism

The studios and ARRK had been fairly thoroughly purged before prominent individuals were seriously attacked in public. This war on artists and critics was intimately connected with the condemnation of "formalism." Formalism at one time had a meaning which was particularly well suited to silent cinema: the emphasis on form (the picture or the technique) over content.

Due to the restrictions imposed by silence, the plot of the silent film must be fairly simple or the titles will overwhelm the viewer. When silent cinema was melodrama with titles, it was surrogate theater; when it concentrated on composition and rhythm, it was an art quite different from, but not inferior to, sound cinema. Because of this aesthetic demand, by the late silent period, as artists matured, silent films tended to become more and more "formalist." This tendency was in harmony with the full flowering of silent cinema as an art, but at odds with the function of cinema in Soviet society as mass entertainment (or as propaganda). Mass audiences in the twenties did not like "difficult" movies any more than do audiences today; for most people, an "artistic" film is not particularly entertaining.

Therefore, at one time formalism had a legitimate meaning in Soviet silent cinema. Without hesitation, I would use this word to describe the work of Eisenstein, Vertov, Dovzhenko, Kozintsev and Trauberg, and Pudovkin (after *Mother*). With slight reservations, I would add most of the films of Room, Kuleshov, and Ermler to this list, which means that all the major artists of the Soviet silent screen (with the exception of Protazanov) were formalists to one degree or another. But it is important to remember that during the course of the purges, the term "formalism" lost its valid application to cinema and became the epithet applied to the victim of the hour.

It is interesting to note that there is only one book of formalist film theory from this period of formalist achievement in cinema. This was the 1927 collection of essays *The Poetics of Cinema* (*Poetika kino*), edited by the literary critic Boris Eikhenbaum.[44] Most of the essays in *The Poetics of Cinema* are concerned with a theoretical justification of the montage theory of silent cinema, which is genuinely "formalist," and which, as we have seen, was early criticized (in connection with Eisenstein, especially) for minimizing the importance of the actor.

The essayists to a man came out for montage as the basis of cinema, Eikhenbaum writing in his contribution that montage is the "syntax of the film."[45] But the most direct statement came from B. Kazanskii in his seminal essay, "The Nature of Cinema" ("Priroda kino"). Kazanskii echoed Kuleshov when he wrote that the film artist needs to "think in shots," but he went beyond Kuleshov with: "Montage is the alpha and omega, the foundation and crown [*venets*] of the creative work of cinema; montage is the 'dramaturgy' of the film in its concrete, screen composition [both] as a whole and in the construction of separate shots."[46] Although the essays also dealt with problems of plot and genre in Soviet cinema, the basis for the charges of formalism which were levelled at the authors stemmed from the defense therein of montage.

Another hallmark of formalism in cinema was support for the idea of "typage," the use of nonprofessional actors in cinema, which we have already discussed in connection with both Eisenstein and the "open letter" of the Leningrad directors. By 1929, an additional sign of formalism was the rejection of a traditional plot (*siuzhet*) in favor of what might be called the plotless (*bessiuzhetnyi*) film. Ippolit Sokolov found the origins of this idea in the naive eagerness to reject the old which characterized the early days of the revolution.

Sokolov realized that some of the best Soviet silent films had been plotless, naming *Strike, The End of St. Peterburg, Arsenal, New Babylon*, and others.

But the genius of the directors involved, not the lack of plot, had accounted for the success of these films. Furthermore, the tendency to "canonize" the plotless film, which could mislead younger and less talented directors, had been reinforced by a series of articles in Leningrad *Cinema* by Eisenstein, Shklovskii, Erenburg, Nedobrovo, and the scenarist Leonidov. Sokolov wrote:

> The nature of cinema as an art of the millions is intensity, drama, intense and fascinating dramatic conflict, and plot [*siuzhet*], and not drawing-room lyricism, not poetical, versified construction of the cinema-shots.[47]

The old argument about the type of film suitable for the Soviet audience was now made part of the debate over formalism ("poetical, versified construction" being a direct reference to *The Poetics of Cinema*). In like manner, the persistent concern over stereotyping was now called "ideological formalism."[48]

Since Ippolit Sokolov had always been an advocate of the traditional entertainment film, his writings of this period represent more a betrayal of his own artistic standards than of genre or style. He pointed to the chasm between critics' and viewers' choices, charging that Soviet critics and directors were forgetting that "art exists for the viewer" and that *"the greatest talent and even genius of the artist consists in his knowing how to see with the eyes of the viewer."* If cinema is mass art, according to Sokolov, it should signify that "cinema exists for the masses, not the masses for cinema."[49]

In the early days of Soviet cinema, the idea of cinema as a mass art meant that cinema was potentially accessible to the masses in a way that no other art was. Now that cinema's raison d'être was serving the mass audience, a true "artist" should see with the "eyes of the masses." At this point Soviet cinema ceased being an art, becoming a medium for propaganda, and at best—but all too rarely—entertainment.

Sokolov's attacks against formalism and his arguments for Socialist Realism were civilized in tone, if wrongheaded. In the real world, the struggle against formalism was a vilification campaign directed against certain individuals, especially those prominent in Leningrad, and most particularly against Adrian Piotrovskii, literary critic, cinema theorist, script writer, and artistic head of the Leningrad studio. As cinema writer for *The Life of Art* (*Zhizn' iskusstva*), he was an outspoken opponent of the aesthetic policy he saw forming in Moscow.[50] In addition to his essay in *The Poetics of Cinema*, Piotrovskii wrote two books on cinema which figured prominently in the debate on formalism.

One was *The Cinefication of the Arts* (*Kinofikatsiia iskusstv*), a self-published look at cinema's influence on other arts, particularly theater and literature. According to Piotrovskii, cinema had something to teach the other arts because through montage it could "surmount the naturalistic laws of the composition of things, the fetish of 'organicness.'"[51] But in the eyes of Piotrovskii's many opponents, this amounted to nothing more than praise of the "dictatorship of the scissors" (montage), a prominent characteristic of formalism in cinema. Piotrovskii was also attacked for his view that, far from being a sign of "maturity," the Soviet viewer's preference for naturalism was "reactionary."[52]

The most important explication of Piotrovskii's views, however, came in his 1930 monograph *Artistic Tendencies in Soviet Cinema* (*Khudozhestvennye techeniia v sovetskom kino*), the preface of which warned readers that Piotrovskii was "very soft" on formalism and unaware of the dangers posed by "intellectual" cinema.[53] Despite the caveat, the book is a useful summary of developments up to this point as well as a prime example of formalist criticism.

Piotrovskii defined the major trends of Soviet cinema as follows. The "right deviation" was characterized by preference for the pseudo-historical film; concentration on the personal, sensational, or erotic; and use of the actor as the main means of expressing emotion. He labelled as rightists the still-active prerevolutionary directors Chardynin, Gardin, Zheliabuzhskii, Protazanov, Ivanovskii, and Sabinskii.[54] The next group was the "formal innovators," among whom he gave Kuleshov and Kozintsev and Trauberg chief honors (although he saw the latter two turning to "intellectual" cinema). Innovators were in danger of becoming reactionaries, meaning elitists.[55]

Piotrovskii's third category was the "intellectual" cinema of Sergei Eisenstein, which he admired as "unarguably one of the greatest tendencies in our cinema." Intellectual cinema was anti-naturalistic, but at the same time a truly socialist style, "not merely new form invented for the sake of form." Piotrovskii admitted that this type was difficult for the viewer, but just as music, literature, and theater were studied in order to appreciate them, so was it necessary to study cinema.[56]

The fourth tendency, the "emotional" cinema of Pudovkin and Dovzhenko, Piotrovskii also found an acceptable socialist style, because although their symbolism was lyrical, not "dialectical," these directors eschewed melodrama. The fifth type was the "cinema of facts" which Vertov and Esfir Shub represented, Piotrovskii dismissing this as propaganda.[57]

The sixth tendency was the "left deviation," and suddenly Piotrovskii became very vague. Who formed the "left deviation" in cinema if not the very people Piotrovskii admired? With the exception of his "right deviation," everybody listed in his other categories belonged to the "left deviation" as far as other critics were concerned. Piotrovskii defined the "ultra-left" as those who made pictures for "specialists"; supported the slogan "The person in cinema is equal to any other thing"; and experimented for the sake of experiment. He feared that the "left deviation" was provoking a blind reaction against innovation, which would lead to the erroneous practice of making films for the lowest common denominator, the rural viewer. An elitist himself, Piotrovskii was appalled, foreseeing a plethora of naturalistic films on peasant and factory life, which were socialist in content but not in form.[58]

Piotrovskii still advocated the kind of revolutionary cinema dreamed of ten years earlier. The rigid but idealistic political and artistic principles expressed in *Artistic Tendencies in Soviet Cinema* are the fullest expression of formalist criticism (distinguished from theory) in Soviet cinema. For this reason, he became a central target in the war against formalism.

The first hint of his troubles had been in the reaction against the "open letter" of the Leningrad directors, which Piotrovskii had signed. Before this, his name had not appeared in the Moscow film press except as a script writer (Kozintsev's and Trauberg's *The Devil's Wheel*, for example). The early part of the attack on formalism in cinema was directed specifically against Leningrad filmworkers and unfailingly against Piotrovskii. One of the first onslaughts (led by Boris Bek and Ia. Rudoi) concerned the Leningrad Higher Art Courses (which included film courses) because the "formalist reactionaries"— Piotrovskii and his henchman, film critic and scenarist Mikhail Bleiman— excluded the "social factor" in film work (presumably as a qualification for entering the school).[59]

For the first time in cinema circles, one can see evidence of guilt by association, whether actual or fabricated. For example, a RAPPist, A. Mikhailov, was "proven" a formalist merely by identifying him with Piotrovskii and Bleiman.[60] Piotrovskii's case was also made worse by an alleged association. He was not only in his own right a "vulgar" formalist and an enemy of the slogan "form understood by the millions," he was now connected with V. Solskii, the RAPPist who had written several interesting, but hard-nosed, essays on cinema in *On Literary Guard* (discussed above). Late in 1929, "Mr." (no more "comrade") Solskii defected to the West on transparent grounds of "ill health." This was not taken kindly,[61] and as a result, Solskii retroactively became a formalist—particularly in connection with his ideas on sound cinema, to be discussed in the next chapter.[62]

Even as *Cinema and Life* derided the arch-formalists Piotrovskii and Bleiman for whimpering about the campaign against them, it was being decided that Viktor Shklovskii, not Piotrovskii, was actually the leader (*vozhd'*) of formalism.[63] Indeed, *Cinema* had since the beginning of 1930 regarded Shklovskii and Boris Eikhenbaum as the heads of the movement, with Piotrovskii, Bleiman, and Viktor Pertsov as mere followers.[64]

The war against formalism and attacks against individuals were proceeding without any clear understanding of what formalism was and why it was dangerous. Ippolit Sokolov was good enough to provide some information about this "most basic danger in Soviet cinema." Formalism was, he wrote, a "metaphysical break of form from content" and an actual *negation* of content in favor of emphasis on form, meaning "technique." Formalism was therefore "in opposition to the 'unity of contradictions' which was part of the dialectic." While this is a reasonable definition of formalism, it does not explain why formalism was considered so invidious. The answer was that formalism was a "product of the petty-bourgeois intelligentsia," therefore part of their social ideology. Who were the members of the petty-bourgeois intelligentsia? The "left cinema-theoreticians." And why were they "petty-bourgeois?" Because they were formalists.[65] Such was the circular logic of the cultural revolution.

Gradually, the definition of formalism became all-encompassing. It was "eclecticism" in criticism, which meant the evaluation of formal aspects of a film without accompanying commentary on the "social-political" effects.[66] It became a synonym for "idealism" and "mechanism" in scripts.[67] It was identified with "art for art's sake," broadly construed to damn those directors of the "right" who were far from being formalists. A film like Protazanov's *The White Eagle*, for example, which is not the least formalist, became "formalist" by virtue of its "subjective psychologism." In fact, any film which allegedly ignored the "social demands" (*sotsial'nyi zakaz*) of the cultural revolution was open to charges of formalism.

Nonetheless, directors on the "right" remained relatively protected from attack. In sharp contrast, young and truly "Soviet" directors like Kuleshov and Vertov were under heavy fire, as were Kozintsev and Trauberg for "romanticism," and Dovzhenko for "biologism." Esfir Shub, her acclaimed film *The Fall of the Romanov Dynasty* notwithstanding, was added to the growing list of "allies" of formalism. Even Eisenstein was not sacred; he was accused of "mechanical materialism." Of "The Five," as the best silent directors—Eisenstein, Kuleshov, Vertov, Dovzhenko, and Pudovkin—were known, only Pudovkin enjoyed a respite.[68]

By 1931, the situation of most important critics and directors was desperate. Despite Sokolov's attempts to save himself from Shklovskii's and Piotrovskii's fates by becoming an ideologue of anti-formalism, he too had fallen in August 1930, as a "short-sighted bourgeois critic cinema specialist [*kinospets*]" overly fond of things American.[69] Mikhail Shneider, whose writings had already disappeared from the press, became the next critic to go, as an "ideologically alien element" and an "unmasked enemy."

Shneider was denounced by Lev Kuleshov in an ARRK meeting. It seems that in 1926 he had written Kuleshov a letter supporting *By the Law* which referred to the "blind fools" criticizing the film and the "oppressive times" in which they were living. Kuleshov, in the process of recanting his sins, read this letter as proof of his sincere desire to reform. ARRK accordingly expelled Shneider on the grounds that *in 1926*, he had been "reactionary, anti-Soviet, anti-social." Shneider had a lone defender in the person of a young, aspiring director who would enjoy an illustrious career in Soviet cinema, Mikhail Romm. Romm was labelled "opportunistic" for pleading leniency in view of Shneider's long service to Soviet cinema.[70]

Kuleshov bought very little time with this ignoble act, since there was a general lull in the attack on individuals during the ARRK purge of 1931. But by late 1931, Kuleshov was again on center stage as a leading light of formalism for his book *The Art of the Cinema* (*Iskusstvo kino*), especially those parts which supported "Americanism" in cinema, montage, and pure action. *The Art of the Cinema* had appeared in 1929; it is difficult to say why there was such a lag in the criticism against it, for in it Kuleshov continued to regard montage as "the foundation of cinematography," despite the fact that by this time, montage theory had definitely been rejected as "formalist." In *The Art of the Cinema*, Kuleshov discussed in some detail his early montage experiments and stressed the manipulative power of editing. He felt that montage was the fundamental principle of cinema, because without it, the only point of view is the camera's (and Kuleshov, as we know, had long opposed Vertov's fetishization of the camera).[71]

In addition to the sin of supporting montage, Kuleshov could also be faulted for his philosophy of actors. He was far from opposing the use of actors; he was, as we know, instrumental in the professionalization of the cinema actor. The problem with his views was that they smacked of "mechanism," because he allegedly wanted his training drills for actors to become as automatic as driving a car.[72] Since *The Art of the Cinema* was intended at least in part as a training manual, Kuleshov gave examples of his exercises which leave no doubt that this charge was valid. He wrote about doing routines to a metronome, for example, "to a pre-arranged plan, in required tempo," and developed a dense jargon of "axes" and "spatial webs" to express his theories. While this may have been a beneficial way of training the actor, it left the impression—despite Kuleshov's denials—that the actor was being denigrated.[73]

The third formalist error discernible in *The Art of the Cinema* is equally, if not more, serious. This was Kuleshov's view on the relationship between form and content. He began his section on the script this way: "Pure action constitutes the basis of the film scenario. Movement, dynamics—these are the basis of the film spectacle." If the scenarist cannot "think in shots," then the director will be the key person in the filmmaking process, for "*content is derived from shots* [emphasis added]."[74] It is difficult to imagine a statement more truly formalist.

Yet Kuleshov's book consistently reveals a profound understanding of cinema as an *industrial* art, one of the demands of the cultural revolution in cinema. Again and again, one learns from Kuleshov the complexity of cinema, the importance of mastery of every detail and technique—acting, lighting, and shot composition. Kuleshov had long urged professionalism in cinema; he had tried to demonstrate that the unevenness of Soviet cinema was the result of imperfect grasp of technique and general unawareness that, especially for cinema, artistic achievement is the result of planning, hard work, and discipline, not genius or class background. He found the success of *Little Red Devils* and *Potemkin* (he steadfastly refused to recognize Eisenstein's greatness) purely accidental, which explained why these directors had yet to do something as good. He wrote: "Resting on one's laurels and the absence of investigation into form will inevitably lead to catastrophe."[75] Kuleshov believed that the "secret" to a better and cheaper Soviet film lay in organization, experience, practice, and training, and he offered concrete examples of how to achieve these.[76] But Kuleshov's sound advice was ignored (to the detriment of Soviet cinema) because it was combined with his pronounced formalist views on cinema as an art. *The Art of the Cinema* was regarded as so heretical that even Pudovkin at last came under attack in connection with it, for he had written the introduction to the book to honor his former teacher.

So it was that Adrian Piotrovskii gradually lost his luster as a formalist, Kuleshov usurping his position.[77] The latter's partners in crime were usually Boris Eikhenbaum and Viktor Shklovskii (now referred to as an "ideologue of Menshevism" for his long-ago flirtation with politics); and sometimes A. Andreevskii, author of *The Construction of the Sound Film* (*Postroenie tonfil'ma*), a study which explored the possibilities of sound montage and the nonrealistic use of sound, rejecting the retention of silent film techniques. It was labelled a "liberal, contrabandist, bourgeois theory of cinema" to which Shklovskii, Sokolov, and Mikhail Levidov allegedly subscribed. There was no longer any effort to make meaningful connections among the theories of these victims; guilt by association, even spurious association, reigned.[78] By 1930 slander and vicious innuendo formed the content of most cinema "discussions."

Old cinema activist and ARK founder Nikolai Lebedev resurfaced in cinema debates after years of silence during which he had been making documentary films to launch a blistering attack on the "vulgar empiricist" Dziga Vertov, who had capitulated before the enemy, the enemy in this case being Art.[79] Lebedev was kicking a very dead horse. A much more significant sign of the deterioration of the position of directors was the extraordinary denunciation of Vsevolod Pudovkin by director Abram Room (who had had his share of trouble with *Third Meshchanskaia Street* and other films) in a four-part article appearing in *Cinema* which claimed that Pudovkin, because of his connections with Kuleshov, was opposed to using *actors* in cinema.[80] Nothing could be more ridiculous than this assertion, and it no more helped Room than Kuleshov's "exposure" of Mikhail Shneider had saved him. ARRK chairman

Iukov quickly recalled that Room, too, had suspect associations, having worked with the arch-formalist Viktor Shklovskii.[81]

The epidemic was spreading. It was suddenly remembered that Trotskii had praised formalist contributions to art in his *Literature and Revolution* (*Literatura i revoliutsiia*); formalism now became "Trotskyite-counter-revolutionary."[82] Olga Preobrazhenskaia and her co-director, Ivan Pravov, "went over" to the Kuleshov "bourgeois formalists," who presumably were worse than the ordinary formalists with whom Preobrazhenskaia had been previously connected. There was in fact considerable refinement in the use of epithets. Protazanov was "bourgeois," while scenarist Valentin Turkin and director Nikolai Okhlopkov were "petty-bourgeois."[83] The rationale behind these distinctions is impossible to fathom.

There were still, however, a few voices of integrity in the wilderness. One was Osip Brik, who dared to defend Kuleshov as a "great master," whose critics only looked at the "unsuccessful parts" of his recent films.[84] Another was Kuleshov, who no longer made any attempt to defend himself but pleaded instead not only for the careers of his associates (Komarov, Khokhlova, Podobed, and Doller were not working), but also for the demoralized and unemployed cadres stigmatized for their expertise by being labelled "specialists" (here he named actress Olga Tretiakova, directors Okhlopkov and Kaufman, and many others). How, asked Kuleshov, could new cadres be created when the old were idle? He urged that the condemned "specialists" at least be permitted to teach.[85]

Although Sergei Eisenstein would be an obvious candidate for leader of the formalist deviation, he had been relatively immune from criticism because from 1929 to 1932 he was abroad, first in Europe, then in Hollywood, and finally in Mexico, working on the ultimately disastrous project, *Que Viva Mexico!* When he returned in 1933, after having been denounced to Stalin by Upton Sinclair, his financial backer on *Que Viva Mexico!*, the new horde of critics awaited him with charges of formalism, mechanism, technical fetishism, and guilt by association (with the "bourgeois aesthetes" in Lef). Eisenstein undertook to defend himself in a most unclear fashion, which unfortunately served as further proof of the accusation that he could not communicate with the masses.[86]

The last attack on a director was the veritable war declared on Abram Room. Although Room had supported the actor and the realistic film throughout the twenties, his dogmatic and self-righteous attacks on others had earned him many enemies; in any case, his "realism" was not the right kind. The major cinema scandal of 1934 was the *Roomovshchina* (an epithet coined from "Room"), which concerned a financial imbroglio over his film *One Summer* (*Odnazhdy letom*). Room was accused of being a coward, a careerist, and an individualist. By this time the artistic independence of the director had been totally subjugated to the demands of society (*sotsial'nyi zakaz*), but Room was apparently the last to realize it.[87] Directors were no longer to be involved in script writing or editing, effectively dividing artistic control over the movie.[88]

By 1934, with the death of the last vestiges of industry independence, an era had decisively ended. ARRK and Sovkino had folded. There was only one cinema publication, the newspaper *Cinema*, and its personnel and priorities had long since changed for the worse. Several major directors—Kuleshov, Eisenstein, Room, Vertov, and Preobrazhenskaia— saw their careers in ruins, not because they had no talent for the sound film, but because they were given no real chance to try.[89] Dovzhenko escaped sustained attack for a little while longer, but his career had effectively ended by the mid-thirties. Pudovkin and Ermler continued to work, as did Protazanov, but without their former verve. Of the major directors, oddly enough, only the talented—and indisputably formalist—Grigorii Kozintsev and Leonid Trauberg survived the thirties with any success, through their "Maksim Trilogy": *The Youth of Maksim (Iunost' Maksima)*, *The Return of Maksim (Vozvrashchenie Maksima)*, and *The Vyborg Side (Vyborgskaia storona)*.

The fates of the critics and publicists is harder to trace. Viktor Shklovskii died only recently, but his significant contributions to cinema ended in the twenties. Nikolai Lebedev, the founder of ARK, was also a consummate survivor and even outlasted the charges of "rootless cosmopolitanism" that were his reward for his fine 1948 history of Soviet silent cinema. Khrisanf Khersonskii, after several years of silence during the purges, began writing once again for *Cinema* in 1934 and even earned a paragraph in *Cinema Dictionary (Kino-slovar')*, although no mention is made of his distinguished career in the twenties. Ippolit Sokolov also received a brief notice in *Cinema Dictionary* (as a teacher); one would never guess that he had ever been a major film critic. Adrian Piotrovskii died in the camps after his 1938 arrest; Sergei Tretiakov suffered the same fate. Mikhail Shneider's byline appeared again in *Cinema* in 1933-34, but his further career is unknown, as is the fate of Mikhail Levidov.

The fates of other important figures in this story were even more difficult to determine. ARK's chairman K. Iukov proved a totally elusive figure. The Glavpolitprosvet personnel connected with *Soviet Cinema*—Katsigras, Meshcheriakov, Veremienko, and others—"vanished" from the scene, as did the Sovkino administrators Shvedchikov, Efremov, and Rafes. I. P. Trainin is remembered in the third edition of *The Great Soviet Encyclopedia (Bol'shaia sovetskaia entsiklopediia)* as an "Old Bolshevik" and prominent jurist who, although born in 1881, had no professional biography before 1931, just about the time he disappeared from the cinema front. Some writers (like Valentin Turkin, who taught for many years at the cinema institute, VGIK) and actors (especially Sergei Gerasimov and Fedor Nikitin who continued to work, Gerasimov as a director) escaped relatively unscathed, but many others for the time being lack histories. This ignominious conclusion to an illustrious chapter in Soviet cultural history someday perhaps will be better understood through more complete availability of sources.

The Last Silent Films

By 1930, the film industry had been almost completely disrupted. It was increasingly difficult to tell that *Cinema*, for example, was a cinema newspaper. Its articles had little to do with films, being concerned instead with the latest campaigns: for the harvest, for maintaining "bolshevik tempo," for achieving the Five Year Plan in four years. The rare movie reviews were most often anonymous or written "collectively," by a "brigade," in the evident hope that numbers would provide security, if the interpretation should prove faulty.

The tempo of filmmaking was far from "bolshevik." As noted previously, as the times became more troubled, fewer and fewer movies were made (see appendix 1). The drop in production was partially due to the fears engendered by intensified political pressures, to be sure, but also due to lack of raw materials and the confusion over the future of sound. This decrease in output of course led to a fall in export of Soviet films, adversely affecting the industry's economic situation.[90] For these reasons, 1929 saw the last brilliant burst of Soviet silent cinema. Although Dovzhenko's final great silent, *Earth (Zemlia)*, was released in 1930, it was already an anomaly. Artistically, the silent era had ended, but due to technological backwardness, silent movies would continue to be made in the USSR until 1935.

The Formalist Films

These last silent films, created in difficult times, serve as an indispensable indication of both the path of Soviet cinema and the validity of the accusations about the state of the silent film. Four major films from this period were invariably labelled "formalist": Eisenstein's *The Old and the New* (*Staroe i novoe*, sometimes called *The General Line*), Kozintsev's and Trauberg's *New Babylon* (*Novyi Vavilon*), Fridrikh Ermler's *Fragment of an Empire* (*Oblomok imperii*), and Vertov's *Man with a Movie Camera*.[91]

In 1926 Sergei Eisenstein had begun work on *The Old and the New*, a film glorifying collective farm life. He interrupted it for *October* and then went back to it in 1928, revising it extensively. The original title, *The General Line*, referred to the Party's "line" for the countryside; the fact that the honor of this title was refused indicates the serious problems Eisenstein once again was having adapting to political reality.

The Old and the New is a rather bad film which depicts how life on a collective farm improves through the acquisition of a bull and a milk separator.

From left, Grigorii Aleksandrov, Eduard Tisse,
Louis Fischer, Sergei Eisenstein, and a Former Priest,
on the Set of *The Old and the New*

Eisenstein seems to be caricaturing his own style. His heroine, the "type" Marfa Lapkina, is a real peasant woman with a stupid and rather unpleasant-looking face, which the camera angles accentuate. Rhythmic editing and titles build anticipation for what is labelled a "wedding." It turns out, however, to be a "marriage" between the new bull and a cow! (The peasants watch the mating lasciviously.) The climax of the movie is whether or not the new separator will produce cream. Cutting on the moving parts of a milk separator does not have the same exalted effect on the viewer as the churning pistons of the battleship Potemkin.

The Old and the New represents the ossification of a great style. Khrisanf Khersonskii admired the agitational aspects of the film,[92] but the review in *Soviet Screen* by B. Alpers was quite negative. He found the actors, and especially Marfa Lapkina, physically repugnant, and their "acting" unconvincing. He found the film as a whole formally uninteresting and old-fashioned. His final remark is a superb comment on Eisenstein's precarious position in the film world: "Three years on *The Old and the New* is the pace of Pushkin's times. In this period, Soviet cinematography has lived through a whole epoch."[93] Alpers was quite correct, but the famous director of revolutionary films was unaware of these changes. Eisenstein continued to support "types" over professional actors and to favor an essentially plotless picture,[94] concepts which were seriously out of step with trends in Soviet filmmaking.

Kozintsev's and Trauberg's final silent, *New Babylon*, a "historical" fable of the Paris Commune of 1870, was a quite different kind of formalist film.[95] Unlike the sad anti-climax that *The Old and the New* provided to Eisenstein's silent oeuvre, *New Babylon* was a brilliant end to the Workshop of the Eccentric Actor (FEKS), which at the same time epitomized the fundamental contradictions and weaknesses of Soviet silent cinema. *New Babylon* is a very experimental film; although there is a heroine—a shop girl (Elena Kuzmina) who is executed for her activity on the barricades—the plot exists to provide an excuse for the pyrotechnics.

New Babylon is extremely interesting visually: titles flashing on different parts of the screen with print of varying sizes, out-of-focus photography, fast-motion, double exposure, and angle shots (which are particularly effective in the cabaret scenes). The montage is excellent: the frenzy of the music hall is contrasted with the preparations for battle; starkly realistic scenes of the common people are juxtaposed with the studied grotesqueness of the bourgeoisie, who are often shot indirectly—through windows—or seen in mirrors. The film is frequently very beautiful, as in the nighttime vigil before battle or the final scene of the execution of the communards in a churchyard in the pouring rain. While *New Babylon* serves as a sterling example of the technical possibilities of the silent film, it does not, in the end, affect the viewer emotionally because of its "coldness" and lack of character development.

New Babylon stirred a storm of controversy, and it perfectly illustrates the gulf between filmmakers and "overly refined" critics, on the one hand, and the mass public, on the other. Movie theater managers were polled about audience reactions, providing a rare and fascinating (but unsurprising) insight into the average Soviet viewer. With few exceptions, theater managers said that the public, whether worker *or* petty-bourgeois, did not like it. People walked out, laughed excitedly at the wrong moments, called for the film to be stopped. Some viewers assumed that the film's technical innovations were the fault of the projection and shouted for "more light!" "Hooligans" were verbally abusive and disruptive.[96] It was the "Rite of Spring" of Soviet cinema.

These reports have the ring of truth; the picture would probably provoke much the same reaction from a culturally unsophisticated audience today. It was not the sort of film that the ordinary viewer could comprehend without considerable preparation. Its most unqualified welcome came in LenARRK, a significant fact, considering the alienation of Leningrad and Moscow circles[97] (although one must also remember that Kozintsev and Trauberg were Leningrad-based).

Dziga Vertov's last silent film, *Man with a Movie Camera,* is the one on which his reputation in the West is primarily based, with good reason. It is a delightful look at Moscow daily life, seen not only through the camera's eye, but also through the photographer's eye. At last the cameraman, and not the camera, is the acknowledged "star" of a Vertov movie. At last Vertov had made a film which was an artful, subtle, and engaging look at life. Yet the wall of rhetoric that he himself had constructed prevented critical acclamation of this charming film in the Soviet Union.

Khrisanf Khersonskii condemned it for "narrow formalism" and "technical fetishism" (a characteristic of all Vertov movies, which was artistically justified in *Man with a Movie Camera*). Khersonskii also criticized the film for its lack of a plot (*siuzhet*) and concluded that "Vertov remains the 'artist-child' of the 'artistic infancy' of Soviet cinema."[98] G. Lenobl agreed that the picture reflected "technological fetishism" because the "person" of the title (*chelovek* can be translated as "person" as well as "man") is only a sometimes-seen shadow. Lenobl saw this as indicative of the way the technical intelligentsia (under fire after the Shakhty trial), and not the proletariat, viewed people.[99]

Khersonskii's and Lenobl's views were typical, but there was still a tiny locus of support for Vertov. A minor scandal erupted concerning the difficulty the picture had getting distributed, although one article asserted that *Man with a Movie Camera* was a financial success.[100] The last full-length defense of the Cinema-eye collective came in 1929 from N. Kaufman (not Vertov's cameraman and brother Mikhail Kaufman). Kaufman rejected all accusations of Vertov's poor planning and supposed "fetishism," and made some countercharges. He said that Vertov's films had been consistently hampered by limited runs and rental "politics," that the first ten numbers of *Cinema Truth* had disappeared, that *Leninist Cinema Truth* and *Cinema Eye* had been shown only once. Kaufman ended plaintively quoting Manet's "'il faut être de son temps'... this did not mean that one needs to keep in step with the century, but that one needs to anticipate the ideas of the century."[101] Kaufman failed to realize that Vertov did not intend to be a *prophet*, but a *spokesman* for the times. Kaufman declared Vertov a Soviet Walt Whitman, which perhaps is not too farfetched;[102] Vertov's vision of Soviet Russia was, after all, a personal and lyrical one, for all his machine-age jargon, and *Man with a Movie Camera* is a wry but affectionate look at his world.

The fourth major formalist movie was Fridrikh Ermler's *Fragment of an Empire*. This is the crowning achievement of Soviet silent cinema, combining as it does a strong plot and a brilliant actor with the very best of silent film techniques. Ermler had already made two good "contemporary" films—*Katka the Apple Seller* and *The Parisian Cobbler* (along with the controversial *The House in the Snowdrifts*)—but it was in *Fragment of a Empire* that he and his star Fedor Nikitin achieved something really special.

Nikitin plays a simple peasant-worker, Fillimonov, who suffers an attack of amnesia during the First World War, recovering ten years after the Revolution. This implausible plot (supposedly based on a true incident) offered many opportunities for the kind of technique and acting in which the silent film excelled. The opening scenes, which take place during the Civil War, are shot in dim light, slightly out-of-focus, to eerie effect (for example, a train rushing out of the darkness). Fillimonov and the peasant woman who has befriended him are stealing boots from a dead soldier.

His memory returns slowly, in a chaos of images intensified by rapid cutting and changing shot perspectives. He then returns to his former home "Peter [Leningrad]," dazzled by the fashions, the new buildings, scenes which could have degenerated into crude cliché if attempted by an actor less sophisticated than Nikitin. *Fragment of an Empire* includes many of the precise details which are a hallmark of Ermler's style. One of the best scenes is when Fillimonov goes to see his prewar employer, now in clearly straitened circumstances. This "former person" enjoys a stolen moment of respect from the befuddled Fillimonov and gives him alms which he can ill afford, a last gesture of self-pride.

Fillimonov finds work in a factory and prevents a drunken worker from attacking an inspector, another example of how socially revealing Ermler's films could be. He finally recalls that he had a wife and manages to find her. Their reunion is wonderfully awkward, for she is now a member of the Soviet bourgeoisie. Her new husband is a well-placed bureaucrat (whom Fillimonov remembers as a murderous White soldier, yet another interesting comment on Soviet life) who treats her with contempt; still, she cannot leave her material comforts. *Fragment of an Empire* is an indictment of NEP society as were Ermler's other movies, but even more complex and ambiguous. It was bound to be controversial.

In the beginning, the reception was enthusiastic. ARRK, which according to one backbiting account usually received films "coldly and pedantically," gave a "hot" reception to *Fragment of an Empire* for showing the "living man" and being "really Soviet."[103] Ippolit Sokolov wrote a particularly incisive review for this late date, finding the picture successful because of its emotion, its artistic unity, its technical mastery, and the credibility of Nikitin's portrayal.[104] B. Alpers also admired the film for these reasons, although he saw a strong but imperfectly assimilated Dovzhenko influence in the slow tempo and pictorial qualities.[105]

Within a few weeks, the Moscow press discovered that this was an incorrect approach to the film. (The Leningrad press, or at least *The Life of Art*, continued to support it as part of their unmistakable opposition to Moscow cinema establishment.)[106] Sokolov—accused of admiring the movie for its artistic, meaning "formalist" qualities—now managed to discern the "battle of sociologism and formalism" in *Fragment of an Empire*.[107] Thereafter, Ermler's picture had definitely joined *New Babylon*, *The Old and the New*, and *Man with a Movie Camera* in the ranks of formalist films. In the minds of the anti-formalist forces, this array attested to the petty-bourgeois influences controlling the best directors in Soviet cinema.[108] But unlike the other films just named, *Fragment of an Empire* is probably a movie that the viewers enjoyed, and it is significant that there was no mention of viewer response in any of the polemics concerning the film.

Although these four were the major movies at which charges of formalism were levelled, there were a number of others which were at least under suspicion. The last two silent films of the Ukrainian director Aleksandr Dovzhenko, *Arsenal* (1929) and *Earth* (1930), fell into this category. *Arsenal* was considered in some quarters to be one of the best films of 1929, which it was, and in others to be "formalist," which it also was.[109] It is a lyrical look at the horrors and chaos of war and revolution, centering on the enigmatic figure of Timosh, a "Ukrainian worker," who functions more as a symbol than as the traditional hero of the developing ethos of Socialist Realism. Dovzhenko sought to evoke his impressions of the pathos, not the grandeur, of the revolutionary struggle, making *Arsenal* unique in the annals of Soviet revolutionary films of the silent period. The action is intentionally difficult to follow, because Dovzhenko wanted to show the rapid flux of events and confused expectations characterizing the Ukrainian situation, in which

Left, Fedor Nikitin, and, *center,* Fridrikh Ermler,
on the Set of *Fragment of an Empire*

nationalism and revolutionary ardor were inseparable. He uses many moving shots and fast-action, especially in the battle scenes, with the freeze-frame providing effective contrast.

Throughout the scenes of war—with its grieving mothers, dying soldiers, expectant workers, cunning Cossacks—moves the figure of Timosh (played by the broodingly handsome Semen Svachenko). In the end, he faces a firing squad, but he cannot be killed. It seems important to remember that he never calls himself a revolutionary or even a worker, but always a "*Ukrainian* [emphasis added] worker." Dovzhenko was willing to debunk the narrow, self-serving nationalism that he saw in the Cossacks, but he was a Ukrainian artist through and through. Considering the innovations and political implications of this work, *Arsenal* received some remarkably good reviews,[110] although Sergei Tretiakov found it a combination of two warring styles: the static, painterly German style and the dynamic Russian style.[111] One of the most insightful commentaries came from the critic B. Alpers, who recognized in Dovzhenko a great and original artist whose work nonetheless required a "highly qualified" viewer.[112] Both admirers and detractors of the film agreed with this assessment, Sovkino's Rafes saying that it was a film neither "understood by the millions, nor oriented toward the millions."[113]

Arsenal is a unique and often fascinating picture, but Dovzhenko reached the height of his genius in *Earth*; in the West, it is an undisputed classic of silent film art. Dovzhenko was the master of the silent film as a moving *picture*, and it is in this film that he shows his background as a painter most clearly. Ostensibly a study of the reaction to the collectivization of a Ukrainian village, *Earth* is in reality a paean to a vanishing way of life, a life which Dovzhenko dearly loved.

It begins with the death of the grandfather, in an apple orchard in the warm summer sun, and climaxes with another death, that of the young hero, Vasil (again, Semen Svachenko), who is murdered while dancing with joy in the moonlight. This famous scene is so remarkably beautiful that no one who has seen it could ever forget it. The denouement—the bitter anguish of the dead man's lover and the crazed guilt of the jealous rich peasant (*kulak*) who murdered Vasil—is constructed to assume a symbolism beyond any literal reading. Dovzhenko turned *Earth* into a fable that transcends class warfare in the countryside. After all, the *kulak* kills Vasil, not because he is the collective's official, but because "he was dancing."

The reaction to *Earth*, considering that it appeared in the midst of the purges of 1930 was predictable, though rarely completely negative. One critic wrote that the beauty and rhythm of the movie "catastrophically *weakened the political purposefulness and clarity of the film.*"[114] Other criticisms were that the Party was not visible enough, and that the film was a defense of the physically strong over the "socially healthy," presumably referring to the village activist being murdered by the *kulak* instead of the other way around.[115]

Ippolit Sokolov could still write a penetrating review, although his conclusions, due to his difficult situation, were predictable. He quite rightly found the "social-ideological point of view" (of class warfare) obscured by the symbolism, by the expressive style, by the obvious nationalism, by the dominance of "negative moments." (Indeed, that the movie's topicality is only superficial is one reason for its greatness.) Given these criticisms, it is a little odd that Sokolov (and others) could complain at the same time that the symbolism rendered the movie "unintelligible" to the masses. (Was that not a blessing under the circumstances?) In any case, Sokolov concluded that Dovzhenko was a "great director" and a "petty-bourgeois artist."[116] (It was generally agreed that Dovzhenko was a "fellow traveller" but not a lost cause.)[117]

Another film of the period which sent confused signals was Abram Room's *The Ghost That Does Not Return* (*Prividenie kotoroe ne vozvrashchaetsia*, 1930), based on a tale of revolutionary activity in a South American country by Henri Barbus (Valentin Turkin wrote the screen adaptation). The plot concerns a revolutionary (José Reál [B. Ferdinandov]) serving a life sentence who receives a day of freedom to visit his family. He is stalked on his way home by a plump, debonair policeman (Maksim Shtraukh) who intends to kill him. The dramatic potential of this plot is marred by the

Abram Room Shooting *The Ghost That Does Not Return*

overly long first part of the movie, located in the prison, which conveys a tendentious social statement about conditions in capitalist countries. This segment of the film relies heavily on technique (primarily very rapid cutting, kaleidoscope patterns, and superimposition) and cliché (the prison director is a deformed dwarf, the prisoners are attacked with hoses). When José Reál finally decides to leave prison to take his day, the picture becomes less self-conscious. The police agent has followed Reál from the start, but it is not until they reach the desert that we know which of the passengers on the train the villain is. In the end, Reál escapes death to lead a revolution.

Room's *Third Meshchanskaia Street* had been characterized by a precise sense of place and the choice of the correct detail; *The Ghost That Does Not Return*, on the other hand, is memorable for its unreality. Only rarely does the movie transcend its coldness and emptiness, primarily through the acting of Shtraukh as the policeman and Olga Zhizhneva as Reál's wife, both of whom lend much-needed warmth to this film. A prerelease review (probably by Ippolit Sokolov) found it a "big and good film but with big shortcomings"—a weak script, confused style, and a hero who appeared to be "mentally ill."[118] A later review discerned elements of formalism in the movie and criticized it for having left the revolutionary situation too much in the background.[119]

Much better than *The Ghost That Does Not Return* was Pudovkin's *The Heir of Genghis Khan* (*Potomok Chingiz-khana*), about the attempts of the British in Mongolia in the early twenties to set up a puppet ruler, the youthful hunter Bair. He turns against them and leads an uprising in a dramatic finale of armed horsemen charging toward the camera. *The Heir of Genghis Khan* is vintage Pudovkin, with powerfully physical scenes in which the objects seem palpable. His sense of drama is intact, particularly in the scene where the Mongol hunter is being marched to a lonely spot for execution. What is most surprising is Pudovkin's feeling for this culture that was alien to him and his ability to transmit this to the screen in such an objective manner. (The movie was in fact attacked for its "favorable" portrayal of the Lama.)[120]

The revolt of the natives, which does not allude to Soviet power in any way, is clearly an elemental force, the renewal of the horde; the implications should have been disquieting, but drew absolutely no comment. Was Pudovkin still coasting from the success of *Mother*, or was this movie overlooked in the frenzy of the purges? *The Heir of Genghis Khan* was considered a success,[121] but it was certainly as formalist (in its emphasis on things, such as the furs at the bazaar) and symbolic (the figure of the hunter Bair is far from typically heroic) as any of the movies discussed above which were labelled "formalist" in no uncertain terms. Moreover, ordinary viewers were not likely to be too interested in the fate of the inscrutable protagonist. The reception of this movie once again demonstrates the capriciousness and unpredictability of critical demands. How was a director to know how much to dare under such circumstances?

Another example of a film with pronounced formalist qualities was the 1933 *The Twenty-six Commissars* (*Dvadtsat'shest' kommissarov*) made by the Georgian director Nikolai Shengelaia (*Eliso*). There had long been talk of filming the 1918 execution of the Baku Soviet that had been carried out by "Mensheviks and SRs" aided by the English. Very late for a major silent effort, *The Twenty-six Commissars* reveals mastery of the full-blown style of the Soviet silents, with its beauty and dramatic weakness. The film is visually evocative, overly long, and ultimately boring. Shengelaia does all that is possible to give interest to the mass scenes, utilizing a good mixture of shots to lend space and variety and a sense of the individuals in the crowd. But it seems like something we have seen before: the foppish socialist revolutionary agitator, the sensuous shots of production (in this case, oil), the scenes of panicked speculation and protracted execution. Shengelaia's personal touch is the figure of a beautiful woman who moves mysteriously throughout the film. Technically, *The Twenty-six Commissars* is very well done, but it *is* a cliché: a caricature not of the worst, but of the best of Soviet cinematography.

By 1933, the situation on the cinema front had quieted down enough so that *The Twenty-six Commissars* could be discussed in relative calm. The film was in general considered "significant" (and it does have an impressive quality), but it was criticized at the same time for its mystical symbolism (the woman), for portraying people "schematically," for not being entertaining.[122]

A fiction film which was not well received and which rather defies categorization was Evgenii Cherviakov's *Cities and Years* (*Goroda i gody*, 1930), an adaptation of the novel by K. Fedin about a Russian artist living in Germany at the beginning of World War I. After dealing briefly with this period, the action resumes with the Civil War (skipping both World War I and the Revolution). Although the artist is fighting with the Reds, he helps a German acquaintance allied with the Whites escape captivity. He commits suicide when threatened with execution for his wrongdoing by another old German friend, this one a Bolshevik. This artist "without will" was certainly not the prototypical hero of the thirties,[123] nor was the "salon-poetic" treatment seen as the correct style.[124]

It is difficult to reconstruct the dramatic tension of *Cities and Years* because two reels have been lost, during which (one surmises) a critical love affair takes place which further erodes whatever spiritual strength the weak protagonist possessed. *Cities and Years* relies on overworked stereotypes (male aristocrats wear makeup, futurist artists declaim grandly in salons) and misses the opportunity to deal with a complicated question of personal morality. The artist faces an unenviable dilemma, but the viewer feels no sympathy. The German had saved him years before from anti-Russian mob violence, so in a sense his action is an affair of honor, yet this is complicated by the fact that we have seen this same German brutally murder a mere boy. The ending is startling and ambiguous; the last image on the screen is a slight, self-satisfied (presumably about the suicide) smile on the icy teutonic face of the German-Bolshevik, a chilling and subtle conclusion. Although *Cities and Years* was made by a director of certain ability and although political restraints undoubtedly prevented a direct confrontation with the moral issue, the film demonstrates that silent cinema too easily became cold and clichéd, even with promising subject matter.

Educational Films

The two major educational feature films (*kul'turfil'my*)—*Turksib* and *Salt for Svanetia* (*Sol' Svanetii*)—also suffered to some degree from formal ossification. *Turksib* (1929), directed by Viktor Turin, was a "documentary" look at the building of the Turkestan-Siberian railroad which concentrated primarily on its economic and social benefits for Turkestan. One learns very little from the film, a serious shortcoming intrinsic to the silent documentary, because information—and propaganda—are better transmitted through speech. There are, however, some charming scenes that suggest how backward the area was: the glee of some young boys at seeing a truck, the alarm of sheep and everyone in the yard at the sight of strangers in a car, a shot of men on camels coming to greet the train. But the drama and hardship of construction are not suggested, and there are too many shots of flowing water and cotton fields. This very modest film was hailed by Ippolit Sokolov, of all people, as a "film understood by the millions" due to its "grandiose" material and "completely iron unity."[125] Another critic found it the first entertaining film on an economic theme, while Valentin Turkin thought it a reasonable compromise between the acted film and the strict documentary.[126]

A more ambitious effort was Mikhail Kalatozov's "ethnographic" film (which meant that the action was staged but based on real material), *Salt for Svanetia* (listed in *Soviet Fiction Films* under the title *Dzhim Shuante*). This film relates the strange customs of an isolated region of the Caucasus. The beginning is long and boring with literary titles and many dull shots of mountain scenery. Then Kalatozov indulges in a lot of "style" as he explores the everyday activities and hardships of these people. The central part of the film concerns an avalanche which kills a man, thereby leading to a depiction of funeral rites. There is heavy use of the closeup, distorted angles, and foreshortening. Finally, the Bolsheviks build a road to this area, ending its historic isolation and proving that the government is "stronger than religion and customs." The bizarre contrast of the gluttony at the funeral with the woman crying for water as she gives birth among the rocks is more than a little sensational and exotic, but *Salt for Svanetia* was seen as a "true Soviet film," unlike most of the movies of the Georgian company Goskinprom Gruzii.[127]

Social Commentaries

Turksib and *Salt for Svanetia* ostensibly answered the new requirements for "art," but it is hard to see their attraction for the viewer. Movies which fulfilled the demands of society (*sotsial'nyi zakaz*) in a more palatable form were *Kain and Artem* (the campaign against anti-Semitism), *Saba* (the campaign against alcoholism), and *Forward* (*Khabarda*, the campaign against religion). P. P. Petrov-Bytov's *Kain and Artem* is an adaptation of Maksim Gorkii's story about a Jewish shoemaker, Kain, who saves the life of a Volga stevedore, Artem. The unselfish humanity and revolutionary ideals of the Jew eventually reform the prejudices of the worker. The film is simple, straightforward, and easily comprehensible, which Petrov-Bytov, as an ideologue of movies for the masses, intended. Khrisanf Khersonskii labelled it an "illustration" of Gorkii's tale, not a real movie, and thought it suffered from a mixture of expressionism and naturalism.[128]

Saba (1929) is a more interesting and satisfying film, exceedingly well made by the Georgian director Mikhail Chiaureli (who was to become a favorite of Stalin's). This beautifully filmed story of an alcoholic child abuser became a drama of the disintegration of a family and the degradation of a man. The details are well chosen: liquor splashing on Saba's long-suffering wife, the smashing of his small son's model airplane, the hopeful gesture of the white tie when he seeks to reconcile with his wife after having been kicked out. It only becomes improbable bathos at the end, when Saba, drunk, steals a tram and accidentally runs over his own son.

Oddly enough, *Saba* was the subject of controversy in ARRK. There was argument over whether the picture should be considered an acted film or an educational film (*kul'turfil'm*). Several speakers felt the picture reflected the backwardness of Georgian film production. But it had an important defender in director Vsevolod Pudovkin, who thought it a movie of "lyrical beauty."[129] Khrisanf Khersonskii was critical of *Saba* in ARRK and in the pages of *Cinema* and *Soviet Screen*, particularly because of the "clichéd apotheosis" of the ending.[130]

Another Chiaureli film from this period is the marvelous satire *Forward* (1931). It succeeded where other anti-religious films had failed in being deft and quite funny. *Forward* begins in misleadingly heavy-handed style with plans to construct a new Tbilisi (a picture of Stalin literally glows in the background). A house collapses, and icons, rather than stones, cut a child. This is followed by a controversy as to whether or not a church is really a historical monument to be saved from demolition for the new housing project, and the fun begins. As the frenzy of the "reactionaries" picks up, the church ages from an eighteenth-century to a fifth-century edifice. The church's supporters march to the "conscience of the country," an old and feeble intellectual literally on his death bed (there is a hilarious funeral dream sequence in which even the filmmakers become part of the film).

Forward is extremely anti-intellectual as well as anti-religious: doctors are incompetent, artists are effete, "cultured" people are unable to settle their differences rationally. The comic power of the film comes from the sharp and skillful way that Chiaureli plays on these prejudices, with genuine good humor—the caricatures are silly without being vicious. Near the end, however, this admittedly fine distinction begins to break down; when shown a document attesting to the age of the church's stones, the worker-leader says: "How can anyone know this was not written by a class-enemy?" Of course, the church turns out not to have been old at all, only a nineteenth-century copy, the implication being that if it had really been old, the people would have "known" it without the fictitious "proofs" of intellectuals.

Iakov Protazanov's Last Silents

A more "bourgeois" approach to the campaign against religion was Protazanov's anti-religious film *St. Jorgen's Holiday* (*Prazdnik sviatogo Iorgena*, 1930). Protazanov undoubtedly wanted to make a "safe" film after *The White Eagle*, with the result that *St. Jorgen's Holiday* is only intermittently funny. It stars Anatolii Ktorov and Igor Ilinskii as two escaped convicts in an unnamed Western country who disguise themselves as nuns and make their way to a place of pilgrimage. Every year at this festival, a "bride" is chosen for St. Jorgen. This year, when the saint, in the person of the international thief Corcoran (Ktorov), "appears" to claim his bride a miracle is proclaimed. The two "villains" escape along with the saint's "bride," the daughter of a Church official. A haggard-looking Ktorov has some fine moments as Corcoran, but this is very slight material. Protazanov's only concession to social comment was in emphasizing the wealth of the Church, but the movie received one very good review in which the only criticism was of Ilinskii's broad acting.[131]

Protazanov's other late silent film, *Ranks and People* (*Chiny i liudi*, 1929), was based on three Chekhov stories and very traditionally made. Protazanov seemed to be getting bored with filmmaking; the backgrounds and costumes for these period pieces are unusually poor and unimaginative. "The Order of St. Anna" ("Anna na shee") is the most successful of the three vignettes. To help her family, a young woman marries an old man who revolts her; yet in the glow of her society success, she forgets all about them. In "Death of a Bureaucrat" ("Smert' chinovnika"), the theater star Ivan Moskvin plays the unfortunate clerk whose obsession with his having accidentally sneezed on a superior leads to his death. Moskvin is indeed quite pathetic and what is worthwhile in this segment is entirely his own doing. The third part, "Chameleon" ("Khameleon"), is an anecdote far too slight to be translated successfully to the screen. It concerns the investigation of whether the dog who bit a man was a nobleman's, or just an ordinary, dog. By 1929, such fluff was unusual fare for a major director, but surprisingly, it received little attention, except for Khrisanf Khersonskii's criticizing it as a "soft" (meaning "uncritical") portrayal of the times.[132]

St. Jorgen's Holiday and *Ranks and People* marked the end of the silent work of one of the best and most underrated of the Soviet directors of the 1920s. Protazanov was professional, prolific, and, most important, popular. Critic B. Alpers admitted that the public adored Protazanov as the master of the entertainment film. Alpers wrote that Protazanov's films were characterized by the "social neutrality and external decorativeness" of the characters and further charged that some of his films (like *St. Jorgen's Holiday*) misleadingly appeared to answer the demands of the day. In reality (according to Alpers), the director was walking "a thin and swaying tightrope of shallow entertainment."[133] Most of the time this was true, but Protazanov was more than a "safe" director, as evidenced by *The White Eagle* and *Don Diego and Pelageia*.

Pyshka

The last major Soviet silent film was also an adaptation of a literary classic. This was Mikhail Romm's first film, *Pyshka* (1934), based on Maupassant's story of a patriotic French prostitute who saves her fellow travellers from being sequestered in an inn by yielding to the demands of a German officer. Most of the early sound films to be discussed in the next chapter were really silent films with sound. *Pyshka* was the opposite, a sound film without sound. Romm, familiar with the static, realistic style and fluid cuts of the early "talkies," made *Pyshka* accordingly.

In addition to these features, the titles are extremely long, another indication that Romm intended this to be a sound film. (That it was not undoubtedly may be explained by economic problems.) All the action takes place in the coach or in the inn, and since the dramatic focus of the movie is in the protracted effort of the good bourgeois passengers to persuade her to set aside her scruples against sleeping with the German, it is obviously a subject unsuited for the silents.

Pyshka is not, however, without power, entirely due to a strong performance by Galina Sergeeva in the title role. The discussion begun in 1933 as to the suitability of this subject[134] continued after its release. Mikhail Shneider, who by late 1933 had been quietly rehabilitated, felt the story poor material for a silent film.[135] A revealing controversy developed based on Schneider's review, which was taken as a slander against the silent film (it was not). *Cinema* charged Shneider with ignorance of the continued political importance of the silent film,[136] but Lev Shatov, on the other hand, admitted there was some justice to Shneider's remarks—Romm did not understand the special audience the silent movie now had. Shatov was specific: the silent film still "reigned" in the countryside,[137] and *Pyshka* obviously was unsuitable for a peasant audience. The affair may of course be read as an indication that Shneider was still in a tenuous position, but another interpretation might be that the continued production of silent films was an embarrassment which needed justification. September 1934 was, after all, a very late date for the "Great Silent" (as silent films were called) to be dominating *any* screens in a country with pretensions to industrial might.

It is unclear exactly how much longer silent cinema reigned in the hinterlands, but considering the expense of changing projection equipment, its dominance probably lasted up to World War II. In 1933, yet another technical manual on editing silent films was published, and the Soviets admit to making fourteen silents as late as 1935; these supposedly were the last.[138] This extraordinarily long life for the silent movie may be explained by the exigencies of poverty exacerbated by the crippling of the industry through purges and censorship and the continued allocation of resources to more pressing priorities.

The period from 1929 to 1935 was a tragic one, in terms of ruined careers and shattered lives and in terms of aesthetic principles. Soviet silent cinema had had its masterpieces but it had never become a genuinely *popular* art ("popular" in the sense of winning public affection and "art" in the sense of having been made according to consistently high standards). In the politically charged atmosphere of the early thirties, the entire history of Soviet filmmaking seemed contemptible. Considering the extent of the industry's demoralization, it could have been 1919 again, but with an important difference—neither revolutionary enthusiasm nor hope for the future was to be found.

9

The Advent of Sound and the Triumph of Realism (1928-35)

The pessimism in the film industry by the end of the decade, even before the purges were in full swing, was extraordinary. Despite the world renown of the films of Pudovkin and Eisenstein, it was widely believed in the USSR that Soviet cinema had failed to achieve any of its goals. Not only did most critics consider most films bad, what was worse was that due to the collapse of the cinefication campaign, films were inaccessible to the masses.[1] Because the demands of industrialization had led to the drastic curtailment of imports (both of equipment and movies), Soviet cinema was becoming ever more isolated from the West at the most critical moment in cinema history—the advent of sound.[2]

What a blow for the Soviet film industry! It had not yet mastered silent film technology, nor produced film stock or equipment, when along came a radical new development which necessitated the complete replacement of existing equipment with sophisticated and expensive devices. The practical effects were enormous, particularly since the coming of sound coincided with the great upheaval of the purges, a dislocation with which no Hollywood studio had to contend.

Sound made the demands of the First Party Conference on Cinema Affairs (discussed in chapter 7) difficult to satisfy. According to one of the conference's mandates, Soviet cinema was supposed to reverse its dependence on foreign films and raw materials, becoming a net exporter instead of importer. But how could more Soviet films be exported if the import of film stock and other items necessary for filmmaking was being curtailed?[3] Even those Soviet films which *were* made were obsolete as far as the foreign market was concerned because they were silent. Sergei Eisenstein, who was abroad from 1929 to 1932, ostensibly to study the sound film, sent a letter to Glaviskusstvo, the central arts administration, warning that Soviet film exports would soon be nonexistent if the industry persisted in making only silents.[4]

The conference's order to the film industry to create new cadres was also complicated by the technical complexity of the sound movie.[5] GTK, the State Cinema Technical Institute, was not equipped to handle sophisticated new technical problems. In addition, sound demanded much more preproduction preparation than silence, as well as a tighter script (which acted as an impetus to restrict further the autonomy of the director).[6] ARRK in its last years devoted a lot of attention to developing a native sound system,[7] but the results were not particularly satisfactory. Even as late as 1932, it was admitted that the technical problems of sound were still so overwhelming that only forty fiction sound films were planned, compared with eighty-five silent. (It was suggested ominously that those who wanted to "bury" the silent film might well be "wreckers.")[8] In 1933 an astonishing figure was revealed to justify the continuation of silent film production: there were only 200 sound projectors in the *entire* country (and 32,000 silent).[9]

But the ramifications of sound were not purely technical and practical. Perhaps even more serious for the development of Soviet cinema was the artistic impact of sound. Sound cinema and silent cinema operate according to the dictates of different aesthetic principles, which helps make the violent opposition to sound from cineasts the world over during the late twenties more understandable. (In the Soviet Union, those connected with the masterful collection of essays on the art of the silent film, *The Poetics of Cinema*—Boris Eikhenbaum and Iurii Tynianov in particular—doggedly resisted the inevitable.) Some moderates hoped that sound and silent cinemas could coexist, but because the technological nature of cinema means that "newer is better," this could not be.

The aesthetic difference between silent and sound films is easily explained. The hallmark of great silent cinema was its montage, a cutting style that was often rapid and unrealistic. Such cutting is impossible in the sound film, because the ear understands more slowly than the eye sees.[10] For this reason the sound film naturally tends to be slower in tempo than the silent, and in its early days, due to the primitiveness of the equipment, it was much more static than it is today. Some Soviet directors, like Eisenstein and especially Pudovkin, hoped to develop a sound montage, that is, to use sound unrealistically for dramatic punctuation (see below), but early sound films did indeed live up to their sobriquet, the *talkies*. Greater realism accompanied the sound film everywhere in the world; therefore, sound has a special significance in the Soviet case, where realism in the arts was already becoming aesthetic dogma for political reasons.

Soviet critics and directors were not oblivious to the artistic dilemma posed by sound. The best known Soviet essay on the sound film, mixing caution and optimism, appeared in August 1928 in *The Life of Art* above the signatures of Sergei Eisenstein, Vsevolod Pudovkin, and Grigorii Aleksandrov

(Eisenstein's collaborator). The three men recognized the difficulties of developing sound in the Soviet Union, but they believed that sound would open exciting new artistic vistas if it were used correctly. Correct use of sound was not, however, dialogue, and they firmly rejected the *talking* film.

If montage were accepted as the basis of silent cinema (as did Eisenstein, Pudovkin, and Aleksandrov), then montage had also to be the basis of sound cinema. The term they devised was "contrapuntal sound," writing: "*The first experimental work with sound must be directed along the line of its distinct non-synchronization with the visual images.*" They saw sound as a way of surmounting the problems of titles and the "explanatory pieces" which had slowed down the tempo in the silent film. At the same time, nonrealistic use of sound could preserve the international character of cinema that dialogue films would destroy (because of language barriers).[11]

A more combative essay supporting the sound film, "The Sound Cinema as a New Art" ("Zvuchashchee kino kak novoe iskusstvo"), came from the "proletarian" critic V. Solskii. Although Solskii was cognizant of the fact that sound cinema necessitated "accurate" montage (cutting tied to dialogue), he had no sympathy for "enemies" of the sound film like Mikhail Levidov, Boris Eikhenbaum, and Iurii Tynianov. Their objections Solskii labelled "aesthetic"—not surprising considering their links to formalism. (Opposition to sound was consistently [and not inaccurately] tied to the formalist heresy already discussed.) Solskii had absolute confidence that Soviet technology would triumph and that all difficulties were short-term.[12]

His point of view, however, was unusually optimistic. Although it is true that some cinema workers right away saw sound cinema as a "new weapon of the proletariat" and as a much more effective means of propaganda than silent cinema,[13] most ARRKists feared that sound meant cinema would once again become theater.[14] Ippolit Sokolov was quite concerned about the demise of fast montage and mourned the end of the silent acting style, which relied heavily on mimicry and gesture. (Sokolov felt that talking restricted the mobility of facial muscles, thereby limiting the range of expression.)[15]

Yet for the same reasons that Sokolov deplored sound, proponents of realism in Soviet cinema saw that they had won their battle. Nikolai Anoshchenko stated in an ARRK discussion that sound cinema was better able to depict the emotions of the "living person than was silent."[16] B. Alpers wrote a penetrating essay on the new course. The sound film, he felt, would guide cinema out of the blind alley into which the limitations of silence had led it. Indeed, the very novelty of the sound medium would make the development of contemporary, truly Soviet themes easier. Alpers further wrote that the reaction against *talking* cinema—he singled out Pudovkin—was completely misguided. Since experimentalism in silent cinema had only served to alienate the viewer, experimentation with sound would have the same sorry result. For this reason, strictly realistic sound was the only sort acceptable for Soviet cinema: the viewer should always be able to tell its source.[17]

As we have seen, Soviet cinema had long exhibited a tendency toward realism in theory (if not in practice). The apparent indifference of the ordinary Soviet viewer to the most famous works of native silent film art and the warm reception accorded foreign and Soviet "bourgeois" films had convinced many critics that Soviet silent cinema—at least its innovative wing—was too far removed from its constituency. As Valentin Turkin had insisted for years, the only way to make Soviet films palatable to their public was through dramaturgically sound plots with strong heroes. Narrative cinema had the support not only of a growing segment of cinema and social critics, but also the support of actors and script writers. Not until the late twenties, however, concomitant with the development of sound and the "restructuring" of the film industry, was this point of view consistently and thoroughly articulated.

There is, of course, a difference between realism in the ordinary sense of the word and what came to be known as Soviet Socialist Realism.[18] One of the most realistic Soviet silent films, Abram Room's 1927 *Third Meshchanskaia Street*, was also one of the most violently abused movies of the decade. To understand why, one must examine in more detail how realism was defined in the Soviet context.

Advocates of realism could be divided into two groups. One faction was connected with the struggle against formalism, which had in part arisen, as discussed above, from a perceived separation of the artist from the public. Ia. Rudoi, in a 1929 article in *Soviet Screen*, had questioned why the path of "art" in Soviet cinema was always shrouded in a "fog" of symbolism, why artistic achievement was inevitably equated with a *break* with realism.[19] This was the "populist" argument in favor of realism. Must art be defined as that which ordinary people do not like and cannot understand?

But there was an alternative way of approaching the question of "realism" in cinema, one not specifically in negative response to artistically innovative works. This view responded instead to the unhealthy influence of the "bourgeois" films, particularly foreign ones. The way of life shown in these films, which for the most part were *not* avant-garde, had an insidious allure for the masses. For this reason, cinema should concentrate on the achievements of the Soviet present, for: "To show in works of art life as it was, even though in the distant past . . . is not only useless, but in many respects harmful."[20] Since "bourgeois" films advertised "philistine 'prettiness,'" Soviet cinema had to dispense with heroes whose chief preoccupation was dressing in the latest fashions. It is clear that this point of view differs markedly from Rudoi's analysis of the crisis in *Soviet Screen*. Here, directors are not being accused of being isolated from the masses, but instead, of pandering to their low tastes, and especially to the Russian love of "psychological" heroes.[21]

Yet both views were valid critiques of Soviet cinema. A few artists answered only to their personal visions, but many more directors made films virtually indistinguishable from Western pictures. The former (and here I am thinking primarily of Eisenstein, Pudovkin, Kuleshov, Kozintsev and Trauberg) did not much value realism. The extreme literalness of Socialist Realism in cinema, the dread of anything that might appear to be "symbolic" or "psychological," and the insistence on exaggerated simplicity of form ("form understood by the millions") reflected the widespread antipathy to the Soviet avant-garde.

The latter, the "bourgeois" directors (which includes all foreigners and Soviets like Protazanov, Gardin, Ivanovskii, and Eggert), were guilty of a different sin. These directors always managed to insert attractive scenes of bourgeois life in their films, and even if the purpose was to show the decadence of the West, no one was much fooled, least of all the critics. Socialist Realism responded to this body of work by emphasizing "life as it should be"— obsession with wholesome heroes and happy lives.[22] Anything truly realistic in the great tradition of critical realism (like the films of Fridrikh Ermler or Room's *Third Meshchanskaia Street*) was labelled "naked naturalism."[23]

By the early thirties the concept of putting drama and the hero back on the screen had lost its noble purpose of making cinema more attractive to the viewer,[24] realistic, heroic cinema becoming just another sterile formula in the rhetoric of the cultural revolution. The content of cinema articles about Socialist Realism may be inferred from titles like this one: "For a Great Epoch—The High Art of Socialist Realism."[25] After a while, it was no longer necessary to posit entertainment value as the raison d'être of Soviet cinema; workers allegedly were demanding films "to teach us how to live."[26] As early as 1930, it became necessary for the director to explicate the theme of a proposed picture with regard to its social purpose before it could be considered for production.[27]

The reaction of the great directors of the silent screen to Socialist Realism can only be imagined. Their first sound films indicate, however, that they resisted in deeds if not words. Defining art through "simplicity" and "intelligibility" was alien to them.

The First Sound Films

Since the primary purpose of this study has been to delineate the evolution of Soviet *silent* cinema, this section does not pretend to look at early sound films systematically. I will, however, discuss several movies which illustrate the problems of the transition to sound and how Socialist Realism was first put into effect in cinema. The conventions and aesthetics of silent cinema resisted change, as indicated above, and the silent era did not pass with the coming of sound.

The film that the Soviets give the honor of being their first sound film is Nikolai Ekk's 1931 *A Start in Life* (*Putevka v zhizn'*).[28] *A Start in Life* suffers from flaws typical of early sound movies, most of all from naturalistic use of sound: the characters are always laughing heartily, whistling shrilly, or singing gaily. The plot concerns the attempts of a commissar (the popular Nikolai Batalov from *Mother* and *Third Meshchanskaia Street)* to reform a gang of thieving orphans (*bezprizorniki*). (Homeless children were again a problem, apparently due to the famine and social dislocation resulting from collectivization.)[29] The children are gradually reformed through work, and the tone of the film for the most part is jolly and optimistic.

A Start in Life's style is quite uneven. It includes several silent film montage sequences, one of which shows "joy" by juxtaposing the boys bathing with the happiness of their warden at learning they had not run away. The best scene, at the end of the movie, is also very "silent" in style. A thief who is trying to woo the boys back to a life of crime kills their leader, Mustafa, on the railroad tracks in the moonlight. The welcome silence and the beautifully composed silhouettes are oddly at variance with the overall crudity of *A Start in Life*.

The movie would certainly seem to conform to the emerging definition of realism. It was contemporary and positive with a plot and a hero. Yet it was received rather critically by some reviewers for not being political enough, by others for being too "schematic" (although well-intended).[30] Nonetheless, the film was alleged to be a "colossal success" with the viewers because of its melodrama and sentimentality[31] (and undoubtedly because of the novelty of sound, although critics did not mention this).

Sergei Iutkevich's first sound film, *Golden Mountains* (*Zlatye gory*, 1931), is a much more complex and satisfying attempt to combine the techniques of sound and silence. The subject is the working-class movement in 1914; Ermler's favorite Fedor Nikitin stars as a simple-minded laborer in league with the owners. It begins with an exciting mixture of techniques, the rhythmic cutting of growing circles of workers, sound, and titles. In general, Iutkevich has fun with sound; for example, he uses the silent film trick of *showing* the factory whistle blowing, but he follows it with the actual sound, delayed. The closeups of machinery so common to the Soviet silent film are now accompanied by the *sound* of machines. There is also a lot of naturalistic music—singing and instrument playing—as opposed to illustrative music, but in most ways *Golden Mountains* is an experiment. Critics recognized that the film attempted to resolve creatively the difficulties of style inherent in the transition to sound but saw it nonetheless as being *too* beautiful. Iutkevich had, as always, "one foot in formalism."[32]

Grigorii Kozintsev's and Leonid Trauberg's first "sound" film, *Alone* (*Odna*, 1931), has more silence than *Golden Mountains* but is less a silent film.

It represents a startling departure from the eccentric style of their FEKS films of the twenties. Elena Kuzmina (who starred in *New Babylon*) plays a teacher who is assigned to a remote central Asian village. She vainly tries to get out of going because it will force her to break with her fiancé. One of the first things she sees upon arrival in her village is the carcass of a dead horse stretched out for a shamanistic ritual. She dreams of teaching the children the marvels of technology, then is jolted back to reality by thoughts of the horse, the shaman, the life going on as it has for centuries. The lonely woman has to contend with a vicious village elder, who forces the children to work instead of attending school, and with the cynical apathy of the Russian chairman of the village council (Sergei Gerasimov). Finally, one of the teacher's confrontations with the elder leaves her frostbitten and dying. The villagers at last realize what she means to them, and as she is flown to a hospital, they accept the miracle of Soviet power and look forward to a new life.

Alone is an extraordinary movie. Although it has very little dialogue, visually it is much more a sound film than most others of this period. The camera work is realistic, almost documentary in style, most of it outdoors; the shots are long; the cuts are fluid. Much of the sound was added later and is unrealistic (babbling voices, clacking typewriters), but Shostakovich's music is illustrative, rather than the "naturalistic" music (like singing) which was all too common in these early efforts.

Alone treats a contemporary problem vividly and poignantly, and the only concession to the new realism is the uplifting ending which was not in fact part of the original plan. (A 1929 production announcement said it was to be based on the true story of a teacher's *suicide*!)[33] *Alone* was praised in the press as a promising effort by Kozintsev and Trauberg to show living people in a simpler way and thus to reform their "petty-bourgeois" and "intellectual" leanings.[34]

Aleksandr Dovzhenko's first sound movie, *Ivan* (1932), has as its subject the building of the great Dniepr dam. Even given this industrial topic, *Ivan* is in many ways a true Dovzhenko film, with the pictorial beauty and troubling ambiguities that characterized his silent work. On the surface, it portrays Ivan, an incompetent but good-hearted peasant lad working on the dam who becomes a Party member. But Ivan's fate is lost in a series of vignettes depicting the resentment and dislocation attending the dam construction.

The most important secondary character is the affectionately and ironically portrayed "idler." Despite his fear of his communist son (who eventually disowns him), the idler fishes and loafs. When a parade of "heroes of labor" triumphantly denounce him, he shouts: "Why don't you stop torturing people?" The "idler" is unable to cope with the disintegration of his world, and it is this man, not Ivan, whom Dovzhenko clearly loves most. The director's sympathies are also with a simple woman whose son is killed at the site. (She unsuccessfully tries to eulogize him at a Party meeting.) Dovzhenko even empathizes with the harassed manager who babbles drunkenly about dialectics and high prices (the only inkling in the film of the terrible inflation of 1932).

None of this affection is apparent for the cold worker-heroes, who are shot from below eye-level, looking up, a technique which serves to distance them further. The scenes of the dam building are very fine; the camera movements accentuate the movement of the machinery, and the cutting on action is superb. Dovzhenko is not against progress in this film, but he does argue for more humanity. He slyly satirizes the battle mentality of the times by suddenly showing a cavalcade of airplanes, tanks, and other military paraphernalia.

The use of sound is both naturalistic—loud laughing and singing—and imaginative—a musical rendition of Ivan's hammering becomes "real" hammering. *Ivan* fails by the dramatic standards of narrative cinema but succeeds as one of the last cinematic attempts to assess the changes in Soviet society critically. Yet *Ivan* was judged not by these serious political implications, but by its dramaturgical shortcomings.[35]

Fridrikh Ermler's first sound effort, *Counterplan* (*Vstrechnyi*, 1932), with Sergei Iutkevich as co-director, is an uneven attempt to exploit the campaign against foreign specialists and "saboteurs" in factories. This ugly theme may explain why Ermler's heart does not seem to be in the movie, which is an unfocussed tale combining the more Ermler-like story of an alcoholic foreman's attempts to reform himself with the topical story of the search for a factory saboteur. Although Ermler's realism had always been pronounced, his last silent, *Fragment of an Empire*, showed that he also had talent for innovation, and he does do some interesting things with sound in *Counterplan*: an off-screen voice indicates a new presence in the room, for example, and Shostakovich's music is used to good purpose. There are also a few nicely lyrical moments which recall the pictorial style of his silents, such as a couple wandering around Leningrad in the "white nights." But Ermler is ill at ease, and nothing is properly developed. Although *Counterplan* has to be judged a failure, viewers reportedly liked the film.[36]

Vsevolod Pudovkin's first planned sound film, *A Simple Case* (*Prostoi sluchai*, 1932), became a silent due to the director's dissatisfaction with the primitiveness of Soviet sound equipment.[37] Therefore, his first realized sound project was *Deserter* (*Dezertir*, 1933), which used the Soviet-developed Tagefon system. The sound quality is terrible, but Pudovkin's experiments with contrapuntal effects are intriguing. Yet the story, of a wavering German worker who fears a commitment to the labor struggle in his own country and takes refuge in the Soviet Union, is not well drawn. More than any other Pudovkin movie, *Deserter* is formalist.

Numerous scenes support this. During a political speech, sounds are muffled, the words only becoming distinct through closeups. In industrial scenes, sounds and images are overlapping. The bottom of a speaker's jaw is at one time the only thing on the screen. At another, there is *nothing* on the screen for several seconds, just sound. It should not be surprising that the reception of this film was less than enthusiastic,[38] and it served as a lesson to other directors (if they were naive enough not to have already realized this) of the foolhardiness of experimenting with sound.

Lev Kuleshov's first sound film, *The Great Consoler* (*Velikii uteshitel'*, 1933), did not deviate from his fondness for American subjects, but unlike his other "American" films, it was fairly well received. *The Great Consoler* is a story within a story: Sidney Porter (O. Henry) is sitting in jail writing a Jimmy Valentine yarn which is cheerfully envisioned in appropriate silent movie style, serving to lighten the grim central story of poor conditions in prison and the dishonest treatment of prisoners. A subplot features Aleksandra Khokhlova as a poor shopgirl who is accused of embezzlement, loses her job, and kills the policeman who has forced her into prostitution.

The Great Consoler is not a unified work, but it has its moments; the part with Khokhlova is particularly successful. The cutting is very "silent film" in style, but the use of sound is realistic. Unlike most of the other movies discussed so far, this is a *talking* picture. The movie was seen as being properly Soviet, representing Kuleshov's rejection of his "bourgeois" formalism.[39]

Boris Barnet's first sound film, *Borderlands* (*Okraina*, 1933), is startlingly good—Barnet had not exactly established himself as a first-rate director with his silent oeuvre: *Miss Mend*, *The House on Trubnaia Square*, *Girl with a Hat Box*, *Moscow in October*. This World War I tale follows the fate of a single family during the war and is first and foremost a rousing war movie which concentrates on action, not message, making it a rarity in Soviet cinema.

Barnet hit on a way to use sound realistically without burdening a film with the conversation that in turn would hamper good camerawork. The extensive use of the moving camera, good parallel cutting among the principals, and the impact of the sound—sirens, shells exploding, bombing— make *Borderlands* very exciting to watch. Moreover, its human interest is strong without crude pathos; for once the viewer really cares when a character—one of the brothers—is killed. *Borderlands* is a marvelously entertaining and well-made movie, one of the very best of the thirties. In general it was praised, although a "brigade" of stuffy—or frightened— Leningrad critics headed by Mikhail Bleiman, found the ideological underpinnings poorly developed.[40]

Dziga Vertov's first sound picture, *Enthusiasm* (*Entuziazm*), had been characteristically innovative and was suppressed. His second film, *Three Songs of Lenin* (*Tri pesni o Lenine*, 1934), somewhat bolstered his sagging reputation, but it also demonstrated the degradation of his style since its peak in 1929, *Man with a Movie Camera*. The worst aspect of the film is its moralistic titles;

dialogue is very limited, and the music is mainly illustrative, although there is some singing and instrument playing. The visuals only briefly show flashes of Vertov's brilliance with a few freeze-frames, angle shots, and subjective motion on a speeding train.

The first segment, "My Face Was in a Dark Prison" ("V chernoi tiur'me bylo litso moe"), shows the liberation of central Asian women from stifling customs and has some documentary value. The second part, "We Loved Him" ("My liubili ego"), is a dreary panegyric to Lenin which resorts to one of Vertov's favorite tricks, the joining of shots without spatial reference. For example, shots of Lenin's funeral are intercut with shots of sorrowing girls who were undoubtedly years and miles away from that scene. The third segment, "In a Big Stone City" ("V bol'shom kamennom gorode"), becomes almost fascistic in its treatment of the People and the Leader and in its emphasis on the human body. This abysmal film marked the bitter end of the career of a great and original director whose artistic politics helped shape the cinema debates of a decade. *Three Songs of Lenin* is typical of what the Soviet "documentary" would become.

The sound films discussed above had been transitional ones, combining silent and sound techniques in the hesitant effort to find a new style. Only one of these is an unqualified and enduring achievement, *Borderlands*, although *Alone* also deserves to be better known. But the first and probably the best film truly to combine the techniques of sound cinema with the tenets of Socialist Realism is a film as central to Soviet cinema history as *Potemkin*. This is *Chapaev* (1934), directed by Sergei Vasilev and Georgii Vasilev (who were *not* brothers, although the press tried to make them so). *Chapaev* received the endorsement of Stalin, the critics, and the Soviet public.

It is based on the memoirs of Dmitrii Furmanov, the writer who was political commissar to the legendary Civil War hero. Even though Chapaev (Boris Babochkin) dies at the end, it is a wonderfully uplifting and high-spirited movie. Chapaev is warm, humorous, and wise (much more appealing than the somewhat foppish and intellectual Furmanov). He empathizes with the people and wins them over to the Bolsheviks, although it is clear that communism is no more than some sort of vaguely good cause to him. *Chapaev* succeeds because it is simple and genuine; Chapaev, although "positive," has enough rough edges to be believable. *Chapaev* marks the beginning of a new era in Soviet cinema and the end of this story.[41]

The 1935 Conference

If anyone had any doubts that the artistic principles of the silent era had ended, these were put to rest by the January 1935 All-Union Creative Conference on Cinematographic Affairs. Here gathered all the greats of silent cinema, along with their new masters, to recant their sins or accuse their colleagues and sometimes both. The tone of the conference was set by its presiding officer, the "critic" and Party bureaucrat, S. Dinamov. Dinamov defined the basis of the new Soviet cinema as optimism, heroism, and theatricality and dispensed with Kuleshov, Eisenstein, Pudovkin, Shklovskii, and ARRK in a few cutting words.[42] Following his lead, the speakers took a dim view of the brilliant and colorful youth of Soviet cinema, with Leonid Trauberg and Aleksandr Dovzhenko trying to outdo each other in their condemnations of the past.[43]

Most of the conference time was spent attacking Sergei Eisenstein, and Dovzhenko's speech was markedly self-serving. He first interpreted his own works as models of realism (conveniently omitting a discussion of the fantastical *Zvenigora*), then separated himself from "narrowly professional" directors who worried about technique and whose works were not "positive" enough.

All of these fine (and self-proclaimed) qualities of Dovzhenko's were in sharp contrast to those of poor Sergei Eisenstein. Dovzhenko said: "I fear that he knows so much, that he has such a 'clear' head, that he evidently will never make another film." And Dovzhenko added that if Eisenstein did not make a picture within a year, then he was finished as a director—and should be.[44] Sergei Iutkevich and Sergei Vasilev did not miss their opportunities to attack Eisenstein either. Iutkevich said that if he knew as much as Eisenstein, he would undoubtedly burst from knowledge; Vasilev urged Eisenstein to "throw away his Chinese robe [*khalat*]" and come out of his study to join the real world.[45]

Eisenstein wryly defended himself, retorting to Vasilev that "...if I sat and worked in my study, it was so you didn't have to...."[46] Nikolai Lebedev also stressed the importance of Eisenstein's creative experiments to his teaching, but this was challenged by a remark from the floor: "Millions of viewers are dearer to us than forty students," to which Lebedev had the temerity to respond: "Millions of viewers will receive forty pictures from forty directors and in each of them will be a part of Eisenstein."[47]

But the most moving defense of Eisenstein came from his old "theoretical enemy," Lev Kuleshov. Kuleshov was now a man with little to lose. After begging for help and accusing the "comrades" of rejoicing over his troubles, Kuleshov said:

> Regarding Sergei Mikhailovich [Eisenstein], whom those on this floor, with very warm, touching, tearful little smiles, want to bury prematurely—a lot of comrades have talked about Sergei Mikhailovich as if he were deceased. I would like to tell him, as a completely alive person, whom I love very much and alone appreciate: dear and beloved Sergei Mikhailovich! Iutkevich said that one can burst from knowledge, and he fears that this will happen with you. Dear Sergei Mikhailovich, one bursts not from knowledge, but from envy.[48]

Kuleshov's speech was not met with the "stormy, prolonged applause" that followed other commentators.

Pudovkin was also criticized at this conference, most of all by Iutkevich, for having gone over to the Eisenstein camp. *Deserter* was a special object of derision.[49] Iutkevich managed to attack Dovzhenko for his "static, painting-like shots."[50] But conspicuously absent from these charges were the former chief whipping boys, Abram Room and Dziga Vertov.[51]

Yet despite the harsh criticism of Eisenstein and others, there was a conciliatory note to this conference. Speakers took care (as usual) to stress that their criticism was intended to help their errant comrades,[52] but this time there seemed to be some truth to it. Directors P. P. Petrov-Bytov and Nikolai Shengelaia spoke of the need to smooth the jealous rivalries in the studios[53] (which had undoubtedly arisen from the purges). The venom unleashed by the purges had outlived its social purpose and was admittedly hampering work, which was proceeding very slowly.[54] The time for rebuilding had begun.

This new attitude was emphasized by the Party's attention to cinema in the January 1935 awards ceremony (at which Eisenstein did not receive the Order of Lenin, a conspicuous insult).[55] It was also reinforced by Soiuzkino head B. Z. Shumiatskii's remarks at the thematic conference in this same month. Shumiatskii admitted the weak position of the industry and promised to strengthen the depleted cadres with young people. Taken as a whole, his remarks are testimony to the great change that had taken place; for the most part, films, disputes, and victims were all new.[56]

It was Sergei Iutkevich who best summed up the attitude toward the future and the past. He said at the All-Union Creative Conference on Cinematographic Affairs:

> The fundamental functions of cinematography are fighting, political functions. From here comes the struggle for the viewer, without which cinematography cannot exist.
>   But what happened? What happened was that we lost the viewer.[57]

Whether the viewer could be regained through films devoted to the exploits of Soviet youth and political education is someone else's story, but the flamboyant past of Soviet cinema had been decisively repudiated. It was the beginning of 1935, and the twenties had ended at last.

Conclusion

Although this work has sought to show that the aesthetics of Soviet silent cinema were in general more conservative than those of Dziga Vertov and its films less brilliant than *Potemkin*, there was nonetheless an extraordinary gravitation of gifted young people to cinema after the Revolution. This is most obvious in the directors, of whom Fridrikh Ermler, Abram Room, Lev Kuleshov, Grigorii Kozintsev, and Leonid Trauberg should by rights be as well known as Eisenstein, Vertov, Pudovkin, and Dovzhenko. It is no exaggeration to say that the appearance of so many first-rate artists in one country in the course of a single decade was nothing short of phenomenal.

More evidence of the high level of Soviet cinema during this period can be seen in the film critics. Despite the prevalent idea that Soviet silent cinema produced primarily theoreticians of montage, the cinema press actually consisted of a number of very talented critics, chief among these being Ippolit Sokolov, Khrisanf Khersonskii, and Viktor Shklovskii. Film criticism—as opposed to theory—is a blend of aesthetic and social analysis of individual films and cinema culture as a whole; Soviet critics of the twenties were definitely not theoreticians. Because NEP Russia provided the opportunity for free discussion (although one must not forget that censorship was an irksome problem even then), the film criticism of this period is indispensible in illuminating the evolution of both cinema and the film industry. Moreover, even if one wants to take issue with their political framework or moral rectitude, the artistic sense of these critics was usually sound. Their writings survive as accurate assessments of the artistic value of these films, no mean feat.

How may the achievements of the silent period be explained? There is no single answer, and "fate" alone is unhistorical. Few artists or critics came to cinema first, many having worked in the theater previously, although some were from the fine arts or literature. Most major Soviet filmworkers were very young indeed, and for them, cinema had the attraction of being an art free from excess cultural baggage. That this would be one of cinema's charms for the young, especially in a time of revolution, is not at all surprising.

But cinema was a revolutionary art in other ways. Despite occasional rhetoric about revolutionary aesthetics, as we have seen, Soviet cinema was rarely revolutionary in the sense of being genuinely avant-garde. It was more often considered revolutionary because it threatened the predominance of both the theater and literature as a source of popular entertainment. This aspect of cinema as a "mass" art, an art for the people, attracted another, artistically more conservative, group to the infant Soviet industry.

Hardworking and dedicated activists like Nikolai Lebedev, the cinema publicist and founder of ARK, or A. Katsigras, the one-man rural cinema lobby from the Commissariat of Enlightenment's Glavpolitprosvet, may be labelled a part of the political left. These Party members, disillusioned with the capitalist regression that the New Economic Policy represented, had no interest in cinema as a revolutionary art form, unlike many of the best directors and critics. Although they were interested in cinema as an "art" in the *service* of the revolution, this must not be construed as an advocacy of the propaganda film. It represented instead an appreciation of the potential cinema had as both an educational tool and a "wholesome" and relatively inexpensive entertainment for a largely illiterate and rural population. That avant-garde cinema could not fulfill this agenda was just one of the problems troubling the times.

The political leftists' interest in cinema was motivated by an idealism which was sincere but more than a little naive. They were right in thinking that Soviet audiences did not want to see Kozintsev's and Trauberg's *The Overcoat* or even Dziga Vertov's "nonfiction" *Cinema Eye*, but they were wrong in assuming that the rural public wanted to watch sober fare like newsreels, educational films, or at lightest, fiction films on peasant life.

The artistic left and center were represented by a diverse group of talented young directors and critics whose only point of unity was an opposition to the "vulgar" and theatrical movie melodramas common to the West. For them, revolutionary cinema was not necessarily anti-realistic, but neither was its subject matter to be the love lives of the privileged classes. The political left, shorter on raw talent, but long on dedication, also opposed such "bourgeois" fare in cinema, although they rarely supported the new alternatives, whether the revolutionary "mass" movies of Sergei Eisenstein or the "problem" dramas of Fridrikh Ermler.

The third major group in Soviet cinema consisted of the much-maligned "Sovkino-ites" and other studio administrators. Despite the criticism levelled at Sovkino and Mezhrabpom by disgruntled filmworkers, there was an abundance of talent and energy in these organizations too. Sovkino's I. P. Trainin and M. P. Efremov were far from being unimaginative bureaucrats or sterile Party hacks. Both Party members of long standing (from before World War I), they were nonetheless rightists in both the political and artistic sense, supporting the principles of NEP *and* traditional "bourgeois" cinema with a plot and actors. Efremov and Trainin were hard-headed pragmatists faced with a formidable task. They took over an industry with serious congenital defects; their successes over the five-year life of Sovkino were staggering. Despite unrelenting financial pressure and ceaseless infighting and enmity, they managed to organize studios that produced some great films.

Was cinema only a challenge to be overcome for Trainin, Efremov, and other studio administrators? I think their public pronouncements also revealed a genuine love of the movies, along with a desire to serve the viewers by producing well-crafted entertainment films. For this reason studio administrators supported unexciting but professional directors like Iakov Protazanov who could be counted on to return the investment with a sound entertainment film that meant good box office receipts. Sovkino's administrators, Trainin in particular, understood the Soviet viewer much better than did well-meaning Glavpolitprosvet workers like Katsigras.

There was a plethora of talent, dedication, and good will in the cinema community. This is why the period was so dynamic and its achievements so numerous. That such people could and did become bitter enemies is a considerable tragedy.

As we have seen, the reasons for the escalating conflict were complex, arising from the contradictory and unreasonably high expectations of the various factions. Everyone expected to be satisfied in every respect. Considering the cultural and financial poverty of the country and its immense social and political problems, this was unreasonable. A decisive factor in determining the course of events for the film industry—the competition for resources—never abated; it was just as frantic by the end of the decade as it was at the beginning. This situation was not due as much to mismanagement (despite a few celebrated scandals) as it was to government priorities. Cinema was never "most important" to either the government or the Party in the twenties, not even as a means of propaganda. Although there was more interest in cinema as propaganda with the advent of the industrialization campaign, industrialization only served to exacerbate the chronic shortages the studios faced, since funds were diverted to heavy industry and imports of film equipment and raw material were drastically curtailed. Given this, centralization seemed to all concerned a rational way of allocating scarce resources to competing directors.

Industrial centralization and the hardening of the aesthetic line were closely linked. Soviet directors, driven by financial imperatives to promote their views vigorously, were frequently intolerant; Dziga Vertov is the supreme example. So long as the fierce disputes and rivalries were contained within the relatively cultured and well-educated group of artists and critics connected with ARK, this was not dangerous, but gradually the furious debates deteriorated into a grim rhetoric that was encouraged and furthered by the appearance in the cinema press of new critics like P. Neznamov or B. Alpers, who, while not without talent, ruthlessly hounded "specialists," whether old or young.

These "new critics" found Soviet cinema in a crisis state. They saw the screens dominated by foreign or foreign-style "fluff" and by elitist experiments. This "crisis" could be interpreted as an excuse for purging the industry, an interpretation which would neatly connect cinema with the sweeping change of "cadres" that the cultural revolution (1928-32) initiated. While the cultural revolution had undeniable impact on cinema at the end of the decade, the cinema crisis was very real.

Like the NEP society of which it was part, Soviet cinema in its "Golden Age" had its seamy and contradictory sides. By the end of the decade, rural areas were still not served on a regular basis by the travelling projectors, and provincial towns received only second- and third-rate films. Vodka drinking was a much more attractive (and lucrative) pastime than moviegoing. In the major cities, commercial theaters attracted audiences despite their high ticket prices, for they could afford to buy the films people wanted to see—not the famous Soviet revolutionary films for which the era is remembered in the West—but foreign films. Although the best Soviet critics, with perfect justice, lavishly praised the films of Dovzhenko and Eisenstein, audiences did not like them. Their favorite Soviet director was Iakov Protazanov. As the decade wore on, the films of the best artists became less and less accessible to the public, as epitomized by the *New Babylon* affaire de scandale.

Soviet film production was unusually graced by genius, and the forms genius took are revealing about the times. But just as revealing are the "ordinary" films, like Protazanov's comedies and melodramas or Ivanovskii's costume extravaganzas, films which were only superficially "Soviet." It is important to remember, moreover, that many, many films of Soviet production were ineptly made and boring, not surprising considering the poverty, inexperience, and isolation of Soviet filmmakers. Therefore, by the late twenties, it could convincingly be argued that the "specialists" (of whom there were precious few) had not come up with a viable Soviet style in cinema.

By the early thirties, in contrast, a Soviet style *had* been articulated. Because Socialist Realism was not unique to cinema and was in fact dogma for all the arts, it is quite easy to regard it as having been dictated from above, reflecting Stalin's primitive personal tastes in culture. Once again, this is not an incorrect view, only an incomplete one. Socialist Realism addressed issues which had been troubling film activists for ten years or more. What forces from within the industry militated toward the triumph of realism, even if a spurious variety?

First, audience tastes definitely favored the superficial, romantic realism of Western films, which featured straightforward plots and likeable heroes—

the kind of movie that Sovkino and Mezhrabpom produced. The promise of good box office returns was undoubtedly one strong motivation for the studio administrators to support such films but another was an apparently genuine commitment to movies as entertainment, not art. Yet despite their rejection of the avant-garde, the studio heads, in their own way splendid idealists, could not and did not triumph, for they scornfully and unequivocally rejected the stereotypes of Socialist Realism as totally unacceptable to the viewer and fatal to the industry. At the same time, studio support of narrative realism, even if not of a socialist stripe, was a powerful force in weakening the influence of nontraditional directors of various persuasions. The political left also favored realism as a matter of principle, but *their* realism was of the tendentious variety. Socialist Realism borrowed from both these sources.

Realism also had important bases of support in two other groups: actors and scenarists. Cinema actors felt themselves a slighted and even abused group. One target of their opprobrium was the young directors, who were often perceived as eschewing use of the professional actor, although the only two consistently guilty of this were Eisenstein and Vertov. But it is true that these younger directors (with the exception of Abram Room and Fridrikh Ermler) did not conceive of cinema as a vehicle for actors. Traditional directors, like Protazanov, were also out of favor with aspiring young actors, for although their films provided strong roles, parts more often than not went to popular and established *theater* actors.

Another group clamoring for realism was movie scenarists. A script has a much more important role in a realistic movie than in an avant-garde film, especially a silent film, which often relied heavily on the visual aspects. Directors of all bents were notoriously loose with scripts, and because of the authorship laws, which favored scenarists for movie royalties, most directors insisted on "co-authoring" screenplays. The advent of Socialist Realism brought an unprecedented reward to the Soviet film writer, whose name is more often than not listed *above* that of the director.

Coupled with these pressures for rejection of artistic innovation was the invention of the sound movie. Therefore, despite the very real political pressures (both internal and external) leading to the establishment of Socialist Realism, the cinema realism of the 1930s was not just a Soviet phenomenon but a *worldwide* trend. At this point society-wide developments merged with changes in the film world.

Although this sad tale has no villains, the only figure who emerges untarnished is Sergei Eisenstein. As far as I can tell, Eisenstein alone never stooped to the character assassination which began in the late twenties and carried on through the thirties. It is not cynical to suggest that his being abroad from 1929 to 1932 helped him retain his integrity, for those were the crucial stress-filled and confused years which nearly brought film production to a halt.

By the end of the twenties, most filmworkers were undoubtedly bewildered by the harsh changes wrought in the course of a single decade, changes for which they were themselves in no small degree responsible. Cinema had indeed become a battle front, one lacking the enthusiastic idealism which had prompted ARK to change its journal's name to *Cinema Front* in 1926. But even with our inestimable benefit of hindsight, it is impossible to fix the point at which everything started to go wrong.

The problems the film industry faced were severe, without clear-cut solutions, and mature, experienced personnel was at a premium. The New Economic Policy had serious shortcomings—it was neither responsive to the political and social dreams of the Revolution's initial supporters nor able to provide a sound financial base for the rebuilding of a shattered society. Both factors had a powerful impact on the evolution of the film industry. It is tempting to judge, but it is better to remember that one of the best (and most realistic) films of the period, Ermler's *The Parisian Cobbler*, ended with the question: "Who is to blame?" But it left the viewer to decide for himself on the basis of the evidence presented.

Appendix 1

Film Production by Studio by Year (1918-35)

Film Production by Studio by Year (1918-35)[1]*

Studio	18	19	20	21	22	23	24	25	26	27	28	29	30	31	32	33	34	35	TOTAL
Armenkino									2	3	2		5	3	5	1	1	(1)	23
Azerbaidjani[2]							3	1	1		3	1	2		1		3	3	18
Belgoskino									1	6	5	6	6	7(1)	5(4)	2(1)	5(3)	(3)	46
Chuvashkino											1		1						2
Goskino						5	25	30	26										86
Goskinprom Gruzii				1	2	4	2	6	8	14	12	6	11	4	3(1)		5(1)	2(1)	80
Gosvoenkino									6	4	10	5							25
Lenfil'm																	10(3)	(6)	16
Leningradkino									7										7
Mezhrabpom (-Rus', -fil'm)							5	11	11	21	22	21	15	10(4)	10(9)	(6)	10(9)	(14)	156
Mosfil'm																		18(14)	18
Moskinokombinat																	15(8)	(2)	17
Proletkino						1	6	5	5										17
Rosfil'm															14(5)	6(2)			20
Sevzapkino					7	7	10	11	1										36

Studio	18	19	20	21	22	23	24	25	26	27	28	29	30	31	32	33	34	35	TOTAL
Sovkino								2	9	52	56	40	14	1					174
Soiuzkino													52(5)	47(13)	28(7)	9(3)	2(11)		138
Tadzhikkino																	2		2
Turkmenfil'm/ Turkmenkino												1		1				2	4
Ukrainian[3]		23	9	4	5	7	11	8	23	27	27	19	27	18(1)	11(3)	4(3)	10(7)	(6)	239
Uzbek[1][4]													3	4	3	1	1	2	22
VFKO			15	5	1														24
Vostokkino		3									1	2	7	8	6	3	2(1)	1	30
Private		20																	20
OTHER[5] (Gov't & Party)	6	11	5	2	1	4	14	15	4	9	8	5	3		4	(3)	(2)	3(2)	99
TOTAL	6	57	29	12	16	28	76	90	105	141	148	106	146	103	90	35	68	63	1319
SOUND													5	19	29	18	35	49	

*(Sound Films in Parentheses Beginning 1930)

1. Data gathered from *Sovetskie khudozhestvennye fil'my*, vols. 1-2. My total of 1,319 films is less than this work's apparent total of 1,326 due to its inconsistent numbering and counting of the different parts of a serial film as separate titles.
2. The Azerbaidjani studio was variously AFKU, Azerfil'm, Azgoskinprom, Azgoskino, and Azerkino.
3. The major Ukrainian studio was VUFKU, which became Ukrainfil'm in 1930.
4. The Uzbeki studio was variously Uzbekfil'm, Uzbekgoskino, and Uzbekkino.
5. Includes Burevestnik, GTK, Iuvkinokomsomol, Kinokontora "Krasnaia zvezda," Kino-Moskva, Kino-Sever, Kino-Sibir', Moskovskii kinokomitet, Petrogradskii kinokomitet.

FEATURE FILM PRODUCTION BY YEAR

SILENT FILMS ———

SOUND FILMS — —

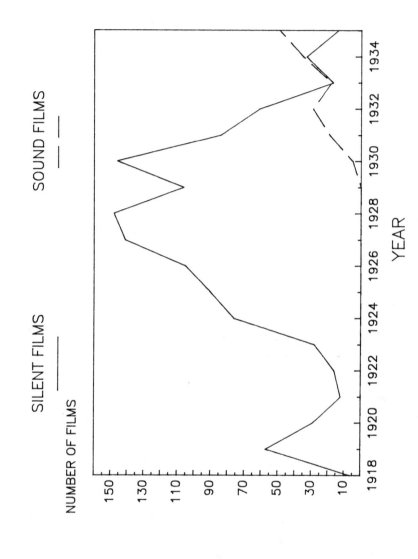

NUMBER OF FILMS

150
130
110
90
70
50
30
10

1918 1920 1922 1924 1926 1928 1930 1932 1934

YEAR

Appendix 2

Genres by Year (1918-35)

Genres by Year (1918-35)[1]

Genres	18	19	20	21	22	23	24	25	26	27	28	29	30	31	32	33	34	35	TOTAL
Agit-film	3	40	21	7	3	1	14	10	2		5	1	9	9	4	1			130
Adventure						4	3	8	10	4		3	1		2	1		6	42
Animated/Children's						1	10	9	2	24	31	21	28	15	23	10	15	24	213
Comedy		1			2	4	17	15	15	23	24	10	13	10	10	1	13	7	165
Contemporary Drama					3	4	8	19	14	38	42	25	67	50	40	12	21	14	357
Educational (Kul'turfil'm)		4					3	4	2	1		4	2						20
Historical					3	3	5	5	18	14	12	5	1	2	4	2	2		76
Literary Adaptation[2]	2	11	5	1	5	6	3	5	12	19	11	8	1	1	1	1	7	4	103
Revolution/Civil War (1905–21)	1	1	3	4		3	13	15	30	16	19	23	16	11	4	7	10	5	181
Other						2				2	4	6	8	5	2			3	32
TOTAL	6	57	29	12	16	28	76	90	105	141	148	106	146	103	90	35	68	63	1319

1. Data from *Sovietskie khudozhestvennye fil'my*, vols. 1-2. Each film was analyzed independently of the classification assigned in ibid. In some categories, my classification was identical: agit-films, animated, comedy, and educational films (*kul'turfil'my*). In other cases, certain films were reassigned to categories which better reflected their content, e.g. adventures and dramas to Revolution/Civil War and dramas to children's.

2. Literary adaptations were only counted as such if they were established literary works not fitting another category. For example, Gorkii's *Mother* was classified "Revolutionary/Civil War," not "Literary Adaptation," while films based on Chekhov, Pushkin, and Tolstoi were "Literary Adaptations," not "Historical." Films based on the works of Soviet novelists were usually classified as contemporary dramas.

CONTEMPORARY DRAMA AS A % OF TOTAL PRODUCTION

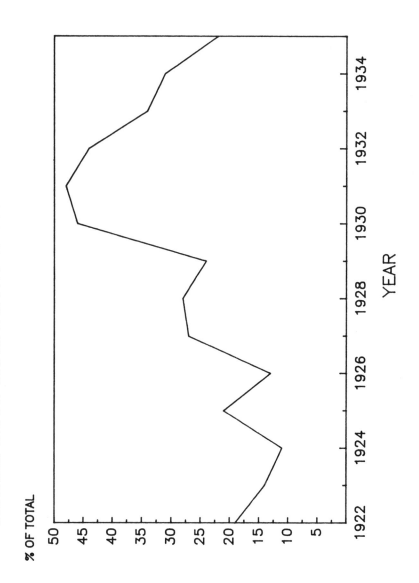

% OF TOTAL

Notes

Preface

1. Foremost (and most prolific) among recent scholars of the twenties is Sheila Fitzpatrick. See her *The Commissariat of Enlightenment: Soviet Organization of Education and the Arts under Lunacharsky, October 1917-1921* (Cambridge, 1970) and *Education and Social Mobility in the Soviet Union, 1921-1934* (Cambridge, 1979), as well as her numerous articles on various aspects of the cultural revolution. For the contributions of other scholars to what is undeniably Fitzpatrick's domain see Fitzpatrick, ed., *Cultural Revolution in Russia, 1928-1931* (Bloomington, Ind., 1978).

   Reformers sometimes proselytize so zealously that they may seem to slight the accomplishments of their predecessors. I am chary of falling into that trap. The pioneering study of Soviet literature and literary groups is Edward J. Brown, *The Proletarian Episode in Russian Literature (1928-1932)* (New York, 1953); another important work in this field is Robert A. Maguire, *Red Virgin Soil: Soviet Literature in the 1920s* (Princeton, NJ, 1968). For developments in the arts see John E. Bowlt, ed. and trans., *Russian Art of the Avant-Garde: Theory and Criticism, 1902-1934* (New York, 1976). Little has been done regarding the institutional developments in Soviet theater in the twenties.

   As far as cinema is concerned, Jay Leyda's *Kino: A History of the Russian and Soviet Film* (New York, 1960; rev. ed., 1983) has long been and undoubtedly will long continue to be the standard introduction in English to Soviet film history for layman and specialist alike. An important early investigation more relevant to this study is Paul Babitsky and John Rimberg, *The Soviet Film Industry* (New York, 1955), which suffers more from paucity of documentation, as is to be expected considering the date of publication, than from conceptualization.

   The three major American doctoral dissertations on Soviet cinema preceding mine have all been by film scholars and have been published in the Arno Press cinema series. See Peter Dart, *Pudovkin's Film and Film Theory* (New York, 1974); Seth Feldman, *Evolution of Style in the Early Works of Dziga Vertov* (New York, 1977); and Louis Harris Cohen, *The Cultural-Political Traditions and Developments of Soviet Cinema, 1927-1972* (New York, 1974). Dart and Feldman are valuable as descriptions and analyses of rare films; Cohen's massive work reads like a Soviet tract and has little to offer by way of original research. The best recent Soviet work is T. F. Selezneva, *Kino-mysl' 20-kh godov* (Moscow, 1976), a brief but intelligent discussion of several important aesthetic issues from a strictly theoretical point of view.

   The most recent scholarly monograph on Soviet cinema in English is Richard Taylor, *The Politics of Soviet Cinema, 1917-1929* (Cambridge, 1979), which primarily addresses the question of the political function—very narrowly defined—of Soviet cinema during this period, positing a "revolution from above." Although my book was not conceived as a polemic with Taylor, it in effect serves as one. Little of the material we cover is the same, and our conclusions are radically different. See my review of Taylor, *Russian Review* 39, no. 2 (April 1980): 272-73.

Introduction

1. Jay B. Sorenson reports that Party membership in Rabis, the Art Workers' Union (which we may take to be the closest approximation to ARK), was 13-14 percent in the twenties. See his *The Life and Death of Soviet Trade Unionism* (New York, 1969), p. 197.

Chapter 1

1. Nikolai Lebedev, *Ocherk istorii kino SSSR: Nemoe kino* (Moscow, 1948), p. 66. Lebedev, an old cinema activist, was denounced for "cosmopolitanism" for this excellent book, still the best Soviet work on silent cinema. Also Taylor, *Politics,* pp. 43-45.

2. Taylor, *Politics*, pp. 45-47; Leyda, *Kino*, p. 133.

3. Taylor, *Politics*, p. 48. Taylor covers the operation of the agit-trains very well, pp. 48-63; cf. his "A Medium for the Masses: Agitation in the Soviet Civil War," *Soviet Studies* 22 (April 1971): 562-74. For descriptions of agit-films, see Leyda, *Kino,* 135ff.

4. Lebedev, *Ocherk*, p. 71. See Leyda, *Kino*, p. 142, for the text of the decree in English.

5. Leyda, *Kino*, pp. 145-47. Leyda vividly describes the ordeal of the filming of *Polikushka.*

6. For a description of the theaters, ibid., pp. 155-56.

7. Taylor, *Politics*, pp. 68-70.

8. Ibid., pp. 72-73. For a full account of the Cibrario affair see Leyda, *Kino*, pp. 126-28.

9. Editorial, *Kino-zhizn'*, no. 2 (1922), p. 3. Journals of this period were irregularly paginated. Page numbers have been included wherever possible.

10. Charli, untitled article, ibid., p. 4.

11. "O novykh postanovkakh, 1922 g.," ibid., no. 3 (1922), p. 1.

12. "Nasha anketa," ibid., p. 6.

13. "Petrogradskie pis'ma," ibid., no. 4 (1922).

14. Advertisements, ibid., no. 5 (1923), p. 5.

15. Aleksei Gan, "Kinematograf i kinematografiia," *Kino-fot*, no. 1 (1922), p. 1.

16. Ippolit [Sokolov?], "Skrizhal veka," ibid., p. 3.

17. B. Arvatov, "Agit-kino," ibid., no. 2 (1922), p. 2.

18. A. V., "Kinematograf i kinoshkola," ibid., no. 1 (1922), pp. 8-9.

19. Lev Liberman, "Kino-delo i kino-pisatel'," ibid., no. 1 (1922), pp. 4-5.

20. A.V., "Molodezhi! Iskusstvo umiraet," ibid., no. 2 (1922), p. 8.

21. Aleksei Gan, "My boiuem," ibid., no. 3 (1922), p. 8; "Khronika GTK," p. 9.

22. Editorial, ibid., no. 4 (1922), p. 1.

23. Aleksei Gan, "*Kino-pravda* (10-ia)," ibid., pp. 3-4.

24. Dziga Vertov, "On i ia," ibid., no. 2 (1922), pp. 9-10. Selected Vertov writings have been translated in *Kino-Eye: The Writings of Dziga Vertov*, ed. Annette Michelson, trans. Kevin O'Brien (Berkeley, Calif., 1984).

25. Lev Kuleshov, "Iskusstvo, sovremennaia zhizn', i kinematografiia," ibid., no. 1 (1922), p. 2.

26. In *Kuleshov on Film: Writings of Lev Kuleshov* (Berkeley, Calif., 1974), Ronald Levaco has translated Kuleshov's *Art of the Cinema* (*Iskusstvo kino*, 1929) and several articles. All of my translations from Kuleshov are, however, my own unless otherwise indicated.

27. Kuleshov, "Amerikanshchina," *Kino-fot*, no. 1 (1922), pp. 14-15. Film historians usually refer to Russian editing theories as "montage" instead of editing or cutting.

28. Kuleshov, "Kamernaia kinematografiia," ibid., no. 2 (1922), p. 3.

29. From Levaco's introduction, *Kuleshov*, p. 8; Lev Kuleshov and Aleksandra Khokhlova, *50 let v kino* (Moscow, 1974), pp. 80-81.

30. Vsevolod Pudovkin, *Film Technique and Film Acting*, translated by Ivor Montagu (New York, 1970), p. 140. This was originally published in 1926.

31. Kuleshov and Khokhlova, *50 let*, p. 69. For a description in English, see Leyda, *Kino*, pp. 159-60.

32. Aleksei Gan, "Po dvum putiam," *Kino-fot*, no. 6 (1923), p. 1.

33. Gan, "'Levyi Front' i kinematografiia," ibid., no. 5 (1922), pp. 1-3.

34. N. Aseev, et al., "Za chto boretsia Lef," *Lef*, no. 1 (1923), pp. 3-7.

35. See note 17.

36. See Aseev, et al., "Za chto"; "V kogo vgryzaetsia Lef," *Lef*, no. 1 (1923), pp. 8-9; "Kogo predosteregaet Lef?," ibid., pp. 10-11; "Comrades, Organisers of Life," ibid., no. 2 (1923), pp. 7-8.

37. *Kinematograf: Sbornik statei* (Moscow, 1919). The earliest Narkompros publication on cinema affairs was *Kino-biulletin kino komiteta Narodnogo kommissariata prosveshcheniia*, vyp. 1-2 (Moscow, 1918). The latter was essentially a repertory list.

38. Boris Kushner, "Izopovest'," *Lef*, no. 3 (1923), pp. 132-34.

39. Dziga Vertov, "Kinoki: Perevorot," ibid., p. 136.

40. Ibid., p. 137.

41. Ibid., p. 138.

42. Ibid., pp. 140-41.

43. Ibid., p. 143.

44. Grigorii Kozintsev, "Ab," in *Ekstsentrizm* (Petrograd, 1921), p. 3.

45. Ibid.

46. Ibid., pp. 3-5.

47. Sergei Iutkevich, "Ekstsentrizm-zhivopis'-reklama," in ibid., pp. 12-15.

48. Ibid., p. 13.

49. "Disput o kino," *Kino-gazeta*, no. 4 (1923), p. 3.

50. Lev Kuleshov, "Chto nado delat'," ibid., no. 3 (1923), p. 1.

51. Vladimir Erofeev, "Za ob"edinenie, za kino-sindikat," ibid., no. 2 (1923), p. 1; and his "Kino-sindikat i akts. o-vo," ibid., no. 4 (1923), p. 1.

52. I. D., "Peremontazh i nadpisi," ibid., no. 11 (1923), p. 1.

53. Vladimir Erofeev, "Bol'noi vopros," ibid., no. 13 (1923), p. 1.

54. "Pochti tezisy," *Proletkino*, no. 1/2 (1923), pp. 3-4; also Vladimir Erofeev, "Segodnia i zavtra," ibid., pp. 21-22.

55. B. Martov, "Kak pisat' stsenarii," ibid., pp. 37-38.

56. TsGALI, f. 985, op. 1, ed. khr. 285, "Protokoly zasedanii pravleniia Goskino," pp. 1, 5.

57. Sevzapkino apparently sponsored this practical manual on script writing: A. Zarin, *Tekhnika stsenariia: Rukovodstvo k izlomeniiu stsenariia dlia kino* (Petrograd, 1923).

58. "Assotsiatsiia revoliutsionnoi kinematografii," *Kino-gazeta*, no. 16 (1923), p. 1.

59. Because our focus is on the feature film (primarily fiction), few agit-films and educational films and no newsreels will be discussed. Since it is also my conviction that movies must be seen in order to pass judgment on them, with very few exceptions, all the movies discussed here are pictures that I have personally screened. I was fortunate to view a large and, I believe, representative selection of what survives; all information on films comes from my notes taken during screenings unless otherwise indicated.

60. This may have been because the titles rotted (a common problem) and were removed to prevent the decay from spreading.

61. Bela Balasz, *Kul'tura kino*, translated by Adrian Piotrovskii (Leningrad-Moscow, 1925). Balasz's work was frequently translated into Russian, an indication that his opinion was highly respected.

62. *Sovetskie khudozhestvennye fil'my: Annotirovannyi katalog,* 3 vols. (Moscow, 1961), 1:27.

63. Valentin Turkin, "*Slesar' i kantsler*," *Kino-gazeta*, no. 15 (1923).

64. L. Kosmatov, "Krest'ianskaia fil'ma," ibid., no. 34 (1924). Kosmatov was identified as an instructor in the Cinema-section of Glavpolitprosvet.

65. I. I-ov, "Nashe kino," ibid., no. 43 (1924). This was a report from a workers' club.

66. For descriptions of some of the *Cinema Truth* series, see Feldman, *Evolution of Style*; for a complete listing, see Feldman, *Dziga Vertov: A Guide to References and Resources* (Boston, 1979), pp. 57-75. (The latter's biographical and critical sections must be used with caution, being riddled with factual and typographical errors.)

67. "Pervaia fil'ma revoliutsii," *Kino-gazeta*, no. 16 (1923), p. 1.

Chapter 2

1. L. V., "Beregite vremia," *Kino-gazeta*, no. 21 (1924), p. 3.

2. "Novosti s zapada," ibid., no. 23 (1924), p. 2.

3.   Daniil Gessen, "Dovol'no?," *Kino-nedelia*, no. 14 (1924), p. 1; Grigorii Boltianskii, "Provintsial'nyi kino-byt," ibid., no. 34 (1924), p. 12.

4.   Nikolai Lebedev, "My stavim voprosy," *Novyi zritel'*, no. 2 (1924), p. 14.

5.   "Vesna," *Kino-gazeta*, nos. 17/18 (1924), p. 1.

6.   Viktor Shklovskii, "Vesna ne povtoritsia," *Kino-nedelia*, no. 8 (1924), p. 1.

7.   Sergei Timoshenko, "Zavtrashnyi den' kino: Kino zavoeval mir," ibid., no. 1 (1924), p. 2. Along the same lines, see "Za rabotu," ibid., no. 20 (1924), p. 1.

8.   "Rezoliutsiia soveshchaniia rabotnikov kinematograficheskikh organizatsii SSSR po voprosu o monopolii," ibid., no. 9 (1924), p. 2.

9.   "Nuzhno-li ob"edinenie?," *Kino-gazeta*, no. 14 (1924), p. 1.

10.   "Glavkizm i initiativa," ibid., no. 20 (1924), p. 1.

11.   "Ne monopoliia a kontrol'," *Kino-nedelia*, no. 15 (1924).

12.   In *Kino-nedelia* (1924) see S. Neimarkh, "K voprosam kino-ekonomiki," no. 23, p. 4; Operator, "K voprosu o proizvodstvennoi statistike," no. 24, p. 4; Petr Veinshtein, "Dorogaia ekonomika," no. 25, p. 1; P. Radetskii, "NOT i kinematografiia," no. 32, p. 5; "Ocherednye zadachi," no. 33, p. 4.

13.   "Resheniia Sovnarkoma," *Kino-gazeta*, no. 21 (1924), p. 1.

14.   "Nuzhno organizovat' prokat," ibid., no. 46 (1924), p. 1.

15.   "Pochemu k nam vvoziat' khlam," ibid., no. 17 (1924), p. 1.

16.   Vladimir Erofeev, "Dovol'no portit' kartiny," ibid., no. 49 (1924), p. 2.

17.   "Kino-rezhisser," ibid., no. 10 (1924), p. 1.

18.   Ar. Ialovyi, "Rezhisser i kino-tekhnika," ibid., no. 10 (1924), p. 2.

19.   Ibid.

20.   N. Shpikovskii, "Bez rezhissera," ibid., no. 33 (1924), p. 1.

21.   Leo Mur, "Rezhisser i kollektiv (Otvet na statiu Shpikovskogo 'Bez rezhissera')," ibid., no. 38 (1924).

22.   Gennadii Fish, "Dovol'no slov," *Kino-nedelia*, no. 34 (1924), p. 11.

23.   "Stsenarnyi krizis," *Kino-gazeta*, no. 44 (1924), p. 1.

24.   A. V. Gol'dobin, "Voprosy kino-obrazovaniia v Agitprope TsK RKP(b)," *Kino-nedelia*, no. 36 (1924), p. 11.

25.   Khrisanf Khersonskii, "O nashem kino-aktere," *Kino-gazeta*, nos. 27-28 (1924).

26.   Lev Kuleshov, "Priamoi put'," ibid., no. 48 (1924), p. 2.

27.   Albert Syrkin, "Mezhdu tekhniki i ideologiei (O kino poputchikakh i partinom rukovodstve)," *Kino-nedelia*, no. 37 (1924).

28.   "Kino-politkomy," ibid., no. 38 (1924), p. 5.

29.   "Rezhisser o politicheskom rukovodstve," ibid., no. 39 (1924).

30.   Glavpolitprosvet, *Kino v derevniu* (Moscow, 1924).

31. Nikolai Lebedev, *Kino: Ego kratkaia istoriia; Ego vozmozhnosti; Ego stroitel'stvo v sovetskom gosudarstve* (Moscow, 1924), pp. 124, 131.

32. Ibid., p. 134. Private entrepreneurs during the New Economic Policy were called NEPmen. At best, the connotation was "bourgeois" and at worst—corrupt, decadent, or gangster-like.

33. Ibid., p. 108.

34. Ibid., p. 143.

35. Ibid., p. 156.

36. Ibid., p. 170.

37. Al. Voznesenskii, *Iskusstvo ekrana: Rukovodstvo dlia kino-akterov i rezhissera* (Kiev, 1924), p. 103.

38. Ibid, p. 28.

39. Ibid., p. 28.

40. Ibid., p. 115.

41. "K sovetskomu realizmu," *Kino-gazeta*, no. 42 (1924), p. 1.

42. N. L., "Kakie nuzhny nam stsenarii?" ibid., no. 14 (1924), p. 3.

43. Ippolit Sokolov, "Istoricheskaia fil'ma," *Novyi zritel'*, no. 35 (1924), pp. 11-12; "Zadachi kinorabkorov," *Kino-gazeta*, no. 39 (1924).

44. *Aelita: Kino lenta na temu romana A. N. Tolstogo* (n.p., n.d.).

45. Vladimir Erofeev, "O proizvodstve 'na zagranitsu,'" *Kino-gazeta*, no. 41 (1924), p. 2.

46. A. Gak, "K istorii sozdaniia Sovkino," *Iz istorii kino*, no. 5 (1962), p. 132. Taylor, *Politics*, puts the date at 1924 without any source cited, but the name Mezhrabpom Rus' was not used this early, as far as I could tell from the press.

47. Erofeev, "O proizvodstve."

48. N. L., "*Aelita*," *Kino-gazeta*, no. 41 (1924), p. 2. *Aelita* came under heavy attack in the Leningrad newspaper *Cinema Week* which tended to be politically much more militant than any of the other cinema journals. Grigorii Boltianskii not only assailed *Aelita* on grounds of faulty ideology but also said it was not even very good cinema. It did, however, prove that: "The dramatization of the red way of life, with its red core, pathos, and spirit and the composition of life in nature is the... creative value of our Soviet cinema." See "*Aelita*," *Kino-nedelia*, no. 36 (1924), p. 3. *Cinema Week* also reported very unfavorable remarks from viewers in Nizhni-Novgorod who could not see the connection between this film and the events of the Civil War. See "Ob *Aelite*," *Kino-nedelia*, no. 47 (1924), p. 3.

49. Advertisement for *Aelita* in *Kino-gazeta* (1924).

50. Vladimir Erofeev, "*Prikliucheniia mistera Vesta*," ibid., no. 17/18 (1924), p. 2.

51. Lev Kuleshov, "Nash byt i amerikanizm," ibid., no. 17/18 (1924), p. 1.

52. Viktor Shklovskii, "*Mister Vest* ne na svoemost'," *Kino-nedelia*, no. 21 (1924), p. 3.

53. Petr Veinshtein, "*Prikliucheniia mistera Vesta*," ibid., no. 16 (1924), p. 4.

54. Ia. M., "*Papirosnitsa ot Mosselproma*," ibid., no. 44 (1924), p. 8. This movie was variously referred to as *Papirosnitsa iz Mosselproma* or as in the title of this article with the preposition "*ot*."

55. *Kino-slovar'*, 2 vols. (Moscow, 1966), 1:586.

56. See in *Kino-nedelia* (1924): Petr Veinshtein, "*Dvorets i krepost'*," no. 1; "Nasha anketa o kartine *Dvorets i krepost'*," no. 1; "Po rabochei auditorii," and "Otkliki pechati," no. 3.

57. "Tov. Zinov'ev o sovetskoi fil'me," ibid., no. 7 (1924), p. 2.

58. Pavel Ozov, "*Dvorets i krepost'*," ibid., no. 8 (1924), p. 5.

59. Vladimir Erofeev, "*Kino pravda*, no. 18," *Kino-gazeta*, no. 8 (1924).

60. Polikarp Malakhov, letter, ibid., no. 27/28 (1924), p. 3.

61. A. Anoshchenko, "Kinokoki," *Kino-nedelia*, no. 2 (1924).

62. Grigorii Boltianskii, "*Kino-glaz* i kinoki," ibid., no. 38 (1924), p. 19.

63. Dziga Vertov, "*Kino-glaz*," ibid., no. 36 (1924), p. 12.

64. Advertisement for *Cinema Eye*, ibid., no. 36 (1924), p. 20.

65. Vladimir Erofeev, "*Kino-glaz*," *Kino-gazeta*, no. 43 (1924) p. 2.

66. Ibid.

67. Khrisanf Khersonskii, "*Kino-glaz*," *ARK*, no. 1 (1925), p. 25.

68. Viktor Shklovskii, "Semantika kino," ibid., no. 8 (1925), p. 5.

69. A. Kurs, "Kto sdelaet kino-khronika," *Sovetskii ekran*, no. 32 (1925), pp. 3-6.

70. Vertov himself saw *Cinema Eye* as a major step forward in proletarian internationalism, especially when combined with another of his schemes, this one for the "Radio Ear." See his "Osnovy *Kino-glaza*," *Kino*, no. 6 (1925), p. 2.

71. "Sem' let," *Kino-nedelia*, no. 40/41 (1924), pp. 8-10.

72. I. P. Trainin, "Puti kino," ibid., no. 40/41 (1924).

73. A. V. Lunacharskii, "Revoliutsionnaia ideologiia i kino," ibid., no. 46 (1924), p. 11.

Chapter 3

1. See Nikolai Lebedev, *Vnimanie: Kinematograf* (Moscow, 1974), p. 55 and Ivan Potemkin, "Dva goda raboty Assotsiatsii revolutsionnoi kinematografii," *Sovetskoe kino*, no. 2 (1927), p. 9. Leningrad ARK (LenARK), founded in 1928, was an independent organization about which I could get almost no information, being denied access to its organ, the Leningrad newspaper *Cinema (Kino)* on the grounds of its being "defective."

2. TsGALI, f. 2494, op. 1, ed. khr. 3, "Ustav i proekt platformy ARK (1924)," p. 1.

3. Ibid., p. 2.

4. Ibid., p. 1.

5. Ibid., pp. 2-3.

6. A. Gak, "K istorii sozdaniia Sovkino," pp. 140-42. See also Taylor, *Politics*, p. 82.

7. Both Gak, p. 144, and Taylor, pp. 82-84, imply that the establishment of Sovkino was the end of Goskino's production activities, although Taylor later corrects this, p. 91.

8. Vladimir Erofeev, "Proizvodstvo plenki," *Sovetskoe kino*, nos. 4-5 (1925), pp. 63, 67.

9.   Vl. F., "O tekhnike osveshcheniia (Beseda s operatorom A. A. Levitskim)," *Sovetskii ekran*, no. 17 (1925). See also: N. Ia., "K organizatsii podsobnoi kino-industrii," *ARK*, no. 3 (1925), p. 40; "Nasha fotokino promyshlennost'," *ARK*, no. 9 (1925), pp. 2-6.

10.   William K. Everson's discussion of the Hollywood scene in *American Silent Film* (New York, 1978) indicates that the American situation was not quite so rosy as the Soviets thought.

11.   E. Kaufman, "Nash eksport-import," *ARK*, no. 10 (1925), pp. 20-23. Terms ranged from only two months to one year. There were 2 million rubles worth of outstanding orders for equipment as of the writing of the article.

12.   Leo Mur, "Trishkin kaftan," in I. N. Bursak, ed., *Kino* (Moscow, 1925), pp. 55-56. This collection of essays was a Proletkul't effort.

13.   Ibid.; Mur was seconded by F. Erastov, "K organizatsii nashego kino-proizvodstva," *Sovetskoe kino*, no. 6 (1925), pp. 31-33.

14.   Erastov, "K organizatsii," p. 33.

15.   K. G., "Zabyvaemye zakony," *Sovetskii ekran*, no. 14 (1925). He went on to add: "And the countryside has nothing except for a travelling projector with a 12-volt light bulb."

16.   "Deiatel'nost' teatrov Goskino," *Kino-gazeta*, no. 4 (1925), p. 3.

17.   Kletchatyi, "Kino-teatry Moskomprom," *Kino*, no. 3 (1925), p. 4. This is the first citation from the new *Cinema*, which started renumbering in 1925.

18.   "Po Moskovskim kino-teatram," ibid., no. 7 (1925), p. 4. S. Frederick Starr reports, on the basis of an interview, that the Malaia Dmitrovka's orchestra was sometimes a jazz band. See his *Red and Hot: The Fate of Jazz in the Soviet Union* (New York, 1983), p. 64.

19.   Kletchatyi, "Moskovskie kino-teatry," ibid., no. 4/5 (1925), p. 7.

20.   V. Ardov, "Chudesa kino: Uplotnennyi seans," *Kino*, no. 4/5 (1925), p. 6.

21.   F. M. Nazarov, "Itogi zimnego sezona Rostova-na-Donu," *Kino-gazeta*, no. 3 (1925), p. 5. Nazarov, identified as a worker correspondent (rabkor), also said that Rostov had not a single well-functioning theater.

22.   Ibid.

23.   F. Kandyba, "Obezdolennyi teatr Kharkhova," *Kino* no. 2 (1925); V. G., "Penzenskaia kino-zhizn'," ibid., no. 4/5 (1925), p. 3; "Kino est—net kartin," ibid., no. 2 (1925), p. 4.

24.   Mikhail Boitler, "Kino-teatry: Neskol'ko myslei praktiki," *ARK*, no. 11/12 (1925), pp. 24-26. Boitler frequently wrote on the state of cinema theaters and was the manager of the Malaia Dmitrovka, Moscow's major movie house.

25.   "Bol'noi vopros," *Kino*, no. 6 (1925), p. 5.

26.   Boitler, "Kino-teatry." It is small wonder that so few of the silents have survived given these conditions. Under any circumstances nitrate film is highly perishable (given to spontaneous combustion).

27.   "5-letnyi iubilei, proshedshim neotmechennym," *Kino-nedelia*, no. 1 (1925), p. 5.

28.   M. P. Efremov, "Direktor tov. Efremov o sovetskoi kinematografii," ibid., pp. 18-19; see also Efremov, "K voprosu ob organizatsii Sovkino," ibid., no. 7 (1925), pp. 3-4.

29.   "Rezoliutsiia TsK VseRabisa o Sovkino," ibid., no. 7 (1925), p. 4.

30. A. Khokhlovkin, "O Sovkino," ibid., no. 9 (1925), p. 4.

31. M. P. Efremov, "Kak sokhranit' i razvit' kino-proizvodstvo," ibid., no. 10 (1925), p. 5.

32. A. Ass., "K organizatsii Sovkino," ibid., no. 10 (1925), p. 5.

33. N. Mukhin, "Sovkino," ibid., no. 12 (1925), p. 6.

34. I. P. Trainin, *Kino-promyshlennost' i Sovkino: Po dokladu na 8-ii konferentsii moskovskogo gubrabisa* (Moscow, 1925).

35. Ibid., p. 4.

36. Ibid., p. 7.

37. Ibid., pp. 13-14.

38. Ibid., p. 10.

39. Ibid., p. 23.

40. Ibid., p. 5.

41. Ibid., p. 26.

42. Ibid., p. 27.

43. Ibid., p. 9.

44. Ibid., p. 28.

45. Ibid., p. 20.

46. Ibid., p. 13.

47. Ibid., p. 12.

48. Ibid.

49. Ibid., p. 16.

50. Ibid., p. 17.

51. Ibid., pp. 15-16.

52. See S. Syrtsov and A. Kurs, *Sovetskoe kino na pod"eme* (Moscow, 1926) for a number of self-congratulatory statements.

53. Boris Fillipov, "Profsoiuzy i Sovkino," *Kino*, no. 7 (1925), p. 5. This received a specific denial from M. P. Efremov, "Po povodu stat'i 'Profsouizy i Sovkino,'" ibid., no. 9 (1925), p. 5.

54. Fillipov, "Sovkino i profsoiuzy," ibid., no. 21 (1925).

55. "Kino na V Vsesoiuznom s"ezde rabotnikov iskusstv," ibid., no. 12 (1925), p. 3.

56. Efremov gave these figures: in 1923 Goskino's average rental price per film was 182 r.; in 1924, 104-47 r., but from March to June 1925 Sovkino's was 69 r. See "O prokatnoi deiatel'nosti Sovkino," *Sovetskoe kino*, no. 4/5 (1925), pp. 42, 45.

57. M. S. Veremienko, "Organizatsionnye formy sovetskoi kinematografii," *Sovetskoe kino*, no. 3 (1926), pp. 1-3. But *Soviet Cinema* could still publish an article that was not too unfriendly to Sovkino; see V. Sol'skii, "Chto nam pokazhut v 1927 g. Sovkino," ibid., no. 8 (1926), pp. 5-6, where the author applauded Sovkino's slogan "Revenue from cinema to the development of cinema." On the other hand, another writer charged that "9/10 of revenues are going to

everything convenient except cinema." See G. Arustanov, "O nekotorykh bol'iachkakh," ibid. no. 2 (1926), p. 9. Arustanov also called for the transfer of theaters to the production companies. How this would have relieved rural problems is not clear.

58. "Deklaratsii: Obshchestvo stroitelei proletarskogo kino," *Kino-nedelia*, no. 33 (1924), p. 6. Since only *Cinema Week* reported on OSPK's activities, I assume this organization was Leningrad-based.

59. K. Mal'tsev, "Kino i sovetskaia obshchestvennost'," *Sovetskoe kino*, no. 1 (1925), pp. 15-16.

60. "OSPK," *ARK*, no. 1 (1925), p. 35. *ARK* also said that the "S" in the acronym stood for "*sodeistvie*" (aid) and not "*stroiteli*" (builders).

61. Nikolai Lebedev, "Zadachi rabochikh kino-kruzhkov," *ARK*, no. 2 (1925), p. 6. See also Bursak, *Kino*, p. 99 and K. G., "Obshchestvo druzei sovetskogo kino," *Sovetskoe kino*, no. 6 (1925), p. 59.

62. Nikolai Lebedev, "Perspektivy ARK," *ARK*, no. 4/5 (1925), pp. 2-4.

63. Lebedev, "Zadachi ODSK," *Kino*, no. 8 (1925) and no. 10 (1925). Also V. P. Uspenskii, *ODSK (Obshchestvo druzei sovetskogo kino)* (Moscow, 1926).

64. Uspenskii, *ODSK*, p. 67.

65. G. Lebedev, "Kino-agropropaganda," *Sovetskoe kino*, no. 2/3 (1925), pp. 37-39.

66. "K voprosu o kinofikatsii derevni," ibid., no. 1 (1925), p. 53.

67. A. Katsigras, "Izuchenie derevenskogo kino-zritelia," ibid., no. 2/3 (1925), p. 50. There were some studies done of viewers, not specifically peasant, which revealed nothing conclusive about audience taste except that educational films were not liked. See M. Zaretskii, "Rabochii podrostok kak zritel' kino," *ARK*, no. 3 (1925), pp. 20-22, and A. Dubrovskii, "Opyty izucheniia zritelia (Anketa ARKa)," ibid., no. 8 (1925), pp. 6-9.

68. M. S. Veremienko, "Kino-peredvizhki ili stantsionarnoe kino dlia derevni," *Sovetskoe kino*, no. 2/3 (1925), p. 43. One of the few to favor the permanent cinema was N. Khazhinskii, "Voprosy kinofikatsii derevni," ibid., no. 6 (1925), p. 46.

69. Kino-sektsiia GPP, "Kakoi kino-apparat nuzhen derevne?," ibid., no. 2/3 (1925), p. 45.

70. Ibid.; also A. Abrosimov, "O prodvizhenii kino v derevne," ibid., no. 1 (1925), p. 44; Ia. A. Ozol', "Bol'nye voprosy derevenskogo kino," ibid., no. 1 (1925), pp. 48-50. Glavpolitprosvet seems to have abandoned the projector-selling operation discussed in chapter 2.

71. TsGALI, f. 2494, op. 1, ed. khr. 7, "Protokol 1 Krest'ianskoi sektsii ARK, 27 avgust 1925," p. 1.

72. *Cinema* printed a few articles on this subject. See V. F., "Kino-peredvizhka ili kino ustanovka," no. 15 (1925) and E. Vii, "O kino-peredvizhke," no. 16 (1925). On lack of electricity see E. Mikheev, "Esche o svete dlia kino v derevne," no. 1 (1925), p. 6, and "Kinofikatsiia derevni," no. 2 (1925), p. 1.

73. V. G., "Kak ne sleduet prodavit' derevne fil'mu," ibid., no. 4/5 (1925), p. 2.

74. M., "Kino v dome krest'ianina," ibid., no. 1 (1925), p. 2.

75. V. K., "Zabytaia tema," ibid., no. 10 (1925), p. 2.

76. V. G., "Kak ne sleduet."

77. V. Katkov, "Eshche o derevenskoi kartine," ibid., no. 8 (1925), p. 4.

78. A. Katsigras, "Opyt fikatsii zritel'skikh interesov," in Bursak, *Kino*, pp. 50-51.

79. Katsigras, "Voprosy derevenskoi kino-raboty," *Sovetskoe kino*, no. 6 (1925), pp. 35-36.

80. N. N. Avdeev, "Kino dlia derevni," ibid., no. 6 (1925), p. 40. A. Katsigras, "Novyi pokhod Sovkino na derevniu," ibid., no. 2 (1926), pp. 18-19.

81. Grigorii Boltianskii, "Kino v derevne," in Bursak, *Kino*, pp. 31-47.

82. B. L., "O fil'me dlia derevni," *Sovetskii ekran*, no. 13 (1925).

83. Katsigras, "Novyi pokhod."

84. V. Meshcheriakov, et al., *Kino-iazva* (Leningrad, 1926), p. 14. The quotation is from Meshcheriakov's article "Kak aktsionernoe obshchestvo Sovkino obratilos' litsom k derevne."

85. M. S. Veremienko, "Kakie kartiny dalo Sovkino dlia derevni?," in ibid., pp. 18-25.

86. A. Katsigras, "Kritika uslovii derevenskogo prokata," in ibid., pp. 26-27.

87. For example, "Itogi kino-konferentsii," *Kino*, no. 47 (1926), p. 2.

88. Katsigras, "Oshibka ili...?," ibid., no. 16 (1926), p. 4.

89. "Nuzhen sindikat," ibid., no. 11 (1926).

90. "Spor o kino-sindikate," ibid., no. 12 (1926), p. 1. Also, "K reorganizatsii kinopromyshlennosti," *ARK*, no. 3 (1926), pp. 3-4.

91. In *Sovetskoe kino*, no. 3 (1926) see "Kino i derevnia," pp. 18-19 and "Po provintsii," pp. 22-23.

92. A. Katsigras, *Kino-rabota v derevne* (Moscow, 1926), pp. 83-87.

93. Ibid., p. 92.

94. Ibid., pp. 58-60.

95. Ibid., pp. 99, 103, 106, 110-11.

96. Ibid., pp. 48-49.

97. L. Grigorov, "Blizhe k derevne," *Kino*, no. 11 (1926), p. 2.

98. Viktor Shklovskii, "O krest'ianskoi lente," ibid., no. 10 (1926), p. 2.

99. A. Katsigras, *Chto takoe kino* (Moscow, 1926). This was a handbook primarily intended to explain cinema to peasants.

100. Khrisanf Khersonskii, "Popravki zritelia," *Kino-front*, no. 1 (1926). *ARK* became *Cinema Front* at this time.

101. See G. Gladkikh, "Nuzhna-li organizatsiia Sel'kino?," *Kino*, no. 5 (1926), p. 4; in the same issue, "Sel'kino," p. 5; "Spor o Sel'kino," ibid., no. 16 (1926), p. 4; "Za Sel'kino," ibid., no. 28 (1926), p. 3.

102. O. Barshak, "ODSK na pod"eme," *Kino-front*, no. 9/10 (1926), p. 32.

103. See for example, O. Barshak, "Druz'ia kino i derevnia," *Kino*, no. 23 (1926), p. 3; "ODSK," ibid., no. 45 (1926), p. 3.

104.   O. Barshak, "Kino-obshchestvennost' v derevne i ODSK," *Kino-front*, no. 5/6 (1926), pp. 22-23.

105.   Uspenskii, *ODSK*, p. 11.

106.   Ibid., p. 12.

107.   Ibid., p. 13.

108.   P. Livanov, "Blizhe k massam," *Sovetskoe kino*, no. 1 (1925), p. 37; also "Proverki kassoi," *Kino*, no. 23 (1925).

109.   Vasil'ev, "O peremontazhe," *Kino-gazeta*, no. 8 (1925), p. 1.

110.   Grigorii Boltianskii, "Rabota kino-ustanovok v SSSR," *Sovetskoe kino*, no. 4/5 (1925), pp. 46-49. Boltianskii saw the clubs as the basis for development of Soviet cinema, for commercial theaters were showing only one Soviet film for every six foreign, p. 49.

111.   A. Rustemoe, "Proizvodstvo i Sovkino," *Kino*, no. 2 (1925), p. 3.

112.   For example, "Redaktsionnye zametki," *Sovetskii ekran*, no. 12 (1926), p. 3; "Vkratse," *Kino*, no. 36 (1926), p. 1.

113.   S. Uritskii, "K voprosu ob organizatsii kino-promyshlennosti," *Kino-front*, no. 4 (1926), p. 2.

114.   Osip M. Brik, "Poslednyi krik," *Sovetskii ekran*, no. 7 (1926), pp. 3-4. Brik referred to Sovkino as their "commercial father." This was the first criticism of Sovkino to appear in *Soviet Screen*.

115.   Vystritskii, "*Znak Zorro*," *Kino*, no. 23 (1925), p. 2.

116.   L., "Prokat i teatry," *ARK*, no. 9 (1925), p. 21. Also P. Livanov, "Ob upriamoi deistvitel'nosti i bol'nykh nervakh," *Sovetskoe kino*, no. 2/3 (1925), p. 20. Livanov went even further. *All* foreign pictures, even scientific ones, were reflections of capitalist ideology and therefore should not be imported.

117.   See for example, "Slovo za chitatelem," *Kino*, no. 12 (1926), p. 5 and no. 13 (1926), p. 4.

118.   "K priezdu Ferbenksa i Pikford," *Kino*, no. 29 (1926), pp. 1-2. Whether this talk ever took place is uncertain. Considering the obsession on the cinema front with the "poisonous" influence of foreign films, it is both ironic and amusing that the big cinema event of 1926 was the July visit of Fairbanks and Pickford to Moscow. *Cinema*, which ordinarily had its fair share of articles denouncing foreign films, devoted many columns to the anticipation of the great event. It was even reported that ARK, the Association of Revolutionary Cinematography, wanted Fairbanks to speak on the state of American cinema at one of its meetings. The headlines in *Cinema* the week of their arrival reflected the extent of the movie "mania" the two American stars aroused; a huge banner on the front page proclaimed: "FAIRBANKS AND PICKFORD IN THE USSR!" Their activities were reported in great detail, including which films they saw and which ones they liked. See "Ferbenks i Pikford v SSSR!," ibid., no. 30 (1926), pp. 1, 3. This was the issue of July 27.

119.   A. Dubrovskii, "Atel'e i natura," *Sovetskii ekran*, no. 27 (1926), p. 5.

120.   Osip Brik, "Kartiny kotorye nam ne pokazyvaiut," *Sovetskoe kino*, no. 2 (1926), p. 9.

121.   G. Nakatov, "Zagranichnye kino-gazy," ibid., no. 2 (1926), p. 3.

122.   "Ponemnogu vytesniaem," *Kino*, no. 15 (1926), p. 4.

123. The film (in Russian translation *A Scandal in Society*), which supposedly starred Charlie Chaplin and Gloria Swanson, must have been a figment of the writer's imagination, for the stars never made a movie together. "Napominanie ob opasnosti," *Sovetskii ekran*, no. 41 (1926), p. 3.

124. See cartoon of a film editor cutting the objectionable material from foreign films, *Kino*, no. 12 (1926).

125. V. Pertsov, "Mesto zarezannykh kadrov," *Sovetskoe kino*, no. 2 (1926), p. 17. Pertsov went on to note that this editing led to more and longer titles, p. 2.

126. "Publika reshaet," *Kino*, no. 7 (1926), p. 2.

127. "Pervoe pis'mo," ibid., no. 12 (1926), p. 2.

128. V. Sol'skii, "Kino na zapade," *Sovetskoe kino*, no. 2/3 (1925), p. 61n.

129. Ibid., p. 64. See also L. R-al, "Chto my videli i khotim videt'," *Kino*, no. 23 (1925). This writer complained that there was a dearth of foreign classics on the screen, only the *latest* hits appearing.

130. "Sto protsentov agitatsii," ibid., no. 15 (1925), p. 1.

131. Ibid.

132. On the hopes for *exporting* Soviet films, see A., "Eksportnaia fil'ma," ibid., no. 7 (1925), p. 4 and G. D., "My—zagranitse, zagranitsa—nam," ibid., no. 23 (1925).

133. This slogan first appeared in *Kino*, no. 26 (1926), p. 2. The rationale behind it was articulated earlier in an article, "Obshchii iazyk," ibid., no. 14 (1926), p. 2, calling for a picture with "Soviet characters and Soviet situations."

134. Kristol, "Dovol'no skazok o nevygodnosti," *Sovetskoe kino*, no. 2 (1926), p. 7.

135. Vl. Erofeev, "Kak my prodvigaemsia za granitsu," *Kino*, no. 3 (1926), p. 5.

136. Mikhail Kresin, "O sovetskom kino-cheloveke," *Sovetskoe kino*, no. 2 (1926), p. 10.

137. TsGALI, f. 2494, op. 1, ed. khr. 6, "Protokoly zasedanii detsko-shkolnoi sektsii ARK." Theater managers were concerned about rowdy behavior.

138. This is the impression I gained from the ARK materials received at TsGALI; due to access politics, it may be misleading.

139. See Taylor, *Politics*, pp. 150-51 for a mistaken interpretation of ARK politics.

140. N. Iakovlev, "O levom rebiachestve v kino," *Sovetskoe kino*, no. 1 (1925), pp. 15-17.

141. E. Cherniavskii, "Eshche o kino-kritike," *Kino*, no. 8 (1925), p. 6.

142. G. Lelevich, "Proletarskaia literatura i kino," *Kino-nedelia*, no. 3 (1925). This cinema section was sometimes called the Union of Proletarian Scenarists. See also A. Grabar, "Chetvertyi mesiats," ibid., no. 10 (1925).

143. Albert Syrkin, et al., "Kino-Voronshchina," ibid., no. 3 (1925), pp. 5-6.

144. Pravlenie kino-sektsiia VAPPa, Biuro sektora rabochikh korrespondentov, "O levykh slovakh i pravykh delakh," ibid., no. 8 (1925), p. 14.

145. N. Bravko, et al., "Komfraktsiia pravleniia ARK," ibid., no. 8 (1925), p. 14.

146. "Khudozhestvennyi sovet GPP o Kino-sektsii VAPPa," ibid., no. 13 (1925), p. 4. This was the last issue of *Cinema Week.*

147. "Vserez i nadolgo," *Kino-front,* no. 4 (1926), p. 1.

148. This slogan appeared at the bottom of page 26, ibid., no. 9/10 (1926).

149. TsGALI, f. 2494, op. 1, ed. khr. 47, "Protokoly zasedanii komissii po pereregistratsii chlenov ARK 20 July-21 December 1926." See especially pp. 5-6, 10. For the public report see "V ARKe: K otchetu komissii po pereregistratsii," *Kino-front,* no. 9/10 (1926).

150. "Chto delat' dal'she?," *Kino,* no. 30 (1926), p. 2, and Osip M. Brik, "Kino i kinoshki," *Sovetskii ekran,* no. 27 (1926), p. 3.

Chapter 4

1. Genri, "Veterany kino-dela," *Sovetskii ekran,* no. 12 (1925), remarks on the continuity in personnel from prerevolutionary days to the present.

2. Cartoon in ibid., no. 5 (1925), p. 1.

3. N. Iudin, "Kino-shkola v SSSR," in Bursak, *Kino,* p. 65; a practical manual for hopefuls was K. Gavriushin, *Ia khochu rabotat' v kino* (Moscow, 1925), which discusses in detail working conditions and wages for all classes of cinema workers, the aim being to discourage any but the most serious from attempting to break into the industry. By contrast, the Leningrad film school, also established in 1919, had graduated its first class by December of that same year. (See G.I. Il'ina, *Kul'turnoe stroitel'stvo v Petrograde* [Leningrad, 1982], p. 103.)

4. K. Gavriushin, "O kino-shkole," *ARK,* no. 3 (1925), p. 30. It is also worth noting that Gavriushin wanted to abolish private schools and strengthen the proletarian composition of GTK.

5. Iudin, "Kino-shkola," p. 72; Gavriushin, "O kino-shkole," p. 30.

6. Valentin Turkin, "Kino-shkola i kino-proizvodstvo," *ARK,* no. 2 (1925), p. 12; also his "Sostoianie kino-obrazovaniia v SSSR," *Sovetskoe kino,* no. 2/3 (1925), p. 72. In the earlier part of the latter article, Turkin traces the history of film education and film schools since the revolution.

7. Gavriushin, *Ia khochu rabotat',* p. 41; see also Umanskii, "Zhizn' kino-rabotnikov," *Kino,* no. 4/5 (1925), p. 6, and B. Fel'dman "Nasha baza," *Kino,* no. 22 (1925), p. 1.

8. V. Arden, "Kino-khudozhnik na zapade i v SSSR," *ARK,* no. 3 (1926), p. 16. Ippolit Sokolov also used this figure of 100,000 r. See "Prezhde vsego organizatsiia," *Kino,* no. 19 (1926), p. 2.

9. Vladimir Shneiderov, "Sovetskaia kino-promyshlennost'," *Sovetskii ekran,* no. 7 (1927), pp. 31-32.

10. Editorial comment to N. Iudin, "Kino-kustary," *Sovetskoe kino,* no. 8 (1926), p. 12.

11. A. Danilov, "Rezhim ekonomii—v pervuiu ochered' uchet," ibid., no. 3 (1926), p. 4. The slogan cited appeared at the end of this article.

12. D-v, "Bolezni proizvodstva kino-kartin," ibid., p. 5.

13. M. Aleinikov, "Organizatsiia kino-proizvodstva," ibid., (1926), p. 8; Sergei Tret'iakov, "Konkretnoe predlozhenie," ibid., p. 9.

14. S. Lur'e, "Rezhim ekonomii v kino," ibid., pp. 10-11.

15.   Izmail Urazov, "Ekonomiia sredstv, no ne ekonomiia vydumka," *Sovetskii ekran*, no. 17/18 (1926), p. 3.

16.   Sergei Tret'iakov, "Dorozhe—deshevle ili deshevle—dorozhe," ibid., no. 39 (1926), p. 3.

17.   "Za rezhim ekonomii," *Kino*, no. 23 (1926).

18.   Viktor Shklovskii, "Volshebniki pervoi stepeni," ibid., no. 17/18 (1926), p. 2.

19.   "Za rezhim ekonomii: Rezoliutsiia ARKa," ibid., no. 22 (1926).

20.   "Za ratsional'izatsiiu proizvodstva," *Kino-front*, no. 7/8 (1926), p. 1.

21.   Sergei A. Timoshenko, *Iskusstvo kino: Montazh fil'ma* (Leningrad, 1926).

22.   Ippolit Sokolov, "NOT v kinoproizvodstve," *Kino-front*, no. 7/8 (1926), pp. 9-13.

23.   Ia. M. Bliokh, "O s"emochnykh gruppakh," *Kino*, no. 26 (1926), p. 3.

24.   Bliokh, "Rezhim ekonomii i kino-fabrika," ibid., no. 25 (1926), p. 3.

25.   V. Shklovskii, "Volshebniki."

26.   Ippolit Sokolov, "Prezhde vsego ...," *Kino*, no. 19 (1926), p. 2.

27.   A. Cherkassov, "Zheleznii stsenarii," *Kino-front*, no. 9/10 (1926), pp. 3-4. The article following, Mikhail Nikanorov, "Stsenarii i proschety v kino-proizvodstve," pp. 5-7, gives examples of a montage list, timetable, etc.

28.   I. P. Trainin, "Na puti k vozrozhdeniiu," *Sovetskoe kino*, no. 1 (1925), p. 13.

29.   "Glavrepertkom: Beseda s zampredom Glavrepertkoma tov. Pel'she," *Kino-gazeta*, no. 3 (1925).

30.   Trainin, *Kino-promyshlennost'*, pp. 28-29.

31.   "Khudozhestvennyi sovet po delam kino pri GPP," *Sovetskoe kino*, no. 1 (1925), pp. 63-64. The charter group included Meshcheriakov, Pelshe, Maltsev, Trainin, Meierkhold, Kerzhentsev, and Shvedchikov, most of whom have more than passing interest for us.

32.   "Khudozhestvennyi sovet po delam kino pri GPP," ibid., no. 2 (1925), pp. 79-80. By the beginning of the year, the figure stood at forty-seven scripts received, sixteen accepted, thirteen conditionally accepted, eighteen rejected.

33.   G. G-zd, "Nashi interviui: Glavpolitprosvet i kino," *Kino-gazeta*, no. 3 (1925). See also N. Iudin, "Na kino-fabrikakh," *Sovetskii ekran*, no. 12 (1925). The plan for the artistic council of the 1st Goskino studio was as follows: (1) systematic manufacture of scripts, (2) involvement in the scenario work of all the best literary circles, (3) evaluation of the script. See Ia. Bliokh, "Rabota khudozhestvennykh sovetov na proizvodstve," *ARK*, no. 9 (1925), pp. 9-10.

34.   O. Barshak, "O perspektivakh," *ARK*, no. 9 (1925), p. 31.

35.   See for example, Khrisanf Khersonskii, "Dramaturgiia kak metod kinoiskusstva," ibid., no. 1 (1925), pp. 14-17, or Boris Gusman, "Eshche o dramaturgii v kino," ibid., no. 4/5 (1925), pp. 15-16. Khersonskii quickly matured into a fine film critic.

36.   A. Seifer, "Gde zhe ideologiia?," *Kino-nedelia*, no. 1 (1925), p. 21.

37.   Valentin Turkin, "Kak naladit' stsenarnoe delo," no. 9 (1925), pp. 7-9.

38. Sergei Tret'iakov, "Stsenarnoe khinshchinichestvo," ibid., no. 10 (1925), pp. 10-11. Tretiakov had been connected with the futurists since 1913 and chaired the art section of the 1st Goskino studio. See "Stsenaristy," ibid., no. 10 (1925), p. 37.

39. Nikolai Anoshchenko, "K voprosu o postroenii stsenariia," ibid., no. 11/12 (1925), p. 13.

40. Evgenii Chvialev, "Rabochaia komissiia po podgotovke derevenskikh stsenariiev," *Sovetskoe kino*, no. 2/3 (1925), pp. 78-79.

41. Leonid Nezhdanov, "O khudozhestvennykh sovetakh na fabrikakh," *Kino*, no. 19 (1925), p. 4.

42. Cartoon, *Kino-gazeta*, no. 9 (1925), p. 1.

43. "Avtorskoe pravo," *Kino*, no. 10 (1925). This debate had another curious feature. Lunacharskii declared that literary works were in the public domain as far as film writers were concerned. See T. Dik, "Avtorskoe pravo," *Kino*, no. 20 (1925), p. 2.

44. A. V. Gol'dobin, *Kak pisat' stsenarii dlia kino-kartin* (Moscow, 1924), pp. 3-4. This book was quite worthless as practical guide.

45. Thirty thousand rubles were at stake in the Sovkino competition. See notice in *Kino*, no. 19 (1925). For other information on this contest, see *Sovetskoe kino*, no. 4/5 (1925). A.V. Lunacharskii was to chair the judging.

46. Osip M. Brik, "100% brak," *Kino*, no. 25 (1926), p. 3.

47. Sergei Tret'iakov, "Opiat' konkurs," *Kino*, no. 31 (1926), p. 1. Growing professionalism was evident in the increasing concern with authors' rights and setting up of pay scales. See "Avtorskie," ibid., no. 11 (1926), p. 4; "Avtorskie," ibid., no. 47 (1926), p. 1; "Oplata stsenariev," ibid., no. 30 (1926), p. 1.

48. For example, see Aller, "Chto takoe stsenarii," ibid., no. 38 (1926), p. 2.

49. Viktor Shklovskii, "Libretto i material," ibid., no. 39 (1926), p. 3.

50. M. S. Veremienko, "Analiz stsenarno-proizvodstvennoi i khudozhestvenno-postanovochnoi raboty proizvodstvennykh-organizatsii," *Sovetskoe kino*, no. 8 (1926), p. 3.

51. Ippolit Sokolov, "O postanovke stsenarnogo delo," *Kino-front*, no. 4 (1926), p. 5.

52. "Kak idet zagotovka stsenariev," ibid., pp. 8-9. Figures on studio acceptance of scripts went as low as 20 percent.

53. Ippolit Sokolov, "Khoroshii stsenarii," ibid., no. 9/10 (1926), pp. 8-12. Another Sokolov variation on the theme was "Organizovannyi stsenarii," *Kino*, no. 29 (1926), p. 2.

54. "Za sovetskoi stsenarii," *Kino-front*, no. 9/10 (1926), pp. 1-2. This went on to denounce *Case of the Three Million* as a film which would satisfy the public of the "bourgeois" theater Ars but never a working-class audience.

55. Sokolov, "Material i forma," ibid., pp. 15-17. Sokolov specifically mentioned the films *The Tripol Tragedy* and *Minaret of Death* which will be discussed later. Shklovskii concurred with the criticism of violence in his "Libretto i material." Preoccupation with violence in cinema was apparently a European-wide phenomenon in the twenties. See Paul Monaco, *Cinema and Society in France and Germany in the 1920s and 1930s* (New York, 1976).
    Trainin took strong exception to this reaction against violence. He believed that without "strong passion" it was impossible to create drama and engage the attention of the viewer. He scoffed that Soviets, not being Tolstoyans, did not shy away from violence. The adventure

was the best cinema genre if it had ideological underpinnings. Rape and murder for their own sakes were not to be permitted, but they would be artistically justifiable if occurring in a Civil War movie, for example. See his "Stseny nasiliia v kino," *Kino*, no. 41 (1926), p. 2.

56. Sokolov, "Material i forma."

57. Ippolit Sokolov, "Kuda idet sovetskoe kino?," *Sovetskii ekran*, no. 37 (1926), p. 3. If dramas were to be permitted, they should about life (*byt*).

58. Sokolov, *Kino-stsenarii* (Moscow, 1926), pp. 57, 63.

59. Ibid., pp. 58, 66.

60. "Slovo za chitatelem," *Kino*, no. 17/18 (1926), p. 4.

61. A. Room, "Sud'ba kino-aktera," ibid., no. 9 (1926), p. 4.

62. "Rezhissery o sebe (Cheslav Sabinskii)," *Sovetskii ekran*, no. 21 (1925). Not all directors from the theater were insensible to the special problems posed by cinema. See K. V. Eggert in "Rezhissery o sebe," ibid., no. 23 (1925). Eggert had worked in the Moscow Art Theater and the Malyi and Kamernyi Theaters before becoming a cinema actor and director.

63. Iurii Tarich, "Rvachestvo," *Kino*, no. 26 (1925), p. 3.

64. TsGALI, f. 2494, op. 1, ed. khr. 33, "Protokoly akterskoi podsektsii ARK," p. 12.

65. Ol'ga Tret'iakova, "Chetvero v kino," *Kino*, no. 12 (1926), pp. 2-3. For her other articles in *Cinema* on the same subject in 1926 see "O kino-geroiakh," no. 14, p. 4 and "Tvorchestvo aktera," no. 25, p. 2.

66. Tretiakova was responding to Leo Mur, "Diktatura rupora," ibid., no. 6 (1926), p. 3. His answer to her criticisms was "Osvobozhdenie konechnostei," ibid., no. 28 (1926). But Tretiakova did not let the "feud" rest. See her "S nachala 'pod kopirku,'" ibid., no. 31 (1926), p. 2.

67. TsGALI, f. 2494, op. 1, ed. khr. 33, "Proekt polozheniia o rabote kino-aktera v proizvodstve," p. 30.

68. Ippolit Sokolov, "Vospitanie kino-aktera," in Bursak, ed., *Kino*, pp. 73-75. Sokolov was a very gifted critic, of whom we shall hear much more.

69. A. Dubrovskii, "Bez aktera," *ARK*, no. 9 (1925). Closely connected to the idea of the actor-model and typage was quite an arcane debate over *amplua*, i.e., that there were classes of roles which should be filled by biological types. To follow this see: Leo Mur, "Sotsial'no-biologicheskoe amplua," ibid., no. 2 (1925), pp. 17-18; Khrisanf Khersonskii, "O dramaturgicheskoi tekhnike amplua aktera," ibid., p. 19.

70. O. Rakhmanova, "O metode vospitaniia aktera," *ARK*, no. 6/7 (1925), pp. 11-12.

71. M. Getmanskii, "Rasskaz o borode [cartoon]," *Sovetskii ekran*, no. 22 (1926), p. 6. On the serious side, ARK had a "trial" (*sud*) on typage in which Tarich and Pudovkin participated with little gain, although the tone of the debate was quite nasty. TsGALI, f. 2494, op. 1, ed. khr. 64, "Stenogramma diskussii o tipazhe v kino," p. 6.

72. Evgenii Petrov, *Chto dolzhen znat' kino-akter* (Moscow, 1926), pp. 38-42. *Kino-slovar'* says that this Petrov was none other than the famous satirist.

73. Valentin Turkin, *Kino-iskusstvo, kino-akter, kino-shkola* (Moscow, 1925), p. 21.

74. Ibid., pp. 24, 32. Turkin thought that Kuleshov was a talented director who should make films and leave the theorizing to others, p. 46.

75. Ibid., pp. 27-28.

76. Ibid., p. 39.

77. Ibid., p. 41.

78. Ibid., p. 49.

79. Ibid., p. 55.

80. Sokolov wrote bitingly of films of this type: "In the peasant picture the February and October coups, cooperation, electrification, ... the emancipation of women, sorcery, anti-religious propaganda, and Soviet construction are shown simultaneously." See "Skhemy vmesto liudei," *Sovetskii ekran*, no. 45 (1926), p. 3.

81. Dziga Vertov, "Kino-glaz i bor'ba za kino-khroniku," ibid., no. 14 (1926), p. 7. See also "Srazhenie prodolzhaetsia," *Kino*, no. 44 (1926), p. 2.

82. Vertov, "Kino-glaz," in V. M. Bliumenfel'd, ed., *Na putiakh iskusstv* (Moscow, 1926), pp. 210-19. Proletkul't, a proletarian culture group founded by A.A. Bogdanov, was subordinated to state control in 1920.

83. Ibid., p. 220.

84. Ibid., p. 229.

85. An exception to the acceptance of the continued existence of theater was Pavel Poluianov's *Gibel' teatra i torzhestvo kino* (Nizhny Novgorod, 1925), self-published. Taylor in *Politics*, pp. 32-33, seems to find this rhetoric representative of the times, but by 1925 it was not. Taking issue with the superiority complex of cinema was An. Mirov, "I. M. Moskvin na ekrane," *Sovetskii ekran*, no. 39 (1925) in which he stated that both cinema and theater have their distinctive virtues.

86. Abram Room, "Kino i teatr," *Sovetskii ekran*, no. 8 (1925). Room had been a theater director, 1919-24. See *Kino-slovar'*, 2:444.

87. Leo Mur, "Sotsial'no-biologicheskoe amplua," p. 16.

88. Ibid.

89. Turkin, *Kino-iskusstvo*, pp. 14-15.

90. Ibid., p. 19.

91. Turkin, "Khudozhestvennaia forma i napravleniia v sovetskom kino," *Sovetskoe kino*, no. 4/5 (1925), pp. 20-21. He cautioned, however, that German expressionism was "simply alien to us." The influence of expressionism on *Aelita* was therefore one reason for the film's failure.

92. A debate vaguely related to the problem of realism was that on photogenics. This was a term devised by the French film theorist Louis Delluc. Photogenics posited that the essence of cinema lay in photographic technique. See Leo Mur, "Fotogeniia," *ARK*, no. 6/7 (1925), pp. 3-4, and Vsevolod Pudovkin, "Fotogeniia," *Sobranie sochinenii*, 3 vols. (Moscow, 1974), 1:90-95. Like *amplua*, photogenics is quite esoteric.

93. Iu. Rist, "*Stachka*," *Sovetskii ekran*, no. 2 (1925).

94. A. I., "Litso *Stachki*," ibid., no. 7 (1925).

95. Nikolai Lebedev, "*Stachka*," *Kino*, no. 12 (1925), p. 2.

96. "My i oni," *ARK*, no. 3 (1925), pp. 1-2. In this article *Strike* was touted as being revolutionary in form as well as content. See also the review, K. I. Sh., "*Stachka*," p. 31, in the same number.

97. A. N. Skachko, "*Stachka*," *Sovetskoe kino*, no. 1 (1925), pp. 61-62.

98. Dziga Vertov, "Kino-glaz o *Stachke*," *Kino*, no. 1 (1925), p. 3.

99. Sergei Eizenshtein, "K voprosu o materialisticheskom podkhode k forme," *ARK*, no. 4/5 (1925), pp. 6-7.

100. Ibid., p. 7-8. Many of Eisenstein's contemporaries unjustly ascribed to him an anti-art attitude. See for example K. Malevich, "I likuiut liki na ekranakh," ibid., no. 10 (1925), pp. 7-9.

101. "Preduprezhdenie," ibid., no. 10 (1925), pp. 1-2. On the politics of art, Trainin wrote a rather uncharacteristic article, "Ob iskusstve bez politiki," *Kino*, no. 3 (1925), p. 2, denouncing director Ivan Perestiani's alleged statements to the effect that art and politics should not mix. This probably had more to do with the struggle between Sovkino and the Georgian studio Goskinprom Gruzii than it did with any deeply held convictions of Trainin's.

102. I. P. Trainin, "Nuzhen li geroi v kartine?," *Kino*, no. 25 (1925), pp. 1, 4, is much more characteristic of Trainin on art.

103. Trainin, "Sovetskaia fil'ma i zritel'," *Sovetskoe kino*, no. 4/5 (1925), pp. 10-18.

104. S. Dashkevich, "Kino v Krasnoi Armii," ibid., p. 38. A favorable but vague review from a "worker correspondent" was M. A., "*Stachka*," *Kino*, no. 10 (1925), p. 2.

105. "Krupnaia pobeda," *ARK*, no. 2 (1926), p. 1.

106. Viktor Shklovskii, "Eizenshtein," ibid., pp. 5-6; in the same issue, Ippolit Sokolov, "Klassicheskii stsenarii," pp. 7-8. See also Sokolov's "Bronenosets—port—more," *Kino*, no. 4 (1926), p. 3.

107. Aleksei Gan (answer to a questionnaire on *Potemkin*), *ARK*, no. 2 (1926), p. 10.

108. TsGALI, f. 2494 (ARK), op. 1, ed. khr. 50, "Stenogramma diskussii *Bronenosets Potemkin*," pp. 6-11.

109. Khrisanf Khersonskii, "Ot *Stachki* k *Potemkinu*," *ARK*, no. 2 (1926), pp. 3-5.

110. TsGALI, f. 2494, op. 1, ed. khr. 50, "Stenogramma," pp. 6-11.

111. Ibid., pp. 1-4.

112. Ibid., pp. 18-19.

113. Viktor Shklovskii, "Doverie vremeni," *Kino*, no. 26 (1926), p. 2.

114. Lev Kuleshov, "Volia, uporstvo, glaz," in *Eizenshtein: Bronenosets Potemkin* (Moscow, 1926), pp. 9-12.

115. Eisenstein expressed his montage theories best in his 1929 articles "The Cinematographic Principle and the Ideogram," "A Dialectic Approach to Film Form," and "Methods of Montage." See his *Film Form*, edited and translated by Jay Leyda (New York, 1949).

116. Timoshenko, *Iskusstvo kino*, pp. 16-17, 19.

117. Ibid., p. 27.

118. Pudovkin's first feature film was the charming 1925 short comedy *Chess Fever* (*Shakhmataia goriachka*) which starred Vladimir Fogel as a chess maniac; *Chess Fever* cleverly incorporated actual footage of an international chess tournament, making it appear as though the grand master Capablanca were part of the movie. The gags are quite funny and the film is not too long to sustain them.

119. *Sovetskie khudozhestvennye fil'my*, 1:13. (I have seen the extant parts of this film.)

120. I. Ch., "Novosti prokata," *Kino*, no. 36 (1926), p. 3.

121. Viktor Shklovskii, "Pudovkin," ibid., p. 1.

122. Khrisanf Khersonskii, "Bor'ba faktov," *Kino-front*, no. 9/10 (1926), p. 24. For analysis of Pudovkin's films in general, see Dart, *Pudovkin's Films*, the only book in English devoted to the director. For an additional analysis of *Mother*, see Richard Taylor, *Film Propaganda: Soviet Russia and Nazi Germany* (New York, 1979), pp. 81-92.

123. P. Neznamov, "Udacha rezhissera (*Bukhta smerti*)," *Kino*, no. 7 (1926), p. 3. Neznamov thought this a "truly Soviet" scene when what it actually was was an exceedingly well-acted scene.

124. Ibid.; also ARK, "Diskussia o *Bukhte smerti*," ibid., or I. S., "*Bukhta smerti*," *Kino-front*, no. 4 (1926), p. 27. I. S. was probably Sokolov, who thought the script weak but the acting and staging good.

125. "Na sud rabochikh," *Kino*, no. 10 (1926), p. 2.

126. See P. A., "Oshibka Vasiliia Guliaeva (*Veter*)," ibid., no. 43 (1926), and Ippolit Sokolov, "*Veter*," ibid., no. 45 (1926), p. 3.

127. A. German, "*Tripol'skaia tragediia*," ibid., no. 15 (1926), p. 3. See also, "Slovo za chitatelem," ibid., where reader A. Renard comments on this.

128. See M. Zaretskii, "Rabochii podrostok," for one account of how much even youth disliked this film.

129. Lev Kuleshov, "Ot eksperimental'no-uchebnoi raboty do *Luchi smerti*," *ARK*, no. 1 (1925), pp. 24-25.

130. N. Shpikovskii, "Masterskaia Kuleshova. *Luch smerti*," *Kino-gazeta*, no. 11 (1925), p. 1.

131. An. Skachko, "*Luch smerti*," *Sovetskoe kino*, no. 1 (1925), p. 63. Others agreed that workers would not like this film, one saying that even the decadent American viewer had rejected it. See also V., "*Luch smerti*," *Kino-gazeta*, no. 12 (1925), p. 2.

132. N. L., "*Luch smerti, ARK*, no. 3 (1925), p. 32. These latter remarks were in regard to a somewhat mystifying comparison he sought to draw between *Death Ray* and Fernand Léger's *Ballet mécanique*.

133. I. P. Trainin, "Sovetskaia fil'ma i zritel'," pt. 2, *Sovetskoe kino*, no. 6 (1925), p. 17.

134. Viktor Shklovskii, "Pochemu troe," *Kino*, no. 15 (1926), p. 2.

135. Lev Kuleshov, "*Vest—Luch—Po zakonu*," ibid., no. 36 (1926), pp. 2-3.

136. Mikhail Levidov, "Novella Kuleshova," ibid., no. 49 (1926), p. 3.

137. Feofan Shipulinskii, "Kak postupit' *Po zakonu*," ibid., p. 3.

138. Viktor Pertsov, "Sotsial'noe znachenie kartiny *Po zakonu*," *Kino-front*, no. 9/10 (1926), pp. 27-28.

139. Arsen, "Sotsial'noe znachenie kartiny *Po zakonu*," ibid., pp. 28-31.

140. "Rezoliutsiia obshchego sobraniia proizvodstvennoi sektsii ARK k kartine *Po zakonu*," ibid., p. 31.

141. TsGALI, f. 2494, op. 1, ed. khr. 32, "Protokoly obshchikh sobranii chlenov ARK (1926)," pp. 6-7.

142. See A. Kurs, "Zametki dlia sebia," *Kino*, no. 36 (1926), p. 2, and "Stanovlenie Kuleshova," ibid., no. 49 (1926), p. 3.

143. In 1924, *Cinema Week* had reported the FEKS collective as having twenty-five members. See "FEKS," *Kino-nedelia*, no. 14 (1924), p. 6. Apparently FEKS had not gotten too tame in its old age, since Sergei Timoshenko was moved to write a hilarious parody of their writing style, "Parodinaia anketa o kino-siuzhete," ibid., no. 11/12 (1926).

> Axiom: FEKS was the best theater of all. Why is *N'T* it now? Thesis: plot [*siuzhet*] = Chaplin's back + the detective story + impudence + skyscraper. Antithesis: I establish a *course* on the USA. The Americanization of cinema is the SR-ization of the plot [*siuzhet*]. Montage is construction. Period. Very good. Very cinema good.

144. Ippolit Sokolov, "*Chertovo koleso*," *Kino-front*, no. 4 (1926), pp. 29-30. S. Gekht agreed that it was "a collection of wonderful frames," rather than a real movie. See "Rabota Feksov," *Kino*, no. 10 (1926), p. 2.

145. See, for example, Lev Kuleshov, "O *Chertovom kolese*," *Kino*, no. 11 (1926), p. 3; A. Kurs, "Molodaia pleiada," *Sovetskii ekran*, no. 8 (1926), pp. 3-4 for less than enthusiastic reviews; for praise, see Sergei Iutkevich, "Romanticheskoe koleso," *Kino*, no. 5 (1926), p. 3.

146. Boris Eikhenbaum, "Literatura i kino," *Sovetskii ekran*, no. 42 (1926), p. 10.

147. Ippolit Sokolov, "*Shinel'*," *Kino-front*, no. 5/6 (1926), p. 28. For agreement that the failure of the film was that it was not "contemporary," see P. Neznamov, "Shineli i livrei," *Kino*, no. 21 (1926), p. 2.

148. "*Shinel'*," *Sovetskoe kino*, no. 3 (1926), p. 3.

149. "Masterstvo," *Kino*, no. 21 (1926), p. 2.

150. Khrisanf Khersonskii, "*Na zhizn' i na smert'* i *Kollezhskii registrator*," *ARK*, no. 10 (1925), p. 27.

151. P. S. Kogan, "Opyt literaturnoi fil'my," *Sovetskoe kino*, no. 6 (1925), p. 13.

152. Advertisement for *Kollezhskii registrator*, *Kino*, no. 18 (1925).

153. G. G., "*Stepan Khalturin*," ibid., no. 4/5 (1925), p. 9. This writer also notes that the movie does not show Khalturin's disagreement with the populists over the workers' question.

154. Ibid. An. Skachko also noted that the impetus behind events seemed to be personal instead of material, "*Stepan Khalturin*," *Sovetskoe kino*, no. 2/3 (1925), p. 77.

155. Skachko, "*Stepan Khalturin*."

156. Viktor Shklovskii, "Nechto, vrode deklaratsii," *Sovetskii ekran*, no. 1 (1926), p. 1.

157.   Shklovskii, "Ne Ioanna, a Ivan," ibid., no. 2 (1926), p. 11.

158.   Izmail Urazov, "*Kryl'ia kholopa*," *Kino*, no. 47 (1926), p. 2.

159.   Sven, "*Kryl'ia kholopa*," ibid., no. 46 (1926), p. 5.

160.   Skachko, "*Stepan Khalturin.*"

161.   V. Kostylev, "Toska po fil'me," *Kino*, no. 21 (1925), p. 3. In Nizhnii-Novgorod, the film attracted "an enormous public." Of course this was mentioned in an article about how few films appeared in Nizhnii so it may be more indicative of how hungry the public was for films rather than how good the films were. This same fact was also noted, however, in Gol'dobin, *Kak pisat' stsenarii*, p. 21.

162.   Boris Gusman, "*Stepan Khalturin*," *ARK*, no. 6/7 (1925), pp. 31-32.

163.   See A. Dvoretskii, "*Abrek Zaur* i prochee," *Sovetskii ekran*, no. 5 (1926), pp. 4-5, which was quite a favorable review; also P. Neznamov, "Kovboi v papkakh," *Kino*, no. 14 (1926), p. 2.

164.   See Khrisanf Khersonskii, "*Namus*," *Kino*, no. 43 (1926), p. 2, and "*Namus*," *Kino-front*, no. 4/5 (1926), pp. 29-30.

165.   One reviewer saw a strong but (happily) popularized FEKS influence in the film. See D. Sven, "*Kat'ka bumazhnii ranet*," *Kino*, no. 51/52 (1926), p. 5. (I cannot agree with this assessment.)

166.   Sovkino was not the only organization open to charges of commercialism. To a lesser extent, Mezhrabpom came under fire as well. We have seen that this began in 1924 with the release of *Aelita*, and by 1926, the chorus was increasing. Shklovskii attacked Mezhrabpom and its chairman Aleinikov for the types of films they produced, writing scornfully:

> We do not want to go back to *The Station Master* [sic! he means *The Collegiate Registrar*]; they can make *The Bear's Wedding* still better in Hollywood. We do not want to give anyone the right to judge questions of art by today's accurate or inaccurate figures at the accountant's.
>
> We are for the airplane, although the first airplane flew worse than a lead balloon.

See "O mezhdu prochem," *Sovetskii ekran*, no. 20 (1926), p. 3. Another accusation was that Mezhrabpom had fulfilled only 55 percent of its production plan. See "Proizvodstvennye plany," *Kino*, no. 16 (1926), p. 2.

167.   I. Falbert, "Zolotaia seriia (*Medvezh'ia svad'ba*)," *Kino*, no. 6 (1926), p. 2.

168.   Ippolit Sokolov, "*Medvezh'ia svad'ba*," *ARK*, no. 3 (1926), p. 27, and L. Kosovitskii in "Slovo za chitatelem," *Kino*, no. 14 (1926), p. 5.

169.   "Miss Mend," *Sovetskoe kino*, no. 8 (1926), p. 31.

170.   Khrisanf Khersonskii, "Lakirovannoe varvarstvo ili 'Miss, vyidite na minutku!,'" *Kino*, no. 49 (1926). Khersonskii also found it shocking that Mezhrabpom could make such a bourgeois film after Pudovkin's *Mother*.

171.   TsGALI, f. 2494, op. 1, ed. khr. 26, "Protokoly obshchikh sobranii chlenov ARK (1926)," pp. 15-16.

172.   For example in Voronezh, "Kupili apparat," *Kino*, no. 7 (1925), p. 4.

173.   This point was also made by M. Zagorskii, "Tapioka—Il'inskii—teatr—kino," *Sovetskii ekran*, no. 38 (1926), p. 5. Zagorskii was more critical of the film's theatricality than its content.

174. Viktor Shklovskii, "Retsenzent," ibid., no. 35 (1925), p. 7.

175. M. B., "*Leninskaia kino-pravda*," *ARK*, no. 3 (1925), p. 34.

176. K. I. Shutko, "Shagaete vse," *Sovetskii ekran*, no. 32 (1926), p. 3.

177. Izmail Urazov, "On shagaet k zhizni kak ona est'," ibid., pp. 5-6. This article was in response to Shklovskii, see next note.

178. Viktor Shlovskii, "Kuda shagaet Dziga Vertov?," ibid., p. 4.

179. Esfir Shub, "Fabrikatsiia faktov," *Kino*, no. 41 (1926), p. 2.

Chapter 5

1. "Net plenki (Beseda s predsedatelem predpravleniia Sovkino K. M. Shvedchikovym)," *Kino*, no. 17 (1927), p. 1.

2. D. Lionov, "Na proizvodstve Sovkino," ibid., no. 14 (1927), p. 4.

3. TsGALI, f. 2494, op. 1, ed. khr. 25, "Sovkino finansovo-kommercheskii plan na 27/28," p. 1. For criticism of the studio construction project see Mikhail Berestinskii, "Chto skazali o Sovkino na dispute v TsDRI," ibid., no. 43 (1927), p. 5. The latter is part of a Rabis discussion.

4. See Vladimir Shneider, "Nuzhny srochnye mery," ibid., no. 47 (1927), p. 2; Nikolai Lukhmanov, "Kino-Chubarovshchina," *Novyi zritel'*, no. 17 (1927), p. 10; "Direktor i rezhisser," ibid., no. 24 (1927), p. 2.

5. "14 dnei i odin god," *Sovetskii ekran*, no. 29 (1927), p. 3.

6. "Protsess kino-rabotnikov," *Kino*, nos. 15-18 (1927). The other sentences ranged from two to eight months.

7. See K. Iukov, "Puti i pereputia sovetskogo kino," *Kino-front*, no. 9/10 (1927), p. 8. Iukov was now the chairman of ARK.

8. See in *Sovetskoe kino*, no. 1 (1927): A. Katsigras, "Kino i derevnia, ob"ektivnye usloviia," p. 18; O. Barshak, "ODSK na putiakh kinofikatsii derevni," p. 19; "Po provintsii, Krasnodarskii okrug," p. 27. In *Sovetskoe kino*, no. 5/6 (1927), see: M. Grinevskii, "Kino-telega," p. 22 (Grinevskii indicates that not all the travelling projectors were equipped with generators, adding to the difficulties) and "ODSK," pp. 24-25.

9. A. Katsigras, "Lik kino-derevni," ibid., no. 7 (1927), pp. 28-30 and "Koren' zla," *Sovetskii ekran*, no. 48 (1927), p. 1.

10. The left opposition, headed by Trotskii, had been effectively silenced by the beginning of 1927, although Trotskii was not ousted from the Party and exiled until the end of the year. Stalin then turned his attention to the right opposition, led by Bukharin. This battle ended in total victory for Stalin when Rykov was ejected from the Politburo in 1930, but the outcome was clear in 1929.

11. V. Sol'skii, "Kino-zadachi i kino-opasnosti," *Na literaturnom postu*, no. 4 (1927), p. 47. Solskii was not the only one to level this charge at, nor to quote this article from a Riga newspaper—remember that Latvia was not part of the USSR at this time—as "proof."

12. Ibid., pp. 48-49.

13. Ibid., p. 49. The term "decadence" (*upadochnichestvo*) had not been levelled earlier at *By the Law*. For another article on decadence in cinema see P. A. Bliakhin, "Upadochnichestvo v kino," *Na literaturnom postu*, no. 1 (1927), pp. 31-33 which also called films like *The Bear's Wedding* and *The Tripol Tragedy* "decadent." Bliakhin saw "cocaine, opium, vodka, the dagger and the bullet" as the "heroes" of the Soviet film. The audience for which these were meant was "petty tradesmen, NEPmen, Soviet ladies [*sovbaryshni*], all manner of intellectuals," etc.

14. Ibid., p. 49. Solskii gave as examples *Lady Macbeth of the Mtsensk District* (*Ledi Makbet Mtsenskogo uezda*) and *The Decembrists*.

15. Ibid., p. 50. Solskii said that *Mother* was not successful at first due to poor advertising. He asserted that *Miss Mend* was an absolute failure.

16. Ibid., pp. 51-52.

17. Ibid., p. 51.

18. Ibid., p. 52.

19. TsGALI, f. 2496, op. 1, ed. khr. 23, "Tematicheskii plan Sovkino postanovki khud. fil'mov na 1927/28," p. 5.

20. Ibid., pp. 2, 11-17.

21. Ibid., pp. 36-37. This was a response to the thematic production plan dated June 6, 1927.

22. See *Kino-front*, no. 9/10 (1927), pp. 28-29 for several anti-Sovkino "advertisements." The salutation is a parody of the familiar "*S komprivetom*," where "*kom*" means "*kommunisticheskim*" (communist) and not "*kommercheskim*" (commercial).

23. A. Katsigras, "Politika prokata Sovkino," *Novyi zritel'*, no. 6 (1927), p. 13; for an exception see Izmail Urazov, "Pobeda polemiki i tsifry," *Sovetskii ekran*, no. 1 (1927), p. 3.

24. For examples see "K soveshchaniiu po delam kino v TsK VKP (b)," *Kino-front*, no. 9/10 (1927), pp. 1-2. Named were *Mary Pickford's Kiss*, *The Man from the Restaurant*, and *Mr. Lloyd's Voyage*.

25. "Nado rashirit' front bor'by," *Sovetskii ekran*, no. 35 (1927), p. 1.

26. See K. M. Shvedchikov, "Sovkino otvechaet," *Kino-front*, no. 1 (1928), p. 31.

27. "Opasnost' *Garemov iz Bukhary*," *Sovetskii ekran*, no. 42 (1927). An early example we have had of retitling was *Commander Ivanov*'s being shown as *The Beauty and the Bolshevik*.

28. "Tri direktivy," *Kino-front*, no. 13/14 (1927), p. 1. These "three directives" were from Lenin, the idea being that films like *Mr. Lloyd's Voyage*, *Mary Pickford's Kiss*, *The Female Journalist*, *Poison*, and *Poet and Tsar* would not have pleased him. Here was the first mention of the idea that cinema revenues must surpass those from the vodka monopoly in order to earn the love of the Party.

29. "Nel'zia dezertirovat'," *Kino*, no. 19 (1927), p. 2.

30. This word play does not translate into English: *klassovoi* (class) and *kassovoi* (box office).

31. "Ideologiia i kassa," *Sovetskii ekran*, no. 43 (1927), p. 3.

32. "Nel'zia dezertirovat'," pointing to Vertov, Shub, and *Potemkin*.

33. R. Pikel', "Ideologiia i kommertsiia," *Kino*, no. 41 (1927), p. 2. Again, in Russian this slogan is catchy: "Daesh' klassovuiu i kassovuiu fil'mu!" For reinforcement, see the remarks by N. B. Eisimont in "Nasha anketa," *Sovetskoe kino*, no. 2 (1927), p. 5.

34. "Good" films were *Turbine no. 3, Little Brother* (*Bratishka*), and *Alarm* (*Trevoga*).

35. VUFKU was also attacked at this time for its anti-Party tendencies, particularly its "narrow nationalism." See A. Shub, "Dva uklona," *Kino*, no. 50 (1927), p. 2.

36. Osip Beskin, "Neigrovaia fil'ma," *Sovetskoe kino*, no. 7 (1927), pp. 9-11.

37. For example see Iukov, "Puti i pereputia," p. 3; P. Livanov, "Ekh, iablochka, kuda kotish'sia!," ibid., no. 8/9 (1927), p. 21, a sarcastic comment on Mezhrabpom's chairman Malkin's excessively "correct" response to a *Soviet Cinema* survey: "Disput o Mezhrabpom-Rusi," *Kino*, no. 4 (1928), p. 6.

38. See "Pechat' o kino," *Sovetskoe kino*, no. 8 (1926), pp. 28-29 for several extracts.

39. The question of workers' needs was largely ignored, but it was definitely believed that Sovkino catered to the first-run theater crowds. See Osip M. Brik, "Protivokinoiadie," *Novyi Lef*, no. 2 (1927), pp. 29-30.

40. See A. Katsigras, "Ne pora li," *Sovetskoe kino*, no. 2 (1927), p. 23; Iurii Saltanov, "Nuzhno sobrat' kinoset'," ibid., no. 5/6 (1927), pp. 8-9 (which reported widespread support from the district executive committees [*gubispolkomy*] for this); I. Piliver, "K voprosu ob organizatsionno-khoziaistvennykh formakh kino-teatral'nogo dela v RSFSR," ibid., no. 2 (1927), pp. 10-11.

41. In ibid., no. 8/9 (1927) see: M. P. Efremov, "Kino i derevnia: Otvet tov. Katsigrasu," pp. 24-25 and A. Katsigras, "Otvet tov. Efremovu," p. 25.

42. "ONO ili Sovkino?," *Sovetskii ekran*, no. 38 (1927), p. 3. For a cautious seconding of this opinion see I. Davydov, "O tsentralizatsii kino seti," *Novyi zritel'*, no. 33 (1927), p. 8, which notes that Sovkino promised to use theater proceeds to help the cinefication campaign in addition to aiding GTK, the film institute.

43. "Za kinematografiiu (Beseda s predsedatelem pravleniia Sovkino K. M. Shvedchikovym)," *Kino*, no. 34 (1927), p. 2.

44. P. A. Bliakhin, "Politika Sovkino," in *Vokrug Sovkino: Stenogramma disputa organizovannogo TsK VLKSM, TsS ODSK i redaktsii gazety Komsomol'skaia pravda 8-15 okt. 1927* (n.p., 1928), pp. 7-16.

45. Kostrov, p. 20 and Meshcheriakov, p. 25 in ibid.

46. Efremov, pp. 43-46, 59 in ibid.

47. Trainin, pp. 48-49 in ibid.

48. L'vovskii, p. 28; Khanin, pp. 29-30; Kirshon, pp. 32-34 in ibid.

49. Kirshon, p. 35; Sosnovskii, p. 36 in ibid.

50. Maiakovskii, pp. 64-65; Smirnov, p. 72 in ibid. (For more on Maiakovskii's experiences with Sovkino and its literary section see "Karaul!," *Novyi Lef*, no. 2 [1927], pp. 23-25.)

51. Bliakhin, pp. 88-89 in ibid.

52. P. A. Bliakhin, "K partsoveshchaniiu," *Novyi zritel'*, no. 50 (1927), p. 14. This refers to the Party Conference on Cinema Affairs which would take place in March 1928.

53.   "'Levye' uklony," *Kino*, no. 43 (1927), p. 1.

54.   A. Kurs, *Samoe mogushchestvennoe* (Moscow-Leningrad, 1927), p. 14.

55.   Ibid., pp. 51-52, 57.

56.   Ibid., p. 51.

57.   Khrisanf Khersonskii, "Khochu snimatsia," *Kino-front*, no. 5 (1927), pp. 4-7. (*Cinema Front* was now bi-weekly.)

58.   "*3-ia Meshchanskaia*: Rezoliutsiia ARK," ibid., no. 4 (1927), p. 21.

59.   K. Ganzenko, "Sovetskii byt na sovetskom ekrane," ibid., no. 1 (1927), pp. 11-12.

60.   For a qualified exception see P. A. Bliakhin, "*Tret'ia Meshchanskaia*," *Kino*, no. 4 (1927), who thought the film successful despite its dubious heroine. He particularly liked the triumph of the maternal instinct; see also Khrisanf Khersonskii, "Rasskaz o meshchanstve," ibid., no. 5 (1927), p. 4.

61.   K. Denisov, "Meshchanstvo v kino," *Sovetskii ekran*, no. 5 (1927), p. 3.

62.   N. Iakovlev, "Pervosortnaia meshchanskaia (diskussionno), *Kino*, no. 5 (1927), p. 3.

63.   "O *Liubvi vtroem*," ibid., no. 13 (1927), p. 14.

64.   "Za preodolenie trudnostei," ibid., no. 15 (1927), p. 2, and Osip Brik, "Polpobedy," p. 3.

65.   Sha, "ARK o *Tret'ei Meshchanskoi*," *Novyi zritel'*, no. 11 (1927), p. 13.

66.   "Chistka," ibid., no. 13 (1927), p. 12.

67.   N. Iakovlev, "Ne tol'ko chto no i tak," *Kino*, no. 12 (1927), p. 3.

68.   Nikolai Lukhmanov, "Bol'naia zhizn'," *Novyi zritel'*, no. 22 (1927), p. 8.

69.   "Ob linii ARK," *Kino*, no. 13 (1927), p. 2.

70.   "*Tret'ia Meshchanskaia* (na prosmotr ODSK)," ibid., no. 12 (1927), pp. 4-5.

71.   Iakovlev, "Ne tol'ko chto no i tak."

72.   O. Barshak, "Nuzhnoe nachinanie," *Kino*, no. 11 (1927), p. 4.

73.   Khersonskii, "Khochu snimatsia," p. 7. A later article stated that the union of ARK and ODSK had been beneficial to both. See "Organizatsiia idei," *Kino-front*, no. 6 (1927), p. 2, but Khersonskii is supported by ARK's complaints against ODSK in TsGALI, f. 2494, op. 1, ed. khr. 71, "Protokoly zasedanii pravleniia ARK."

74.   Vladimir Kirshon, "Zametki ob ARK i ODSK," *Kino-front*, no. 9/10 (1927), pp. 14-17. Unfortunately I have no idea what Shklovskii said, but he was in an unenviable position due to his connection with *Wings of a Serf* and now *Third Meshchanskaia Street*, and may have been currying favor with one faction or another.

75.   Ibid., p. 18.

76.   TsGALI, f. 2494, op. 1, ed. khr. 74, "Protokol obshchego sobraniia chlenov ARK ot 20-go okt. 1927," p. 45.

77.   M. Nikanorov, "Nekotorye itogi," *Kino-front*, no. 9/10 (1927), pp. 13-14.

78.   Ibid., bottom of p. 12.

79.   Ibid., p. 15.

80.   See Sheila Fitzpatrick, "The 'Soft' Line on Culture and Its Enemies: Soviet Cultural Policy, 1922-1927," *Slavic Review* 33 (June 1974): 267-87; "Culture and Politics under Stalin: A Reappraisal," *Slavic Review* 35 (June 1976): 211-31; "The Emergence of Glaviskusstvo: Class War on the Cultural Front, Moscow, 1928-29," *Soviet Studies* 23, no. 2 (October 1971): 236-53; and "Cultural Revolution in Russia, 1928-32," *Journal of Contemporary History* 9 (January 1974): 33-52. In the last mentioned article, Fitzpatrick says the term "cultural revolution" was used in December 1927 in a "Leninist" sense, that is, to mean that educational levels had to be increased as a prerequisite to expansion, p. 38. The references in the film press in 1927, however, clearly use "cultural revolution" to mean class warfare, which Fitzpatrick believes is a later development.

81.   See "Pered novym pokhodom," *Kino-front*, no. 11/12 (1927), pp. 1-2.

82.   K. Iukov, "Desiat' let i kino," ibid., pp. 2-6.

83.   V. Sol'skii, "Diskussii o Sovkino," ibid., pp. 6-10.

84.   TsGALI, f. 2494, op. 1, ed. khr. 71, "Rezoliutsiia po dokladu t. Trainina," pp. 40-42.

85.   TsGALI, f. 2494, op. 1, ed. khr. 74, "Tezisy doklada t. Iukova ob itogakh i perspektivakh raboty ARK na obshchem sobranii chlenov ARK 20-go okt. 27," pp. 47-48.

86.   Partial membership lists appeared in *Kino-front*, no. 1 (1927), pp. 25-26 and no. 4 (1927), p. 28.

87.   "Nigilisty iz ARKa," *Sovetskii ekran*, no. 3 (1928), p. 3.

88.   "O kharaktere kritiki," ibid., no. 49 (1927).

89.   V. Sol'skii, "Nekotorye itogi kino-diskussii," *Na literaturnom postu*, no. 1 (1928), p. 65.

90.   Ibid., p. 66.

91.   Ibid., pp. 66-68.

92.   Ibid., p. 70.

93.   On the "Sovietization of adultery" see also V. Meshcheriakov, "Kuda derzhit kurs Sovkino," in K. A. Mal'tsev, ed., *Sovetskoe kino pered litsom obshchestvennosti* (n.p., 1928), pp. 109-16. It is not clear from the internal evidence whether all or only part of the essays in this book originated before the conference.

94.   S. Krylov, *Kino vmesto vodki: K Vsesoiuznom partsoveshchaniiu po voprosam kino* (Moscow-Leningrad, 1928), pp. 3-5, 7-8, 11-16. This 80 percent figure was repeated by V. Meshcheriakov, "Kogo i kak obsluzhivaet Sovkino," in Mal'tsev, *Sovetskoe kino*, p. 168.

95.   Krylov, *Kino*, pp. 17, 19-20.

96.   Ibid., pp. 21-26.

97.   Ibid., 28-30.

98.   Ibid., pp. 50-70. For further information on conditions in workers' clubs, see A. L'vovskii, "Kino v kul'trabote profsoiuzov," in Mal'tsev, *Sovetskoe kino*, pp. 146-152. Lvovskii supported Krylov's complaints that films often started as much as one hour late.

99.   Efraim Lemberg, *Kinopromyshlennost' SSSR: Ekonomika sovetskoi kinematografii* (Moscow, 1930), pp. 176ff.

100.   Vladimir Kirshon, "Listki iz bloknota," *Kino-front*, no. 2 (1928), pp. 6-7.

101.   "Ne vzryv a ispravlenie," ibid., no. 1 (1928), pp. 1-2.

102.   Osip Beskin, "Nekotorye cherty iz zhizni Sovkino," *Sovetskoe kino*, no. 1 (1928), pp. 2-4.

103.   I. Davydov, "Order na zhizn'," ibid., p. 6

104.   G. Arustanov, "Nashi oshibki," ibid., pp. 8-10.

105.   *Deiatelnost' Vserossiskogo foto-kinematograficheskogo aktsionernogo o-va sovetskogo kino "Sovkino" s 1-go marta 1925 po 1-oe oktiabria 1927* (Moscow, 1928), pp. 3-30. Sovkino published this itself in 300 copies.

106.   I. P. Trainin, *Kino na kul'turnom fronte* (Leningrad, 1928), pp. 7-12.

107.   Ibid., pp. 13-18.

108.   Ibid., pp. 29-41. See also Trainin's "Raboche-krest'ianskii byt v sovetskom kino" in Mal'tsev, *Sovetskoe kino*, pp. 76-90.

109.   Ibid., pp. 42-52.

110.   Ibid., pp. 52-59. Trainin argued the merits of *Third Meshchanskaia Street* ending with a poignant comment on the nature of criticism: it had, with a few swift strokes, destroyed a film that had been a year in the making.

111.   Ibid., pp. 62-70.

112.   Ibid., p. 77. Trainin here indicted one Smirnov, former editor of *Worker's Gazette*, who "directly demanded the burning of all our pictures on Red Square, the expulsion of all non-Party directors and so forth."

113.   Ibid., pp. 87-88.

114.   Ibid., pp. 92-96.

115.   Ibid., pp. 103-7.

116.   This was always given in terms of *copies*, not titles, which could mean that there were ten copies of one Soviet film and seven copies of seven foreign films, enabling Sovkino to say that there were "more" Soviet films in circulation.

117.   "Rabochoe slovo na nashem kino," *Kino*, no. 1 (1928), p. 2.

118.   See M. P. Efremov, "Itogi i perspektivy sovetskoi kinematografii," in Mal'tsev, *Sovetskoe kino*, pp. 21-38; also his "Kino na sluzhbe u trudiashchikhsia," ibid., pp. 133-46.

119.   A. V. Lunacharskii, *Kino na zapade i u nas* (Moscow, 1928), pp. 10, 14.

120.   Ibid., pp. 30-31.

121.   Ibid., p. 63.

122.   Ibid., pp. 67, 69.

123.   Ibid., pp. 70-71.

124.   A. V. Lunacharskii, "Sovetskoe kino na pod"eme," in Mal'tsev, *Sovetskoe kino*, pp. 13-14.

125.   Leningradskii oblastnoi komitet VKP(b), *Rezoliutsii Leningradskogo oblastnogo partsoveshchaniia po voprosam kinematografii, 2-3 marta 1928* (Leningrad, 1928), pp. 4-13.

126. See Famarin, "Kino ne teatr," *Sovetskoe kino*, no. 2 (1927), pp. 2-3 or "Khudozhnik i 'material'naia sreda' v igrovoi fil'me: Beseda s khudozhnikom A.M. Rodchenko," ibid., no. 5/6 (1927), pp. 14-15, for two different views on the nature of cinema realism (whether it should be "life" or an approximation of reality).

127. Vadim Shershenevich, "Kino-slovar'," in *Kino-kalendar'* (n.p., 1927).

Chapter 6

1. G. Arustanov, "Rentabel'nost'," *Sovetskoe kino*, no. 8/9 (1927), p. 10. For actual production figures, see appendix 1.

2. P. A. Bliakhin, "O stsenarnom rezerve," *Kino*, no. 15 (1927), p. 2.

3. See the announcement in *Sovetskii ekran*, no. 14 (1927), p. 2. The results were wittily reported on by Izmail Urazov in several articles titled "Notes on Our Competition" ("Zametki o nashem konkurse"). One comment he made was that the repetition of themes was quite popular, especially films on the order of *His Call*. See ibid., no. 42 (1927), p. 10. He also joked that amateur writers took the term "underground" literally and set their revolutionary stories in catacombs. Police could always be identified by their half-masks. See ibid., no. 43 (1927), p. 10.

4. "Ob osnovom," ibid., no. 50 (1927), p. 3. This was seconded by Mikhail Shneider in "Stsenariev net," *Kino*, no. 9 (1927), p. 3.

5. Ippolit Sokolov, "Mnogo stsenariev, a khoroshikh net," *Kino*, no. 39 (1927). Viktor Shklovskii also continued to insist on professional *cinema* writers. See his *Motalka: O kino-remesle* (Moscow-Leningrad, 1927), p. 22.

6. K. Denisov, "O stsenariiakh," *Kino-front*, no. 4 (1927), pp. 11-12. Denisov also indicated there was continued wrangling among various organizations in charge of reviewing scripts, see pp. 10, 12.

7. Viktor Pertsov, "Razmyshleniia neorganizovannogo cheloveka," *Sovetskoe kino*, no. 8/9 (1927), p. 13.

8. Viktor Shklovskii, "Kinematografiia nachinaetsia s liudei," *Kino*, no. 33 (1927), p. 2. Shklovskii also criticized scenarists for adapting other writers' works without their permission.

9. Abram Room, "Den'gi i uvazhenie," ibid., no. 42 (1927), p. 2.

10. Viktor Pertsov, "Vnimanie pisateliu," ibid.

11. Fedor Gladkov, "Pochemu net khoroshikh stsenariev," ibid., no. 40 (1927), p. 2.

12. L. Goldenveizer, "Net sviazi," ibid.

13. M. S. Veremienko, "Chto nado delat'," ibid., no. 45 (1927), p. 2.

14. Ippolit Sokolov, "Proizvodstvo sostoianiia stsenarnogo dela," *Kino-front*, no. 11/12 (1927), pp. 15-18.

15. "Stsenarnoi golod," *Kino*, no. 10 (1927), p. 2.

16. "Ob osnovom."

17. See Izmail Urazov, "Vtoroi konets pal'ki," *Sovetskii ekran*, no. 11 (1927), p. 3; Ippolit Sokolov, "Nauka o kino i nauchno-issledovatel'skaia rabota v kino," *Kino-front*, no. 6 (1927), p. 5.

18.   Izmail Urazov, "Nuzhno soglasovanie planov," *Sovetskii ekran*, no. 6 (1927), p. 3. Urazov was now the editorial secretary of *Soviet Screen*.

19.   Ippolit Sokolov, "Sostoianie stsenarnogo dela," *Kino-front*, no. 13/14 (1927), pp. 22-26.

20.   Urazov, "Nuzhno soglasovanie planov."

21.   P. A. Bliakhin in "Protokol no. 8: Zasedaniia stsenarnoi masterskoi (1927)," TsGALI, f. 2496, op. 1, ed. khr. 14, p. 14.

22.   Arsen, "O sovetskoi teme i o stsenarnom krizise," *Sovetskii ekran*, no. 14 (1927), p. 3.

23.   Viktor Pertsov, "Basnia i nravouchenie: O sovetskoi bytovoi fil'me," *Kino*, no. 7 (1927).

24.   TsGALI, f. 2496, op. 1, ed. khr. 23, "Templan Sovkino," pp. 50-51.

25.   Ibid., pp. 45, 48.

26.   Ibid., p. 45; also "Sovetskaia komicheskaia," *Kino*, no. 16 (1927) p. 2.

27.   Osip Brik, "Na podstupakh v sovetskoi komedii (Anketa)," ibid., p. 3.

28.   Ippolit Sokolov, "Kak sozdat' sovetskuiu komediiu," *Kino-front*, no. 3 (1927), p. 14. In this vein see also Pochtar', "Smekh i ideologiia," *Kino*, no. 2 (1927), p. 4. Sokolov really was an intelligent critic but like all Soviet critics in these sad times, he could now and then be counted on to write an embarrassing article.

29.   Vladimir Kirshon, "Listki iz bloknota," *Kino-front*, no. 13/14 (1927), p. 10.

30.   TsGALI, f. 2496, op. 1, ed. khr. 23, "Sovkino templan 1927/28," p. 45. Also "Psevdo-natsional'nye proizvodstva," *Sovetskii ekran*, no. 27 (1927), p. 3. To my great regret, I was not allowed to see these films.

31.   Ship., "Vse v proshlom," *Novyi zritel'*, no. 14 (1927), p. 12.

32.   Nikolai Lukhmanov, "Psevdo-klassitsizm," ibid., no. 16 (1927), p. 12.

33.   Osip Brik, "Po sushchestvu stsenarnogo krizis," *Sovetskoe kino*, no. 8 (1928), p. 11.

34.   See "*Kino-glaz*," *Kino*, no. 34 (1926), p. 13.

35.   "*Shestaia chast' mira* (Beseda s Dzigoi Vertovym)," ibid., pp 3-5.

36.   Izmail Urazov, "Pafos i deistvii," *Kino*, no. 39 (1926), p. 1.

37.   Urazov, "Nashi velikie pobedy," *Sovetskii ekran*, no. 40 (1926), p. 3. The other "great victory" was *By the Law* which indicates that Urazov's taste was both catholic and highly developed.

38.   See the unpublished letter from Sovkino to the editors of *Kino-front*, TsGALI, f. 2494, op. 1, ed. khr. 69, pp. 16-17.

39.   Viktor Shklovskii, "Kinoki i nadpisi," *Kino*, no. 44 (1926), p. 3.

40.   Vladimir Korolevich, "Samaia deshevaia veshch'," p. 13.

41.   N. Aseev, "Shestaia chast' vozmozhnostei," *Kino*, no. 43 (1926), p. 2. Aseev thought the film the only weapon against the "immanent laws of art."

42.   "*Shestaia chast' mira*," ibid., p. 5.

43.   See for example N. Iakovlev, "Protiv arkheologii," *Sovetskii ekran*, no. 46 (1926), p. 3.

44.   Ippolit Sokolov, "*Shestaia chast' mira*," *Kino-front*, no. 2 (1927), pp. 9-12.

45. "*Shestaia chast' mira* (Diskussionnyi prosmotr v ARKe)," ibid., p. 2.

46. Sokolov, "*Shestaia chast'*," p. 12.

47. Dziga Vertov, untitled letter, *Kino-front*, no. 4 (1927), p. 32.

48. Ippolit Sokolov, untitled letter, ibid., no. 7/8 (1927), pp. 31-32.

49. Nikolai Lebedev, letter in ibid. D. Borisov had early claimed that 30-40 percent of the picture was not original. See "*Shestaia chast' mira,*" *Kino*, no. 3 (1927), p. 2. For a recently uncovered Vertov scandal, see V. Listov, "Dve *Kino-nedeli,*" *Iskusstvo kino*, no. 5 (1968), pp. 93-100. Listov asserts that Vertov falsified footage in his *newsreels*.

50. Sokolov, letter. Sokolov admired Pudovkin's scientific film *Mechanics of the Brain* (*Mekhanika golovnogo mozga*), Shub's *Fall of the Romanov Dynasty*, and Kaufman's and Kopalin's *Moscow* (*Moskva*) among others. Sokolov also noted that his opinion of *One-Sixth of the World* had been formed many months before his association with Sovkino. This is the first indication I saw that Sokolov also worked for Sovkino; I have no idea in what capacity.

51. "My ishchem," *Novyi Lef*, no. 11/12 (1927), pp. 1-2. This issue was devoted to cinema, particularly to the question of the nonacted film.

52. Osip Brik, "Protiv zhanrovykh kartinok," *Kino*, no. 27 (1927), p. 3. Brik expanded on this in "Fiksatsiia fakta," *Novyi Lef*, no. 11/12 (1927), pp. 44-50.

53. But cf. Viktor Pertsov, "'Igra' i demonstratsiia," *Novyi Lef*, no. 11/12 (1927), pp. 33-44.

54. See Brik's remarks in "Lef i kino," ibid., pp. 63-66.

55. TsGALI, f. 2494, op. 1, ed. khr. 74, "Protokol sobraniia chlenov ARK 18/IV-27," p. 18. This was a report from Iukov, who disagreed that Eisenstein was a Lef product. Shklovskii and one Potemkin then protested Iukov's "abuse" of Lef.

56. See Grigorii Boltianskii, "Usloviia razvitiia kino-khroniki," *Sovetskoe kino*, no. 5/6 (1927), pp. 78-79 and an editorial "Zhizn' pered ob"ektivom," *Sovetskii ekran*, no. 40 (1927), p. 1; there was also a long questionnaire on the subject of educational films "Nasha anketa," *Sovetskoe kino*, no. 8/9 (1927), pp. 1-7, to which a number of cinema workers responded. Pudovkin and Room protested any idea that only educational films (*kul'turfil'my*) should be produced, to which the editors responded that they merely wanted to draw deserved attention to nonfiction cinema.

57. See Abram Room in "Nasha anketa," p. 7.

58. "Bol'noe mesto v kino," *Kino-front*, no. 5 (1927), p. 1.

59. Vladimir Korolevich, "Kino ili zagovor imperiatritsy," ibid., pp. 8-9.

60. S. I., "Novye liudi," *Kino-front*, no. 3 (1927), p. 6. He also named Okhlopkov, Eggert, Ktorov, and Kuindzhi, even though he was quite hostile to such "specialists."

61. A. Cherkassov, "Masterstvo artista v kino," ibid., pp. 2-4; also n. 63, chap. 4.

62. Korolevich, "Kino ili zagovor imperiatritsy."

63. S. I., "Novye liudi."

64. Sokolov rejected the Stanislavskii method of "feeling" (*perezhivanie*) which he saw as being based on "instinct" or "hysteria" or perhaps even drug addiction! He supported instead "performance" (*predstavlenie*) which was by contrast "technique, mastery, training,

performance." This should not be based on Delsartism or Dalcroism (like the Kuleshov method) but on reflexology. For details of this approach see his "Metody igry pered kino-apparatom," in *Kino-front*, no. 5 (1927), pp. 10-14 and the second part in no. 6, pp. 11-13. Along this line, Sokolov also began to develop a special jargon for his acting theories and invested words like role (*amplua*), mask, type, image, and character with the most minute shades of meaning. See his "Amplua, tipazh, maska: Kharakter obraza," ibid., no. 3 (1927), pp. 18-22. For the previous discussion of these methods, see chapter 4.

65. For a statement against typage see "Kino-akter," *Kino*, no. 21 (1927), p. 3. This also opposed "dramatic actors and prima ballerinas" in cinema.

66. Fridrikh Ermler, "Kadr i akter," ibid., no. 9 (1927), p. 3.

67. Abram Room, "Rezhisser...v koridore," ibid., no. 21 (1927), p. 3.

68. Lev Kuleshov, "O nashem kinoaktere," ibid. This was one of the rare occasions in which the normally civilized Kuleshov was very sharp-tongued.

69. See V. Muskin, "Podvodnye kontsy," *Sovetskii ekran*, no. 15 (1927), pp. 3-4. This was specifically directed at understanding why the viewers did not like *Potemkin*.

70. An early detailed critique by A. Kurs of Soviet film criticism appeared in *Soviet Cinema* in 1925. He felt that most film reviews were not written with the mass viewer in mind and that the general and Party press was not concerned enough with artistic values in films. See "Kino-kritika v SSSR," *Sovetskoe kino*, no. 4/5 (1925), pp. 22-28. This was not the only article on film criticism that appeared at this time. See also Abram Room, "Kakoi dolzhna byt' kino-kritika," *Kino*, no. 2/5 (1925), p. 6 for a director's viewpoint; P. Kb., "Kino-zhurnal *ARK*," *Kino*, no. 5 (1925), p. 4; E. Cherniavskii, "Kak pisat' kino-retsenzii," *Kino*, no. 10 (1925), p. 6.

71. Ippolit Sokolov, "Ne dolzhen pisat' obyvatel'," *Kino*, no. 43 (1927), p. 2.

72. Mikhail Levidov, "Tovarishchei zhal'ko," ibid. See also Pavel Potemkin, "Slovo massovomu zriteliu," ibid., no. 44 (1927), p. 2.

73. Sergei Iutkevich, "O kino-kritike," ibid., no. 44 (1927), p. 2.

74. For other adverse criticisms see M. Bystritskii, "S tochki zreniia teorii," ibid., no. 2 (1927), p. 3, which attacked the film for its "American" montage. Even its own scenarist Viktor Shklovskii criticized it in his *Motalka*, pp. 38-39. (Shklovskii was in a great deal of trouble for *Third Meshchanskaia Street*, which could explain this action). See also Ippolit Sokolov, "Kryl'ia kholopa," *Kino-front*, no. 1 (1927), pp. 12-13.

75. Il'ia Erenburg, *Materializatsiia fantastiki* (Moscow-Leningrad, 1927), p. 26.

76. Arsen, "*Dekabristy*," *Kino-front*, no. 5 (1927), pp. 15-17.

77. See "*Dekabristy*," *Sovetskoe kino*, no. 2 (1927), p. 31 and M. Babenchikov, "Kino—geroi—byt," *Sovetskii ekran*, no. 39 (1927), p. 13, which also lists *Poet and Tsar, The Collegiate Registrar,* and *The Overcoat* as representing "half-life." Also see "*Dekabristy*," *Kino*, no. 3 (1927), p. 34.

78. P. Neznamov, "*Poet i tsar'*," *Kino*, no. 39 (1927), p. 3.

79. "Pushkinisty o *Poete i tsare*," *Sovetskii ekran*, no. 43 (1927), p. 4.

80. Mikhail Shneider, "*Poet i tsar'*," *Kino-front*, no. 11/12 (1927), pp. 27-29.

81. For a brief plot summary see *Sovetskie khudozhestvennye fil'my*, 1:225-26. The unlucky director was M. Verner, about whom I have heard nothing else.

82. Mikhail Shneider, "*Solistka ego velichestva,*" *Kino-front,* no. 7/8 (1927), pp. 13-14.

83. Mikhail Shneider, "*Gospoda Skotininy,*" ibid., no. 4 (1927), pp. 18-20 and "*Gospoda Skotininy:* Rezoliutsiia ARKa," ibid., pp. 21-22. The resolution quite unaccountably added that the picture showed that successful screen adaptations were possible. P. Neznamov in "Po poverkhnosti epokhi," *Kino,* no. 3 (1927), p. 4 found the picture "ornamental and naive." See also "*Gospoda Skotininy,*" *Sovetskoe kino,* no. 2 (1927), p. 30.

84. P. Neznamov, "*S.V.D.,*" *Kino,* no. 35 (1927), p. 3.

85. Mikhail Shneider, "*S.V.D.,*" *Kino-front,* no. 9/10 (1927), pp. 19-20.

86. Ippolit Sokolov, "*S.V.D.,*" ibid., pp. 20-23.

87. Ganzenko, "Sovetskii byt." On the other hand, a favorable review came from *Soviet Cinema.* See "*Kat'ka bumazhnyi ranet,*" no. 2 (1927), pp. 30-31.

88. For criticism of M. Chekhov's acting see P. Neznamov, "Chekhov—krupnym planom," *Kino,* no. 34 (1927), p. 4.

89. Ippolit Sokolov, "*Chelovek iz restorana,*" *Kino-front,* no. 9/10 (1927), pp. 23-24. (Sokolov accused the press of receiving it "softly and even warmly.") See also Mikhail Shneider, "Po tu storonu 17-go goda," *Kino,* no. 36 (1927), p. 3.

90. See Iakov Lev, "*Iad,*" *Kino,* no. 37 (1927), p. 3; F. A., "Kak delalsia stsenarii *Iada* (Iz nashego obsledovaniia)," ibid.; for a technical evaluation see S. I., "*Iad,*" *Kino-front,* no. 9/10 (1927), pp. 29-30. See also K. Denisov, "O stsenariiakh," *Kino-front,* no. 4 (1927), p. 12.

91. Preobrazhenskaia's first film as a director was the 1916 *Lady Peasant* (*Baryshnia krest'ianka*). On the posters she was inadvertently listed as Preobrazhen*skii* (masculine suffix) apparently because theater managers were unable to believe that a woman could be a director. See TsGALI, f. 2356, op. 1, ed. khr. 46a, "Avtobiografiia (1963)," pp. 1-3.

92. TsGALI, f. 2494, op. 1, ed. khr. 94, "Stenogramma diskussii po obsuzhdeniiu kinofil'ma *Baby riazanskie* 17-22 noia. 1927," pp. 1-3.

93. Ibid., pp. 8-27, particularly pp. 8-10, 15, 17-18, 21, 23, 27. Part of the discussion, pp. 4-8, was missing.

94. P. Neznamov, "*Baby riazanskie,*" *Kino,* no. 52 (1927). For more information on this film see TsGALI, f. 2356, op. 1, ed. khr. 8, which contains clippings and some notations by Preobrazhenskaia.

95. "Baby riazanskie," *Sovetskoe kino,* no. 8/9 (1927), p. 31.

96. Sergei M. Eizenshtein, "Pochemu opozdal *Oktiabr',*" *Kino,* no. 51 (1927), p. 4. He did mention editing problems.

97. Mikhail Levidov, "*Konets Sankt-Peterburga,*" ibid., no. 47 (1927), p. 2.

98. Khrisanf Khersonskii, "*Konets Sankt-Peterburga,*" *Kino-front,* no. 1 (1928), pp. 16-18. The editors issued a disclaimer to this.

99. Khersonskii, "*Moskva v Oktiabre,*" *Kino,* no. 47 (1927), p. 3. It is true that since one-half the film is now missing I cannot be an authority on the continuity, but my impressions are compatible with the critical assessments of those who saw it in its entirety.

100. Civil War films were seen to be responsible for a trend of excessive violence in Soviet cinema, now known as the "bloody deviation" (*krovavyi uklon*). See "Krov' na ekrane," *Sovetskii*

ekran, no. 32 (1927), pp. 4-6. Vertov was quoted here as saying that the fiction feature film was preoccupied with "love, naked women, and violence," p. 6.

101. See "Na temu grazhdanskoi voiny (O *Sorok pervom*)," *Kino*, no. 11 (1927), p. 4 and Khrisanf Khersonskii, "*Sorok pervyi*," ibid., no. 12 (1927), p. 3.

102. Arsen, "*Sorok pervyi*," *Kino-front*, no. 6 (1927), pp. 15-19.

103. Quoted disapprovingly by Arsen, ibid., p. 18.

104. Iakov Lev, "*Devushka s korobkoi*," *Kino*, no. 18 (1927), p. 2.

105. For example see M. Bystritskii, "Besprizornaia (Po povodu *Potselui Meri*)," ibid., no. 38 (1927), p. 3; Pikel', "Ideologiia i kommertsiia." There are others too numerous to mention.

106. *Sovetskie khudozhestvennye fil'my*, 1:222.

107. Khrisanf Khersonskii, "*Reis mistera Lloida*," *Kino*, no. 39 (1927), p. 3.

108. Nikolai Lukhmanov, "Lovite vora!," ibid., no. 38 (1928).

109. Osip Brik, "Pobeda fakta," ibid., no. 14 (1927), p. 3.

110. Lev Kuleshov, "Ekran segodnia," *Novyi Lef*, no. 4 (1927), pp. 31-34; Mikhail Shneider, "*Padenie dinastii romanovykh*," *Kino-front*, no. 7/8 (1927), pp. 15-18; "*Padenie dinastii romanovykh*," *Sovetskoe kino*, no. 4 (1927).

111. Viktor Shklovskii, "Po povodu kartiny Esfir Shub," *Novyi Lef*, no. 8/9 (1927), pp. 52-54; Sergei Tret'iakov, "Kino k iubileiu," ibid., no. 10 (1927), pp. 28-29.

112. P. A. Bliakhin, "*Velikii put'*," *Kino*, no. 44 (1927), p. 3.

Chapter 7

1. A. I. Krinitskii in B. S. Ol'khovyi, ed., *Puti kino: Pervoe Vsesoiuznoe partiinoe soveshchanie po kinematografii* (Moscow, 1929), pp. 22-41.

2. Krinitskii, p. 43; Ryskulov, pp. 95-96 (who noted that the so-called "Eastern" films were unconvincing when shown to the natives they were portraying); Zastenkov, p. 107 in ibid.

3. Meshcheriakov, p. 102; Krylov, p. 142 in ibid. Lunacharskii's "middle line" was also attacked by one Martynenko, p. 122.

4. Kirshon, ibid., p. 79. See also Tsekhev, p. 75; Mandel'shtam, p. 90.

5. Miuntsenberg, ibid., p. 119.

6. On import policies see Ol'khovyi, ibid., p. 164; on export policies see Chernin, pp. 194-95 and Krinitskii, pp. 45-46.

7. Trainin, ibid., pp. 136-39.

8. Shvedchikov, ibid., pp. 153-56.

9. Krinitskii, ibid., pp. 220-26.

10. Shvedchikov, "Organizatsionnye i khoziaistvennye voprosy sovetskoi kinematografii," in ibid., pp. 235-53. Since Sovkino already was a joint-stock company, it is not clear what advantage reorganizing would provide.

11. Arustanov, ibid., pp. 272-73; Brigdanov, p. 282, Altaitsev, p. 295; Makarian, pp. 354-57; Sharikian, p. 359; Vinogradskii, p. 326.

12. Arustanov, ibid., p. 274; Kiva, p. 303.

13. Shvedchikov, ibid., pp. 365-68.

14. Mal'tsev, ibid., pp. 386-90.

15. Kirshon, ibid., pp. 416-17; Mal'tsev, p. 424.

16. N. I. Smirnov, "Pechat' i kino," in ibid., pp. 397-405. For a rebuttal from Teakinopechat' see Orlinskii, pp. 417-21.

17. Ibid., pp. 429-44.

18. S. Kosior, "K itogam voprosov kino," *Revoliutsiia i kul'tura*, no. 6 (1928), pp. 5-7. On the continued shortage of raw film see M. Paushkin, "Direktivy Sovnarkoma RSFSR o plane kinofikatsii," *Sovetskii ekran*, no. 29 (1928), p. 6 and G. Dalmatov, "Za sovetskuiu kino-plenku," *Kino*, no. 14 (1928), p. 4.

19. "To, chego my ne umeem ekonomit'," *Sovetskii ekran*, no. 15 (1928), p. 3.

20. "Doloi!," ibid., no. 26 (1928), p. 3. This issue has several articles on the subject of foreign films. See also "Nasha pochta," ibid., no. 42 (1928).

21. "Davno pora," *Kino*, no. 20 (1928), p. 1. See also "Soobshchenie Glavrepertkoma," ibid.

22. "Eshche odna seriia sniatykh kartin," ibid., no. 21 (1928), p. 2.

23. "Udachnaia operatsiia: Ekran ochishchen ot khlama," ibid., no. 47 (1928), p. 6.

24. TsGALI, f. 2496, op. 1, ed. khr. 31, "Stenogramma soveshchanii po obsuzhdeniiu tematicheskogo plana Sovkino 11-17 iiulia 1928." I have no way of knowing for certain if this outside interference had been allowed before, but I saw no documents indicating that it had.

25. *Tematicheskii plan Sovkino na 1928/29 g. utverzhdennyi plenumom khudozhestvennogo soveta ot 11/VII zasedaniem pravleniia Sovkino ot 13/VIII s. g.* (n.p., 1928), pp. 3-6.

26. See A. A. Levitskii and E. K. Tisse in "Nasha anketa sredi deiatelei kino," *Na literaturnom postu*, no. 1 (1928), pp. 74-75.

27. R. Pikel', "Ukhaby na kino-fronte," *Revoliutsiia i kul'tura*, no. 3/4 (1928), pp. 45-49. This was printed as a "discussion."

28. Vladimir Kirshon, "O kino-kritike," in his *Na kino-postu* (Moscow-Leningrad, 1928), pp. 114-59.

29. "Kino-kritiki i obshchestvennost'," *Kino*, no. 9 (1928), p. 1. See also "Diskussiia o kino-kritike," ibid. This is the first and last time I read about such a critics' association.

30. For an example from an unlikely source, see V. Sol'skii, "V zashchitu *Zemli v plenu*," ibid., no. 10 (1928), p. 3.

31. "Davno pora."

32. See "Kino pod ogon' samokritiki," *Kino*, no. 23 (1928), p. 1; K. Riutin, "Pochistik ob"ektiv," ibid., no. 41 (1928), p. 2; S. Bogatirev, "Protiv passivnosti i podpol'shchiny," ibid.

33. "Samokritika" (cartoon), *Kino*, no. 27 (1928), p. 1.

34. Prodavtsy slavy, "Teakinopechat' pered sudom rabochikh," *Kino*, no. 12 (1929), p. 2.

35. See A. Mil'kin, "Pod svoe tiazhestvo," ibid., no. 15 (1929), p. 3; untitled obituary, *Sovetskii ekran*, no. 16 (1929), p. 4. The tone of the former is especially unsavory.

36. "Na novye rel'sy," *Sovetskii ekran*, no. 19 (1929), p. 3. The journal promised to stop serving the petty-bourgeoisie.

37. See *Kino*, no. 2 (1930), p. 1. The purge continued through the spring; see ibid., no. 26 (1930).

38. G. Ivashchenko, "O perekvalifikatsii kino-mekhanikov," ibid., no. 16 (1928), p. 2.

39. TsGALI, f. 2494, op. 1, ed. khr. 139, "Stenogramma sobraniia ARK po obsuzhdenii doklada Sharikiana o Gosudarstvennom tekhnikume kinematografii 14 avg. 28," pp. 1-32. The title page, however, says this was an ODSK report.

40. "V zashchitu GTK," *Kino*, no. 36 (1928).

41. E. Sharikian, "Itogi priema v GTK," ibid., no. 38 (1928).

42. "Bor'ba s protektsionizmom," ibid., no. 34 (1928), p. 6. At this time Osip Brik was chief of the literary section of the Mezhrabpom studio.

43. "Kumovstvo na kino-fabrike," ibid., no. 14 (1928), p. 6.

44. "Novye v bytu kino-akterov," ibid., no. 17 (1928), p. 6.

45. "Sovetskaia obshchestvennost' ne pozvolit sryvat' rabotu professional'nykh organizatsii...," ibid., no. 25 (1928), p. 2. Because I was denied access to Leningrad *Cinema*, I must use this biased version of the letter.

46. Ibid.

47. M. Donskoi and M. Averbakh, "Akter i tipazh," ibid., no. 26 (1928), p. 2.

48. "Rezoliutsiia ARKa," ibid., no. 28 (1928), p. 5.

49. A. Zh., "Obshchestvennyi sud nad tipazhem," ibid., no. 31 (1928), p. 4. See also Valentin Turkin, "O zhivykh liudiakh," *Sovetskii ekran*, no. 20 (1929), p. 7.

50. For earlier opposition to the "dictatorship of the director," see Grigorii Boltianskii, *Kul'tura kino-operatora* (Moscow-Leningrad, 1927), p. 11 and P. S. Radetskii, *Chto takoe kino* (Moscow-Leningrad, 1927), p. 3.

51. V. Sutyrin, "Literatura, teatr, kino," *Na literaturnom postu*, no. 10 (1929), pp. 35-45. Sutyrin wrote a similar article attacking directors in "O stsenarii i stsenariste," *Sovetskii ekran*, no. 16 (1929), p. 8.

52. Sergei A. Timoshenko, *Chto dolzhen znat' kino-rezhisser, inzhener fil'my* (Moscow-Leningrad, 1929), especially p. 25. Timoshenko here refined his views expressed elsewhere on the place of the director in the filmmaking process. By calling the director the "engineer" of the film, Timoshenko hoped to connect the director in a positive way with the drive for industrialization.

53. See P. A. Bliakhin, "Na vtoroi den'," *Kino*, no. 15 (1929), p. 1; A. Novogrudskii, "Zametki o 'krizise,'" ibid., no. 46 (1929), p. 2.

54. TsGALI, f. 2494, op. 1, ed. khr. 211, "Stenogramma zasedaniia ARRK o kino-iazyke stsenariia (1929)," p. 13. Mikhail Shneider suggested that the script was sometimes unfairly blamed for the director's lack of ability, p. 11.

55. See Kolin, ibid., l. 18. Also TsGALI, f. 2494, op. 1, ed. khr. 206, "Protokoly organizatsionnogo sobraniia i zasedanii biuro rezhisserskoi sektii ARRK (1929)," p. 15. These comments of course came from directors, but it seems fair to resolve the controversy by saying that there were two stages of creation in film production, both important. (This was part of a broader discussion entitled, "Who Is the Author of a Cinema Picture?")

56. Ippolit Sokolov, "Prichiny poslednikh neudach," *Kino*, no. 46 (1928), pp. 4-5.

57. G. Lenobl', "Cherez porazheniia k pobedam," ibid., no. 47 (1928), p. 5.

58. Arsen, "O krizise," ibid., no. 48 (1928), pp. 2-3.

59. Vak-zal [L. Vaks?], "Kino-obshchestvennost': Est' ili net?," ibid., no. 49 (1928), p. 1.

60. See Sergei Tret'iakov, "Chem zhivo kino," *Novyi Lef*, no. 5 (1928), pp. 23-28.

61. See for example, "Liudei i deneg kul'turnoi lente," *Sovetskii ekran*, no. 40 (1928), p. 1 or "Neosushchestvliaemaia proportsiia," ibid., no. 41 (1928), p. 3.

62. Nikolai Lukhmanov, "Zhizn' kak ona dolzhna byt'," ibid., no. 15 (1928), p. 6.

63. K. Iukov, "Novyi etap (K voprosu o 'krizise' v kino)," *Kino*, no. 51 (1928), pp. 2-3.

64. V. Kartinov, et al., "Otkliki na statiu 'Na tsentral'noi fabrike Sovkino,'" ibid., no. 6 (1929), p. 3.

65. "Novyi kurs Sovkino," *Sovetskii ekran*, no. 1 (1929), p. 4; "Summirovat' i uchest'," *Kino*, no. 2 (1929), p. 4; TsGALI, f. 645, op. 1, ed. khr. 385, "Rezoliutsiia soveshchaniia pravleniia i khudozhestvennykh rabotnikov Sovkino," p. 151.

66. "Novyi kurs," p. 3.

67. M. P. Efremov, "O prokatnoi politike Sovkino," *Kino i kul'tura*, no. 4 (1929), pp. 3-9.

68. "Proizvodstvennaia konferentsiia Sovkino," *Kino*, no. 7 (1929), p. 6.

69. A. I. Krinitskii, *Zadachi sovetskogo kino* (n.p., 1929), especially pp. 4, 35.

70. TsGALI, f. 645, op. 1, ed. khr. 360, "Spravka o vypolnenii kino-organizatsii proizvodstvennoi programmy po khud. fil'me za vremia s 1/X-1929 po 20/1-1930," p. 7. See also Khrisanf Khersonskii, "Oshibka Sovkino," *Kino*, no. 11 (1929), p. 4 on the script shortage.

71. "Organizatsiia stsenarnoi raboty: Tezisy tov. Rafesa k soveshchaniiu v Glaviskusstve," *Kino*, no. 11 (1929), p. 1.

72. M. Rafes, "Na poroge novogo sezona," ibid., no. 39 (1929), pp. 4-5.

73. TsGALI, f. 2494, op. 2, ed. khr. 199, "Protokoly zasedanii pravleniia ARRK," p. 10 (the date of this report is tentatively 1929). Without *Cinema Front* and because of the incomplete look at the ARK/ARRK archive I was permitted, it is difficult to be certain of events at this point.

74. See Kino-rabotnik, "Ne pora li peresmotret' funktsii ARRKa," *Sovetskii ekran*, no. 8 (1929).

75. See "Proletarskie pisateli na kinofronte," *Kino*, no. 40 (1929), p. 2.

76. "Kino: Rezoliutsiia priniataia po dokladu t. Kirshona...," *Na literaturnom postu*, no. 2 (1930), pp. 62-70.

77. For an assessment of Mezhrabpom's production see P. A. Bliakhin, "Osnovnye voprosy," in Mal'tsev, *Sovetskoe kino*, pp. 90-104.

78. Lemberg, *Kinopromyshlennost'*, p. 270.

79. K. I. Shutko, "Mezhrabpom-fil'm," *Sovetskii ekran*, no. 39 (1928). This attack on "Rus'" and its Moscow Art Theater tendencies continued in K. Fel'dman, "Itogi goda Mezhrabpom-fil'm," ibid., no. 42 (1928), p. 6.

80. "Tam gde delaiut krizis kinematografii," *Kino*, no. 50 (1928), pp. 2-3.

81. See, for example, "K smotru kino-sezona," *Sovetskii ekran*, no. 20 (1929), p. 5; Prim, "General'naia liniia Mezhrabpomfil'ma," ibid., p. 6.

82. B. Mal'kin, "Neobkhodimyi otvet: O rabote Mezhrabpomfil'ma," *Kino*, no. 16 (1929), p. 5.

83. See Taylor, *Film Propaganda*, for his essay, pp. 92-102.

84. For a good contemporary analysis see Boris Gusman, "Po teatram i kino," *Revoliutsiia i kul'tura*, no. 5 (1928), pp. 87-90. Gusman noted that the drawbridge scene is the only memorable one in the movie because it uses pictorial language. Gusman thought *October* a logical step for Eisenstein but an artistic dead end.

85. For an analysis along these lines see Osip Brik's very good essay "*Oktiabr'* Eizenshteina," in the collective review article "Ring Lefa," *Novyi Lef*, no. 4 (1928), pp. 29-33.

86. See N. K. Krupskaia's remarks in the survey "*Oktiabr'*," *Kino*, no. 12 (1928), p. 4.

87. "*Oktiabr'*," ibid., no. 11 (1928), p. 4.

88. "*Oktiabr'*," ibid., no. 12 (1928), p. 1.

89. Z-v, "Provintsial'naia pressa ob *Oktiabre*," ibid., no. 15 (1928), p. 3.

90. See Brik, Pertsov, and Shklovskii in "Ring Lefa," pp. 27-36. The "left front" of the arts was disintegrating, and Eisenstein broke with Lef in March 1928. For an account, see Yon Barna's excellent *Eisenstein: The Growth of a Cinematic Genius* (Boston and Toronto, 1973), pp. 126-27.

91. M. Bystritskii, "Shag vpered (*Don Diego i Pelageia*)," *Kino*, no. 3 (1928), p. 3. See also the favorable comments of B. Gusman, "Po teatram i kino," *Revoliutsiia i kul'tura*, no. 3/4 (1928), p. 114. For a more negative view, charging that peasants preferred drama (specifically criticizing this film), see L. B., "O sovetskoi komedii," *Kino*, no. 19 (1928), p. 6.

92. See "Rezoliutsiia po kartine *Don Diego i Pelegeia*," *Kino-front*, no. 2 (1928), p. 16 and A. Aravskii, "*Don Diego i Pelageia*," ibid., pp. 20-21.

93. See Boris Gusman, "Po teatram i kino," *Revoliutsiia i kul'tura*, no. 3/4 (1928), p. 114; P. A. Bliakhin, "*Dva druga, model', podruga*," *Kino*, no. 51 (1927), p. 3.

94. "*Dom na Trubnoi*," *Kino*, no. 38 (1928), p. 6.

95. See K. Fel'dman, "Na putiakh k sovetskoi komedii," *Kino*, no. 40 (1928), p. 3.

96. *Diplomatic Pouch* did not appear in Moscow until nine months after its Kiev premiere. See *Sovetskie khudozhestvennye fil'my*, 1:519.

97. See V. Isn., "*Sumka dipkur'era*," *Kino*, no. 5 (1928), p. 3.

98. Grigorii Aleksandrov, *Epokha i kino* (Moscow, 1976), p. 240. For Eisenstein's slightly different version, see his "Birth of an Artist" in *Notes of a Film Director* (New York, 1970), pp. 140-45.

99. Viktor Pertsov, "*Zvenigora*," *Novyi Lef*, no. 1 (1928), pp. 46-47.

100. TsGALI, f. 2494, op. 1, ed. khr. 190, "Stenogramma diskussii po obsuzhdeniiu kinofil'ma *Elisso* [sic]," pp. 2-18. ODSK also reviewed it favorably. See "V Obshchestve druzei sov. kinem. *Eliso*," *Kino*, no. 39 (1928).

101. Vitalii Zhemchuzhnyi, *"Khaz-push,"* *Kino*, no. 5 (1928), p. 3; Izmail Urazov, "Chto na ekrane," *Sovetskii ekran*, no. 5 (1928), p. 3.

102. TsGALI, f. 2494, op. 1, ed. khr. 171, "Protokol diskussii po obsuzhdeniiu kinofil'ma *Parizhskii sapozhnik* 24 ian. 28," pp. 112-13.

103. "ODSK o *Parizhskom sapozhnike,"* *Kino*, no. 7 (1928), p. 3.

104. Mikhail Shneider, *"Parizhskii sapozhnik,"* *Kino-front*, no. 2 (1928), pp. 22-25. See also K. Fel'dman, "Chto na ekrane," *Sovetskii ekran*, no. 6 (1928), p. 13 and Gusman, "Po teatram i kino," *Revoliutsiia i kul'tura*, no. 3/4 (1928), pp. 11-14. Gusman disagreed that the film's ending was inconclusive.

105. K. Fel'dman, *"Dom v sugrobakh,"* *Kino*, no. 14 (1928), p. 3.

106. TsGALI, f. 2494, op. 1, ed. khr. 149, "Stenogramma diskussii po obsuzhdeniiu kinofil'ma *Dom v sugrobakh* 6 apr. 1928," pp. 2-17.

107. See K. G., "O *Kruzhevakh,"* *Kino*, no. 17 (1928), p. 3.

108. Khrisanf Khersonskii, *"Kruzheva,"* *Sovetskii ekran*, no. 16 (1928), p. 10. (This was a pre-release review.) Sovkino was also opposed to the film; see L. Vaks, "Na prosmotre *Kruzhev,"* *Kino*, no. 21 (1928), p. 5.

109. Lev Shatov, *"Salamandra,"* *Kino*, no. 51 (1928).

110. L. M., *"Odinnadtsatyi,"* ibid., no. 7 (1928), p. 3. In the same issue the film was criticized by workers for not showing collective labor. See "Rabochie ob *Odinnadtsatom,"* p. 3.

111. See Brik in "Ring Lefa," pp. 27-28.

112. V. Svilova, "Gde *Odinnadtsatyi?,"* *Kino*, no. 16 (1928), p. 3. To be fair, a favorable review came from K. I. Shutko, *"Odinnadtsatyi,"* *Kino-front*, no. 2 (1928), pp. 17-19. (Shutko was an advocate of educational films [*kul'turfil'my*]).

Chapter 8

1. "Vazhneishii vopros," *Sovetskii ekran*, no. 14 (1929), p. 3. There was, however, still resistance to the crisis theory on the grounds that it was harmful to Soviet cinema. See Stekliannyi glaz, "Obzor pechati," ibid., no. 33 (1929), p. 10.

2. "Nachalos' obsledovanie kinoorganizatsii," ibid., no. 23 (1929), p. 2.

3. L. Vaks, "Chistka v Sovkino," ibid., no. 31 (1929), p. 3.

4. "Chistka v Belgoskino," *Kino*, no. 43 (1929), p. 2; A. Shvidler, "Itogi i chistki," ibid., no. 51 (1929).

5. Vaks, "Chistka."

6. "Mezhrabpomfil'm—organizatsiia nuzhdaiushchaiasia v korennoi perestroike," *Kino*, no. 5 (1930), p. 2.

7. "Pered chistki," ibid., no. 27 (1930), p. 1.

8. TsGALI, f. 2497, op. 1, ed. khr. 10, "Informatsionnyi biulleten informbiuro Soiuzkino (1930)," p. 2.

9. "Shag vpered," *Kino*, no. 37 (1930), p. 1.

10. TsGALI, f. 2497, op. 1, ed. khr. 10, "Informatsionnyi biulletin," pp. 3-4.

11. TsGALI, f. 2498, op. 1, ed. khr. 32, "Biulletin informbiuro Soiuzkino," p. 2.

12. Chernov, "Ugroza kinoproizvodstva," *Kino*, no. 56 (1930).

13. Igor' Vsevolozhskii, "Kak Soiuzkino obsluzhivaet Krasnuiu armiiu," *Kino i zhizn'*, no. 29/30 (1930), p. 15.

14. "Nachalos' chistka Soiuzkino," *Kino*, no. 64 (1930), p. 1. Vostokkino was also included in the November purge.

15. "Tov. B. Z. Shumiatskii—pred. prav. Soiuzkino," ibid., no. 65 (1930), p. 1.

16. "Vnimanie chistke kinoorganizatsii," ibid.

17. "Tvorcheskie kadry na chistku," ibid., no. 67 (1930), p. 1.

18. "Reshitel'naia bor'ba s opportunizmom v kino," *Kino i zhizn'*, no. 34/35 (1930), p. 5.

19. A. Mil'kin, "Chistka v ARRKe," *Kino*, no. 9 (1930), p. 9.

20. "Chistka LenARRKa," ibid., no. 24 (1930), p. 1. For a similar opinion of LenARRK see Stekliannyi glaz, "Obzor pechati," *Kino i zhizn'*, no. 7 (1930). LenARRK had just changed the name of their newspaper *Cinema* to *Cinema Front*, the last name of the defunct ARK journal, surely a symbolic gesture.

21. See Stekliannyi glaz, "Obzor pechati," *Kino i zhizn'*, no. 23, (1930), p. 14.

22. "Udarnye templany," ibid.

23. N. Bodrov, "Litso opportunistov," *Kino*, no. 54 (1930), p. 3. If there were a byline by this time, it was frequently a new name. This individual was an inquisitor in the December ARRK purge.

24. Vladimir Kirshon, K. Iukov, and Vsevolod Pudovkin, "Protiv demagogii i travili," ibid., no. 62 (1930).

25. "K rabochim-udarnikam v kino," ibid., no. 65/66 (1930), p. 3.

26. "Na novom etape," *Kino i zhizn'*, no. 31 (1930), pp. 3-4.

27. "Na chistke ARK [sic]," *Kino*, no. 68 (1930).

28. V. Strel'tsov, and L. Al'tsev, "Pomozhem ARRK perestroit'sia," ibid., no. 6 (1931), p. 2.

29. TsGALI, f. 2494, op. 1, ed. khr. 362, "Stenogramma obshchego sobraniia chlenov ARRK po obsuzhdeniiu doklada K. L. Gavriushina 'O strukture ARRK,'" pp. 1-11.

30. "ARRK nado reorganizovat'," *Kino*, no. 58 (1931).

31. K. Iukov, "Sil'nee ogon' po burzhuaznym teoriiam v kino i liberal'nomu k nim otnosheniiu," ibid., no. 1 (1932). See also note 81.

32. Brigada gazety *Kino*, "Politicheskii schet dolzhen byt' ARRKom oplachen," ibid., no. 9 (1932).

33. For a different report in *Kino* on RAPP's dissolution see "Itogi perestroiki," no. 57 (1932), pp. 1-2.

34. I. Bachelis, M. Dolonolov, and Z. Ostrovskii, untitled article, ibid., no. 45 (1933), p. 2.

35. See for example R. Katsman, "Nevypolnennye zadachi," ibid., no. 20 (1934), p. 2; A. Z-ov, "'Tvorcheskaia' beskhoziaistvennost'," ibid.; P. R., "Pochemu plokho rabotaet ARRK?," ibid., no. 30 (1934), p. 1.

36. See "ARRK," *Kino-slovar'*, 1:114.

37. TsGALI, f. 2494, op. 1, ed. khr. 206, "Protokoly organizatsionnogo sobraniia i zasedanii biuro rezhisserskoi sektsii ARRKa (1929)," pp. 5-7.

38. TsGALI, f. 2494, op. 1, ed. khr. 216, "Stenogramma disputa 'Mesto pisateli v kino' (1929)," pp. 28-39.

39. Grigorii Boltianskii, "Kino-kadry i ODSK," *Kino i zhizn'*, no. 8 (1930).

40. Fedor Ivanov, "Reorganizovat' ODSK," *Kino*, no. 18 (1930), p. 1.

41. "ODSK k XVI Parts"ezdu," ibid., no. 35 (1930), p. 1.

42. See *Kino*, no. 50 (1930).

43. TsGALI, f. 2494, op. 1, ed. khr. 356, "Stenogramma sobraniia s chlenov ARRK o sviazi s obshchestvennym organizatsiami (1930)," p. 4.

44. Most of *The Poetics of Cinema* has been translated in Herbert Eagle, *Russian Formalist Film Theory*, Michigan Slavic Publications, no. 19 ([Ann Arbor,] 1981), pp. 55-166.

45. Boris Eikhenbaum, "Problemy kino-stylistiki," in Eikhenbaum, ed., *Poetika kino* (Moscow-Leningrad, 1927; rpt., Berkeley, Calif., 1984), p. 33.

46. B. Kazanskii, "Priroda kino," in ibid., pp. 122-23.

47. Ippolit Sokolov, "Za interesnyi siuzhet," *Sovetskii ekran*, no. 22 (1929), p. 8.

48. See Sergei Tret'iakov, "Stsenarnyi krizis," *Kino i kul'tura*, no. 3 (1929), p. 10. Tretiakov was in a great deal of trouble by this time, and his theory of "ideological formalism" did not get very far.

49. Ippolit Sokolov, "Rabotat' na massovogo kino-zritelia," *Kino i zhizn'*, no. 2 (1929).

50. As examples of Piotrovskii's articles in *Zhizn' iskusstva* (1928) see: "Kino-romantiki i geroiki," no. 31, p. 2 and "Est' li krizis v sovetskoi kinematografii," no. 48, pp. 6-7. In 1929 see "Platforma Petrova-Bytova i sovetskaia kinematografiia," no. 19 and "Dialekticheskaia forma v kino i front kino-reaktsii," no. 41, p. 3.

51. Adrian Piotrovskii, *Kinofikatsiia iskusstv* (Leningrad, 1929), p. 11.

52. I. F. Popov, "Sensatsiia Adriana Piotrovskogo," *Kino i zhizn'*, no. 1 (1929). The "sensation" was caused by Piotrovskii's article "Dialekticheskaia forma," note 50.

53. See the introduction by I. F. Popov to Adrian Piotrovskii, *Khudozhestvennye techeniia v sovetskom kino* (Leningrad-Moscow, 1930), pp. 5-6.

54. On the right deviation, ibid., pp. 11-19.

55. Ibid., pp. 20-23.

56. Ibid., pp. 24-30.

57. Ibid., pp. 32-41.

58. Ibid., pp. 42-47. Actually, Piotrovskii is confusing artistic leftists (the experimenters) with political leftists (those who wanted to make pictures for the masses).

59. Boris Bek, "Pis'ma iz Leningrada," *Kino i zhizn'*, no. 8 (1930), p. 15. See also Ia. Rudoi, "Na ideologicheskom fronte," *Kino*, no. 11 (1930), p. 2 for an attack on Piotrovskii-Bleiman; and on Piotrovskii's and Bleiman's alleged disregard for proletarian cadres in script work, see Boris Bek, "Pod flagom revoliutsionnosti," *Kino*, no. 16 (1930), p. 2.

60. Ia. Rudoi, "Zamaskirovannaia zashchita kinoformalizma," *Kino i zhizn'*, no. 15 (1930), pp. 7-9 and I. F. Popov, "V kino eto delaetsia ochen' prosto," ibid., no. 36 (1930), p. 8. I was denied access to the pertinent works of the unfortunate Mikhailov: "Kino i zhivopis'" in *Iskusstvo v SSSR i zadachi khudozhnikov* (n.p., 1928); "Voinstvuiushchaia organichennost'," *Na literaturnom postu*, no. 3 (1930); and "Sovetskaia kinematografiia i zhurnal Kino i zhizn'," *Kniga i revoliutsiia*, no. 26 (1930).

61. See Predatel' [Traitor], "Gospodin Sol'skii 'bolen,'" *Kino*, no. 49 (1929), p. 6.

62. See Popov, "V kino," p. 9.

63. See "Formalisty iz LenARRKa boriutsia s . . . 'formalizmom,'" *Kino i zhizn'*, no. 13 (1930), pp. 8-9.

64. "Sovetskaia kinematografiia v periode rekonstruktsii," *Kino*, no. 2 (1930), p. 5. Dziga Vertov was also labelled a formalist herein.

65. Ippolit Sokolov, "Korni formalizma," *Kino*, no. 17 (1930), p. 3.

66. "Za marksistskuiu kino-kritiku," ibid., no. 14 (1930), pp. 6-7.

67. "Izzhit' stsenarnyi krizis," *Kino i zhizn'*, no. 17 (1930), pp. 3-4.

68. Ia. Rudoi, "Zametki o tvorcheskikh putiakh sovetskoi kinematografii," ibid., no. 24 (1930), pp. 7-11. This was continued in no. 25, pp. 4-5; no. 26, pp. 6-7; and no. 27, pp. 6-7. Rudoi's series was the most comprehensive attack on directors; his views were typical and repeated in many articles by other authors. (Rudoi published another article under the same title in no. 28 but this was a description of "proletarian style.") For criticism of Shub, see Kudriatsev, "Dokumentalizm— soiuznik formalizma," *Kino*, no. 44 (1930), p. 2. This was on Shub's film *Today* (*Segodnia*) which I did not see; the charge was that it could easily be used for propaganda by the Soviet Union's enemies. Shub had a champion, however, in I. Dollinskii, "Soiuznik formalizma li dokumentalizm?," *Kino*, no. 47 (1930), p. 3.

69. See Viktor Geiman, "Protiv prikazchikov burzhuaznogo iskusstva—za izuchenie tvorcheskikh metodov sovetskogo kino," *Kino*, no. 48 (1930), p. 3. Geiman was particularly amused at the pretensions of that "specialist" on Lillian Gish, Ippolit Sokolov.

70. Mei, "Ideologichesko-chuzhdym elementam net mesta v sovetskoi kinematografii," ibid., no. 5 (1931), p. 1.

71. This important work of Kuleshov's has been translated in Levaco's *Kuleshov on Film*, pp. 41-123. All my references refer to this translation. See especially pp. 78-79. Another book on montage which was viewed as intermittently formalist in nature was S. D. Vasil'ev, *Montazh kino-kartiny* (Leningrad, 1929). It was devoted in the main to technical matters, but Vasilev (the director of *Chapaev*) went so far as to say that "the role in cinema is created by montage," p. 51.

72. Kuleshov, *Art of the Cinema*, in Levaco, *Kuleshov*, p. 67.

73. Ibid., pp. 99-115. The Kuleshovian theory of the actor was still very popular as evidenced by these books on physical training for actors: N. Oznobishin, *Fizkul'tura kino-aktera* (Moscow, 1929), which had lots of diagrams for exercises and a translation of Guido Sieber's *Tekhnika kino-triuka* (Moscow, 1929), for which Eisenstein wrote the introduction.

74. Kuleshov, *Art of the Cinema*, in Levaco, *Kuleshov*, p. 91.

75. Ibid., p. 97.

76. Ibid., see pp. 116-21.

77. See V. Sutyrin, *Problemy sotsialisticheskoi rekonstruktsii sovetskoi kinopromyshlennosti* (n.p., 1932), p. 14. Sutyrin was also sharply critical of montage, p. 60. By 1934, Kuleshov had become the founder of the formalist "school" in cinema. See N. Iezuitov, *Puti khudozhestvennogo fil'ma, 1919-1934* (n.p., 1934), p. 48.

78. K. Iukov, "Sil'nee ogon'." Iukov still headed ARRK but the precariousness of his position is indicated by the editor's note that Iukov had overstated ARRK's activities in fighting formalism. For Abram Room's attack on Kuleshov (and Pudovkin) see "Akter—polpred ideii," *Kino*, no. 7 (1932).

79. Nikolai Lebedev, "Pol'naia kapitulatsiia," *Kino*, no. 10 (1932), p. 3.

80. See Room, "Akter—polpred ideii," ibid., nos. 7, 11, 15, 17 (1932).

81. M. S., "O rekonstruktsii sovetskoi kinematografii i zadachakh ARRK," ibid., no. 19 (1932), p. 3.

82. See E. Orlikova, T. Rokotov, untitled article, ibid., no. 17 (1932), p. 3. This was another attack on Andreevskii.

83. M. S., "O rekonstruktsii."

84. Osip Brik, "Put' Kuleshova," *Kino*, no. 22 (1932).

85. Lev Kuleshov, "Zabytye liudi," ibid., no. 30 (1932). This theme was repeated in E. Kuznetsova, "Govorit akter," *Kino*, no. 59 (1932), p. 2.

86. For the attack on Eisenstein see S. Bartenev, M. Kolotozov, "Obraz i dramaturgiia v tvorchestve S. M. Eizenshteina," ibid., no. 29 (1933), p. 3. For Eisenstein's response see "Vyglazka klassovykh druzei," ibid., no. 30 (1933), pp. 2-3, and no. 31, pp. 2-3. Jay Leyda says that Eisenstein's article Perspectives ("Perspektivy") published in *Art* (*Iskusstvo*) in 1929 immediately aroused a storm of protest over its formalism. While I was not able to verify this, it is quite probable. For a translation see Eisenstein, *Film Essays and a Lecture* (New York, 1970), pp. 35-47.

87. In *Kino* (1934) see E. Kuznetsova, "Korni bezotvetstvennosti," no. 15; B. Dorin, "Pokonchit' s Roomovshchinoi," ibid.; R. Katsman, "Platsdarm samokritiki," no. 6; "Rabotat' po bolshevistku," no. 17.

88. Sutyrin, *Problemy sotsialisticheskoi rekonstruktsii*, pp. 58-59.

89. Kuleshov was briefly rehabilitated in 1933 due to his film *The Great Consoler*. See Osip Brik, "Svoe litso," *Kino*, no. 53 (1933), p. 2 and chapter 9, note 39.

90. L. V-a, "Pechal'nye itogi," *Kino i zhizn'*, no. 18 (1930); also Lemberg, *Kinopromyshlennost'*, pp. 77ff, 90.

91. These four films were thus branded in "K itogam kinosezona," *Kino i zhizn'*, no. 15 (1930), pp. 3-5. Admired were *Turksib*, *The Heir of Genghis Khan*, *Earth*, *The Ghost That Does Not Return*.

92. Khrisanf Khersonskii, "Chernovnye vpechatleniia," *Kino*, no. 12 (1929), p. 5.

93. B. Alpers, "*Staroe i novoe*," *Sovetskii ekran*, no. 40 (1929).

94. Actress Olga Tretiakova was also displeased with the use of Lapkina. See TsGALI, f. 2494, op. 1, ed. khr. 214, "Stenogramma vechera ARRK 'O kinoaktere' (1929)," p. 6.

95. Iurii Tynianov, the film's scenarist, explained that *New Babylon* was not intended as a historical work. See his "O Feksakh," *Sovetskii ekran*, no. 14 (1929), p. 10.

96. TsGALI, f. 2494, op. 1, ed. khr., 272, "Stenogramma diskussii po obsuzhdeniiu kinofil'ma *Novyi Vavilon*," pp. 4-28. See also Lev Shatov, *"Novyi Vavilon," Kino*, no. 14 (1929), p. 4.

97. See E. A-n, *"Novyi Vavilon* v LenARKe," ibid., no. 13 (1929), p. 3.

98. Khrisanf Khersonskii, *"Chelovek s kinoapparatom,"* ibid., no. 7 (1929), p. 4. For a somewhat more favorable review by Khersonskii see *"Chelovek s kinoapparatom," Sovetskii ekran*, no. 18 (1929). For a very favorable assessment see E. Vilenskii, "Geroi fil'my—apparat," *Kino*, no. 2 (1929), p. 3.

99. G. Lenobl', *"Chelovek s kinoapparatom," Kino*, no. 17 (1929), p. 3. (The cultural revolution is considered to have been launched by the announcement in March 1928 that a group of Donbass mining engineers would be tried for treason and sabotage.)

100. "V chem zhe delo: Snova o *Cheloveke s kinoapparatom*," ibid., no. 17 (1929), p. 3.

101. N. Kaufman, "Kinoki," *Sovetskii ekran*, no. 4 (1929), pp. 8-9.

102. See Kaufman's *"Chelovek s kinoapparatom*," ibid., no. 5 (1929). In the same issue see K. Fel'dman, "Kino i Aristotl'," also on Vertov's work; and in ibid., no. 7 see N., "Nadpis' i razvitie u kinokov."

103. *"Oblomok imperii* v ARRKe," *Kino*, no. 35 (1929), p. 5.

104. Ippolit Sokolov, *"Oblomok imperii*," ibid., no. 38 (1929), p. 2.

105. B. Alpers, *"Oblomok imperii*," *Sovetskii ekran*, no. 38 (1929).

106. In *Zhizn' iskusstva* (1929) see Vladimir Nedobrovo, *"Oblomok imperii*," no. 36, p. 7; Piotrovskii, "Dialekticheskaia forma" and "Za materialistichskuiu dialektiku v kino protiv nastupaiushchei kino-reaktsii," no. 47, pp. 2-3. For a fascinating though heavily edited transcript of Sovkino's discussion of the film (preserved in the Leningrad State Archive of Literature and Art [LGALI]) see Fridrikh Ermler, *Dokumenty, stat'i, vospominaniia* (Leningrad, 1974), pp. 114-20.

107. Mikhail Room, "Oblomok formalizma," *Kino*, no. 41 (1929), p. 3. For Sokolov's response see "Bor'ba sotsiologii s fiziologiei," ibid., no. 42 (1929). This "struggle" could be discerned in *The Old and the New* and *Arsenal* as well. See also Sokolov, "Korni formalizma," for his later views.

108. See "K itogam kinosezona."

109. See Il'in's comments in TsGALI, f. 2494, op. 1, ed. khr. 265, "Stenogramma diskussii po obsuzhdeniiu kinofil'ma *Zolotoi kliuv* (1929)," p. 14.

110. See for example G. Lenobl', "Poezd sovremennosti," *Kino*, no. 8 (1929), p. 3. Lenobl', one of the new critics who came to *Cinema* on the eve of the purges, was not usually noted for his critical acuity.

111. Sergei Tret'iakov, "Uroki iarosti," *Kino i kul'tura*, no. 3 (1929), p. 54.

112. See B. Alpers, *"Arsenal* Dovzhenko," *Sovetskii ekran*, no. 16 (1929), p. 5. For a concurring opinion on *Arsenal* see Ia. Rudoi, "Nasha kinematografiia i massovoi zritel'," ibid., no. 37 (1929). Rudoi saw it as a decidedly experimental film.

113. See Viktor Geiman, "Pochemu zriteliu nravitsia odno, a kritiku—drugoe," *Kino*, no. 19 (1929), pp. 2-3; M. Rafes's remarks in TsGALI, f. 2494, op. 1, ed. khr. 213, "Stenogramma zasedaniia rezhisserskoi sektsii ARRK o stsenarnom krizise (1929)," pp. 5-9. Rafes evidently wanted to take a pot-shot at VUFKU, for he mentioned Vertov in this regard.

114. Benia, "*Zemlia*," *Kino*, no. 19 (1930), p. 3.

115. See "Vokrug *Zemli*," ibid., no. 18 (1930), p. 5; D., "*Zemlia* v ARRKe," ibid., no. 19 (1930), p. 3.

116. Ippolit Sokolov, "*Zemlia*," ibid., no. 21 (1930), pp. 4-5.

117. See "*Zemlia* Dovzhenko," *Kino i zhizn'*, no. 12 (1930), pp. 5-6 for various comments.

118. I. S., "*Prividenie kotoroe ne vozvrashchaetsia*," *Sovetskii ekran*, no. 22 (1929), p. 5.

119. Lev Shatov, "*Prividenie kotoroe ne vozvrashchaetsia*," *Kino i zhizn'*, no. 10 (1930), p. 6.

120. See Mikhail Bronskii, "Klassovoi vrag v okopakh kinopechati," *Kino*, no. 34 (1930), perhaps the most vicious article to appear in this troubled period.

121. See "K itogam kinosezona," p. 5.

122. "Obsuzhdaem fil'mu N. Shengelaia *26 komissarov*," *Kino*, no. 2 (1933), p. 2. Also see Mikhail Room, "Khorosho no ne tak, kak nuzhno," ibid., no. 3 (1933), p. 2, and Viktor Shklovskii, "Emkost' kinoproizvedeniia *26 komissarov*," ibid., p. 3.

123. See Brigada rabkora, "*Goroda i gody*," ibid., no. 2 (1931), p. 3. This is an example of the collective review which came into vogue.

124. B. Alpers, "*Goroda i gody*," *Kino i zhizn'*, no. 34/35 (1930), pp. 7-8.

125. See Ippolit Sokolov, "Fil'ma poniatnaia millionam," *Kino*, no. 41 (1929), p. 3. See also "*Turksib* i ego avtor Turin," *Kino i zhizn'*, no. 9 (1930), pp. 7-8 for an explanation of how use of contemporary themes can turn a bad director into a good one!

126. A. Urenin, "Khlopok, khleb, les: O *Turksibe*," *Kino*, no. 40 (1929), p. 63; Valentin Turkin, "Uroki *Turksiba*," *Sovetskii ekran*, no. 23 (1929), p. 4.

127. See V. Kh., "Sozdadim podlinnuiu proletarskuiu kinematografiiu," *Kino*, no. 12/13 (1931).

128. Khrisanf Khersonskii, "*Kain i Artem*," *Kino*, no. 49 (1929), p. 4.

129. TsGALI, f. 2494, op. 1, ed. khr. 279, "Stenogramma diskussii po obsuzhdeniiu kinofil'ma *Saba* (1929)," pp. 3-13.

130. Khrisanf Khersonskii, "*Saba*," *Kino*, no. 38 (1929). See also his "*Saba*—igrovaia kul'turfil'ma," *Sovetskii ekran*, no. 27 (1929), p. 7.

131. A. V., "*Prazdnik sv. Iorgena*," *Kino*, no. 51 (1930), p. 4.

132. Khrisanf Khersonskii, "*Chiny i liudi*," ibid., no. 40 (1929), p. 5.

133. B. Alpers, "*Prazdnik sviatogo Iorgena*," *Kino i zhizn'*, no. 25 (1930), pp. 7-8.

134. See V. Voloshchenko, "Kogda zhe mozhno postavit' *Pyshku*?," *Kino*, no. 30 (1933), p. 2 and continued in no. 32.

135. Mikhail Shneider, "Pol'no-krovnyi pamflet," ibid., no. 37 (1934).

136. "*Pyshka*," ibid., no. 45 (1934), p. 1. This was the lead article for the week.

137. Lev Shatov, "Eshche o *Pyshke*," ibid., no. 41 (1934).

138. See entries for 1935 in *Sovetskie khudozhestvennye fil'my*, vol. 1, and also N. Trofimov, *Ratsionalizatsiia montazha kinofil'm* (Moscow, 1933).

Chapter 9

1. Lemberg, *Kinopromyshlennost'*, p. 192. Lemberg offers a very detailed look at the economic problems of the period.

2. *The Jazz Singer* (1927) is officially the first sound movie, although experimental films preceded it.

3. Evgenii Chvialev, *Sovetskie fil'my za granitsei* (Leningrad, 1929), p. 78. Chvialev also pointed out that many filmworkers were opposed to an active export policy, p. 81.

4. TsGALI, f. 2494, op. 1, ed. khr. 303, "Stenogramma doklada Nikulina 'V zvukovom kino za granitsei,' 17/II-1930," pp. 29-30.

5. Viktor Pertsov, "Chto izmenil zvuk," *Kino*, no. 34 (1932), p. 1.

6. A. Gol'dman, "Kadry v kinopiatiletke," *Kino i zhizn'*, no. 22 (1930), pp. 3-4.

7. See, for example, TsGALI, f. 2494, op. 1., ed. khr. 218, 219, 234, 235, 246, 248, and 256 for various technical discussions on sound. The two Soviets most involved in work on sound were P. G. Tager and A. F. Shorin. For an account of their work see Leyda, *Kino*, pp. 278-79.

8. Iu. Liss, "Organizatsiia templana 1933 goda," *Kino*, no. 38 (1932), p. 2.

9. E. Kuznetsova, "Vokrug templana," ibid., no. 5 (1933), p. 1.

10. Many realized this point. See, for example, Viktor Shklovskii, "Laboratoriia stsenariia," *Kino i zhizn'*, no. 17 (1930), pp. 6-7.

11. S. M. Eisenstein, V. I. Pudovkin, G. V. Aleksandrov, "A Statement," in Eisenstein, *Film Form*, edited and translated by Jay Leyda (New York, 1949), pp. 257-59. Leyda believes that Eisenstein was the actual author of this piece.

12. V. Sol'skii, "Zvuchashchee kino kak novoe iskusstvo," *Na literaturnom postu*, no. 2/3 (1928), pp. 37-43. See also his "Zvukovoe kino," *Kino*, no. 31 (1928), p. 3.

13. *Kino*, no. 1 (1929) inaugurated the New Year with a spread entitled "Za zvukovoe kino—novoe oruzhie proletariata," pp. 2-3. On the propaganda value of sound cinema, see Nikolai Anoshchenko, "Zvukovoe kino na sluzhbe kul'turnoi revoliutsii," *Kino i zhizn'*, no. 7 (1930), pp. 15-16.

14. See Shneider's remarks in L. Vaks, "O zvukovom kino (Disput v ARRKe)," *Kino*, no. 1 (1929), p. 4. Also see "O zadachakh zvukovogo kino," *Sovetskii ekran*, no. 41 (1929).

15. Ippolit Sokolov, "Na putiakh k zvukovomu kino," *Sovetskii ekran*, no. 41 (1929).

16. Vaks, "O zvukovom kino."

17. B. Alpers, "Khudozhestvennye puti zvukovoi fil'my," *Kino i zhizn'*, no. 15 (1930), pp. 7-8.

18. The term Socialist Realism was first used in the cinema press in December 1932. See "Itogi perestroiki," *Kino*, no. 57 (1932), p. 2. (This article discusses the dissolution of RAPP.) There is a vast literature on the subject. See for example, Herman Ermolaev, *Genesis of Socialist Realism in Literature* (Berkeley, Calif., 1964) or Margaret M. Bullitt, "Toward a Marxist

Theory of Aesthetics: The Development of Socialist Realism in the Soviet Union," *Russian Review* 35 (January 1976): 53-74.

19. Ia. Rudoi, "Nasha kinematografiia i massovoi zritel'," *Sovetskii ekran*, no. 37 (1929). See also O. Barshak, "Vazhneishii opyt," *Kino*, no. 22 (1929), p. 1 and "Kino-tvorchestvo i massovoi zritel'," *Kino i zhizn'*, no. 18 (1930), p. 6. The last article urged greater attention to the lowest common denominator.

20. Nikolai Lukhmanov, "Zhizn', kakoi ona dolzhna byt'," *Kino i kul'tura*, no. 1 (1929), p. 30.

21. Iurii Gromov, "Za novyi byt geroev fil'my," *Sovetskii ekran*, no. 25 (1929), p. 6. Also see Mikhail Levidov, "Nashchet geroev v kino i literature," ibid., no. 48 (1928).

22. See for example, "Daite siuzhet," *Kino*, no. 17 (1934), p. 1, or "Na poroge vtoroi piatiletki," ibid., no. 60 (1932), p. 1, which call for "courageous and life-loving" films.

23. See "Bezotvetstvennoe vystuplenie," *Kino i zhizn'*, no. 22 (1930), pp. 8-9. This was in response to an article by V. Sedin in *The Book and Revolution (Kniga i revoliutsiia)*, a journal to which I was denied access.

24. For some of the later expressions of this point of view on the actor see Valentin Turkin, *Kino-akter* (Moscow, n.d. [probably 1929]), especially p. 71 and TsGALI, f. 2494, op. 1, ed. khr. 214, "Stenogramma vechera ARRK 'O kino-aktere,'" pp. 3-28.

25. "Velikoi epokhe—vysokoe iskusstvo sotsialisticheskogo realizma," *Kino*, no. 19 (1933), p. 3.

26. See B. Levman, *Rabochii zritel' i kino: Itogi pervoi rabochei kino-konferentsii* (n.p., 1930), p. 41, a fascinating look at what workers allegedly wanted in cinema.

27. See a script outline by Petrov-Bytov, director of *Kain and Artem*, in TsGALI, f. 2387, op. 1, ed. khr. 2, "*Chudo*, kratkoe libretto i literaturnoi stsenarii (1930)," pp. 1, 3. This hackneyed revolutionary tale is just as primitive as an agit-film.

28. The honor should actually belong to Dziga Vertov's *Enthusiasm (Entuziazm)*, (alternate title *Symphony of the Donbass [Simfonia Donbassa]*) which was released before *A Start in Life*. This film has recently been reconstructed. For a discussion see Lucy Fisher, "*Enthusiasm*: From Kino-Eye to Radio-Eye," *Film Quarterly* (Winter 1977-78), pp. 24-25.

29. Hans von Herwarth with S. Frederick Starr, *Against Two Evils* (New York, 1981), pp. 37-38. Herwarth was attached to the German Embassy in Moscow during the thirties.

30. See G. D., "*Putevka v zhizn'* na obshchestvennom prosmotre v Kolosse," *Kino*, no. 28 (1931), p. 4 and I. V., "*Putevka v zhizn'*," *Kino*, no. 33 (1931), p. 4.

31. TsGALI, f. 2494, op. 1, ed. khr. 362, "Stenogramma obshchego sobraniia chlenov ARRK po obsuzhdeniiu doklada K. L. Gavriushina 'O strukture ARK [sic]," p. 9. (ARRK was criticized for not discussing the film.) See also L. Macheret, "O razvlekatel'nosti, uspekhe u zritelia i nekotorykh drugikh veshchakh," *Kino*, no. 59 (1932).

32. K. Fel'dman, "*Zlatye gory*: Na pereput'ia," *Kino*, no. 62 (1931).

33. See "Khronika zvukovogo kino," ibid., no. 34 (1929), p. 1.

34. N. Iukov, "*Odna*," ibid., no. 58 (1931).

35. See for example, Viktor Shklovskii, "Dve neudachi," ibid., no. 55 (1932), p. 1. The other "failure" was *Counterplan*.

36. Macheret, "O razvlekatel'nosti."

37. This film was heavily criticized throughout its making, drastically revised, and little seen (I unfortunately did not see it, either). See for example, A. Amasovich, *"Ochen' khorosho zhivetsia* v ARRK," *Kino,* no. 4 (1931), p. 4. (This was the film's first title.) See also Leyda, *Kino,* pp. 279-80, 294-95. Peter Dart is of the opinion that *A Simple Case* was intended from the beginning as a silent, *Pudovkin's Films,* pp. 27-28.

38. See for example, Brigada Lenbiuro RosARRK, *"Dezertir," Kino,* no. 47 (1933), p. 3. For more favorable reviews see in ibid., no. 48 (1933), *"Dezertir:* Rezoliutsiia prosmotrogo plenuma LOSPS" and L. Voloshchenko, "Epokha krupnym planom."

39. N. Iakovlev, "Dve pobedy *(Velikii uteshitel')*," ibid., no. 52 (1933). This article also re-evaluated *By the Law* as a masterpiece of "psychological realism!" But for less favorable reviews see *"Velikii uteshitel':* Vystuplenie tov. Shumiatskogo na tvorcheskoi kollegii GUFK," and I. F. Popov, "Itogi ili perspektiva," ibid., no. 55 (1933), p. 2.

40. For praise of *Borderlands* see ibid., no. 11 (1933), p. 3. For criticism, see Bleiman, et al., "Bez chetkogo ideinogo zamysla (Ob *Okraine*)," ibid., no. 23 (1933), p. 2.

41. On *Chapaev,* see ibid., nos. 53 and 54 (1934) and *Za bol'shoe kinoiskusstvo* (Moscow, 1935) for numerous references. For an interesting evaluation by a historian see Marc Ferro, "The Fiction Film and Historical Analysis," in Paul Smith, ed., *The Historian and Film* (Cambridge, 1976), pp. 80-94.

42. See S. Dinamov's remarks in *Za bol'shoe kinoiskusstvo* (Moscow, 1935), pp. 8-15.

43. Ibid., pp. 56, 70.

44. Ibid., pp. 59-73.

45. Ibid., pp. 100, 113.

46. Ibid., p. 163.

47. Ibid., pp. 140-41.

48. Ibid., p. 121.

49. Ibid., see pp. 87, 99, 102-5, 128.

50. Ibid., pp. 93, 100.

51. Lebedev also dared to defend *Vertov* for his important pioneering work, ibid., p. 139.

52. See for example Iukov's remarks, ibid., p. 126.

53. Ibid., see pp. 122, 137.

54. Ibid., p. 77.

55. Leyda, *Kino,* p. 318.

56. *Za bol'shoe kinoiskusstvo,* pp. 169-96.

57. Ibid., p. 83.

Bibliography

Primary Sources

Archival

Tsentral'nyi gosudarstvennyi arkhiv literatury i iskusstvo (TsGALI).
F[ond] 645:Glavnoe upravlenie po delam khudozhestvennoi literatury i iskusstvo NKP RSFSR (Glaviskusstvo).

F. 985:	Goskino.
F. 1921:	Iakov Protazanov.
F. 1923:	Sergei Eizenshtein.
F. 2014:	Grigorii Grebner.
F. 2057:	Grigorii Boltianskii.
F. 2091:	Dziga Vertov.
F. 2354:	Iurii Zheliabuzhskii.
F. 2356:	Ol'ga Preobrazhenskaia.
F. 2384:	Valentin Turkin.
F. 2387:	P. P. Petrov-Bytov.
F. 2489:	Vostokkino.
F. 2494:	Assotsiatsiia revoliutsionnoi kinematografii (ARK); after 1928, Assotsiatsiia rabotnikov revoliutsionnoi kinematografii (ARRK).
F. 2496:	Goskino/Sovkino.
F. 2497:	Gosudarstvennoe vsesoiuznoe foto-kino ob"edinenie Soiuzkino.
F. 2498:	Moskovskaia ob"edinennaia kinofabrika Sovkino.
F. 2647:	Iurii Tarich.
F. 2680:	Dmitrii Bassalygo.

Newpapers and Journals Systematically Reviewed

ARK
Kino
Kino i kul'tura
Kino i zhizn'
Kino-fot
Kino-front
Kino-gazeta
Kino-nedelia
Kino-zhizn'

Lef
Na literaturnom postu
Novyi Lef
Novyi zritel'
Proletarskoe kino
Proletkino
Revoliutsiia i kul'tura
Sovetskii ekran
Sovetskoe kino
Zhizn' iskusstva

296   Bibliography

Books and Articles

A. "Eksportnaia fil'ma." *Kino*, no. 7 (1925), p. 4.
A. Ass. "K organizatsii Sovkino." *Kino-nedelia*, no. 10 (1925), p. 5.
Abrosimov, A. "O prodvizhenii kino v derevniu." *Sovetskoe kino*, no. 1 (1925), pp. 44-48.
Aelita: Kinolenta na temu romana A. N. Tolstogo. N.p., 1924.
"*Aelita.*" *Kino-nedelia*, no. 36 (1924), p. 3.
Aleinikov, M. "Organizatsiia kino-proizvodstva." *Sovetskoe kino*, no. 3 (1926), p. 8.
A. I. "Litso *Stachki.*" *Sovetskii ekran*, no. 7 (1925).
Aller. "Chto takoe stsenarii." *Kino*, no. 38 (1926), p. 2.
Alpers, B. "*Arsenal* Dovzhenko." *Sovetskii ekran*, no. 16 (1929), p. 5.
_____. "*Oblomok imperii.*" *Sovetskii ekran*, no. 38 (1929).
_____. "*Staroe i novoe.*" *Sovetskii ekran*, no. 40 (1929).
_____. "Khudozhestvennye puti zvukovoi fil'my." *Kino i zhizn'*, no. 15 (1930), pp. 7-8.
_____. "*Prazdnik sviatogo Iorgena.*" *Kino i zhizn'*, no. 25 (1930), pp. 7-8.
_____. "*Goroda i gody.*" *Kino i zhizn'*, no. 34/35 (1930), pp. 7-8.
Amasovich, A. "*Ochen' khorosho zhivetsia* v ARRKe." *Kino*, no. 4 (1930), p. 4.
Andreevskii, A. *Postroenie tonfil'ma.* Moscow and Leningrad, 1931.
Anoshchenko, A. "Kinokoki." *Kino-nedelia*, no. 2 (1924).
_____. *Tainy kino: Raskrytie chudes ekrana.* Moscow, 1924.
Anoshchenko, Nikolai. "K voprosu o postroenii stsenariia." *ARK*, no. 11/12 (1925), p. 13.
_____. *Kino.* Moscow, 1929.
_____. *Chudesa kinoapparata.* Leningrad, 1930.
_____. *Zvuchashchaia fil'ma v SSSR i za granitsei.* Moscow, 1930.
_____. "Zvukovoe kino na sluzhbe kul'turnoi revoliutsii." *Kino i zhizn'*, no. 7 (1930), pp. 15-16.
Aravskii, A. "*Don Diego i Pelageia.*" *Kino-front*, no. 2 (1928), pp. 20-21.
Arden, V. "Kino-khudozhnik na zapade i v SSSR," *ARK*, no. 3 (1926), p. 16.
Ardov, V. "Chudesa kino: Uplotnennyi seans." *Kino*, no. 4/5 (1925), p. 6.
ARK. "Diskussiia o *Bukhte smerti.*" *Kino*, no. 7 (1926), p. 3.
Arnoldi, E. *Komicheskoe v kino.* Moscow and Leningrad, 1928.
_____. *Avantiurnyi zhanr v kino.* Leningrad and Moscow, 1929.
"ARRK nado reorganizovat'." *Kino*, no. 58 (1931).
Arsen. "Sotsial'noe znachenie kartiny *Po zakonu.*" *Kino-front*, no. 9/10 (1926), pp. 28-31.
_____. "*Dekabristy.*" *Kino-front*, no. 5 (1927), pp. 15-17.
_____. "*Sorok pervyi.*" *Kino-front*, no. 6 (1927), pp. 15-19.
_____. "O sovetskoi teme i o stsenarnom krizise." *Sovetskii ekran*, no. 14 (1927), p. 3.
_____. "O krizise." *Kino*, no. 48 (1928), pp. 2-3.
Arustanov, G. "O nekotorykh bol'iachkakh." *Sovetskoe kino*, no. 2 (1926), p. 9.
_____. "Rentabel'nost'." *Sovetskoe kino*, no. 8/9 (1927), p. 10.
_____. "Nashi oshibki." *Sovetskoe kino*, no. 1 (1928), pp. 8-10.
Arvatov, B. "Agit-kino." *Kino-fot*, no. 2 (1922).
Aseev, N. "*Shestaia chast' mira.*" *Kino*, no. 43 (1926), p. 5.
_____. Arvatov, B.; Brik, O.; Kushner, B.; Maiakovskii, V.; Tret'iakov, S.; Chuzhak, N. "Za chto boretsia Lef." *Lef*, no. 1 (1923), pp. 3-7.
"Assotsiatsiia revoliutsionnoi kinematografii." *Kino-gazeta*, no. 16 (1923), p. 1.
A. V. "Kinematograf i kinoshkola." *Kino-fot*, no. 1 (1922), pp. 8-9.
_____. "Molodezhi! Iskusstvo umiraet." *Kino-fot*, no. 2 (1922), p. 8.
_____. "*Prazdnik sv. Iorgena.*" *Kino*, no. 51 (1930), p. 4.
Avdeev, N. N. "Kino dlia derevni." *Sovetskoe kino*, no. 6 (1925), pp. 39-42.
"Avtorskie." *Kino*, no. 11 (1926), p. 4; no. 47 (1926), p. 1.

"Avtorskoe pravo." *Kino*, no. 10 (1925).

A. Zh. "Obshchestvennyi sud nad tipazhem." *Kino*, no. 31 (1928), p. 4.

A. Z-ov. "Tvorcheskaia beskhoziaistvennost'." *Kino*, no. 20 (1934), p. 5.

Babenchikov, M. "Kino—geroi—byt." *Sovetskii ekran*, no. 39 (1922), p. 13.

"Baby riazanskie." *Sovetskoe kino*, no. 8/9 (1927), p. 31.

Bachelis, I.; Dolonolov, M.; Ostrovskii, Z. Untitled article. *Kino*, no. 45 (1933), p. 2.

Balasz, Bela. *Kul'tura kino.* Translated by Adrian Piotrovskii. Leningrad and Moscow, 1925.

Bartenev, S.; Kolotozov, M. "Obraz i dramaturgiia v tvorchestve S. M. Eizenshteina." *Kino*, no. 39 (1933), p. 3.

Barshak, O. "O perspektivakh." *ARK*, no. 9 (1925), p. 31.

_____. "Kino-obshchestvennost' v derevne i ODSK." *Kino-front*, no. 5/6 (1926), pp. 22-23.

_____. "ODSK na pod"eme." *Kino-front*, no. 9/10 (1926), p. 32.

_____. "Druz'ia kino i derevnia." *Kino*, no. 23 (1926), p. 3.

_____. "ODSK na putiakh kinofikatsii derevni." *Sovetskoe kino*, no. 1 (1927), p. 19.

_____. "Nuzhnoe nachinanie." *Kino*, no. 11 (1927), p. 4.

_____. "Vazhneishii opyt." *Kino*, no. 22 (1929), p. 1.

Bek, Boris. "Pis'ma iz Leningrada." *Kino i zhizn'*, no. 8 (1930), p. 15.

_____. "Pod flagom revoliutsionnosti." *Kino*, no. 16 (1930), p. 2.

Benia. *"Zemlia."* *Kino*, no. 19 (1930), p. 3.

Berestinskii, Mikhail. "Chto skazali o Sovkino na dispute v TsDRI." *Kino*, no. 43 (1927), p. 5.

Beskin, Osip. "Neigrovaia fil'ma." *Sovetskoe kino*, no. 7 (1927), pp. 9-11.

_____. "Nekotorye cherty iz zhizni Sovkino." *Sovetskoe kino*, no. 1 (1928), pp. 2-4.

"Bezotvetstvennoe vystuplenie." *Kino i zhizn'*, no. 22 (1930), pp. 8-9.

B. L. [Levman, B.?]. "O fil'me dlia derevni." *Sovetskii ekran*, no. 13 (1925).

Bleiman, Mikhail. *O kino: Svidetel'skie pokazaniia.* Moscow, 1973.

_____. Kalatozov; Krinkin; Kovarskii; Trauberg. "Bez chetkogo ideinogo zamysla (Ob *Okraine*)." *Kino*, no. 23 (1933), p. 2.

Bliakhin, P. "Upadochnichestvo v kino." *Na literaturnom postu*, no. 1 (1927), pp. 31-33.

_____. *"Tret'ia Meshchanskaia."* *Kino*, no. 4 (1927), p. 3.

_____. "O stsenarnom rezerve." *Kino*, no. 15 (1927), p. 2.

_____. *"Velikii put'."* *Kino*, no. 44 (1927), p. 3.

_____. "K partsoveshchaniiu." *Novyi zritel'*, no. 50 (1927), p. 14.

_____. *"Dva druga, model', i podruga."* *Kino*, no. 51 (1927), p. 3.

_____. "Na vtoroi den'." *Kino*, no. 15 (1929), p. 1.

Bliokh, Ia. M. "Rabota khudozhestvennykh sovetov na proizvodstve." *ARK*, no. 9 (1925), pp. 9-10.

_____. "Rezhim ekonomii i kino-fabrika." *Kino*, no. 25 (1926), p. 3.

_____. "O s"emochnykh gruppakh." *Kino*, no. 26 (1926), p. 3.

Bodrov, N. "Litso opportunistov." *Kino*, no. 54 (1930), p. 3.

Bogatirev, S. "Protiv passivnosti i podpol'shchiny." *Kino*, no. 41 (1928), p. 2.

Boitler, Mikhail. "Kino-teatry: Neskol'ko myslei pratiki." *ARK*, no. 11/12 (1925), pp. 24-26.

_____. *Kino-teatr: Organizatsiia i upravlenie.* Moscow, 1926.

_____. *Reklama i kino-reklama.* Moscow, 1926.

"Bol'noe mesto v kino." *Kino-front*, no. 5 (1927), p. 1.

"Bol'noi vopros." *Kino*, no. 6 (1925), p. 5.

Boltianskii, Grigorii. "Provintsial'nyi kino byt." *Kino-nedelia*, no. 34 (1924), p. 12.

_____. *"Kino-glaz i kinoki."* *Kino-nedelia*, no. 38 (1924), p. 19.

_____. "Rabota kino-ustanovok v SSSR." *Sovetskoe kino*, no. 4/5 (1925), pp. 46-49.

_____. *Kino-khronika i kak ee snimat'.* Moscow, 1926.

————. *Kul'tura kino-operatora: Opyt issledovaniia osnovannyi na rabotakh E. K. Tisse.* Moscow and Leningrad, 1927.

————. "Usloviia razvitiia kino-khroniki." *Sovetskoe kino,* no. 5/6 (1927), pp. 78-79.

————. "Kino-kadry i ODSK." *Kino i zhizn',* no. 8 (1930).

"Bor'ba s protektsionizmom." *Kino,* no. 34 (1928), p. 6.

Borisov-Vladimirov, N. *Iskusstvo kadra: Praktika kino-stsenariia.* Khar'kov, 1926.

Bravko, N. "Komfraktsiia pravleniia ARK." *Kino-nedelia,* no. 8 (1925), p. 14.

Brigada gazety *Kino.* "Politicheskii schet dolzhen byt' ARRKom oplachen." *Kino,* no. 9 (1932), p. 3.

Brigada Lenbiuro RosARRK. *"Dezertir."* *Kino,* no. 47 (1933), p. 3.

Brigada rabkora. *"Goroda i gody."* *Kino,* no. 2 (1931), p. 3.

Brik, Osip. "Kartiny, kotorye nam ne pokazyvaiut." *Sovetskoe kino,* no. 2 (1926), p. 9.

————. "Poslednyi krik." *Sovetskii ekran,* no. 7 (1926), pp. 3-4.

————. "100% brak." *Kino,* no. 25 (1926), p. 3.

————. "Kino i kinoshki." *Sovetskii ekran,* no. 27 (1926), p. 3.

————. "Protivokinoiadie." *Novyi Lef,* no. 2 (1927), pp. 29-30.

————. "Po sushchestvu stsenarnogo krizisa." *Sovetskoe kino,* no. 8 (1927), p. 11.

————. "Fiksatsiia fakta." *Novyi Lef,* no. 11/12 (1927), pp. 44-50.

————. "Pobeda fakta." *Kino,* no. 14 (1927), p. 3.

————. "Polpobedy." *Kino,* no. 15 (1927), p. 3.

————. "Protiv zhanrovykh kartinok." *Kino,* no. 27 (1927), p. 3.

————. "Put' Kuleshova." *Kino,* no. 22 (1932).

————. "Svoe litso." *Kino,* no. 53 (1933), p. 2.

Bronenosets Potemkin: Sbornik. Moscow, 1926.

Bronskii, Mikhail. "Klassovoi vrag v okopakh kinopechati." *Kino,* no. 34 (1930), p. 1.

Bugoslavskii, S.; Messman, V. *Muzyka i kino.* Moscow, 1926.

Bursak, I. N., ed. *Kino.* Moscow, 1925.

Bystritskii, M. "S tochki zreniia teorii." *Kino,* no. 2 (1927), p. 3.

————. "Besprizornaia (Po povodu *Potselui Meri*)." *Kino,* no. 38 (1927), p. 3.

————. "Shag vpered (*Don Diego i Pelageia*)." *Kino,* no. 3 (1928), p. 3.

Charli. Untitled article. *Kino-zhizn',* no. 2 (1922), p. 4.

Cherkasov, A. "Zheleznyi stsenarii." *Kino-front,* no. 9/10 (1926), pp. 3-4.

————. "Masterstvo artista v kino." *Kino-front,* no. 5 (1927), pp. 2-4.

Cherniavskii, E. "Eshche o kino-kritike." *Kino,* no. 8 (1925), p. 6.

Chernov. "Ugroza kinoproizvodstva." *Kino,* no. 56 (1930), p. 1.

"14 dnei i odin god." *Sovetskii ekran,* no. 29 (1927), p. 3.

"Chistka." *Novyi zritel',* no. 13 (1927), p. 12.

"Chistka LenARRKa." *Kino,* no. 24 (1930), p. 1.

"Chistka v Belgoskino." *Kino,* no. 43 (1929), p. 2.

"Chto delat' dal'she?" *Kino,* no. 30 (1926), p. 2.

Chvialev, Evgenii. "Rabochaia komissiia po podgotovke derevenskikh stsenariev." *Sovetskoe kino,* no. 2/3 (1925), pp. 78-79.

————. *Sovetskie fil'my za granitsei: Tri goda za rubezhom.* Leningrad, 1929.

"Comrades, Organisers of Life!" *Lef,* no. 2 (1923), pp. 7-8.

D. "*Zemlia* v ARRKe." *Kino,* no. 19 (1930), p. 3.

"Daite siuzhet." *Kino,* no. 17 (1934), p. 1.

Dalmatov, G. "Za sovetskuiu kino-plenku." *Kino,* no. 14 (1928), p. 4.

Danilov, A. "Rezhim ekonomii: V pervuiu ochered' uchet." *Sovetskoe kino,* no. 3 (1926), p. 4.

Dashkevich, S. "Kino v Krasnoi armii." *Sovetskoe kino,* no. 4/5 (1925), p. 38.

"Davno pora." *Kino,* no. 20 (1928), p. 1.

Davydov, I. "O tsentralizatsii kino-set'." *Novyi zritel'*, no. 33 (1927), p. 18.

_____. "Order na zhizn'." *Sovetskoe kino*, no. 1 (1928), p. 6.

"Deiatel'nost' teatrov Goskino." *Kino-gazeta*, no. 4 (1925), p. 3.

Deiatel'nost' Vserossiskogo foto-kinematograficheskogo aktsionernogo o-va sovetskogo kino "Sovkino" s 1-go marta 1925 po 1-oe oktiabria 1927. Moscow, 1928.

"*Dekabristy*." *Sovetskoe kino*, no. 2 (1927), p. 31.

"*Dekabristy*." *Kino*, no. 3 (1927), p. 4.

"Deklaratsiia: Obshchestvo stroitelei proletarskogo kino." *Kino-nedelia*, no. 33 (1924), p. 6.

Denisov, K. "O stsenariiakh." *Kino-front*, no. 4 (1927), pp. 11-12.

_____. "Meshchanstvo v kino." *Sovetskii ekran*, no. 5 (1927), p. 3.

Derzhavin, Konstantin. *Dzhekii Kugan i deti v kino*. Leningrad, 1926.

"*Dezertir*: Rezoliutsiia prosmotrogo plenuma LOSPS." *Kino*, no. 48 (1933).

Dik, T. "Avtorskoe pravo." *Kino*, no. 20 (1925), p. 2.

"Direktor i rezhisser." *Kino*, no. 24 (1927), p. 2.

"Diskussiia o kino-kritike." *Kino*, no. 9 (1928), p. 1.

"Disput o kino." *Kino-gazeta*, no. 4 (1923), p. 3.

"Disput o Mezhrabpom-Rusi." *Kino*, no. 4 (1928), p. 6.

"Disput v dome pechati." *Kino*, no. 36 (1929), p. 2.

Dollinskii, I. "Soiuznik formalizma li dokumentalizm?" *Kino*, no. 47 (1930), p. 3.

"Doloi!" *Sovetskii ekran*, no. 26 (1928), p. 3.

"*Dom na Trubnoi*." *Kino*, no. 38 (1928), p. 6.

Donskoi, M.; Averbakh, M. "Akter i tipazh." *Kino*, no. 26 (1928), p. 2.

Dorin, B. "Pokonchit' s Roomovshchinoi." *Kino*, no. 15 (1934), p. 2.

Dovzhenko, Aleksandr. "The Dovzhenko Papers." Translated by Marco Carynnyk. *Film Comment* 7 (Fall 1971): 35-41.

_____. *The Poet as Filmmaker: Selected Writings*. Edited and translated by Marco Carynnyk. Cambridge, Mass. and London, 1973.

Dramaturgiia: Pervyi sbornik stsenariev. Moscow, 1934.

Dubrovskii, A. "Opyty izucheniia zritelia (Anketa ARK)." *ARK*, no. 8 (1925), pp. 6-9.

_____. "Bez aktera." *ARK*, no. 9 (1925).

_____. "Atel'e i natura." *Sovetskii ekran*, no. 27 (1926), p. 5.

D-v. "Bolezni proizvodstva kino-kartin." *Sovetskoe kino*, no. 5 (1926), p. 5.

Dvoretskii, A. "*Abrek Zaur* i prochee." *Sovetskii ekran*, no. 5 (1926), pp. 4-5.

E. A-n. "*Novyi Vavilon* v LenArke." *Kino*, no. 13 (1929), p. 3.

Editorial (untitled). *Kino-fot*, no. 4 (1922), p. 1.

Efremov, M. P. "Direktor tov. Efremov o sovetskoi kinematografii." *Kino-nedelia*, no. 1 (1925), pp. 18-19.

_____. "K voprosu ob organizatsii Sovkino." *Kino-nedelia*, no. 7 (1925), pp. 3-4.

_____. "O prokatnoi deiatel'nosti Sovkino." *Sovetskoe kino*, no. 4/5 (1925) pp. 40-43.

_____. "Po povodu stat'i 'Profsoiuzy i Sovkino.'" *Kino*, no. 9 (1925), p. 5.

_____. "Kak sokhranit' i razvit' kinoproizvodstvo." *Kino-nedelia*, no. 10 (1925), p. 5.

_____. "Kino i derevnia: Otvet tov. Katsigrasu." *Sovetskoe kino*, no. 8/9 (1927), pp. 24-25.

_____. "O prokatnoi politike Sovkino." *Kino i kul'tura*, no. 4 (1929), pp. 3-9.

Eikhenbaum, Boris. "Literatura i kino." *Sovetskii ekran*, no. 42 (1926), p. 10.

_____, ed. *Poetika kino*. Moscow and Leningrad, 1927. Rpt., Berkeley, Calif., 1984.

Eisenstein, Sergei. See next entry.

Eizenshtein, Sergei. "K voprosu o materialisticheskom podkhode k forme." *ARK*, no. 4/5 (1925), pp. 6-8.

_____. "Pochemu opozdal *Oktiabr'*." *Kino*, no. 51 (1927), p. 4.

_____. "Vyglazka klassovykh druzei." *Kino*, no. 30 (1933), pp. 2-3; no. 31 (1933), pp. 2-3.

————. *The Film Sense.* Translated and edited by Jay Leyda. New York, 1942.

————. *Film Form.* Translated and edited by Jay Leyda. New York, 1949.

————. *Film Essays and a Lecture.* Edited by Jay Leyda. New York, 1970.

————. *Notes of a Film Director.* New York, 1970.

————. *Three Films.* Edited by Jay Leyda and translated by Diana Matias. New York, 1974.

Eizenshtein: Bronenosets Potemkin. Moscow, 1926.

Ekstsentrizm. Petrograd, 1921.

Erastov, F. "K organizatsii nashego kino-proizvodstva." *Sovetskoe kino,* no. 6 (1925), pp. 31-33.

Erenburg, Il'ia. *Materializatsiia fantastiki.* Moscow and Leningrad, 1927.

Ermler, Fridrikh. "Kadr i akter." *Kino,* no. 9 (1927), p. 3.

————. *Dokumenty, stat'i, vospominaniia.* Leningrad, 1974.

Erofeev, Vladimir. "Segodnia i zavtra." *Proletkino,* no. 1/2 (1923), pp. 21-22.

————. "Za ob"edinenie, za kino-sindikat." *Kino-gazeta,* no. 2 (1923), p. 1.

————. "Kino-sindikat ili akts. o-vo?" *Kino-gazeta,* no. 4 (1923), p. 1.

————. "Bol'noi vopros." *Kino-gazeta,* no. 13 (1923), p. 1.

————. *"Kino-pravda, no. 18." Kino-gazeta,* no. 10 (1924), p. 2.

————. *"Prikliucheniia mistera Vesta." Kino-gazeta,* no. 17/18 (1924), p. 2.

————. "O proizvodstve 'na zagranitsu.'" *Kino-gazeta,* no. 41 (1924), p. 2.

————. *"Kino-glaz." Kino-gazeta,* no. 42 (1924), p. 2.

————. "Dovol'no portit' kartinu." *Kino-gazeta,* no. 49 (1924), p. 2.

————. "Proizvodstvo plenki." *Sovetskoe kino,* no. 4/5 (1925), pp. 63-67.

————. "Kak my prodvigaemsia za granitsu." *Kino,* no. 3 (1926), p. 5.

————. "Protiv kabinetnogo tvorchestva." *Kino,* no. 37 (1926), p. 3.

"Eshche odna seriia sniatykh kartin." *Kino,* no. 21 (1928), p. 2.

E. Vii [Vilenskii, E.?]. "O kino-peredvizhke." *Kino,* no. 16 (1925).

F. A. "Kak delalsia stsenarii *Iada* (Iz nashego obsledovaniia)." *Kino,* no. 37 (1927), p. 3.

Fal'bert, I. "Zolotaia seriia (*Medvezh'ia svad'ba*)." *Kino,* no. 6 (1926), p. 2.

Famarin. "Kino ne teatr." *Sovetskoe kino,* no. 2 (1927), pp. 2-3.

"FEKS." *Kino-nedelia,* no. 14 (1924), p. 6.

Fel'dman, B. "Nasha baza." *Kino,* no. 22 (1925), p. 1.

Fel'dman, K. I. "Chto na ekrane." *Sovetskoe ekran,* no. 6 (1928), p. 13.

————. *"Dom v sugrobakh." Kino,* no. 14 (1928), p. 3.

————. "Itogi goda Mezhrabpom-fil'm." *Sovetskii ekran,* no. 42 (1928), p. 6.

————. "Na putiakh k sovetskoi komediiu." *Kino,* no. 40 (1928), p. 3.

————. "Kino i Aristotl'." *Sovetskii ekran,* no. 5 (1929).

————. *"Zlatye gory:* Na pereput'ia." *Kino,* no. 62 (1931).

"Ferbenks i Pikford v SSSR!" *Kino,* no. 30 (1926), pp. 1, 3.

Fillipov, Boris, "Profsoiuzy i Sovkino." *Kino,* no. 7 (1925), p. 5.

————. "Sovkino i profsoiuzy." *Kino,* no. 21 (1925).

————. *Kino v rabochem klube.* Moscow, 1926.

Fish, Gennadii. "Dovol'no slov." *Kino-nedelia,* no. 34 (1924), p. 11.

"Formalisty iz LenARRKa boriutsia s... 'formalizmom.'" *Kino i zhizn',* no. 13 (1930), pp. 8-9.

Furduev, V. V. *Kino zavtra.* Moscow and Leningrad, 1929.

Gak, A. M., ed. *Samoe vazhnoe iz vsekh iskusstv: Lenin i kino (Sbornik dokumentov i materialov).* 2nd ed. Moscow, 1973.

Gan, Aleksei. "Kinematograf i kinematografiia." *Kino-fot,* no. 1 (1922), p. 1.

————. "My boiuem." *Kino-fot,* no. 3 (1922), p. 8.

————. "Kino-pravda (10-ia)." *Kino-fot,* no. 4 (1922), pp. 3-4.

————. "'Levyi Front' i kinematografiia." *Kino-fot,* no. 5 (1922), pp. 1-3.

————. "Po dvum putiam." *Kino-fot,* no. 6 (1923), p. 1.

Ganzenko, K. "Sovetskii byt na sovetskom ekrane." *Kino-front*, no. 1 (1927), pp. 11-12.

Garri, A. *I. I. Mozhukhin*. Moscow and Leningrad, 1927.

Gavriushin, K. *Ia khochu rabotat' v kino: Posobie pri vybore professii*. Moscow, 1925.

_____. "O kino-shkole." *ARK*, no. 3 (1925), p. 30.

G. D. [Dalmatov, G.?]. "My—zagranitse, zagranitsa—nam." *Kino*, no. 23 (1925).

_____. "*Putevka v zhizn*': Na obshchestvennom prosmotre v Kolosse." Kino, no. 28 (1931), p. 4.

Geiman, Viktor. "Pochemu zriteliu nravitsia odno, a kritiku—drugoe." *Kino*, no. 19 (1929), pp. 2-3.

_____. "Protiv prikazchikov burzhuaznogo iskusstva za izuchenie tvorcheskikh metodov sovetskogo kino." *Kino*, no. 48 (1930), p. 3.

Gel'mont, A. M., ed. *Kino, deti, shkola: Metodicheskii sbornik*. Moscow, 1929.

Genri. "Veterany kino-dela." *Sovetskii ekran*, no. 12 (1925).

German, A. "*Tripol'skaia tragediia*." *Kino*, no. 15 (1926), p. 3.

Gessen, Daniil. "Dovol'no." *Kino-nedelia*, no. 14 (1924), p. 1.

G. G. "*Stepan Khalturin*." *Kino*, no. 4/5 (1925), p. 9.

G. G-zd. "Nashi interviui: Glavpolitprosvet i kino." *Kino-gazeta*, no. 3 (1925).

Gladkikh, G. "Nuzhna-li organizatsii Sel'kino?" *Kino*, no. 5 (1926), p. 4.

Gladkov, Fedor. "Pochemu net khoroshikh stsenariev." *Kino*, no. 40 (1927), p. 2.

"Glavkizm i initiativa." *Kino-gazeta*, no. 20 (1924), p. 1.

Glavpolitprosvet. *Kino v derevniu*. Moscow, 1924.

"Glavrepertkom (Beseda s zampredom Glavrepertkoma tov. Pel'she)." *Kino-gazeta*, no. 3 (1925).

Gol'denveizer, L. "Net sviazi." *Kino*, no. 40 (1927), p. 2.

Gol'dman, A. *U poroga kino-proizvodstva (Zametki o kino-aktere)*. Leningrad and Moscow, 1929.

_____. "Kadry v kinopiatiletke." *Kino i zhizn'*, no. 22 (1930), pp. 3-4.

Gol'dobin, A. V. "Voprosy kino-obrazovaniia v Agitprope TsK RKP(b)." *Kino-nedelia*, no. 36 (1924), p. 11.

_____. *Kino na territoriiu SSSR (po materialam provintsial'noi pressy)*. Moscow, 1924.

_____. *Kak pisat' stsenarii dlia kino-kartin: Prakticheskoe rukovodstvo*. Moscow, 1925.

Gol'dovskii, E. M. *Zvukovoe kino*. Leningrad, 1930.

Gosfil'mofond SSSR. *Mat'*. Moscow, 1975.

_____. *Arsenal*. Moscow, 1977.

"*Gospoda Skotininy*." *Sovetskoe kino*, no. 2 (1927), p. 30.

"*Gospoda Skotininy*: Rezoliutsiia ARKa." *Kino-front*, no. 4 (1927), pp. 21-22.

Grabar, A. "Chetvertyi mesiats." *Kino-nedelia*, no. 10 (1925), p. 6.

Grigorov, L. "Blizhe k derevne." *Kino*, no. 11 (1926), p. 2.

Grinevskii, M. "Kino-telega." *Sovetskoe kino*, no. 5/6 (1927), p. 22.

Gromov, Iurii. "Za novyi byt geroev fil'my." *Sovetskii ekran*, no. 25 (1929), p. 6.

Gusman, Boris. "Eshche o dramaturgii v kino." *ARK*, no. 4/5 (1925), pp. 15-16.

_____. "*Stepan Khalturin*." *ARK*, no. 6/7 (1925), pp. 31-32.

_____. "Po teatram i kino." *Revoliutsiia i kul'tura*, no. 3/4 (1928), pp. 112-14; no. 5 (1928), pp. 89-90.

Iakovlev, N. "O levom rebiachestve v kino." *Sovetskoe kino*, no. 1 (1925), pp. 25-27.

_____. "Protiv arkheologii." *Sovetskii ekran*, no. 46 (1926), p. 3.

_____. "Pervosortnaia meshchanskaia (Diskussionno)." *Kino*, no. 5 (1927), p. 3.

_____. "Ne tol'ko chto no i tak." *Kino*, no. 12 (1927), p. 3.

_____. "Dve pobedy (*Velikii uteshitel'*)." *Kino*, no. 52 (1933).

Ialovyi, Ar. "Rezhisser i kino-tekhnika." *Kino-gazeta*, no. 10 (1924), p. 2.

Ia. M. "*Papirosnitsa ot* [sic] *Mosselproma*." *Kino-nedelia*, no. 44 (1924), p. 8.

I. Ch. "Novosti prokata." *Kino*, no. 36 (1926), p. 3.

I. D. "Peremontazh i nadpisi." *Kino-gazeta*, no. 11 (1923), p. 1.

"Ideologiia i kassa." *Sovetskii ekran*, no. 43 (1927), p. 3.

Iezuitov, N. *Puti khudozhestvennogo fil'ma: 1919-1934*. N.p., 1934.

I. I-ov. "Nashe kino." *Kino-gazeta*, no. 43 (1924), p. 4.

Ippolit [Sokolov, Ippolit?]. "Skrizhal veka." *Kino-fot*, no. 1 (1922), p. 3.

I. S. [Sokolov, Ippolit?]. "*Bukhta smerti.*" *Kino-front*, no. 4 (1926), p. 27.

―――. "*Prividenie kotoroe ne vozvrashchaetsia.*" *Sovetskii ekran*, no. 22 (1929), p. 5.

"Itogi kino-konferentsii." *Kino*, no. 47 (1927), p. 2.

"Itogi perestroiki." *Kino*, no. 57 (1932), pp. 1-2.

Iudin, N. "Kino-kustary." *Sovetskoe kino*, no. 8 (1926), p. 12.

Iukov, K. "Puti i pereput'ia sovetskogo kino." *Kino-front*, no. 9/10 (1927), p. 8.

―――. "Desiat' let i kino." *Kino-front*, no. 11/12 (1927), pp. 2-6.

―――. "Novyi etap (K voprosu o 'krizise' v kino)." *Kino*, no. 51 (1928), pp. 2-3.

―――. "*Odna.*" *Kino*, no. 58 (1931).

―――. "Sil'nee ogon' po burzhuaznym teoriam v kino i liberal'nomu k nim otnosheniiu." *Kino*, no. 1 (1932).

Iu. Rist. "*Stachka.*" *Sovetskii ekran*, no. 2 (1925).

Iutkevich, Sergei. "Romanticheskoe koleso." *Kino*, no. 5 (1926), p. 3.

―――. "O kino-kritike." *Kino*, no. 44 (1927), p. 2.

I. V. [Vsevolozhskii, Igor?]. "*Putevka v zhizn'.*" *Kino*, no. 33 (1931), p. 4.

Ivanov, Fedor. "Reorganizovat' ODSK." *Kino*, no. 18 (1930), p. 1.

Ivashchenko, G. "O perekvalifikatsii kino-mekhanikov." *Kino*, no. 16 (1928), p. 2.

Iz istorii Lenfil'ma: Stat'i, vospominaniia, dokumenty (1920-1930-e gody). 3 vols. Leningrad, 1970-1973.

Izrailevich, L. *Kak delaiutsia kino-triuki*. Leningrad, 1927.

"Izzhit' stsenarnyi krizis." *Kino i zhizn'*, no. 17 (1930), pp. 3-4.

"Kak idet zagotovka stsenariev." *Kino-front*, no. 4 (1926), pp. 8-9.

Kandyba, F. "Obezdolennyi teatr Kharkov." *Kino*, no. 2 (1925).

Kartinov, V.; Pavlovskii, V.; Zorich, B.; Aleksandrov, G.; Pertsov, V.; Sheffer, L.; Razumnyi, A. "Otkliki na stat'iu 'Na tsentral'noi fabrike Sovkino.'" *Kino*, no. 6 (1929), p. 3.

"*Kat'ka bumazhnii ranet.*" *Sovetskoe kino*, no. 2 (1927), pp. 30-31.

Katkov, V. "Eshche o derevenskoi kartine." *Kino*, no. 8 (1925), p. 4.

Katsigras, A. "Izuchenie derevenskogo kino-zritelia." *Sovetskoe kino*, no. 2/3 (1925), pp. 50-52.

―――. "Voprosy derevenskoi kino-raboty." *Sovetskoe kino*, no. 6 (1925), pp. 35-36.

―――. *Chto takoe kino: Pochemu figury dvizhutsia na ekrane*. Moscow, 1926.

―――. *Kino-rabota v derevne*. Moscow, 1926.

―――. "Novyi pokhod Sovkino na derevniu." *Sovetskoe kino*, no. 2 (1926), pp. 18-19.

―――. "Oshibka ili...?" *Kino*, no. 16 (1926), p. 4.

―――. "Kino i derevnia, ob"ektivnye usloviia." *Sovetskoe kino*, no. 1 (1927), p. 18.

―――. "Ne pora li." *Sovetskoe kino*, no. 2 (1927), p. 23.

―――. "Politika prokata Sovkino." *Novyi zritel'*, no. 6 (1927), p. 13.

―――. "Otvet tov. Efremovu." *Sovetskoe kino*, no. 8/9 (1927), p. 25.

Katsman, R. "Platsdarm samokritiki." *Kino*, no. 6 (1934), p. 1.

―――. "Nevypolnennye zadachi." *Kino*, no. 20 (1934), p. 2.

Kaufman, E. "Nash eksport-import." *ARK*, no. 10 (1925), pp. 20-23.

Kaufman, N. "Kinoki." *Sovetskii ekran*, no. 4 (1929), pp. 8-9.

―――. "*Chelovek s kinoapparatom.*" *Sovetskii ekran*, no. 5 (1929).

K. G. "Obshchestvo druzei sovetskogo kino." *Sovetskoe kino*, no. 6 (1925), p. 59.

―――. "Zabyvaemye zakony." *Sovetskii ekran*, no. 14 (1925).

―――. "O *Kruzhevakh.*" *Kino*, no. 17 (1928), p. 3.

Khazhinskii, N. "Voprosy kinofikatsii derevni." *Sovetskoe kino*, no. 6 (1925), p. 46.

Khersonskii, Khrisanf. "O nashem kino-aktere." *Kino-gazeta*, no. 27/28 (1924), p. 1.

———. "Dramaturgiia kak metod kinoiskusstva." *ARK*, no. 1 (1925), pp. 14-17.

———. "*Kino-glaz*." ARK, no. 1 (1925), p. 25.

———. "O dramaturgicheskoi tekhnike amplua aktera." *ARK*, no. 2 (1925), p. 15.

———. "*Na zhizn' i na smert'* i *Kollezhskii registrator*." *ARK*, no. 10 (1925), p. 27.

———. "Popravki zritelia." *Kino-front*, no. 1 (1926).

———. "Ot *Stachki* k *Potemkinu*." *ARK*, no. 2 (1926), pp. 3-5.

———. "*Namus*." *Kino-front*, no. 4/5 (1926), pp. 29-30.

———. "Bor'ba faktov." *Kino-front*, no. 9/10 (1926), p. 24.

———. "*Namus*." *Kino*, no. 43 (1926), p. 2.

———. "Lakirovannoe varvarstvo ili 'Miss, vyidite na minutku!'" *Kino*, no. 49 (1926).

———. "Khochu snimatsia." *Kino-front*, no. 5 (1927), pp. 4-7.

———. "Rasskaz o meshchanstve." *Kino*, no. 5 (1927), p. 4.

———. "*Sorok pervyi*." *Kino*, no. 12 (1927), p. 3.

———. "*Reis mistera Lloida*." *Kino*, no. 39 (1927), p. 3.

———. "*Moskva v Oktiabre*." *Kino*, no. 47 (1927), p. 3.

———. "*Konets Sankt-Peterburga*." *Kino-front*, no. 1 (1928), pp. 16-18.

———. "*Kruzheva*." *Sovetskii ekran*, no. 16 (1928), p. 10.

———. "*Chelovek s kinoapparatom*." *Kino*, no. 7 (1929), p. 4.

———. "Oshibka Sovkino." *Kino*, no. 11 (1929), p. 4.

———. "Chernovnye vpechatleniia." *Kino*, no. 12 (1929), p. 5.

———. "*Chelovek s kinoapparatom*." *Sovetskii ekran*, no. 18 (1929), p. 5.

———. "*Saba*: Igrovaia kul'turfil'ma." *Sovetskii ekran*, no. 27 (1929), p. 7.

———. "*Saba*." *Kino*, no. 38 (1929), p. 5.

———. "*Chiny i liudi*." *Kino*, no. 40 (1929), p. 5.

———. "*Kain i Artem*." *Kino*, no. 49 (1929), p. 4.

Khokhlovkin, A. "O Sovkino." *Kino-nedelia*, no. 9 (1925), p. 4.

"Khronika GTK." *Kino-fot*, no. 3 (1922), p. 3.

"Khronika zvukovogo kino." *Kino*, no. 34 (1929), p. 1.

"Khudozhestvennyi sovet GPP o kino-sektsii VAPPa." *Kino-nedelia*, no. 13 (1925), p. 4.

"Khudozhestvennyi sovet po delam kino pri GPP." *Sovetskoe kino*, no. 1 (1925), pp. 63-64; no. 2 (1925), pp. 79-80.

"Khudozhnik i 'material'naia sreda' v igrovoi fil'me: Beseda s khudozhnikom A. M. Rodchenko." *Sovetskoe kino*, no. 5/6 (1927), pp. 14-15.

Kinematograf: Sbornik stat'ei. Moscow, 1919.

Kino. Odessa, 1928.

"Kino-akter." *Kino*, no. 21 (1927), p. 3.

Kino-biulletin kino komiteta Narodnogo kommissariata prosveshcheniia. Moscow, 1918.

"Kino est'—net kartin." *Kino*, no. 2 (1925), p. 4.

"Kinofikatsiia derevni." *Kino*, no. 2 (1925), p. 1.

"Kino i derevnia." *Sovetskoe kino*, no. 3 (1926), pp. 18-19.

"*Kino-glaz*." *Kino*, no. 34 (1926), p. 13.

Kino-kalendar'. N.p., 1927.

"Kino-kritiki i obshchestvennost'." *Kino*, no. 9 (1928), p. 1.

"Kino na V Vsesoiuznom s"ezde rabotnikov iskusstva." *Kino*, no. 12 (1925), p. 3.

"Kino pod ogon' samokritiki." *Kino*, no. 23 (1928), p. 1.

"Kino-politkomy." *Kino-nedelia*, no. 38 (1924), p. 5.

Kino-rabotnik. "Ne pora li peresmotret' funktsii ARRKa." *Sovetskii ekran*, no. 8 (1929).

"Kino-rezhisser." *Kino-gazeta*, no. 10 (1924), p. 1.

"Kino: Rezoliutsiia priniataia po dokladu t. Kirshona." *Na literaturnom postu*, no. 2 (1930), pp. 62-70.

Kino-sektsiia GPP. "Kakoi kino-apparat nuzhen derevne." *Sovetskoe kino*, no. 2/3 (1925), p. 45.

"Kino-tvorchestvo i massovoi zritel'." *Kino i zhizn'*, no. 18 (1930), p. 6.

Kirshon, Vladimir. "Zametki ob ARK i ODSK." *Kino-front*, no. 9/10 (1927), pp. 14-18.

―――. "Listki iz bloknota." *Kino-front*, no. 13/14 (1927), p. 10; no. 2 (1928), pp. 6-7.

―――. *Na kino-postu*. Moscow and Leningrad, 1928.

―――; Iukov, K.; Pudovkin, V. "Protiv demagogii i travili." *Kino*, no. 62 (1930), p. 4.

K. I. Sh. [Shutko, K.?]. *"Stachka." ARK*, no. 3 (1925), p. 31.

"K itogam kinosezona." *Kino i zhizn'*, no. 15 (1930), pp. 3-5.

Kletchatyi. "Kino-teatry Moskomproma." *Kino*, no. 3 (1925), p. 4.

―――. "Moskovskie kino-teatry." *Kino*, no. 4/5 (1925), p. 7.

Kogan, P. S. "Opyt literaturnoi fil'my." *Sovetskoe kino*, no. 6 (1925), p. 13.

"Kogo predosteregaet Lef." *Lef*, no. 1 (1923), pp. 10-11.

Komarov, B. *Zlodei v kino*. Moscow and Leningrad, 1929.

Korolevich, Vladimir. "Samaia deshevaia veshch'." *Sovetskii ekran*, no. 40 (1926), p. 13.

―――. "Kino ili zagovor imperiatritsy." *Kino-front*, no. 5 (1927), pp. 8-9.

―――. *Nata Vachnadze*. Moscow, 1927.

―――. *Zhenshchina v kino*. N.p., 1928.

Korennye voprosy sovetskoi kinematografii: Vsesoiuznoe soveshchanie po tematicheskomu planirovaniiu khudozhestvennykh fil'm na 1934. Moscow, 1933.

Kosior, S. "K itogam voprosov kino." *Revoliutsiia i kul'tura*, no. 6 (1928), pp. 5-7.

Kosmatov, L. "Krest'ianskaia fil'ma." *Kino-gazeta*, no. 34 (1924), p. 1.

Kostylev, V. "Toska po fil'me." *Kino*, no. 21 (1925), p. 3.

"K priezdu Ferbenksa i Pikford." *Kino*, no. 29 (1926), pp. 1-2.

"K rabochim-udarnikam v kino." *Kino*, no. 65/66 (1930), p. 3.

"K reorganizatsii kinopromyshlennosti." *ARK*, no. 3 (1926), pp. 3-4.

Kresin, Mikhail. "O sovetskom kino-cheloveke." *Sovetskoe kino*, no. 2 (1926), p. 10.

Krinitskii, A. I. *Zadachi sovetskogo kino*. N.p., 1929.

Kristol'. "Dovol'no skazok o nevygodnosti." *Sovetskoe kino*, no. 2 (1926), p. 7.

"Krov' na ekrane." *Sovetskii ekran*, no. 32 (1927), pp. 4-6.

"Krupnaia pobeda." *ARK*, no. 2 (1926), p. 1.

Krylov, S. *Kino vmesto vodki: K Vsesoiuznom partsoveshchaniiu po voprosam kino*. Moscow and Leningrad, 1928.

"K smotru kino-sezona." *Sovetskii ekran*, no. 20 (1929), p. 5.

"K soveshchaniiu po delam kino v TsK VKP(b)." *Kino-front*, no. 9/10 (1927), pp. 1-2.

"K sovetskomu realizmu." *Kino-gazeta*, no. 42 (1924), p. 1.

Kudriatsev. "Dokumentalizm—soiuznik formalizma." *Kino*, no. 44 (1930), p. 2.

Kuleshov, Lev. "Iskusstvo, sovremennaia zhizn', i kinematografiia." *Kino-fot*, no. 1 (1922), p. 2.

―――. "Amerikanshchina." *Kino-fot*, no. 1 (1922), pp. 14-15.

―――. "Kamernaia kinematografiia." *Kino-fot*, no. 2 (1922), p. 3.

―――. "Chto nado delat'." *Kino-gazeta*, no. 3 (1923), p. 1.

―――. "Nash byt i amerikanizm." *Kino-gazeta*, no. 17/18 (1924), p. 1.

―――. "Priamoi put'." *Kino-gazeta*, no. 48 (1924), p. 2.

―――. "Ot eksperimental'no-uchebnoi raboty do *Luchi smerti*." *ARK*, no. 1 (1925), pp. 24-25.

―――. "O *Chertovom kolese*." *Kino*, no. 11 (1926), p. 3.

―――. "*Vest—Luch—Po zakonu*." *Kino*, no. 36 (1926), pp. 2-3.

―――. "O nashem kinoaktere." *Kino*, no. 21 (1927), p. 3.

―――. "Ekran segodnia." *Novyi Lef*, no. 4 (1927), pp. 31-34.

―――. "Zabytye liudi." *Kino*, no. 30 (1932).

_____. *Kuleshov on Film: Writings by Lev Kuleshov.* Translated and edited by Ronald Levaco. Berkeley and Los Angeles, 1977.

"Kumovstvo na kino-fabrike." *Kino,* no. 14 (1928), p. 6.

"Kupili apparat." *Kino,* no. 7 (1925), p. 4.

Kurs, A. "Kto sdelaet kino-khroniku." *Sovetskii ekran,* no. 32 (1925), pp. 3-6.

_____. "Molodaia pleiada." *Sovetskii ekran,* no. 8 (1926), pp. 3-4.

_____. "Zametki dlia sebia." *Kino,* no. 36 (1926), p. 2.

_____. "Stanovlenie Kuleshova." *Kino,* no. 49 (1926), p. 3.

_____. *Samoe mogushchestvennoe.* Moscow and Leningrad, 1927.

Kushner, Boris. "Izopovest'." *Lef,* no. 3 (1923), pp. 132-34.

Kuznetsova, E. "Govorit akter." *Kino,* no. 59 (1932), p. 2.

_____. "Vokrug templana." *Kino,* no. 5 (1933), p. 1.

_____. "Korni bezotvetstvennosti." *Kino,* no. 15 (1934), p. 1.

"K voprosu o kinofikatsii derevni." *Sovetskoe kino,* no. 1 (1925), pp. 51-55.

L. "Prokat i teatry." *ARK,* no. 9 (1925), p. 21.

L. B. "O sovetskoi komedii." *Kino,* no. 19 (1928), p. 6.

Lebedev, G. "Kino-agropropaganda." *Sovetskoe kino,* no. 2/3 (1925), pp. 37-39.

Lebedev, Nikolai. *Kino: Ego kratkaia istoriia; ego vozmozhnosti; ego stroitel'stvo v sovetskom gosudarstve.* Moscow, 1924.

_____. "My stavim voprosy." *Novyi zritel',* no. 2 (1924), p. 14.

_____. "Zadachi rabochikh kino-kruzhkov." *ARK,* no. 2 (1925), p. 6.

_____. "Perspektivy ARK." *ARK,* no. 4/5 (1925), pp. 2-4.

_____. "Zadachi ODSK." *Kino,* no. 8 (1925), p. 4; no. 10 (1925), p. 5.

_____. "Stachka." *Kino,* no. 12 (1925), p. 2.

_____. Untitled letter. *Kino-front,* no. 7/8 (1927), p. 32.

_____. *Vnimanie: Kinematograf!* Moscow, 1974.

"Lef i kino." *Novyi Lef,* no. 11/12 (1927), pp. 50-70.

Lelevich, G. "Proletarskaia literatura i kino." *Kino-nedelia,* no. 3 (1925).

Lemberg, Efraim: *Kinopromyshlennost' v SSSR: Ekonomika sovetskoi kinematografii.* Moscow, 1930.

Leningradskii oblastnoi komitet VKP(b). *Rezoliutsii Leningradskogo oblastnogo partsovesh-chaniia po voprosam kinematografii (2-3 marta 1928).* Leningrad, 1928.

Lenobl', G. "Cherez porazhenie k pobedam." *Kino,* no. 47 (1928), p. 5.

_____. "Poezd sovremennost'." *Kino,* no. 8 (1929), p. 3.

_____. "*Chelovek s kinoapparatom.*" *Kino,* no. 17 (1929), p. 3.

Lev, Iakov [Iakovlev, N.?]. "*Devushka s korobkoi.*" *Kino,* no. 18 (1927), p. 2.

_____. "*Iad.*" *Kino,* no. 37 (1927), p. 3.

Levidov, Mikhail. "Novella Kuleshova." *Kino,* no. 49 (1926), p. 3.

_____. *Chelovek i kino: Estetiko-sotsiologicheskii etiud.* Moscow, 1927.

_____. "Tovarishchei zhal'ko." *Kino,* no. 43 (1927), p. 2.

_____. "Konets Sankt-Peterburga." *Kino,* no. 47 (1927), p. 2.

_____. "Nashchet geroev v kino i literature." *Sovetskii ekran,* no. 48 (1928).

Levman, B. *Rabochii zritel' i kino: Itogi pervoi rabochei kino-konferentsii.* N.p., 1930.

"'Levye' uklony." *Kino,* no. 43 (1927), p. 1.

Liberman, Lev. "Kino-delo i kino-pisatel'." *Kino-fot,* no. 1 (1922), pp. 4-5.

Lionov, D. "Na proizvodstve Sovkino." *Kino,* no. 14 (1927), p. 4.

Liss, Iu. "Organizatsiia templana 1933 goda." *Kino,* no. 38 (1932), p. 2.

Liublinskii, P. *Kinematograf i deti.* Moscow, 1925.

"Liudei i deneg kul'turnoi lente." *Sovetskii ekran,* no. 40 (1928), p. 1.

Livanov, P. "Blizhe k massam." *Sovetskoe kino,* no. 1 (1925), pp. 37-38.

———. "Ob upriamoi deistvitel'nosti i bol'nykh nervakh." *Sovetskoe kino*, no. 2/3 (1925), p. 26.

———. "Ekh, iablochka, kuda kotish'sia." *Sovetskoe kino*, no. 8/9 (1927), p. 21.

L. M. [Mur, Leo?]. *"Odinnadtsatyi." Kino*, no. 7 (1928), p. 3.

L. R-al'. "Chto my videli i khotim videt'." *Kino*, no. 23 (1925).

Lukhmanov, Nikolai. "Psevdo-klassitsizm." *Novyi zritel'*, no. 16 (1927), p. 12.

———. "Kino-chubarovshchina." *Novyi zritel'*, no. 17 (1927), p. 10.

———. "Bol'naia zhizn'." *Novyi zritel'*, no. 22 (1927), p. 8.

———. "Zhizn' kak ona dolzhna byt'." *Sovetskii ekran*, no. 15 (1928), p. 6.

———. "Lovite vora!" *Kino*, no. 38 (1928), p. 4.

———. "Zhizn' kakoi ona dolzhna byt'." *Kino i kul'tura*, no. 1 (1929), p. 30.

Lunacharskii, Anatolii. "Revoliutsionnaia ideologiia i kino." *Kino-nedelia*, no. 46 (1924), p. 11.

———. *Kino na zapade i u nas*. Moscow, 1928.

Lur'e, S. "Rezhim ekonomii v kino." *Sovetskoe kino*, no. 3 (1926), pp. 10-11.

L. V. "Beregite vremia." *Kino-gazeta*, no. 21 (1924), p. 3.

L. V-a. "Pechal'nye itogi." *Kino i zhizn'*, no. 18 (1930), pp. 17-18.

M. "Kino v dome krest'ianina." *Kino*, no. 1 (1925), p. 2.

M. A. [Aleinikov, M.?]. *"Stachka." Kino*, no. 10 (1925), p. 2.

Macheret, L. "O razvlekatel'nosti uspekhe u zritelia i nekotorykh drugikh veshchakh." *Kino*, no. 59 (1932).

Maiakovskii, Vladimir. "Karaul!" *Novyi Lef*, no. 2 (1927), pp. 23-25.

———. *Teatr i Kino*. Moscow, 1954.

Malakhov, Polikarp. Untitled letter. *Kino-gazeta*, no. 17/18 (1924), p. 3.

Malevich, K. "I likuiut liki na ekranakh." *ARK*, no. 10 (1925), pp. 7-9.

Mal'kin, B. "Neobkhodimyi otvet: O rabote Mezhrabpomfil'ma." *Kino*, no. 16 (1929), p. 5.

Mal'tsev, K. A. "Kino i sovetskaia obshchestvennost'." *Sovetskoe kino*, no. 1 (1925), pp. 15-16.

———, ed. *Sovetskoe kino pered litsom obshchestvennosti*. N.p., 1928.

Martov, B. "Kak pisat' stsenarii." *Proletkino*, no. 1/2 (1923), pp. 37-38.

Marchand, René; Veinshtein, Petr [Weinstein, Pierre]. *Le cinéma*. Paris, 1927.

"Masterstvo." *Kino*, no. 21 (1926), p. 2.

M. B. [Boitler, Mikhail?]. *"Leninskaia kino-pravda." ARK*, no. 3 (1925), p. 34.

Mei. "Ideologichesko-chuzhdym elementam net mesta v sovetskoi kinematografii." *Kino*, no. 5 (1931), p. 1.

Meshcheriakov, V.; Veremienko, M.; Katsigras, A. *Kino-iazva (Ob uprazhneniiakh Sovkino nad derevne)*. Leningrad, 1926.

"Mezhrabpomfil'm: Organizatsiia nuzhdaiushchaiasia v korennoi perestroike." *Kino*, no. 5 (1930), p. 2.

Mikheev, E. "Eshche o svete dlia kino v derevne." *Kino*, no. 1 (1925), p. 6.

Mil'kin, A. "Chistka v ARRKe." *Kino*, no. 9 (1930), p. 9.

———. "Pod svoe tiazhestvo." *Kino*, no. 15 (1929), p. 3.

Mirov, An. "I. M. Moskvin na ekrane." *Sovetskii ekran*, no. 39 (1925).

"Miss Mend." Sovetskoe kino, no. 8 (1926), p. 31.

M. S. [Shneider, Mikhail?]. "O rekonstruktsii sovetskoi kinematografii i zadachakh ARRK." *Kino*, no. 19 (1932), p. 3.

Mukhin, N. "Sovkino." *Kino-nedelia*, no. 12 (1925), p. 6.

Mur, Leo. "Rezhisser i kollektiv (Otvet na stat'iu Shpikovskogo 'Bez rezhissera')." *Kino-gazeta*, no. 38 (1924), p. 2.

———. "Sotsial'no-biograficheskoe amplua." *ARK*, no. 2 (1925), pp. 17-18.

———. "Fotogeniia." *ARK*, no. 6/7 (1925), pp. 3-4.

———. "Diktatura rupora." *Kino*, no. 6 (1926), p. 3.

———. "Osvobozhdenie konechnosti." *Kino*, no. 28 (1926).

_____. *Fabrika serykh tenei (Den' kinofabriki).* Moscow and Leningrad, 1927.

_____. *Bumazhnye bronenosetsy.* Moscow and Leningrad, 1929.

Muskin, V. "Podvodnye kontsy." *Sovetskii ekran,* no. 15 (1927), pp. 3-4.

"My i oni." *ARK,* no. 3 (1925), pp. 1-2.

"My ishchem." *Novyi Lef,* no. 11/12 (1927), pp. 1-2.

N. "Nadpis' i razvitie u kinokov." *Sovetskii ekran,* no. 7 (1929).

"Nachalos' chistka Soiuzkino." *Kino,* no. 64 (1930), p. 1.

"Nachalos' obsledovanie kinoorganizatsii." *Kino,* no. 23 (1929), p. 2.

"Na chistke ARK [sic]," *Kino,* no. 68 (1930).

"Nado rashirit' front bor'by." *Sovetskii ekran,* no. 35 (1927), p. 1.

Nakatov, G. "Zagranichnye kino-gazy." *Sovetskoe kino,* no. 2 (1926), p. 3.

"Na novom etape." *Kino i zhizn',* no. 31 (1930), pp. 3-4.

"Na novye rel'sy." *Sovetskii ekran,* no. 19 (1929), p. 3.

"Na podstupakh v sovetskoi komedii (Anketa)." *Kino,* no. 16 (1927), p. 3.

"Napominanie ob opasnosti." *Sovetskii ekran,* no. 41 (1926), p. 3.

"Na poroge vtoroi piatiletki." *Kino,* no. 60 (1932), p. 1.

"Nasha anketa." *Kino-zhizn',* no. 3 (1922), p. 6.

"Nasha anketa." *Sovetskoe kino,* no. 2 (1927), p. 5; no. 8/9 (1927), pp. 1-7.

"Nasha anketa o kartine *Dvorets i krepost'.*" *Kino-nedelia,* no. 1 (1924), p. 3.

"Nasha anketa sredi deiatelei kino." *Na literaturnom postu,* no. 1 (1928), pp. 50-54.

"Na sud rabochikh." *Kino,* no. 10 (1926), p. 2.

"Na temu grazhdanskoi voiny (O *Sorok pervom*)." *Kino,* no. 11 (1927), p. 4.

Nazarov, F. M. "Itogi zimnego sezona Rostova-na-Donu." *Kino-gazeta,* no. 3 (1925), p. 5.

"Ne monopoliia a kontrol'." *Kino-nedelia,* no. 15 (1924).

"Ne vzryv a ispravlenie." *Kino-front,* no. 1 (1928), pp. 1-2.

Neimarkh, S. "K voprosam kino-ekonomiki." *Kino-nedelia,* no. 23 (1924), p. 4.

"Nel'zia dezertirovat'." *Kino,* no. 19 (1927), p. 2.

"Neosushchestvliaemaia proportsiia." *Sovetskii ekran,* no. 41 (1928), p. 3.

"Net plenki (Beseda s predsedatelem predpravleniia Sovkino K. M. Shvedchikovym)." *Kino,* no. 17 (1927), p. 1.

Nezhdanov, Leonid, "O khudozhestvennykh sovetakh na fabrikakh." *Kino,* no. 19 (1925), p. 4.

Neznamov, P. "Udacha rezhissera (*Bukhta smerti*)." *Kino,* no. 7 (1926), p. 3.

_____. "Kovboi v papkakh." *Kino,* no. 14 (1926), p. 2.

_____. "Shineli i livrei." *Kino,* no. 21 (1926), p. 2.

_____. "Po poverkhnosti epokhi." *Kino,* no. 3 (1927), p. 4.

_____. "Chekhov—krupnym planom." *Kino,* no. 34 (1927), p. 4.

_____. "*S.V.D.*" *Kino,* no. 35 (1927), p. 3.

_____. "*Poet i tsar'.*" *Kino,* no. 39 (1927), p. 3.

_____. "*Baby riazanskie.*" *Kino,* no. 52 (1927).

"Nigilisty iz ARKa." *Sovetskii ekran,* no. 3 (1928), p. 3.

Nikanorov, Mikhail. "Nekotorye itogi." *Kino-front,* no. 9/10 (1927), pp. 13-14.

_____. "Stsenarii i proschety v kino proizvodstve." *Kino-front,* no. 9/10 (1926), pp. 5-7.

N. Iu. [Iudin, N.?]. "Na kino-fabrikakh." *Sovetskii ekran,* no. 12 (1925).

N. L. [Lebedev, Nikolai?]. "Kakie nuzhny nam stsenarii." *Kino-gazeta,* no. 14 (1924), p. 3.

_____. "*Aelita.*" *Kino-gazeta,* no. 41 (1924), p. 2.

_____. "*Luch smerti.*" *ARK,* no. 3 (1925), p. 32.

Novogrudskii, A. "Zametki o 'krizise.'" *Kino,* no. 46 (1929), p. 2.

"Novosti s zapada." *Kino-gazeta,* no. 23 (1924), p. 2.

"Novye v byte kino-aktera." *Kino,* no. 17 (1928), p. 6.

"Novyi kurs Sovkino." *Sovetskii ekran,* no. 1 (1929), pp. 2-4.

"Nuzhen sindikat." *Kino*, no. 11 (1926).
"Nuzhno-li ob"edinenie." *Kino-gazeta*, no. 14 (1924), p. 1.
"Nuzhno organizovat' prokat." *Kino-gazeta*, no. 46 (1924), p. 1.
"Ob *Aelite*." *Kino-nedelia*, no. 47 (1924), p. 3.
"*Oblomok imperii* v ARRKe." *Kino*, no. 35 (1929), p. 5.
"Ob osnovom." *Sovetskii ekran*, no. 50 (1927), p. 3.
"Obshchii iazyk." *Kino*, no. 14 (1926), p. 2.
"Obsuzhdaem fil'mu N. Shengelaia *26 komissarov*." *Kino*, no. 2 (1933), p. 2.
"Obsuzhdaem *Tanku*." *Kino*, no. 35 (1929), p. 2.
"Ocherednye zadachi." *Kino-nedelia*, no. 33 (1924), p. 4.
"ODSK." *Sovetskoe kino*, no. 5/6 (1927), pp. 24-25.
"ODSK k XVI parts"ezdu." *Kino*, no. 35 (1930), p. 1.
"ODSK o *Parizhskom sapozhnike*." *Kino*, no. 7 (1928), p. 3.
"O kharaktere kritiki." *Sovetskii ekran*, no. 49 (1927).
"*Okraina*." *Kino*, no. 11 (1933), p. 3.
"*Oktiabr'*." *Kino*, no. 11 (1928), p. 4; no. 12 (1928), p. 1.
"*Oktiabr'* (Anketa)." *Kino*, no. 12 (1928), p. 4.
Ol'ga Tret'iakova. Moscow, 1926.
Ol'khovyi, B. S., ed. *Puti kino: Pervoe Vsesoiuznoe partiinoe soveshchanie po kinematografii.* Moscow, 1929.
"O linii ARK." *Kino*, no. 13 (1927), p. 2.
"O *Liubvi vtroem*." *Kino*, no. 13 (1927), p. 14.
"ONO ili Sovkino." *Sovetskii ekran*, no. 38 (1927), p. 3.
"O novykh postanovkakh, 1922 g." *Kino-zhizn'*, no. 3 (1922), p. 1.
"Opasnost' *Garemov iz Bukhary*." *Sovetskii ekran*, no. 42 (1927).
Operator. "K voprosu o proizvodstvennoi statistike." *Kino-nedelia*, no. 24 (1924), p. 4.
"Oplata stsenariev." *Kino*, no. 30 (1926), p. 1.
"Organizatsiia ideia." *Kino-front*, no. 6 (1927), p. 2.
"Organizatsiia stsenarnoi raboty: Tezisy tov. Rafesa k soveshchaniiu v Glaviskusstve." *Kino*, no. 11 (1929), p. 1.
Orgbiuro (VAPP). "K kino-rabkorovskoi konferentsii." *Kino-nedelia*, no. 7 (1925), p. 8.
"OSPK." *ARK*, no. 1 (1925), p. 35.
"Otkliki pechati." *Kino-nedelia*, no. 3 (1924), p. 5.
"O zadachakh zvukovogo kino." *Sovetskoe ekran*, no. 41 (1929).
Oznobishin, N. *Fizkul'tura kino-aktera: Prakticheskoe rukovodstvo.* Moscow, 1929.
Ozol', Ia. A. "Bol'nye voprosy derevenskogo kino." *Sovetskoe kino*, no. 1 (1925), pp. 48-50.
P. A. "Oshibka Vasiliia Guliaeva (*Veter*)." *Kino*, no. 43 (1926).
"*Padenie dinastii romanovykh*." *Sovetskoe kino*, no. 4 (1927).
"Pechat' o kino." *Sovetskoe kino*, no. 8 (1926), pp. 28-29.
"Pered chistke," *Kino*, no. 27 (1930), p. 1.
"Pered novym pokhodom." *Kino-front*, no. 11/12 (1927), pp. 1-2.
"Pervaia fil'ma revoliutsii." *Kino-gazeta*, no. 16 (1923), p. 1.
"Pervoe pis'mo." *Kino*, no. 12 (1926), p. 2.
Pertsov, Viktor. "Mesto zarezannykh kadrov." *Sovetskoe kino*, no. 2 (1926), p. 17.
_____. "Sotsial'noe znachenie kartiny *Po zakonu*." *Kino-front*, no. 9/10 (1926), pp. 27-28.
_____. "Basnia i nravouchenie: O sovetskoi bytovoi fil'me." *Kino*, no. 7 (1927), p. 2.
_____. "Razmyshleniia neorganizovannogo cheloveka." *Sovetskoe kino*, no. 8/9 (1927), p. 13.
_____. "'Igra' i demonstratsiia." *Novyi Lef*, no. 11/12 (1927), pp. 33-44.
_____. "Vnimanie pisateliu." *Kino*, no. 42·(1927), p. 2.
_____. "*Zvenigora*." *Novyi Lef*, no. 1 (1928), pp. 46-47.

————. "Chto izmenil zvuk." *Kino*, no. 34 (1932), p. 1.

"Petrogradskie pis'ma." *Kino-zhizn'*, no. 3 (1922).

Petrov, Evgenii. *Chto dolzhen znat' kino-akter*. Moscow, 1926.

————. *Akter pered kino-apparatom: Prakticheskoe rukovodstvo*. Moscow, 1929.

"5 letnyi iubilei, proshedshim neotmechennym." *Kino-nedelia*, no. 1 (1925), p. 5.

Pikel', R. "Ideologiia i kommertsiia." *Kino*, no. 41 (1927), p. 2.

————. "Ukhaby na kino-fronte." *Revoliutsiia i kul'tura*, no. 3/4 (1928), pp. 45-49.

Piliver, I. "K voprosu ob organizatsionno-khoziaistvennykh formakh kino-teatral'nogo dela v RSFSR." *Sovetskoe kino*, no. 2 (1927), pp. 10-11.

Piotrovskii, Adrian. "Kino-romantiki i geroiki." *Zhizn' iskusstva*, no. 31 (1928), p. 2.

————. "Est' li krizis v sovetskoi kinematografii." *Zhizn' iskusstva*, no. 48 (1928), pp. 6-7.

————. "Platforma Petrova-Bytova i sovetskaia kinematografiia." *Zhizn' iskusstva*, no. 19 (1929), p. 7.

————. "Dialekticheskaia forma v kino i front kinoreaktsii." *Zhizn' iskusstva*, no. 41 (1929), p. 3.

————. *Kinofikatsiia iskusstv*. Leningrad, 1929.

————. *Khudozhestvennye techeniia v sovetskom kino*. Leningrad and Moscow, 1920.

————. *Teatr, kino, zhizn'*. Leningrad, 1969.

"Pochemu k nam vvoziat khlam." *Kino-gazeta*, no. 17 (1924), p. 1.

Pochtar'. "Smekh i ideologiia." *Kino*, no. 2 (1927), p. 4.

"Pochti tezisy." *Proletkino*, no. 1/2 (1923), pp. 3-4.

Poluianov, Pavel. *Gibel' teatra i torzhestvo kino*. Nizhni-Novgorod, 1925.

"Po moskovskim kino-teatram." *Kino*, no. 7 (1925), p. 4.

"Ponemnogo vytesniaem." *Kino*, no. 15 (1926), p. 4.

Popov, I. F. "Sensatsiia Adriana Piotrovskogo." *Kino i zhizn'*, no. 1 (1929).

————. "V kino eto delaetsia ochen' prosto." *Kino i zhizn'*, no. 36 (1930), p. 8.

————. "Itogi ili perspektiva." *Kino*, no. 55 (1933), p. 2.

"Po provintsii." *Sovetskoe kino*, no. 3 (1926), pp. 22-23.

"Po provintsii (Krasnodarskii okrug)." *Sovetskoe kino*, no. 1 (1927), p. 22.

"Po rabochei auditorii." *Kino-nedelia*, no. 3 (1924), p. 4.

Potemkin, Pavel. "Slovo massovomu zritel'iu." *Kino*, no. 44 (1927), p. 2.

P. R. [Radetskii, P.?]. "Pochemu plokho rabotaet ARRK." *Kino*, no. 30 (1934), p. 1.

Pravlenie kino-sektsiia VAPPa. Biuro sektora rabochikh korrespondentov. "O levykh slovakh i pravykh delakh." *Kino-nedelia*, no. 8 (1925), p. 14.

Predatel'. "Gospodin Sol'skii 'bolen.'" *Kino*, no. 49 (1929), p. 6.

"Preduprezhdenie." *ARK*, no. 10 (1925).

Prim. "General'naia liniia Mezhrabpomfil'ma." *Sovetskii ekran*, no. 20 (1929), p. 6.

Prodavtsy slavy. "Teakinopechat' pered sudom rabochikh." *Kino*, no. 12 (1929), p. 2.

"Proizvodstvennaia konferentsiia Sovkino." *Kino*, no. 7 (1929), p. 6.

"Proizvodstvennye plany." *Kino*, no. 16 (1926), p. 2.

"Proletarskie pisateli na kinofronte." *Kino*, no. 40 (1929), p. 2.

"Protsess kino-rabotnikov." *Kino*, nos. 15-18 (1927).

"Proverki kassoi." *Kino*, no. 23 (1925), p. 1.

"Psevdo-natsional'nye proizvodstva." *Sovetskii ekran*, no. 27 (1927), p. 3.

"Publika reshaet." *Kino*, no. 7 (1926), p. 2.

Pudovkin, Vsevolod. *Film Technique and Film Acting*. Translated and edited by Ivor Montagu. New York, 1958.

————. *Sobranie sochinenii*. 3 vols. Moscow, 1974-76.

————; Dovzhenko, Aleksandr. *Two Russian Film Classics: Mother and Earth*. New York, 1973.

"Pushkinisty o *Poet i tsare*." *Sovetskii ekran*, no. 43 (1927), p. 4.

"*Pyshka*." *Kino*, no. 45 (1934), p. 1.

"Rabochoe slovo na nashem kino." *Kino*, no. 1 (1928), p. 2.
"Rabochie ob *Odinnadtsatom*." *Kino*, no. 7 (1928), p. 3.
"Rabotat' po bolshevistku." *Kino*, no. 17 (1934), p. 1.
Radetskii, P. "NOT i kinematografiia." *Kino-nedelia*, no. 32 (1924), p. 5.
_____. *Chto takoe kino (Ot stsenariia k ekranu)*. Moscow and Leningrad, 1927.
Rafes, M. "Na poroge novogo sezona." *Kino*, no. 39 (1929), pp. 4-5.
Rakhmanova. "O metode vospitaniia aktera." *ARK*, no. 6/7 (1925), pp. 11-12.
"Redaktsionnye zametki." *Sovetskii ekran*, no. 12 (1926), p. 3.
"Resheniia Sovnarkoma." *Kino-gazeta*, no. 21 (1924), p. 1.
"Reshitel'naia bor'ba s opportunizmom v kino." *Kino i zhizn'*, no. 34/35 (1930), p. 5.
"Rezhissery o politicheskom rukovodstve." *Kino-nedelia*, no. 39 (1924).
"Rezhissery o sebe." *Sovetskii ekran*, nos. 21, 23 (1925).
"Rezoliutsiia ARKa." *Kino*, no. 28 (1928), p. 5.
"Rezoliutsiia disputa v dome pechati." *Kino*, no. 37 (1929), p. 2.
"Rezoliutsiia obshchego sobraniia proizvodstvennoi sekstsii ARKa k kartine *Po zakonu*." *Kino-front*, no. 9/10 (1926), p. 31.
"Rezoliutsiia po kartine *Don Diego i Pelageia*." *Kino-front*, no. 21 (1928), p. 16.
"Rezoliutsiia soveshchaniia rabotnikov kinematograficheskikh organizatsii SSSR po voprosu o monopolii." *Kino-nedelia*, no. 9 (1924), p. 2.
"Rezoliutsiia TsK VseRabisa o Sovkino." *Kino-nedelia*, no. 7 (1925), p. 4.
"Ring Lefa." *Novyi Lef*, no. 4 (1928), pp. 27-36.
Riutin, K. "Pochistik ob"ektiv." *Kino*, no. 41 (1928), p. 2.
Room, Abram. "Kino i teatr." *Sovetskii ekran*, no. 8 (1925).
_____. "Sud'ba kino aktera." *Kino*, no. 9 (1926), p. 4.
_____. "Rezhisser.... v koridore." *Kino*, no. 21 (1927), p. 3.
_____. "Den'gi i uvazhenie." *Kino*, no. 42 (1927), p. 2.
_____. "Akter, pol'pred ideii," *Kino*, nos. 7, 11, 15, 17 (1932).
Room, Mikhail. "Oblomok formalizma." *Kino*, no. 41 (1929), p. 3.
_____. "Khorosho, no ne tak, kak nuzhno." *Kino*, no. 3 (1933), p. 2.
Rudoi, Ia. "Nasha kinematografiia i massovoi zritel'." *Sovetskii ekran*, no. 37 (1929).
_____. "Na ideologicheskom fronte." *Kino*, no. 11 (1930), p. 2.
_____. "Zamaskirovannaia zashchita kinoformalizma." *Kino i zhizn'*, no. 15 (1930), pp. 7-9.
_____. "Zametki o tvorcheskikh putiakh sovetskoi kinematografii." *Kino i zhizn'*, no. 24 (1930), pp. 7-11; no. 25 (1930), pp. 4-5; no. 26 (1930), pp. 6-7; no. 27 (1930), pp. 6-7.
Rustemoe, A. "Proizvodstvo i Sovkino." *Kino*, no. 2 (1925), p. 3.
Rynin, N. A. *Kinematografiia*. Leningrad, 1924.
Saltanov, Iurii. "Nuzhno sobrat' kinoset'." *Sovetskoe kino*, no. 5/6 (1927), pp. 8-9.
Seifer, A. "Gde zhe ideologiia." *Kino-nedelia*, no. 1 (1925), p. 1.
"Sel'kino." *Kino*, no. 5 (1926), p. 5.
Serpinskii, S. V. *Chto takoe kino*. Moscow and Leningrad, 1928.
Sieber, Guido [Zeber, Gvido]. *Tekhnika kino-triuka*. Moscow, 1929.
Sha [Shatov, Lev?]. "ARK o *Tret'ei Meshchanskoi*." *Novyi zritel'*, no. 11 (1927), p. 13.
"Shag vpered." *Kino*, no. 37 (1930), p. 1.
Sharikian, E. "Itogi priema v GTK." *Kino*, no. 38 (1928), p. 5
Shatov, Lev. "*Salamandra*." *Kino*, no. 51 (1928), p. 4.
_____. "*Novyi Vavilon*." *Kino*, no. 14 (1929), p. 4.
_____. "*Prividenie kotoroe ne vozvrashchaetsia*." *Kino i zhizn'*, no. 10 (1930), p. 6.
_____. "Eshche o *Pyshke*." *Kino*, no. 41 (1934).
"*Shestaia chast' mira*." *Kino*, no. 3 (1927), p. 2.
"*Shestaia chast' mira* (Beseda s Dzigoi Vertovym)." *Kino*, no. 34 (1926), pp. 3-5.

"*Shestaia chast' mira* (Diskussionnyi prosmotr v ARKe)." *Kino-front*, no. 2 (1927), p. 2.

"*Shinel'.*" *Sovetskoe kino*, no. 3 (1926), p. 3.

Ship [Shipulinskii, Feofan?]. "Vse v proshlom." *Novyi zritel'*, no. 14 (1927), p. 12.

Shipulinskii, Feofan. "Kak postupit' *Po zakonu.*" *Kino*, no. 49 (1926), p. 3.

Shklovskii, Viktor. *Literatura i kinematograf.* Berlin, 1923.

————. "Vesna ne povtoritsa." *Kino-nedelia*, no. 8 (1924), p. 1.

————. "*Mister Vest* ne na svoemost'." *Kino-nedelia*, no. 21 (1924), p. 3.

————. "Semantika kino." *ARK*, no. 8 (1925), p. 5.

————. "Retsenzent." *Sovetskii ekran*, no. 35 (1925), p. 7.

————. "Nechto, vrode deklaratsii." *Sovetskii ekran*, no. 1 (1926), p. 1.

————. "Eizenshtein." *ARK*, no. 2 (1926), pp. 5-6.

————. "Ne Ioanna, a Ivan." *Sovetskii ekran*, no. 2 (1926), p. 11.

————. "O krest'ianskoi lenti," *Kino*, no. 10 (1926), p. 2.

————. "Pochemu troe." *Kino*, no. 15 (1926), p. 2.

————. "Volshebniki pervoi stepeni." *Kino*, no. 17/18 (1926), p. 2.

————. "O mezhdu prochem." *Sovetskii ekran*, no. 20 (1926), p. 3.

————. "Doverie vremeni." *Kino*, no. 26 (1926), p. 2.

————. "Kuda shagaet Dziga Vertov?" *Sovetskii ekran*, no. 32 (1926), p. 4.

————. "Pudovkin." *Kino*, no. 36 (1926), p. 1.

————. "Libretto i material'." *Kino*, no. 39 (1926), p. 3.

————. "Kinoki i nadpisi." *Kino*, no. 44 (1926), p. 3.

————. "Po povodu kartiny Esfir Shub." *Novyi Lef*, no. 8/9 (1927), pp. 52-54.

————. "Kinematografiia nachinaetsia s liudei." *Kino*, no. 33 (1927), p. 2.

————. *Ikh nastoiashchee.* Moscow and Leningrad, 1927.

————. *Motalka: O kino-remesle.* Moscow and Leningrad, 1927.

————. "Laboratoriia stsenariia." *Kino i zhizn'*, no. 17 (1930), pp. 6-7.

————. *Kak pisat' stsenarii.* Moscow and Leningrad, 1931.

————. "Dve neudachi." *Kino*, no. 55 (1932), p. 1.

————. "Emkost' kinoproizvedeniia *26 komissarov.*" *Kino*, no. 3 (1933), p. 3.

————. *Za sorok let.* Moscow, 1965.

Shershenevich, Vadim. *Smeshno o kino.* Moscow, 1928.

Shneider, Mikhail. "*Gospoda Skotininy.*" *Kino-front*, no. 4 (1927), pp. 18-20.

————. "*Solistka ego velichestva.*" *Kino-front*, no. 7/8 (1927), pp. 13-14.

————. "*Padenie dinastii romanovykh.*" *Kino-front*, no. 7/8 (1927), pp. 15-18.

————. "*S.V.D.*" *Kino-front*, no. 9/10 (1927), pp. 19-20.

————. "Stsenariev net." *Kino*, no. 9 (1927), p. 3.

————. "*Poet i tsar'.*" *Kino-front*, no. 11/12 (1927), pp. 27-29.

————. "Po tu storonu 17-go goda." *Kino*, no. 36 (1927), p. 3.

————. "*Parizhskii sapozhnik.*" *Kino-front*, no. 2 (1928), pp. 22-25.

————. "Pol'no-krovnyi pamflet." *Kino*, no. 37 (1934).

Shneiderov, Vladimir. "Sovetskaia kino-promyshlennost'." *Sovetskii ekran*, no. 7 (1927), pp. 31-32.

————. "Nuzhny srochnye mery." *Kino*, no. 47 (1927), p. 2.

————. *Tekhnika i organizatsiia kino-s"emochnoi raboty.* Moscow, 1928.

Shpikovskii, N. "Bez rezhissera." *Kino-gazeta*, no. 33 (1924), p. 1.

————. "Masterskaia Kuleshova: *Luch smerti.*" *Kino-gazeta,* no. 11 (1925), p. 1.

Shub, A. "Dva uklona." *Kino*, no. 50 (1927), p. 2.

Shub, Esfir. "Fabrikatsiia faktov." *Kino*, no. 41 (1926), p. 2.

Shutko, K. I. "Shagaete vse." *Sovetskii ekran*, no. 32 (1926), p. 3.

————. "*Odinnadtsatyi.*" *Kino-front*, no. 2 (1928), pp. 17-19.

_____. "Mezhrabpom-fil'm." *Sovetskii ekran*, no. 39 (1928).

Shvedchikov, K. I. "Sovkino otvechaet." *Kino-front*, no. 1 (1928), p. 31.

Shvidler, A. "Itogi i chistki." *Kino*, no. 51 (1929), p. 4.

S. I. "Novye liudi." *Kino-front*, no. 3 (1927), p. 6.

_____. "*Iad.*" *Kino-front*, no. 9/10 (1927), pp. 29-30.

Skachko, An. "*Luch smerti.*" *Sovetskoe kino*, no. 1 (1925), p. 63.

_____. "*Stachka.*" *Sovetskoe kino*, no. 1 (1925), pp. 61-62.

_____. "*Stepan Khalturin.*" *Sovetskoe kino*, no. 2/3 (1925), pp. 77-78.

"Slovo za chitatelem." *Kino*, nos. 12-17/18 (1926).

Sokolov, Ippolit. "Istoricheskaia fil'ma." *Novyi zritel'*, no. 35 (1924), pp. 11-12.

_____. "Klassicheskii stsenarii." *ARK*, no. 2 (1926), pp. 7-8.

_____. "*Medvezh'ia svad'ba.*" *ARK*, no. 3 (1926), p. 27.

_____. "Bronenosets—port—more." *Kino*, no. 4 (1926), p. 3.

_____. "O postanovke stsenarnogo dela." *Kino-front*, no. 4 (1926), p. 5.

_____. "*Chertovo koleso.*" *Kino-front*, no. 4 (1926), pp. 29-30.

_____. "*Shinel'.*" *Kino-front*, no. 5/6 (1926), p. 28.

_____. "NOT v kinoproizvodstve." *Kino-front*, no. 7/8 (1926), pp. 9-13.

_____. "Khoroshii stsenarii." *Kino-front*, no. 9/10 (1926), pp. 8-12.

_____. "Material i forma." *Kino-front*, no. 9/10 (1926), pp. 15-17.

_____. "Prezhde vsego organizatsiia." *Kino*, no. 19 (1926), p. 2.

_____. "Organizovannyi stsenarii." *Kino*, no. 29 (1926), p. 2.

_____. "Kuda idet sovetskoe kino?" *Sovetskii ekran*, no. 37 (1926), p. 3.

_____. "*Veter.*" *Kino*, no. 45 (1926), p. 3.

_____. "Skhemy vmesto liudei." *Sovetskii ekran*, no. 45 (1926), p. 6.

_____. *Kino-stsenarii: Teoriia i tekhniki.* Moscow, 1926.

_____. "*Kryl'ia kholopa.*" *Kino-front*, no. 1 (1927), pp. 12-13.

_____. "*Shestaia chast' mira.*" *Kino-front*, no. 2 (1927), pp. 9-12.

_____. "Kak sozdat' sovetskuiu komediiu." *Kino-front*, no. 3 (1927), p. 14.

_____. "Amplua, tipazh, maska: Kharakter obraza." *Kino-front*, no. 3 (1927), pp. 18-22.

_____. "Metody igry pered kino-apparatom." *Kino-front*, no. 5 (1927), pp. 10-14; no. 6 (1927), pp. 11-13.

_____. "Nauka o kino i nauchno-issledovatel'skaia rabota v kino," *Kino-front*, no. 6 (1927), p. 5.

_____. Untitled letter. *Kino-front*, no. 7/8 (1927), pp. 31-32.

_____. "*S.V.D.*" *Kino-front*, no. 9/10 (1927), pp. 20-23.

_____. "*Chelovek iz restorana.*" *Kino-front*, no. 9/10 (1927), pp. 23-24.

_____. "Proizvodstvo sostoianiia stsenarnogo dela." *Kino-front*, no. 11/12 (1927), pp. 15-18.

_____. "Sostoianie stsenarnogo dela." *Kino-front*, no. 13/14 (1927), pp. 22-26.

_____. "Mnogo stsenariev, a khoroshikh net." *Kino*, no. 39 (1927).

_____. "Ne dolzhen pisat' obyvatel'." *Kino*, no. 43 (1927), p. 2.

_____. "Prichiny poslednikh neudach." *Kino*, no. 46 (1928), pp. 4-5.

_____. "Rabotat' na massovogo kino-zritelia." *Kino i zhizn'*, no. 2 (1929).

_____. "Za interesnyi siuzhet." *Sovetskii ekran*, no. 22 (1929), p. 8.

_____. "*Oblomok imperii.*" *Kino*, no. 38 (1929), p. 2.

_____. "Fil'ma poniatnaia millionam." *Kino*, no. 41 (1929), p. 3.

_____. "Na putiakh k zvukovomu kino." *Sovetskii ekran*, no. 41 (1929).

_____. *Analiz igry kinoaktera: Masterstvo Lilian Gish.* Leningrad, 1929.

_____. "Korni formalizma." *Kino*, no. 17 (1930), p. 3.

_____. "*Zemlia.*" *Kino*, no. 21 (1930), pp. 4-5.

Sol'skii, V. "Kino na zapade." *Sovetskoe kino*, no. 2/3 (1925), pp. 61-67.

_____. "Chto nam pokazhut v 1927 g. Sovkino." *Sovetskoe kino*, no. 8 (1926), pp. 5-6.

_____. "Kino-zadachi i kino-opasnosti." *Na literaturnom postu*, no. 4 (1927), pp. 47-52.
_____. "Diskussii o Sovkino." *Kino-front*, no. 11/12 (1927), pp. 6-10.
_____. "Nekotorye itogi kino-diskussii." *Na literaturnom postu*, no. 1 (1928), pp. 65-70.
_____. "Zvuchashchee kino kak novoe iskusstvo." *Na literaturnom postu*, no. 2/3 (1928), pp. 37-43.
_____. "V zashchitu *Zemli v plenu*." *Kino*, no. 10 (1928), p. 3.
_____. "Zvukovoe kino." *Kino*, no. 31 (1928), p. 3.
_____. *Zvuchashchee kino*. Leningrad, 1929.
"Soobshchenie Glavrepertkoma." *Kino*, no. 20 (1928), p. 1.
"Sovetskaia kinematografiia v periode rekonstruktsii." *Kino*, no. 2 (1930), p. 5.
"Sovetskaia komicheskaia." *Kino*, no. 16 (1927), p. 2.
"Sovetskaia obshchestvennost' ne pozvolit sryvat' rabotu professional'nykh organizatsii." *Kino*, no. 25 (1928), p. 2.
Soviet Cinema. Moscow, 1935.
"Spor o kino-sindikate." *Kino*, no. 12 (1926), p. 1.
"Spor o Sel'kino." *Kino*, no. 16 (1926), p. 4.
Stekliannyi glaz. "Obzor pechati." *Sovetskii ekran*, no. 33 (1929), p. 10.
_____. "Obzor pechati." *Kino i zhizn'*, no. 7 (1930); no. 23 (1930), p. 14.
Stepanov, N. Ia. *Zametki po iskusstvu kino-ekrana*. Vladivostok, 1928.
"Sto protsentov agitatsii." *Kino*, no. 15 (1925), p. 1.
Strel'tsov, V; Al'tsev, L. "Pomozhem ARRK perestroit'sia." *Kino*, no. 6 (1931), p. 2.
"Stsenaristy." *ARK*, no. 10 (1925), p. 37.
"Stsenarnyi golod." *Kino*, no. 10 (1927), p. 2.
"Stsenarnyi krizis." *Kino-gazeta*, no. 44 (1924), p. 1.
Sukharebskii, L. *Uchebnoe kino*. Moscow, 1929.
"Summirovat' i uchest'." *Kino*, no. 2 (1929), p. 4.
Sutyrin, V. "Literatura, teatr, kino." *Na literaturnom postu*, no. 10 (1929), pp. 35-45.
_____. "O stsenarii i stsenariste." *Sovetskii ekran*, no. 16 (1929), p. 8.
_____. *Problemy sotsialisticheskoi rekonstruktsii sovetskoi kinopromyshlennosti*. N.p., 1932.
Sven, D. "*Kryl'ia kholopa*." *Kino*, no. 46 (1926), p. 5.
_____. "*Kat'ka bumazhnii ranet*." *Kino*, no. 51/52 (1926), p. 5.
Svilova, V. "Gde *Odinnadtsatyi*?" *Kino*, no. 16 (1928), p. 3.
Syrkin, Albert. "Mezhdu tekhniki i ideologiei (O kino poputchikakh i partinom rukovodstve)." *Kino-nedelia*, no. 37 (1924).
_____; Lelevich, G.; Furmanov, D.; Grabar, L.; Gladkov, F.; Minaev, K. "Kino-Voronshchina." *Kino-nedelia*, no. 3 (1925), pp. 5-6.
Syrtsov, S.; Kurs, A. *Sovetskoe kino na pod"eme*. Moscow, 1926.
"Tam gde delaiut krizis kinematografii." *Kino*, no. 50 (1928), pp. 2-3.
Tarich, Iurii. "Rvachestvo." *Kino*, no. 26 (1925), p. 3.
Tematicheskii plan Sovkino na 1928/29 g. utverzhdennoi plenumom khudozhestvennogo soveta ot 11/VII i zasedaniem pravleniia Sovkino ot 13/VII s.g. N.p., 1928.
Timoshenko, Sergei. "Zavtrashnyi den' kino: Kino zavoeval mir." *Kino-nedelia*, no. 1 (1924), p. 2.
_____. "Parodinaia anketa o kino-siuzhete." *Kino-nedelia*, no. 11/12 (1924).
_____. *Iskusstvo kino: Montazh fil'ma*. Leningrad, 1926.
_____. *Chto dolzhen znat' kino-rezhisser, inzhener fil'my*. Moscow and Leningrad, 1929.
"To, chego my ne umeem ekonomit'." *Sovetskii ekran*, no. 15 (1928), p. 3.
Tolstoi, Aleksei. "Vozmozhnosti kino." *Kino-nedelia*, nos. 1-2 (1924).
"Tov. B. Z. Shumiatskii—pred. prav. Soiuzkino." *Kino*, no. 65 (1930), p. 1.
"Tov. Zinov'ev o sovetskoi fil'me." *Kino-nedelia*, no. 7 (1924), p. 2.
Trainin, I. P. "Puti kino." *Kino-nedelia*, no. 40/41 (1924), pp. 8-10.

————. "Na puti k vozrozhdeniiu." *Sovetskoe kino*, no. 1 (1925), p. 13.

————. "Ob iskusstve bez politiki." *Kino*, no. 3 (1925), p. 2.

————. "Sovetskaia fil'ma i zritel'." *Sovetskoe kino*, no. 4/5 (1925), pp. 10-18; no. 6 (1925), p. 17.

————. "Nuzhen li geroi v kartine." *Kino*, no. 25 (1925), pp. 1, 4.

————. *Kino-promyshlennost' i Sovkino: Po dokladu na 8-ii konferentsii moskovskogo gubrabisa.* Moscow, 1925.

————. "Stseny nasiliia v kino." *Kino*, no. 41 (1926), p. 2.

————. *Kino na kul'turnom fronte.* Leningrad, 1928.

Tret'e vserossiiskoe soveshchanie po voprosam kinofikatsiia RSFSR. Moscow, 1935.

"*Tret'ia Meshchanskaia* (Na prosmotre ODSK)." *Kino*, no. 12 (1927), pp. 4-5.

"*3-ia Meshchanskaia:* Rezoliutsiia ARK." *Kino-front*, no. 4 (1927), p. 21.

Tret'iakov, Sergei. "Stsenarnoe khinshchinichestvo." *ARK*, no. 10 (1925), pp. 10-11.

————. "Konkretnoe predlozhenie." *Sovetskoe kino*, no. 3 (1926), p. 9.

————. "Opiat' konkurs." *Kino*, no. 31 (1926), p. 1.

————. "Dorozhe—deshevle ili deshevle—dorozhe." *Sovetskii ekran*, no. 39 (1926), p. 3.

————. "Kino k iubileiu." *Novyi Lef*, no. 10 (1927), pp. 28-29.

————. "Chem zhivo kino." *Novyi Lef*, no. 5 (1928), pp. 23-28.

————. "Stsenarnyi krizis." *Kino i kul'tura*, no. 3 (1929), p. 10.

————. "Uroki iarosti." *Kino i kul'tura*, no. 3 (1929), pp. 52-55.

Tret'iakova, Ol'ga. "Chetvero v kino." *Kino*, no. 12 (1926), pp. 2-3.

————. "O kino-geroiakh." *Kino*, no. 14 (1926), p. 4.

————. "Tvorchestvo aktera." *Kino*, no. 25 (1926), p. 2.

————. "Snachala 'pod kopirku.'" *Kino*, no. 31 (1926), p. 2.

"Tri direktivy." *Kino-front*, no. 13/14 (1927), p. 1.

Trofimov, N. *Ratsionalizatsiia montazha kinofil'm.* Moscow, 1933.

Troianovskii, A. V.; Elizarov, P. I. *Izuchenie kino-zritelia (Po materialom issledovatel'skoi teatral'noi masterskoi).* Moscow and Leningrad, 1928.

Turkin, Valentin. "*Slesar' i kantsler.*" *Kino-gazeta*, no. 15 (1923), p. 2.

————. "Kino-shkola i kino-proizvodstvo." *ARK*, no. 2 (1925), p. 12.

————. "Sostoianie kino-obrazovaniia v SSSR." *Sovetskoe kino*, no. 2/3 (1925), pp. 68-72.

————. "Khudozhestvennaia forma i napravleniia v sovetskom kino." *Sovetskoe kino*, no. 4/5 (1925), pp. 19-22.

————. "Kak naladit' stsenarnoe delo." *ARK*, no. 9 (1925), pp. 7-9.

————. *Kino-iskusstvo, kino-akter, kino-shkola.* Moscow, 1925.

————. "O ratsional'noi postanovke stsenarnogo dela." *Kino-front*, no. 7/8 (1926), pp. 6-7.

————. "O zhivykh liudiakh." *Sovetskii ekran*, no. 20 (1929), p. 7.

————. "Uroki Turksiba." *Sovetskii ekran*, no. 23 (1929), p. 4.

————. *Kino-akter.* Moscow, 1929.

"*Turksib* i ego avtor Turin." *Kino i zhizn'*, no. 9 (1930), pp. 7-8.

"Tvorcheskie kadry na chistke." *Kino*, no. 67 (1930), p. 1.

Tynianov, Iurii. "O Feksakh." *Sovetskii ekran*, no. 14 (1929), p. 10

————. *Poetika, istoriia literatury, kino.* Moscow, 1977.

"Udarnye templany." *Kino i zhizn'*, no. 23 (1930), pp. 3-5.

Umanskii. "Zhizn' kino-rabotnikov." *Kino*, no. 4/5 (1925), p. 6.

Urazov, Izmail. "Ekonomiia sredstv, no ne ekonomiia vydumki." *Sovetskii ekran*, no. 17/18 (1926), p. 3.

————. "On shagaet k zhizni kak ona est'." *Sovetskii ekran*, no. 32 (1926), pp. 5-6.

————. "Pafos i deistvii." *Kino*, no. 39 (1926), p. 1.

————. "Nashi velikie pobedy." *Sovetskii ekran*, no. 40 (1926), p. 3.

————. "*Kryl'ia kholopa.*" *Kino*, no. 47 (1926), p. 2.

_____. "Pobeda polemiki i tsifry." *Sovetskii ekran*, no. 1 (1927), p. 3.

_____. "Nuzhno soglasovanie planov." *Sovetskii ekran*, no. 6 (1927), p. 3.

_____. "Vtoroi konets palki." *Sovetskii ekran*, no. 11 (1927), p. 3.

_____. "Zametki o nashem konkurse." *Sovetskii ekran*, nos. 42-43 (1927).

_____. "Chto na ekrane." *Sovetskii ekran*, no. 5 (1928), p. 3.

Urenin, A. "Khlopok, khleb, les: O *Turksibe*." *Kino*, no. 40 (1929), p. 3.

Uritskii, S. "K voprosu ob organizatsii kino-promyshlennosti." *Kino-front*, no. 4 (1926), p. 2.

Uspenskii, V. P. *ODSK (Obshchestvo druzei sovetskogo kino)*. Moscow, 1926.

V. *Luch smerti*. *Kino-gazeta*, no. 12 (1925), p. 2.

Vainshtok, Vladimir; Iakobson, Dmitri. *Kino i molodezh'*. Moscow and Leningrad, 1926.

Vaks, L. "Na prosmotre *Kruzhev*." *Kino*, no. 21 (1928), p. 5.

_____. "O zvukovom kino (Disput v ARRKe)." *Kino*, no. 1 (1929), p. 4.

_____. "Chistka v Sovkino." *Kino*, no. 31 (1929), p. 3.

Vak-zal [Vaks, L.?]. "Kino-obshchestvennost': Est' ili net?" *Kino*, no. 49 (1928), p. 1.

"V ARKe: K otchetu komissii po pereregistratsii." *Kino-front*, no. 9/10 (1926).

"Vazhneishii vopros." *Sovetskii ekran*, no. 14 (1929), p. 3.

Vasil'ev, [Sergei?]. "O peremontazhe." *Kino-gazeta*, no. 8 (1925), p. 1.

Vasil'ev, Sergei. *Montazh kino-kartiny*. Leningrad, 1929.

"V chem zhe delo: Snova o *Cheloveke s kinoapparatom*." *Kino*, no. 17 (1929), p. 3.

Veinshtein, Petr. "*Prikliucheniia mistera Vesta*." *Kino-nedelia*, no. 16 (1924), p. 4.

_____. "Dorogaia ekonomika." *Kino-nedelia*, no. 25 (1924), p. 1.

_____. "*Dvorets i krepost'*." *Kino-nedelia*, no. 1 (1924), p. 1.

Veisenberg, E. *Kombinirovannaia kino-s"emka*. Moscow and Leningrad, 1928.

_____. *Konets nemogo kino*. Leningrad and Moscow, 1929.

"*Velikii uteshitel'*: Vystuplenie tov. Shumiatskogo na tvorcheskoi kollegii GUFK." *Kino*, no. 55 (1933), p. 2.

"Velikoi epokhe: Vysokoe iskusstvo sotsialisticheskogo realizma." *Kino*, no. 19 (1933), p. 3.

Vel'tman, S. *Zadachi kino na Vostoke*. Moscow, 1927.

Veremienko, M. S. "Kino-peredvizhki ili stantsionarnoe kino dlia derevnii." *Sovetskoe kino*, no. 2/3 (1925), pp. 40-43.

_____. "Organizatsionnye formy sovetskoi kinematografii." *Sovetskoe kino*, no. 3 (1926), pp. 1-3.

_____. "Analiz stsenarno-proizvodstvennoi i khudozhestvenno-postanovochnoi raboty proizvodstvennykh-organizatsii." *Sovetskoe kino*, no. 8 (1926), p. 3.

_____. "Chto nado delat'." *Kino*, no. 45 (1927), p. 2.

Vertov, Dziga. "On i ia." *Kino-fot*, no. 2 (1922), pp. 9-10.

_____. "Kinoki: Perevorot." *Lef*, no. 3 (1923), pp. 136-43.

_____. "Kino-glaz." *Kino-nedelia*, no. 36 (1924), p. 12.

_____. "Kino-glaz o *Stachke*." *Kino*, no. 1 (1925), p. 3.

_____. "Osnovy *Kino-glaza*." *Kino*, no. 6 (1925), p. 2.

_____. "*Kino-glaz* i bor'ba za kino-khroniku." *Sovetskii ekran*, no. 14 (1926).

_____. "Srazhenie prodolzhaetsia." *Kino*, no. 44 (1926), p. 2.

_____. "Kino-glaz." In V. M. Bliumenfel'd, ed., *Na putiakh iskusstv* (Moscow, 1926), pp. 210-29.

_____. Untitled letter. *Kino-front*, no. 4 (1927), p. 32.

_____. "The Vertov Papers." Translated by Marco Carynnyk. *Film Comment* 8 (Spring, 1972): 46-51.

_____. *Kino-Eye: The Writings of Dziga Vertov*. Edited by Annette Michelson. Translated by Kevin O'Brien. Berkeley, Calif., 1984.

"Vesna." *Kino-gazeta*, no. 17/18 (1924), p. 1.

V. F. "Kino peredvizhka ili kino-ustanovka." *Kino*, no. 15 (1925).

V. G. "Penzenskaia kino-zhizn'." *Kino*, no. 4/5 (1925), p. 3.

Vilenskii, E. "Geroi fil'my—apparat." *Kino*, no. 2 (1929), p. 3.

V. Isn. *"Sumka dipkur'era." Kino*, no. 5 (1928), p. 3.

V. K. "Zabytaia tema." *Kino*, no. 10 (1925), p. 2.

V. Kh. "Sozdadim podlinnuiu proletarskuiu kinematografiiu." *Kino*, no. 12/13 (1931).

"V kogo vgryzaetsia Lef." *Lef*, no. 1 (1923), pp. 8-9.

"Vkratse." *Kino*, no. 36 (1926), p. 1.

Vl. F. "O tekhnike osveshcheniia (Beseda s operatorom A. A. Levitskim)." *Sovetskii ekran*, no. 17 (1925).

"Vnimanie chistke kinoorganizatsii." *Kino*, no. 65 (1930), p. 1.

"Vnimanie kino-rabkoru." *Kino-nedelia*, no. 6 (1925), p. 5.

V. O. "Kak ne sleduet prodavit' derevne fil'mu." *Kino*, no. 4/5 (1925), p. 2.

"V Obshchestve druzei sov. kinem.: *Eliso.*" *Kino*, no. 39 (1928), p. 5.

Vokrug Sovkino: Stenogramma disputa organizovannogo TsK VLKSM, TsS ODSK i redaktsiei gazety Komsomol'skaia pravda, 8-15 okt. 1927. N.p., 1928.

"Vokrug *Zemli.*" *Kino*, no. 18 (1930), p. 5.

Voloshchenko, V. "Kogda zhe mozhno postavit' *Pyshku?*" *Kino*, no. 30, 32 (1933), p. 2.

————. "Epokha krupnym planom." *Kino*, no. 48 (1933).

Voznesenskii, Al. *Iskusstvo ekrana: Rukovodstvo dlia kino-akterov i rezhisserov.* Kiev, 1924.

[V. P. Uspenskii, untitled obituary]. *Sovetskii ekran*, no. 16 (1929), p. 4.

"Vserez i nadolgo." *Kino-front*, no. 4 (1926), p. 1.

"Vsesoiuznaia konferentsiia proletarskikh pisatelei o kino." *Kino-nedelia*, no. 4 (1925), p. 12.

Vsevolozhskii, Igor'. "Kak Soiuzkino obsluzhivaet Krasnuiu armiiu." *Kino i zhizn'*, no. 29/30 (1930), p. 15.

Vystritskii. *"Znak Zorro." Kino*, no. 23 (1925), p. 2.

"V zashchitu GTK." *Kino*, no. 36 (1928).

Za bol'shoe kinoiskusstvo. Moscow, 1935.

"Zadachi kinorabkorov." *Kino-gazeta*, no. 39 (1924).

Zagorskii, M. "Tapioka—Il'inskii/teatr—kino." *Sovetskii ekran*, no. 38 (1926), p. 5.

"Za kinematografiiu (Beseda s predsedatelem pravleniia Sovkino K. M. Shvedchikovym)." *Kino*, no. 34 (1927), p. 2.

"Za marksistskuiu kino-kritiku." *Kino i zhizn'*, no. 14 (1930), pp. 6-7.

"Za preodolenie trudnostei." *Kino*, no. 15 (1927), p. 2.

"Za rabotu." *Kino-nedelia*, no. 20 (1924), p. 1.

"Za ratsionalizatsiiu proizvodstva." *Kino-front*, no. 7/8 (1926), p. 1.

Zaretskii, M. "Rabochii podrostok kak zritel' kino." *ARK*, no. 3 (1925), pp. 20-22.

"Za rezhim ekonomii." *Kino*, no. 23 (1926).

"Za rezhim ekonomii: Rezoliutsiia ARKa." *Kino*, no. 22 (1926).

Zarin, A. *Tekhnika stsenarii: Rukovodstvo k izlozheniiu stsenariia dlia kino.* Petrograd, 1923.

"Za Sel'kino." *Kino*, no. 28 (1926), p. 3.

"Za sovetskoi stsenarii." *Kino-front*, no. 9/10 (1926), pp. 1-2.

"Za zvukovoe kino: Novoe oruzhie proletariata." *Kino*, no. 1 (1929), pp. 2-3.

"*Zemlia* Dovzhenko." *Kino i zhizn'*, no. 12 (1930), pp. 3-5.

Zhemchuzhnyi, Vitalii. "*Khaz-push.*" *Kino*, no. 5 (1928), p. 3.

"Zhizn' pered ob"ektivom." *Sovetskii ekran*, no. 4 (1927), p. 1.

Z-v. "Provintsial'naia pressa ob *Oktiabre.*" *Kino*, no. 15 (1928), p. 3.

Films

*Indicates Sound Film
+Indicates Nonfiction Film

Abrek Zaur. Directed by Boris Mikhen. 1926.

Aelita. Directed by Iakov Protazanov. 1924.

Arsen Dzhordzhiashveli. Directed by Ivan Perestiani. 1921.

Arsenal. Directed by Aleksandr Dovzhenko. 1929.

Baby riazanskie (Peasant Women of Riazan). Directed by Ol'ga Preobrazhenskaia. 1927.

Belyi orel (The White Eagle). Directed by Iakov Protazanov. 1928.

Bronenosets Potemkin (Battleship Potemkin). Directed by Sergei Eizenshtein. 1926.

Bukhta smerti (Death Bay). Directed by Abram Room. 1926.

*Chapaev. Directed by Sergei Vasil'ev and Georgii Vasil'ev. 1934.

Chelovek iz restorana (The Man from the Restaurant). Directed by Iakov Protazanov. 1927.

+*Chelovek s kinoapparatom* (Man with a Movie Camera). Directed by Dziga Vertov. 1929.

Chertovo koleso (The Devil's Wheel). Directed by Grigorii Kozintsev and Leonid Trauberg. 1926.

Chiny i liudi (Ranks and People). Directed by Iakov Protazanov. 1929.

Chudotvorets (The Miracle Worker). Directed by Aleksandr Panteleev. 1922.

Dekabristy (The Decembrists). Directed by Aleksandr Ivanovskii. 1927.

Devushka s korobkoi (The Girl with a Hat Box). Directed by Boris Barnet. 1927.

*Dezertir (Deserter). Directed by Vsevolod Pudovkin. 1933.

Dom na Trubnoi (The House on Trubnaia Square). Directed by Boris Barnet. 1928.

Dom v sugrobakh (The House in the Snowdrifts). Directed by Fridrikh Ermler. 1928.

Don Diego i Pelageia. Directed by Iakov Protazanov. 1928.

Dva dnia (Two Days). Directed by Georgii Stabovoi. 1927.

Dva druga, model', i podruga (Two Friends, a Model, and a Girlfriend). Directed by Aleksei Popov. 1928.

Dvadtsat' shest' kommissarov (The Twenty-six Commissars). Directed by Nikolai Shengelaia. 1933.

Dvorets i krepost' (Palace and Fortress). Directed by Aleksandr Ivanovskii. 1924.

Ego prizyv (His Call). Directed by Iakov Protazanov. 1925.

Eliso. Directed by Nikolai Shengelaia. 1928.

General'naia liniia. See *Staroe i novoe.*

Goroda i gody (Cities and Years). Directed by Evgenii Cherviakov. 1930.

Gospoda Skotininy (The Skotinins). Directed by Grigorii Roshal'. 1927.

Iad (Poison). Directed by Evgenii Ivanov-Barkov. 1927.

Iagodka liubvi (Love Berries). Directed by Aleksandr Dovzhenko. 1926.

*Ivan. Directed by Aleksandr Dovzhenko. 1932.

Kain i Artem. Directed by P. P. Petrov-Bytov. 1929.

Kat'ka bumazhnii ranet (Katka the Apple Seller). Directed by Fridrikh Ermler. 1926.

Khabarda! (Forward!). Directed by Mikhail Chiaureli. 1931.

Khaz-push (The Mob). Directed by Amo Bek-Nazarov. 1928.

+*Kino-glaz* (Cinema Eye). Directed by Dziga Vertov. 1924.

Kino-pravda, no. 21, *Leninskaia* (Leninist Cinema-Truth). Directed by Dziga Vertov. 1925.

Kollezhskii registrator (The Collegiate Registrar). Directed by Iurii Zheliabuzhskii. 1925.

Kombrig Ivanov (Commander Ivanov). Directed by Aleksandr Razumnyi. 1922.

Konets Sankt-Peterburga (The End of St. Petersburg). Directed by Vsevolod Pudovkin. 1927.

Krasnye d'iavoliata (Little Red Devils). Directed by Ivan Perestiani. 1922.

Krest' i mauzer (Cross and Mauser). Directed by Vladimir Gardin. 1925.

Kruzheva (Lace). Directed by Sergei Iutkevich. 1928.

Kryl'ia kholopa (Wings of a Serf). Directed by Iurii Tarich. 1926.

Luch smerti (Death Ray). Directed by Lev Kuleshov. 1925.

Mat' (Mother). Directed by Aleksandr Razumnyi. 1919.

Mat' (Mother). Directed by Vsevolod Pudovkin. 1926.

Medvezh'ia svad'ba (The Bear's Wedding). Directed by Konstantin Eggert. 1926.

Miss Mend. Directed by Fedor Otsep and Boris Barnet. 1926.

Mister Vest. See *Neobychainye....*

Moskva v Oktiabre (Moscow in October). Directed by Boris Barnet. 1927.

Namus (Honor). Directed by Amo Bek-Nazarov. 1926.

Neobychainye prikliucheniia mistera Vesta v strane bolshevikov (The Extraordinary Adventures of Mr. West in the Land of the Bolsheviks). Directed by Lev Kuleshov. 1924.

Novyi Vavilon (New Babylon). Directed by Grigorii Kozintsev and Leonid Trauberg. 1929.

Oblomok imperii (Fragment of an Empire). Directed by Fridrikh Ermler. 1929.

+*Odinnadtsatyi* (The Eleventh). Directed by Dziga Vertov. 1928.

*Odna (Alone). Directed by Grigorii Kozintsev and Leonid Trauberg. 1931.

*Okraina (Borderlands). Directed by Boris Barnet. 1933.

Oktiabr' (October). Directed by Sergei Eizenshtein. 1928.

+*Padenie dinastii romanovykh* (The Fall of the Romanov Dynasty). Directed by Esfir Shub. 1927.

Papirosnitsa iz Mosselproma (The Cigarette Girl from Mosselprom). Directed by Iurii Zheliabuzhskii. 1924.

Parizhskii sapozhnik (The Parisian Cobbler). Directed by Fridrikh Ermler. 1928.

Poet i tsar'. Directed by Evgenii Cherviakov. 1927.

Potemkin. See *Bronenosets Potemkin.*

Potomok Chingiz-khana (The Heir of Genghis Khan). Directed by Vsevolod Pudovkin. 1929.

Potselui Meri Pikford (Mary Pickford's Kiss). Directed by Sergei Komarov. 1927.

Po zakonu (By the Law). Directed by Lev Kuleshov. 1926.

Polikushka. Directed by Aleksandr Sanin. 1919.

Prazdnik sviatogo Iorgena (St. Jorgen's Holiday). Directed by Iakov Protazanov. 1930.

Prividenie kotoroe ne vozvrashchaetsia (The Ghost That Does Not Return). Directed by Abram Room. 1930.

Protsess o trekh millionakh (The Case of the Three Million). Directed by Iakov Protazanov. 1926.

*Putevka v zhizn' (A Start in Life). Directed by Nikolai Ekk. 1931.

Pyshka. Directed by Mikhail Romm. 1934.

Saba. Directed by Mikhail Chiaureli. 1929.

Salamandra (Salamander). Directed by Grigorii Roshal'. 1928.

Serp i molot (Sickle and Hammer). Directed by Vladimir Gardin. 1921.

+*Shagai Sovet!* (Stride, Soviet!). Directed by Dziga Vertov. 1926.

Shakhmataia goriachka (Chess Fever). Directed by Vsevolod Pudovkin. 1925.

+*Shestaia chast' mira* (One-Sixth of the World). Directed by Dziga Vertov. 1926.

Shinel' (The Overcoat). Directed by Grigorii Kozintsev and Leonid Trauberg. 1926.

Slesar' i kantsler (Locksmith and Chancellor). Directed by Vladimir Gardin. 1923.

Sol' Svanetii (Salt for Svanetia). Directed by Mikhail Kalatozov. 1930.

Sorok pervyi (The Forty-first). Directed by Iakov Protazanov. 1927.

Stachka (Strike). Directed by Sergei Eizenshtein. 1925.

Stepan Khalturin. Directed by Aleksandr Ivanovskii. 1925.

Staroe i novoe (The Old and the New). Directed by Sergei Eizenshtein. 1929.

Sumka dipkur'era (Diplomatic Pouch). Directed by Aleksandr Dovzhenko. 1927.

S.V.D. (Union of the Great Cause). Directed by Grigorii Kozintsev and Leonid Trauberg. 1927.

+**Tri pesni o Lenine* (Three Songs of Lenin). Directed by Dziga Vertov. 1934.

Tri zhizni (Three Lives). Directed by Ivan Perestiani. 1925.
Tripol'skaia tragediia (The Tripol' Tragedy). Directed by A. Anoshchenko. 1926.
Tret'ia Meshchanskaia (Third Meshchanskaia Street). Directed by Abram Room. 1927.
Turksib. Directed by Viktor Turin. 1929.
Uplotnenie (Overcrowding). Directed by Aleksandr Panteleev. 1918.
Vasha znakomaia (Your Acquaintance). Directed by Lev Kuleshov. 1927.
+*Velikii put'* (The Great Way). Directed by Esfir Shub. 1927.
**Velikii uteshitel'* (The Great Consoler). Directed by Lev Kuleshov. 1933.
Veter (Wind). Directed by L. Sheffer. 1926.
**Vstrechnyi* (Counterplan). Directed by Fridrikh Ermler and Sergei Iutkevich. 1932.
Zakroishchik iz Torzhka (The Tailor from Torzhok). Directed by Iakov Protazanov. 1925.
Zemlia (Earth). Directed by Aleksandr Dovzhenko. 1930.
Zhurnalistka. See *Vasha znakomaia.*
**Zlatye gory* (Golden Mountains). Directed by Sergei Iutkevich. 1931.
Zvenigora. Directed by Aleksandr Dovzhenko. 1928.

Selected Secondary Sources

Abramov, N. P. *Dziga Vertov.* Moscow, 1962.
Aleksandrov, Grigorii. *Epokha i kino.* Moscow, 1976.
Amiredzhibi, Natia. *Na zare gruzinskogo kino.* Tbilisi, 1978.
Babitsky, Paul; Rimberg, John. *The Soviet Film Industry.* New York, 1955.
Bann, Stephen; Bowlt, John, eds. *Russian Formalism.* New York, 1973.
Barna, Yon. *Eisenstein: The Growth of a Cinematic Genius.* Translated by Lise Hunter. Boston and Toronto, 1973.
Borovkov, V. *Fedor Nikitin.* Moscow, 1977.
Bowlt, John. "Russian Art in the 1920s." *Soviet Studies* 22 (April 1971): 575-94.
Bordwell, David. "Dziga Vertov: An Introduction." *Film Comment* 8 (Spring 1972): 38-45.
Bratoliubov, S. *Na zare sovetskoi kinematografii.* Leningrad, 1976.
Carter, Huntly. *The New Spirit in the Russian Theatre, 1917-1928.* New York and London, 1929.
———. *The New Spirit in the Cinema.* London, 1930.
Dart, Peter. *Pudovkin's Films and Film Theory.* New York, 1974.
Dikov, E. *A. V. Lunacharskii: Kino dramaturg i teoretik kinoiskusstva.* Moscow, 1971.
Eagle, Herbert. *Russian Formalist Film Theory.* Michigan Slavic Materials, no. 19 ([Ann Arbor, Mich.], 1981).
Enzenburger, Masha. "Dziga Vertov." *Screen* 13 (Winter 1972-73): 90-107.
Everson, William K. *American Silent Film.* New York, 1978.
Feldman, Seth. *Evolution of Style in the Early Work of Dziga Vertov.* New York, 1977.
———. *Dziga Vertov: A Guide to References and Resources.* Boston, 1979.
Fevral'skii, A. *Puti k sintezu: Meierkhol'd i kino.* Moscow, 1978.
Fisher, Lucy. "*Enthusiasm*: From Kino-eye to Radio-eye." *Film Quarterly* (Winter 1977-78), pp. 24-35.
Fitzpatrick, Sheila. *The Commissariat of Enlightenment: Soviet Organization of Education and the Arts under Lunacharsky, October 1917-1921.* Cambridge, 1970.
———. "The Emergence of Glaviskusstvo: Class War on the Cultural Front, Moscow, 1928-29." *Soviet Studies* 23, no. 2 (October 1971): 236-53.
———. "Cultural Revolution in Russia, 1928-32." *Journal of Contemporary History* 9 (January 1974): 33-52.
———. "The 'Soft' Line on Culture and Its Enemies: Soviet Cultural Policy, 1922-1927." *Slavic Review* 33 (June 1974): 267-87.

————. "Culture and Politics under Stalin: A Reappraisal." *Slavic Review* 35 (June 1976): 211-31.

————, ed. *Cultural Revolution in Russia, 1928-1931.* Bloomington, Ind. and London, 1978.

————. *The Russian Revolution.* Oxford, 1982.

Fülop-Miller, Rene. *The Mind and Face of Bolshevism: Cultural Life in Soviet Russia.* New York, 1927.

Furhammar, Leif; Isaksson, Folke. *Politics and Film.* Translated by Kersti French. New York, 1971.

Gak, A. "Dokument solidarnosti trudiashchikhsia." *Iskusstvo kino,* no. 11 (1961), pp. 129-31.

————. "K istorii sozdaniia Sovkino." *Iz istorii kino,* no. 5 (1962), p. 132.

Glovatskii, B. "U istokov." *Iskusstvo kino,* no. 11 (1966), pp. 5-13.

Grashchenkova, I. *Abram Room.* Moscow, 1977.

Harper, Samuel. *Civic Training in Soviet Russia.* Chicago, 1929.

Herwarth, Hans von, with S. Frederick Starr. *Against Two Evils.* New York, 1981.

Huaco, George. *The Sociology of Film Art.* New York and London, 1965.

Il'ina, G. I. *Kul'turnoe stroitel'stvo v Petrograde: Oktiabr' 1917-1920 gg.* Leningrad, 1982.

Iurenev, Rostislav. *Sovetskoe kinovedenie.* Moscow, 1977.

————. *Kratkaia istoriia sovetskogo kino.* Moscow, 1979.

Iutkevich, Sergei. *O kino iskusstve.* Moscow, 1962.

Kino-slovar'. 2 vols. Moscow, 1966.

Kovacs, Steven. "Kuleshov's Aesthetics." *Film Quarterly* (Spring 1976), pp. 34-40.

Kozintsev, Grigorii. *Glubokii ekran.* Leningrad, 1973.

Kuleshov, Lev; Khokhlova, Aleksandra. *50 let v kino.* Moscow, 1974.

Kushnirov, M. *Zhizn' i fil'my Borisa Barneta.* Moscow, 1977.

Lebedev, Nikolai. *Ocherk istorii kino SSSR.* Vol. 1: *Nemoe kino.* Moscow, 1948.

————. *Voznikovenie sovetskogo kino (1918-1921).* Moscow, 1959.

————. "Boevye dvadtsatye gody." *Iskusstvo kino,* no. 8 (1971), pp. 128-39.

Leyda, Jay. *Kino: A History of the Russian and Soviet Film.* New York, 1960; rev. ed. 1983.

Listov, V. "Dve *Kinonedeli.*" *Iskusstvo kino,* no. 5 (1968), pp. 93-100.

London, Kurt. *Seven Soviet Arts.* London, 1937.

L'vunin, Iu.; Polianskii, I. "Blagodaria lichnomu sodeistviiu V. I. Lenina." *Iskusstvo kino,* no. 1 (1970), pp. 3-9.

Monaco, Paul. *Cinema and Society in France and Germany in the 1920s and 1930s.* New York, 1976.

Montagu, Ivor. *With Eisenstein in Hollywood.* New York, 1967.

Moussinac, Leon. *Sergei Eisenstein.* Translated by D. Sandy Petry. New York, 1970.

Ocherki istorii sovetskogo kino. Vol. 1: *1917-1939.* Moscow, 1956.

O'Connor, Timothy Edward. *The Politics of Soviet Culture: Anatolii Lunacharskii.* Studies in the Fine Arts: The Avant-Garde, no. 42. Ann Arbor, Mich., 1983.

Pleynet, Marcel. "The Left Front of Art: Eisenstein and the Old Young Hegelians." *Screen* 13 (Spring 1972): 101-19.

"Rasskazy stareishikh kinematografistov." *Iskusstvo kino,* no. 8 (1959), pp. 35-49.

Razumnyi, Aleksandr. "Pervye." *Iskusstvo kino,* no. 11 (1967), pp. 51-54.

Rimberg, John. *The Motion Picture in the Soviet Union, 1918-1925.* New York, 1973.

Schnitzer, Luda; Schnitzer, Jean; Martin, Marcel, eds. *Cinema in Revolution: The Heroic Era of the Soviet Film.* Translated by David Robinson. New York, 1973.

Selezneva, T. F. *Kinomysl' 1920-kh godov.* Leningrad, 1972.

Seton, Marie. *Sergei M. Eisenstein.* New York, 1960.

Shklovskii, Viktor. *Eizenshtein.* Moscow, 1973.

Shub, Esfir. *Krupnym planom.* Moscow, 1959.

Sovetskie khudozhestvennye fil'my: Annotirovannyi katalog. Vol. 1: *Nemye fil'my (1918-1935).* Moscow, 1961.

Starr, S. Frederick. *Red and Hot: The Fate of Jazz in the Soviet Union, 1917-1980.* New York, 1983.

Swallow, Norman. *Eisenstein: A Documentary Portrait.* New York, 1977.

Taylor, Richard. "A Medium for the Masses: Agitation in the Soviet Civil War." *Soviet Studies* 22 (April 1971): 562-74.

_____. *Film Propaganda: Soviet Russia and Nazi Germany.* New York, 1979.

_____. "From October to *October*: The Soviet Political System in the 1920s and Its Films." In M. J. Clark, ed., *Politics and the Media: Film and Television for the Political Scientist and Historian* (Oxford, 1979), pp. 31-42.

_____. *The Politics of the Soviet Cinema: 1917-1929.* New York and London, 1979.

_____. "The Spark That Became a Flame: The Bolsheviks, Propaganda, and the Cinema." In T. H. Rigby, Archie Brown, and Peter Reddaway, eds., *Authority, Power, and Policy in the USSR* (New York, 1980), pp. 57-76.

Trauberg, Leonid. *Fil'm nachinaetsia.* Moscow, 1977.

Vogel, Amos. *Film as a Subversive Art.* New York, 1974.

Index